DICTIONARY OF ALBANIAN LITERATURE

ROBERT ELSIE

Greenwood Press
NEW YORK · WESTPORT, CONNECTICUT · LONDON

Library of Congress Cataloging-in-Publication Data

Elsie, Robert, 1950–
  Dictionary of Albanian literature.

  Bibliography: p.
  Includes index.
  1. Albanian literature—Dictionaries.   I. Title.
PG9602.E47   1986   891′.991′03   85-31693
ISBN 0-313-25186-X (lib. bdg. : alk. paper)

Copyright © 1986 by Robert Elsie

All rights reserved. No portion of this book may be
reproduced, by any process or technique, without the
express written consent of the publisher.

Library of Congress Catalog Card Number: 85-31693
ISBN: 0-313-25186-X

First published in 1986

Greenwood Press, Inc.
88 Post Road West, Westport, Connecticut 06881

Printed in the United States of America

The paper used in this book complies with the
Permanent Paper Standard issued by the National
Information Standards Organization (Z39.48-1984).

10 9 8 7 6 5 4 3 2 1

Dictionary
of
Albanian
Literature

CONTENTS

Preface vii

Dictionary of Albanian Literature 1

Bibliography 157

Index 161

PREFACE

In research on Eastern European and the Balkans, there has long been a gap, if not a chasm, when it comes to Albania. Romanian has always attracted fringe interest from students and experts in Romance studies. Bulgarian and Serbo-Croatian are firmly embedded in Slavonic studies. Modern Greek benefits from a long-standing interest in Classics and from direct contacts which have arisen as a result of mass tourism. Albanian has long been ignored not only because it does not fit into any of these convenient patterns, but also because of the lack of adequate grammars and primers to learn the language, because of the paucity of readable translations of Albanian literature, and no doubt because of Albania's traditional political isolation and its comparative inaccessibility.

The present work serves to provide the Western reader with basic information on Albanian literature from its origins to the present day. It contains entries on over five hundred Albanian writers and literature-related topics, including in most cases fundamental biographical and bibliographical data.

As to the eternal question of inclusion or exclusion, I have tried to keep the dictionary as eclectic as possible, i.e., better too many than too few. Inevitably, however, a few authors will have been overlooked which should by no means be interpreted as a statement about their literary qualities. Nor is inclusion in the dictionary to be understood as automatic recognition of literary merit. Excluded as a rule are scholars, journalists, and publishers of little relevance to Albanian literature itself.

It must be noted from the start that such a dictionary can only be as good as the sources upon which it is based. Primary sources for Albanian literature are frequently difficult and occasionally impossible to trace; and secondary sources, both those from Albania itself, from Kosovo, and those from the West, are eminently unreliable. Inaccurate and conflicting data are endemic to virtually all works to date. Titles and years of publication contradict one another from source to source with an alarming regularity, which caused me at times to wonder whether such a probject was indeed feasible. The reader may rest assured that I have done my best to eliminate as many inaccuracies as possible and not to introduce any of my own, but should keep the above word of caution in mind.

In conclusion, a word or two on methods. The dictionary is ordered according to the English alphabet and not according to the Albanian: thus *Dhosi* before *Dodani,* etc. Authors with more than one name (e.g., Italian and Albanian names for Arbëresh writers) have been entered under that most commonly used, with a cross-reference to the other(s). The original titles of older works are provided where available; otherwise the titles are in modern Albanian. Albanian place-names are normally given without the post-positive definite article: thus *Tiranë* not *Tirana, Shkodër* not *Shkodra*. General sources are all listed in the bibliography, whereas specific literature on individual entries is included in the corpus itself. For many authors, information is unfortunately scant, but I have chosen, nevertheless, to publish here what could be elicited from the sources available in the hope that the compilation may help and encourage others to pursue further research in this much neglected field.

It remains for me simply to thank all those who have helped and encouraged me during the four years leading to the completion of this project, including: Martin Camaj (Munich), Johannes Faensen (Berlin), Xhevat Lloshi (Tiranë), Arshi Pipa (Minneapolis), and Agim Vinca (Prishtinë).

Dictionary of Albanian Literature

A

ABDALLI, Mulla Fejzo (fl. 1841). Moslem priest and poet from Gjirokastër. Author of a historical poem written in Arabic script and dated 1841, dealing with a battle against a Turkish pasha during the reign of Sultan Mahmud II (1808–1839).

ABDIHOXHA, Ali (1923–   ). Prose writer born in Elbasan. After taking part in the resistance movement during World War II, he studied at the Gorky Institute of World Literature in Moscow. He has since held various positions in the fields of journalism, education, and culture and is now a professional writer.

Abdihoxha is the author of novels, short stories, and literary criticism, the former dealing to a great extent with World War II. Among his works are *Në malet tona,* Tiranë 1952 (In our mountains); *Ëndra dhe dritë,* Tiranë 1958 (Dreams and light); *Mirazh,* Tiranë 1958 (Mirages); *Një vjeshtë me stuhi,* Tiranë 1959 (Stormy autumn); *Tri ngjyra të kohës,* Tiranë 1965–1972 (Three colours of time); *Probleme të zhvillimit të letërsisë sonë,* Tiranë 1970 (Problems of the development of our literature); *Vepra 1–5,* Prishtinë 1970 (Works 1–5); *Tregime të zgedhura,* Tiranë 1973 (Selected tales); *Dueli i madh,* Tiranë 1975 (The great duel); *Vila në periferi,* Tiranë 1982 (Villa in the suburbs); and *Kronika e një nate,* Tiranë 1984 (Chronicle of a night).

ADAE, Guillelmus (fl. 1332). Also known as *Brocardus monacus* or *frère Brochard.* French monk and author of a Latin work entitled *Directorium ad passagium faciendum* (1332), written for the Crusades. He was appointed Archbishop of Antivari in 1324 and is known to have left Albania in 1330 for Avignon. He died before 1341.

His work is noted for its first reference to the existence of Albanian literature: *Licet Albanenses aliam omnino linguam a latina habeant et diversam, tamen litteram latinam habent in uso et in omnibus suis libris* (The Albanians indeed have a language quite different from Latin, however, they use Latin letters in all their books).

AGIMI SOCIETY. Literary and cultural society (Engl. "The dawn") founded in Shkodër in 1901 by Ndre Mjeda (q.v.). Among the activities of the society were the creation of an Albanian alphabet, the so-called Agimi alphabet, and the publication of school texts.

AGOLLI, Dritëro (1931–   ). Poet of the soil and one of the leading writers of contemporary Albania. Agolli was born in Menkulas in the Devoll region near Korçë of a peasant family. He finished secondary school in Gjirokastër in 1952 and continued his studies at the Faculty of Arts of the University of Leningrad. On his return to Albania he took up journalism, working for *Zëri i Popullit* (The People's Voice) for fifteen years. In 1973, he became president of the Albanian Union of Writers and Artists and is a deputy in the People's Assembly.

Agolli is the author of novels, plays, and film scenarios but is particularly noted as one of the best and most popular contemporary poets. He made his literary debut with the collection *Në udhë dola,* Tiranë 1958 (I went out on the street); followed by *Hapat e mija në asfalt,* Tiranë 1961 (My steps on the pavement); *Shtigje malesh dhe trotuare,* Tiranë 1965 (Mountain paths and sidewalks); and the poems *Devoll, Devoll,* Tiranë 1964 (Devoll, Devoll) and *Baballarët,* Tiranë 1969 (The fathers). perhaps best known is his poem *Nënë Shqipëri,* Tiranë 1974 (Mother Albania), written for the thirtieth anniversary of the liberation and which had a circulation of over 100,000 copies. More recently he has published the collections: *Të pagjumet,* Prishtinë 1980 (The insomniacs) and *Udhëtoj i menduar,* Tiranë 1985 (I travel pensively). Among his novels are *Komisari Memo,* Tiranë 1970 (Engl. transl. *The bronze bust,* Tiranë 1975), about the role of a political commissar in the partisan movement of World War II; *Shkëlqimi dhe rënia e shokut Zylo,* Tiranë 1973 (The splendour and fall of comrade Zylo); *Njeriu i mirë,* Prishtinë 1973 (The good man); *Njeriu me top,* Tiranë 1975 (Engl. transl. *The man with a gun,* Tiranë 1981), portraying once again the national liberation struggle; and *Trëndafili në gotë,* Tiranë 1979 (Rose in a glass).

His works have been collected in *Poezi,* Tiranë 1979 (Poetry) and *Vepra letrare,* Tiranë 1980 (Literary works). Both his poetry and prose have been translated in Tiranë into Western languages.

Lit.: ÇULI, Diana, *Poemat e Dritëro Agollit.* in: Studime Filologjike 32 (1978) 3, p. 91–120; KALLULLI, Adriatik, *Mbi krijimtarinë poetike të Dritëro Agollit.* in: Nëntori (1973) 7, p. 55–70.

ALBANO, Albanus. See VASA, Pashko.

ALIAJ, Hamit (1954–   ). Poet. Born in Tropojë in the northern Albanian alps. He graduated from secondary school in Shkodër and studied Albanian language and literature in Tiranë. He is the author of the verse collection *Bjeshkët janë mbiemri im,* Tiranë 1974 (The alpine meadows are my name), and now teaches in Tropojë.

ALIAJ, Tasim T. (1939–   ). Prose writer and dramatist. Born in Kurvelesh, he is a graduate of the Faculty of Economics in Tiranë. He has also worked as a journalist and editor.

Aliaj is best known for his satirical novels and short stories, although he has also written several plays. Among his publications are *Muret e pamposhtura,* Tiranë 1967 (The inflexible walls); *Stuhi në sirtar,* Tiranë 1968 (Storm in a drawer); *Njeriu që nuk qesh,* Tiranë 1972 (The man who doesn't laugh); and *Kur dola në jetë,* Tiranë 1972 (When I entered life).

ALIU, Ali (1934–). Kosovo critic born on Lake Prespa in Macedonia. He went to school in Bitola and Skopje and studied Albanian language and literature at the University of Belgrade. Aliu finished his doctorate in philology at the University of Prishtinë, where he now lectures. He has published: *Kërkime,* Prishtinë 1971 (Research); *Shqyrtime,* Prishtinë 1974 (Observations); *Koha dhe krijuesi,* Prishtinë 1975 (Time and the creative writer); *Rrjedhave të letërsisë,* Prishtinë 1977 (The ways of literature); *Kritika,* Prishtinë 1980 (Criticism); and *Artikuj kritikë,* Prishtinë 1983 (Articles of criticism).

ALIU, Mulla (fl. 1730). Moslem priest and poet. Great rival of his better known contemporary Nezim Frakulla (q.v.) in Berat.

ALIU, Sylejman (1947–). Kosovo short story writer. Born in Kashtanjevë near Ferizaj, he studied Albanian language and literature at the University of Prishtinë. He now works for the Kosovo daily newspaper *Rilindja* (Rebirth). His short stories have been published in the following volumes: *Ankthi,* Prishtinë 1978 (Fear); *Shtëpia në pluhur,* Prishtinë 1978 (The house in dust); and *Fillimi i vjeshtës,* Prishtinë 1980 (The beginning of autumn).

ALJAMIADO LITERATURE. Term denoting literature written in Arabic script but in a vernacular language, in this case Albanian, and strongly influenced by Islamic culture. The process of Islamization in Albania began with the Turkish conquest in the fifteenth century and lasted well into the twentieth century. Writing in Albania, in particular in the Islamic cultural centres of Berat and Elbasan, was for several centuries strongly influenced by Turkish and Persian models. Among the major authors of Albanian Aljamiado literature are Nezim Frakulla (q.v.), Sulejman Naibi (q.v.), Muhamet Kyçyku (q.v.), Hasan Zyko Kamberi (q.v.), Tahir Boshnjaku (q.v.), Dalip Frashëri (q.v.), Shahin Frashëri (q.v.), and Hafëz Ali Ulqinaku (q.v.).

Lit.: KALEŠI, Hasan, *Albanska Aljamiado Književnost.* in: Prilozi za orijentalnu filologiju, 16/17 (Sarajevo 1966–1967), p. 49–76.

ALTIMARI, Francesco (1955–). Arbëresh (q.v.) poet from San Demetrio Corone. Student of Albanian language and literature and teacher at the University of Cosenza. He has contributed numerous articles on Arbëresh literature to the periodical *Zjarri* (The fire) which has also published his poetry.

ANDONI, Sotir (1924–). Prose writer. Born in Ziçisht near Korçë, he took part in the partisan movement during World War II. He has subsequently taken up a teaching career.

Andoni is known primarily for his short stories, among which the publications: *Maleve në Shënëndre,* Tiranë 1958 (In the mountains in December); *Tregime nga Morava,* Tiranë 1960 (Tales from Morava); *Dasmë e çuditëshme,* Tiranë 1963 (A strange wedding); *Kur merrnim fluturim,* Tiranë 1967 (When we took wing); *I dërguar nga klasa,* Tiranë 1970 (Expelled from class); *Pran-*

vera e madhe, Tiranë 1971 (The great spring); *Hije, flakë dhe dritë,* Prishtinë 1971 (Shade, flame and light); *Hëna kishte marrë tatëpjetë,* Prishtinë 1973 (The moon had slanted); *Trokthet e kuajve nëpër natë,* Tiranë 1973 (Gallop in the night); and *Tregime nga Voskopoja,* Tiranë 1980 (Tales from Voskopojë).

Lit.: GJERGO, Edor, *Personazhet dhe gjuha e Sotir Andonit.* in: Nëntori (1973) 11, p. 79–87.

ANGELUS, Paulus (ca. 1417–1470). Alb. *Pal Engjëll.* Author of the first datable sentence of written Albanian, the so-called Baptismal Formula (Alb. *Formula e pagëzimit*), 1462.

Angelus was the archbishop of Durrës and a close friend and counsellor of Scanderbeg (q.v.). In a pastoral letter on the occasion of a synod held in the church of the Holy Trinity in Mati on November 8, 1462, Angelus provided an Albanian translation of a baptismal formula for use by non-Latin speakers. It read: *Unte paghesont premenit Atit et birit et spertit senit* (I baptize you in the name of the father, the son and the holy ghost). This oldest document in the Albanian language is preserved in the Laurentian Library (Ashburnham 1167) in Florence.

ANONIMI I ELBASANIT. The so-called anonymous seventeenth century manuscript from Elbasan. Discovered in 1949 and preserved in Tiranë, it contains parts of the four Gospels in Elbasan dialect and is now attributed to Theodhor Bogomili (q.v.) or Papa Totasi (q.v.), a priest from the Shpati region. The codex is written in an original alphabet of forty letters and is indeed the oldest known example of an original Albanian alphabet. The language of the text is more archaic than that of Theodhor Haxhifilipi (q.v.) (Dhaskal Todhri) who was active in the second half of the seventeenth century.

Lit.: DOMI, Mahir, *Rreth autorit dhe kohës së dorëshkrimit elbasanas me shqipërim copash të ungjillit.* in: Konferenca I e Studimeve Albanologjike, Tiranë 1965; SHUTERIQI, Dhimitër, *Anonimi i Elbasanit.* in: Buletini i Institutit të Shkencave, 1949, no. 1; *Shkrimet shqipe në vitet 1322–1850,* Tiranë 1976, p. 91–93; ZAMPUTI, Injac, *Dorëshkrimi i Anonimit t'Elbasanit.* in: Buletin i Institutit të Shkencave 5 (1951), 3–4, p. 64–131.

ARANITI, Midhat (20th century). Journalist and humourist from Tiranë. Active collaborator in the right-wing periodical *Revistë letrare.* Arrested in the late 1940s by the Communist authorities, he spent long years in prison. Fate unknown.

Araniti, using the pseudonym *Rem Vogli,* published among other things, light-hearted sketches and portraits in Tiranë dialect.

ARAPI, Fatos (1930–   ). Poet. Born in the port of Vlorë, Arapi studied economics at the Karl Marx Institute in Sofia. Upon his return to Albania, he took up careers as an economist, journalist, and, since 1960, lecturer in economics and Albanian at the University of Tiranë.

He is the author of a novel and several short stories but is known mainly for his impulsive poetry mirroring the reciprocity of bonds between the inner life of the individual and the profound social changes of the postwar period.

Among his poetic works are the collections: *Shtigje poetike,* Tiranë 1962 (Poetic paths); *Poema dhe vjersha,* Tiranë 1966 (Poems and verses); *Ritme të hekurta,* Tiranë 1968 (Iron rhythms); *Kaltërsira,* Prishtinë 1971 (Blues); *Drejt qindra shekujsh shkojmë,* Tiranë 1977 (We're marching towards hundreds of centuries); and *Fatet,* Prishtinë 1979 (The fates). He has also published the prose works' *Patat e egra,* Tiranë 1969 (The wild geese); *Dhjetori i shqetë suar,* Tiranë 1970 (Uneasy December); and *Dikush më buzëqeshte,* Tiranë 1972 (Someone smiled at me).

ARBËRESH. Term for the Italo-Albanians, i.e., the Albanian minority in Italy, the descendents of refugees who fled Albania after the death of Scanderbeg (q.v.) and settled in southern Italy. The first wave of refugees left southern Albania between 1468 and 1478 to settle in Basilicata, Molise, Apulia, and especially in Calabria. A second wave of Albanians fled Greece in 1532–1533 after Turkish encroachments in the Morea and settled mostly in Sicily. A small group from the Himarë district in southern Albania settled in 1744 in Villa Badessa near Pescara. Due to a more favourable political climate than in the homeland, the Arbëresh were able to make a decisive contribution to the evolution of Albanian literature and culture and to the nationalist movement in the nineteenth century. Early Albanian literature is indeed to a large extent Arbëresh literature. As a linguistic minority, the Arbëresh now consist of about 90,000 speakers, most of whom live in the mountain villages of Cosenza in Calabria and in the vicinity of Palermo in Sicily.

Lit.: KELLNER, Heidrun, *Die albanische Minderheit in Sizilien, eine ethnosoziologische Untersuchung,* Wiesbaden 1972; NASSE, George Nicholas, *The Italo-Albanian villages of southern Italy.* in: U.S. National Academy of Sciences. National Research Council Publication 1149, Washington 1964; ROTHER, Klaus, *Die Albaner in Süditalien.* in: Mitteilungen der Österreichischen Geographischen Gesellschaft 110. 1 (Vienna 1968); SHKURTAJ, G. *Shpirti i arbrit rron,* Tiranë 1984; ZLLATKU, Rexhep, *Me Arbëreshët,* Prishtinë 1976.

ARGONDICA, Anton (1839–1918). Ital. *Antonio Argondizza.* Arbëresh (q.v.) folklorist and poet. Born in San Giorgio Albanese, he finished his studies at the college of Sant' Adriano where he later taught. He collaborated in a great number of periodicals with articles on Albanian folklore and language. In 1890, he visited Spain, France, and the United States where he founded the newspaper *L'emigrato italiano.* In 1902, he also visited Albania. Argondica is chiefly remembered as editor of the Albanian periodical *Ili i Arbreshëvet* (The star of the Arbëresh), founded in 1896.

Aside from his writings on folklore and linguistics, he was also the author of poetry of varying quality written in his native dialect.

ARGONDIZZA, Antonio. See ARGONDICA, Anton.

ARGYROKASTRITIS, Grigorios. See GJIROKASTRITI, Grigor.

ARNAUTI, Abdylatif (1941–   ). Syrian-Albanian author and translator. Brother of Abdylkader (q.v.), Ajshe (q.v.), and Hatixhe Arnauti (q.v.). He was born in Damascus of a family which originated from the village of Dobërllukë near Vuçitërnë in Kosovo and finished his studies in Arabic language and literature in Damascus. The surname Arnauti means simply "the Albanian."

Arnauti is the author of novels, short stories, translations, and poetry both in Arabic (using the pseudonym *Ibn Kosova*) and Albanian. Among his Albanian works are two novels, children's short stories from Syria, and a collection of poetry entitled *Përtej maleve, deteve,* Prishtinë 1981 (Beyond mountains and seas), imbued with the nostalgic reflection of those in exile. In Arabic, he has compiled and translated anthologies of Albanian, Kosovo, and Yugoslav poetry and has translated novels of Dritëro Agolli (q.v.), Ismail Kadare (q.v.), and the late Croatian writer Miroslav Krleža.

ARNAUTI, Abdylkader (1936–   ). Syrian-Arabic painter and poet of Albanian origin. Brother of Abdylatif (q.v.), Ajshe (q.v.), and Hatixhe Arnauti (q.v.). He studied art in Rome and Paris where he finished his doctorate and now teaches at the Faculty of Fine Arts in Damascus. He is the author of the Arabic verse collection "Ashes on a cold land," Damascus 1973.

ARNAUTI, Ajshe (1946–   ). Syrian-Arabic poetess and short story writer of Albanian origin. Sister of Abdylatif (q.v.), Abdylkader (q.v.), and Hatixhe Arnauti (q.v.). She studied French language and literature at the University of Damascus and now lives in Paris. She started writing at an early age and attained something of the reputation of a Syrian Sagan. Some of her work has recently appeared in an American anthology of Arabic verse.

ARNAUTI, Hatixhe (1934–   ). Syrian-Arabic poetess and short story writer of Albanian origin from Damascus. Sister of Abdylatif (q.v.), Abdylkader (q.v.), and Ajshe Arnauti (q.v.). Her romantic verse, often concerned with the lost homeland and plight of emigration, has been published in two collections: "Springtime of a heart," Damascus 1954 and "Sorrowful verse is in my house," Damascus 1958.

ARNAUTI, Maruf (1892–1948). Syrian-Arabic novelist and playwright of Albanian origin. Born in Beirut of a family from Vlorë, he studied in the Lebanese capital and moved to Istanbul in 1916 where he served as an officer in the Ottoman army. He took part in the Arab uprising that year which started in Mecca and later in the movement to free Syria of French occupation. For the latter, he was sentenced to death in 1920 but released shortly afterwards under an amnesty. He thereafter lived in Damascus until his death. Arnauti was the author of the first four novels of Arabic literature in Syria.

Lit.: MUFAKU, Muhamed, *Tregime siriane (1931-1981),* Prishtinë 1981.

ARNAUTI, Muhamed Barakat Latif (1935–   ). Syrian-Arabic poet of Albanian origin from Damascus. He went to school in the Syrian capital, received professional training in the German Democratic Republic, and now works for the railway. Arnauti first became known as a poet at the age of forty and developed into quite a phenomenon in Syrian literature. He published several volumes of Arabic poetry, among which the collection entitled "The songs of the engine driver," Damascus 1979.

ARNAUTI, Raxha (1946–   ). Syrian-Arabic poetess of Albanian origin. She was born in Damascus and studied French literature in Algeria. She is the author of translations of French poetry and of original verse which has appeared in a number of periodicals.

ARTIOTI, Maksim (1480–1556). Latin scholar of Albanian origin. He was born in Arta, Greece, and studied Latin, Greek, philosophy, and theology in Florence. In 1514, he was called to the court of Basil III in Moscow to translate several religious texts. Artioti is the author of a number of works of philosophy, theology, and ethics.

ASCURI, Costantino (1810–1871). Arbëresh (q.v.) writer and poet. Little is known of Ascuri aside from the fact that he studied at the college in San Demetrio Corone.

He is the author of two works plus a historical poem entitled *Kënka*, dated 1834, dealing with events in Eianina (Porcile) and Frascineto during the French occupation from 1799 to 1806.

ASDRENI (1872–1947). Pseudonym of *Aleks Stavre Drenova*. Lyric poet. He was born of poor parents in the village of Drenovë near Korçë. After six years of elementary schooling in his native village, he began to study at the Greek secondary school in Korçë until the untimely death of his father forced him to give up school. As a teenager, he emigrated with his brothers to Romania, where a community of exiles with an Albanian press and school was gradually flourishing. There he worked as a coal-boy and apprentice and later continued his studies, both on his own and for a short time at the Faculty of Political Science of the University of Bucharest, where he came into contact with the ideas and ideals of the nationalist movement in exile.

Dominant themes in his romantic poetry, rich in expression, are the Albanian countryside, the ardent patriotism of the nationalist movement, and the beauties of nature. His three volumes of verse, *Rreze dielli,* Bucharest 1904 (Sunbeams); *Ëndra e lotë,* Bucharest 1912 (Dreams and tears); and *Psallme murgu,* Bucharest 1930 (Psalms of a monk), have been republished recently in two volumes: *Vepra 1–2,* Tiranë 1976, 1980 (Works 1–2).

Lit.: QOSJA, Rexhep, *Asdreni, jeta dhe vepra e tij,* Prishtinë 1972.

ASHKIU, Mehmet (fl. 1750). Moslem poet from Berat. Contemporary of Nezim Frakulla (q.v.).

ASLLAN bej Puçe (1807–1830). Poet. Son of Ago Myhyrdari who was secretary to Ali Pasha Tepelena. He died at the young age of twenty-three, together with other Albanian nobles in the massacre of Monastir on August 30, 1830.

ASLLANI, Ali (1884–1966). Lyric and satirical poet and diplomat from Vlorë. He studied in Ioannina (Greece) and Istanbul where he worked as a civil servant in the Ottoman administration. He also managed, however, to play an active role in the struggle for Albanian independence, for which he was imprisoned for a time. He served as secretary in the independent government of Ismail Qemali in 1912. In the 1930s, he represented Albania at its diplomatic missions in Trieste, Sofia, and Athens.

Asllani is best known for his folksy narrative poem *Hanko Halla,* Tiranë 1942, the best verse of this genre in Albanian literature. In it, he depicts the struggles and apprehensions of a colourful aristocratic lady constantly at odds with new-fangled Western ways. His writings have been reedited in *Vepra 1– 2,* Prishtinë 1984 (Works 1–2).

AVATI, Francesco (1717–1800). Arbëresh (q.v.) folklorist. Born in the village of Macchia Albanese in Calabria, as was de Rada (q.v.). He studied at the Arbëresh college of San Benedetto Ullano where he later taught and became rector. He died as a teacher of Greek at Urbino in 1800.

Avati is remembered as the first scholar to have collected material on Arbëresh folklore in Calabria, in particular folksongs.

Lit.: SHUTERIQI, Dhimitër, *Autorë dhe tekste,* Tiranë 1977, p. 160–178.

AVRAMI, Thoma (fl. 1900). Journalist and poet from Korçë. Before Albanian independence in 1912, Avrami travelled extensively to places of Albanian settlement abroad (Sofia, Bucharest, Egypt, and Constantinople), inciting nationalist fervour as a journalist and editor. In 1903, he became editor of the Albanian periodical *Vetëtima* (Lightening) published in Sofia. He also collaborated in other exile newspapers and periodicals such as *Albania, Drita, Shqipëria, Përlindja Shqipëtare* (Bucharest 1903), *Besa* (Cairo 1904), and *Përlindja Arësimtare* (Korçë). In 1908, he represented Korçë at the Congress of Monastir (q.v.).

In addition to his journalistic activities, he was the author of prose, poetry, and translations from Greek and Arabic. His lyric poetry, often on a nationalist theme, was published in a number of periodicals of the time, such as *Shqipëria* and *Albania.*

AZI. See REXHA, Zekeria.

AZZOPARDUS, Franciscus (fl. 1635). Author of a six-line Latin poem serving as a dedication to the Latin-Albanian dictionary of Frang Bardhi (q.v.), dated 1635. He was a Maltese student at the College of the Propaganda Fide in Rome where he came into contact with Bardhi and other Albanians.

B

BABI, Pashko (1843–1905). Catholic writer and dramatist. Born in Shkodër, he received a religious education there and later became a parish priest.

He is the author of a school book for religious instruction entitled *Vakinat e lighes t'hershem e lighes t'ree,* Shkodër 1882 (Stories from the Old and New Testaments) and one of the first Albanian plays *I biri i çifutit* (The son of the Jew).

BAFFA, Pasquale (–1799). Arbëresh (q.v.) philologist from the village of Santa Sofia, Cosenza.

BAFFA, Stefano (–1808). Arbëresh (q.v.) author from the village of Santa Sofia in Cosenza. He is known to have written an Albanian poem, now lost, about the sacking of the college of Sant' Adriano in San Demetrio Corone. Nothing else is known about Baffa except that he was the teacher of Angelo Masci (q.v.).

BAGERI, Josef (fl. 1910). Also known as *Josef Bageri Rekas* from Dibër. Journalist and poet. Editor of the small but vociferous periodical *Shqypeja e Shqypënisë* (The Albanian eagle) which began publication in Sofia in 1909 and of the weekly *Ushtimi i Krujës* (The Krujë echo) which started in 1914 in Durrës. He is also the author of a volume of poetry and prose written in his native dialect, entitled *Kopësht Malsori msime të shqyptarvetë dhe vjersha,* Sofia 1910.

BALA, Muhamet (fl. 1940). Author of a number of articles on Moslem subjects in the Tiranë journal *Kultura islame* (Islamic culture).

BALA, Vehbi (1923–   ). Critic and poet. Born in Shkodër, he studied philology in Bucharest after World War II and later taught literature in Tiranë and Shkodër.

Bala is the author of works on literary theory, several volumes of poetry, and monographs on Dora d'Istria (q.v.), Fan Noli (q.v.) and Pashko Vasa (q.v.). Among his publications are *Shtigje drite,* Shkodër 1946 (Paths of light); *Vjer-*

sha, Tiranë 1954 (Poetry); *Gjaku i falun,* Tiranë 1955 (Absolved blood); *Një përrallë e vërtetë,* Tiranë 1957 (A true story); *Burim poezie,* Tiranë 1977 (Source of poetry); *Epigrame,* Tiranë 1979 (Epigrams); and *Përsiatje,* Tiranë 1982 (Meditation).

Lit.: KASTRATI, Jup, *Mbi poezinë e Vehbi Balës.* in: Shkodra (1963) 1, 3, p. 136–186.

BALASHI, Adelina (contemporary). Poetess from Korçë. She has studied Albanian literature at the Faculty of History and Philology of the University of Tiranë and has published the collection *Përgjigje,* Tiranë 1983 (Answer).

BALLACI, Sinan (1922–1944). Poet, partisan, and Communist activist. Born in Delvinë, he joined the resistance movement in the war and was a member of the "Thoma Lulo" batallion. He was killed in fighting during the liberation of Sarandë.

Some of his patriotic and satirical verse from the war years was put to music and widely sung.

BALLANCA, Faik (1945–1978). Short story writer. Born in Tiranë where he studied at the Faculty of History and Philology. He published several collections of short stories, among which: *Rrëmbimi,* Tiranë 1970 (The theft); *Mbasdite të lagura,* Tiranë 1971 (Wet afternoons); *Katër orë larg shtëpisë,* Tiranë 1972 (Four hours from home); *Letra anonime,* Tiranë 1973 (Anonymous letters); and *Tregime të zgjedhura,* Tiranë 1976 (Selected tales).

BALLAURI, Elsa (contemporary). Poetess. She works at the "Enver Hoxha" industrial complex in Tiranë and has published the collection *Mëngjes,* Tiranë 1983 (Morning).

BALLIU, Fahri (1954–   ). Short story and film script writer. Born in Elbasan, he studied Albanian language and literature at the University of Tiranë.

Balliu´has published two volumes of short stories entitled *Udhë të çelura,* Tiranë 1977 (Open roads); and *Dita e nesërme,* Tiranë 1980 (One day and the next).

BANUSHI, Aleksandër (1920–   ). Poet. He was active in a Communist literary group in Shkodër during the war and was one of the founding members of the writers' union in 1945. Banushi is author of the volumes: *Ylberi,* Tiranë 1952 (The rainbow); *Rrugë të ndrituna,* Tiranë 1955 (Shining roads); *Nën qiell të kaltër,* Tiranë 1957 (Under a blue sky); and *Dasma,* Tiranë 1960 (The wedding).

BAPTISMAL FORMULA. See ANGELUS, Paulus.

BARBACI, Giovanni Tommaso. See BARBAÇI, Gjon Thoma.

BARBAÇI, Gjon Thoma (1742–1791). Ital. *Giovanni Tommaso Barbaci.* Arbëresh (q.v.) poet. Born in Mezzoiuso, Sicily. Parish priest of the Orthodox church in Naples and chaplain of the Imperial Macedonian Regiment created by the King of the Two Sicilies. He is also said to have taught Greek in Trapani.

Barbaçi is remembered for one religious poem *O ti çë helme shkove,* dedicated to the Virgin Mary.

BARÇA, Zef (18th century). Ital. *Giuseppe Barcia*. Arbëresh (q.v.) poet from Palazzo Adriano in Sicily. Nothing is known of his life. He is the author of one didactic poem written in 1755 entitled *Njeriu i harroshëm* (The careless man).

BARCIA, Giuseppe. See BARÇA, Zef.

BARDHI, Frang (1606–1643). Also known as (Alb.) *Frano Bardhi, Frangu i Bardhë;* (Lat.) *Franciscus Blancus* or *Blanchus;* (Ital.) *Francesco Blanco*. Author of the first Albanian dictionary and one of the prime figures in early Albanian literature.

Bardhi was born in Kallmeti in the Zadrimë region of northern Albania of a family which had long been in the service of the Republic of Venice. His uncle was the Bishop of Sapë. Bardhi was sent to Italy where he studied theology at Loreto College near Ancona and later at the College of the Propaganda Fide in Rome. In 1635, he was appointed Bishop of Sapë, replacing his uncle who became Archbishop of Bar (Antivari). In 1641, two years before his death, he is known to have travelled back to Rome to submit to the Pope a report on the diocese of Sapë.

It was during his last year at the College of the Propaganda Fide that Bardhi published the Latin-Albanian dictionary for which he is best known. The work, bearing the title *Dictionarium latino-epiroticum, una cum nonnullis usitatioribus loquendi formulis* (Rome 1635), consists of about 5000 words translated from Latin into Albanian, supplemented by a list of phrases and proverbs. It has been reprinted recently under the title *Fjalor latinisht-shqip 1635*, Prishtinë 1983. Bardhi also published a seventy-six-page work in Latin on Scanderbeg (q.v.), entitled *Georgius Castriottus Epirensis vulgo Scanderbegh, Epirotarum Princeps fortissimus ac invictissimus suis et Patriae restitutus* (Venice 1636), in which he refuted the assertion by the Bosnian bishop, Tomeus Marnavitius, that the Albanian national hero was of Bosnian origin.

Lit.: GECI, Pashko, *Frang Bardhi dhe fjalori i tij latin-shqip.* in: Studime Filologjike (1965) 2, p. 121–128; ROQUES, Mario, *Le dictionnaire albanais de 1635*, Paris 1932.

BARDHI, Pashko (1870–   ). Writer and journalist from Shkodër. He was an active collaborator in the periodical *Hylli i Dritës* (The day-star).

BARLETI, Marin (ca. 1450-ca. 1512). Lat. *Marinus Barletius*. First Albanian historian. He is thought to have been born around 1450 in Shkodër where he lived and survived the second siege of the city by the Turks in 1478. When Shkodër was finally taken, Barleti fled to Italy, living in Venice and Rome, where he came into contact with the culture and ideas of the Italian Renaissance.

Barleti, although he wrote exclusively in Latin, is considered the father of Albanian historiography. His first work on the siege of Shkodër, entitled *De obsidione Scodrensi* (Venice 1504), describes the events he experienced at first hand. More important is his history of Scanderberg (q.v.): *Historia de vita et gestis Scanderbegi, Epirotarum Princeps* (Rome ca. 1508–1510), which was widely read and has been translated into many European languages. It constitutes a basic source of our knowledge of fifteenth century Albania. His last work on the lives of the popes and Roman emperors, *Compendium vitarum summorum pontificium* was published posthumously in Rome in 1555.

Lit.: PALL, F., *Marino Barlezio, uno storico umanista*, Bucharest 1938; SHUTERIQI, Dhimitër, *Mbi Barletin dhe shkrime të tjera*, Tiranë 1979.

BARLETIUS, Marinus. See BARLETI, Marin.

BASHA, Eqrem (1948–   ). Kosovo poet. Born in Dibër, he studied Albanian language and literature at the University of Prishtinë and is now editor of the drama section of Prishtinë television. Among his publications are *Opuset e maestros*, Prishtinë 1971 (The works of the maestro); *Shetitje nëpër mjegull*, Prishtinë 1971 (Walk through the fog); *Stacionet e fisnikëve*, Prishtinë 1972 (The stations of the nobles); *Polip-ptikon*, Prishtinë 1974; *Yjedet*, Prishtinë 1977 (Sea stars); *Mëngjesi i një pasditeje*, Prishtinë 1978 (The breakfast one afternoon); and *Atleti i ëndrrave të bardha*, Prishtinë 1982 (The athlete of white dreams). Basha has also translated Sartre, Camus, Ionesco, and Malraux.

BASHKIMI SOCIETY. Literary and cultural society (Engl. "The union") founded in Shkodër in 1899 on the initiative of Preng Doçi (q.v.) and in collaboration with the Catholic clergy. Among its other members were Gjergj Fishta (q.v.), Luigj Gurakuqi (q.v.), Ndre Mjeda (q.v.), and Lazër Mjeda. The society, having no specific formal structure, was devoted primarily to the creation of an Albanian alphabet, the so-called Bashkimi alphabet, and to the publication of texts for Catholic schools.

BASILE, Angelo (1813–1848). Arbëresh (q.v.) folklorist and writer. Born in Plataci, a mountain village in Cosenza, he was sent as a priest to Naples where he took part in the revolution of 1848.

Of his many works, only one Italian play, *Ines de Castro* (Naples 1847), was published during his lifetime. He is remembered for his collection of Arbëresh folksongs translated into Italian, entitled *Raccolta di canti popolari albanesi*, which was published by his close friend de Rada (q.v.).

Lit.: SHUTERIQI, Dhimitër, *Gjurmime letrare*, Tiranë 1974.

BASILE, Vincenzo (fl. 1845). Italian Jesuit priest and missionary in Shkodër. He is the author, in Albanian, of *Ruga e parrisit*, Rome 1845 (The road to paradise), recounting the legend of the flight of the Madonna of Shkodër to Italy in 1566 after the city had been taken by the Turks. He is also thought to have been the coauthor with Giuseppe Gualiata (q.v.) of an unpublished grammar of Albanian, written in Italian and now lost.

BASTARI, Zenel (early 19th century). Bektash (q.v.)-Moslem poet from the village of Bastar near Tiranë. He worked as a tailor. Little else is known of his life. Bastari is the author of about 200 stanzas of poetry, including Bektash religious verse, love lyrics, and caustic fragments on his rivals.

Lit.: GJYLI, Arif, *Zenel Bastari, vjershëtar i gjysmës së parë të shek. XIX*. in: Buletin i Universitetit Shtetëror të Tiranës. Seria Shkenc. Shoq. (1961) 1, p. 148–180.

BAZHDARI, Gjon (1877–1915). Jesuit priest and editor, born in Shkodër. Bazhdari was editor of the Jesuit periodical *Përparimi* (Progress) from 1914 until his death.

BECICHEMUS, Marinus. See BEÇIKEMI, Marin.

BEÇIKEMI, Marin (1468–1526). Lat. *Marinus Becichemus.* Latin author of Albanian origin. He was from Shkodër and studied and taught in Dubrovnik and Brescia before becoming professor of rhetoric at the University of Padua. He is the author of a number of Latin works, including a panegyric published in Venice in 1503 dealing with the sieges of his native Shkodër in 1474 and 1478.

Lit.: *Marin Beçikemi, nji humanist shkodran (kah 1468–1526).* in: Leka 10 (1938), p. 264–269, 336–344 and 11 (1939), p. 99-103, 116–119.

BEDO, Resul (1927–   ). Author of memoirs and partisan literature from World War II: *Nga Kuçi në Vishegrad,* Tiranë 1958 (From Kuçi to Vishegrad); *Në zemër të maleve,* Tiranë 1960 (In the heart of the mountains); *Njëqind episode partizane,* Tiranë 1963 (One hundred partisan episodes); *Operacioni 'Nepërka',* Tiranë (Operation 'Viper'); *Goditje—kronikë letrare,* Tiranë 1972 (Attack—literary chronicle); and *Gjurmë të ndezura,* Tiranë 1980 (Burning tracks).

BEJTEXHI. Term for a popular poet in the Moslem tradition.

BEKTASHI. Religious order of dervishes founded in Asia Minor in the thirteenth century by Haci Bektaş Veli (Alb. *Haxhi Bektash Veli*). In the fifteenth century, the Bektashi exercised considerable political power in the Ottoman empire due to their influence among the janissaries. It was no doubt via these elite troops that the sect spread to Albania where it flourished. Among its adherents in the nineteenth century was Naim Frashëri (q.v.). Though the Bektashi and all other dervish orders were banned in Turkey in the autumn of 1925, they survived in Albania as an independent religious community up to the 1950s. During the nineteenth century, the Bektashi were instrumental in smuggling and distributing books in Albania and their *tekes* (monasteries) served as covert centres of national culture and learning.

Lit.: BARTL, Peter, *Die albanischen Muslime zur Zeit der nationalen Unabhängigkeitsbewegung (1878–1912),* Wiesbaden 1968, p. 99–111; BIRGE, John Kingsley, *The Bektashi order of dervishes,* London 1937; FRASHËRI, Naim, *Fletore e Bektashinjet,* Bucharest 1896; JOKL, Norbert, *Die Bektaschis von Naim Be Frashëri.* in: Balkan-Archiv 2 (Leipzig 1926), p. 226–256; KISSLING, H.J., *Über die Anfänge des Bektaschitums in Albanien.* in: Oriens 15 (1962), p. 281–286; MYDERRIZI, Osman, *Letërsia fetare e bektashive.* in: Buletin për Shkencat Shoqërore (1955) 3, p. 131–142.

BELIÇI, Domeniko. See UJKO, Vorea.

BELLIZZI, Domenico. See UJKO, Vorea.

BELLUÇI, Konstantin (1796–1867). Ital. *Costantino Bellucci Sciaglia.* Arbëresh (q.v.) poet from San Demetrio Corone. He studied at the Albanian college in his home town and made his living as a tailor and later as a forester.

He was a satirical poet, quite popular at the time, whose verse was published in part by de Rada (q.v.) in 1844 and translated into Italian by Salvatore Braile (q.v.) in 1924 under the title *La commediante, satira ai galantuomini di S. Demetrio Corone.*

BELLUSCI, Michele. See BELLUSHI, Miqel.

BELLUSHI, Miqel (1754–1806). Ital. *Michele Bellusci.* Arbëresh (q.v.) bishop and writer. He was born in Frascineto, Cosenza, and studied at the Arbëresh college of San Benedetto Ullano. He is the author of various writings in Albanian, all of which have been lost.

BELMONTE, Vincenzo (1945–   ). Arbëresh (q.v.) poet. Born in Strigari, Cosenza, he studied philosophy and literature at the University of Rome and now teaches philosophy in Corigliano Calabro. His first collection of poetry, *Vento di Ponente* (West wind), was published in 1973.

BENUSI, Gasper (1850–1931). Also known as *Caspar Benussi Skodrani.* Writer of the Rilindja (q.v.) period. He was born in Shkodër and attended a school of commerce. From about 1876 on, he organized an Albanian private school in his home, as his father George Benusi had done. From 1888 to 1892, he taught at the school of commerce of the Saverian college in Shkodër and from 1892 on, worked as a translator for the Austrian consulate.

Benusi is the author of a bilingual Albanian reader *Scciyptari i msuem n'ghiuh t'vet,* Shkodër 1897 (The learned Albanian in his own language), written in the old Latin alphabet of northern Albanian. He also published an Albanian primer *Abetare e gjuhese scyp,* written in the Istanbul alphabet, in the periodical *Dituria* (Knowledge), Bucharest 1890.

BENUSSI SKODRANI, Caspar. See BENUSI, Gasper.

BEQIRI, Shaip (1954–   ). Kosovo poet. Born in the village of Gllamnik near Podujevë, he studied Albanian language and literature at the University of Prishtinë. He now works for the Kosovo periodical *Zëri i rinisë* (The voice of youth). Beqiri has published two volumes of poetry: *Fontana e etjeve,* Prishtinë 1976 (The fountain of thirst); and *Flatrat e gjymta,* Prishtinë 1983 (The broken wings).

BERATI, Kostandin (ca. 1745–ca. 1825). Also known as *Kostë Berati* or *Constantine of Berat.* Orthodox monk and writer from Berat. He is known only for having possessed a codex from 1764 to 1822, presumably the 152-page manuscript preserved in the National Library of Tiranë. Some authors doubt his existence.

The Codex of Kostandin Berati, or simply Codex of Berat, contains various and sundry works in Greek and Albanian: blessings and prayers in Albanian written in the Greek alphabet; an Albanian poem translated from Greek entitled *Zonja Shën Mëri përpara kryqësë* (The Virgin Mary before the cross); two Greek-Albanian dictionaries comprising a total of 1710 words; an original alphabet for Albanian based on Glagolitic script; and religious notes and a chronicle of events between 1764 and 1789 written in Greek. Some of the religious texts later circulated for teaching purposes among the Orthodox communities of central and southern Albania. From a linguistic point of view, the codex provides useful information about the dialect of eighteenth century Berat.

Lit.: HETZER, Armin, *Der sogenannte Kodex von Berat. II.* in: Südostforschungen 41 (1982), p. 131–179; *Griechisches in Südalbanien im Zeitalter der Aufklärung.* in: Münchner Zeitschrift für Balkankunde 4 (1981–82), p. 169–218.

BERATI, Kostë. See Berati, Kostandin.

BERATI, Nezi (fl. 1920). Author of the play *Zëmra e shpirtit* (The heart of the soul).

BERATI, Nezim. See FRAKULLA, Nezim.

BERISHA, Anton (1946–   ). Kosovo critic and writer from the village of Dobërdol near Klinë. He attended school in Gllarevë and Ujmir and studied Albanian language and literature at the University of Prishtinë. Berisha finished his postgraduate studies at the University of Zagreb in 1981 with a doctoral dissertation on poetic correspondences in oral and written Albanian literature. He has also done research at the University of Göttingen in Germany and now works for the Folklore Department of the Albanological Institute in Prishtinë.

Among his publications are *Përkime poetike,* Prishtinë 1978 (Poetic correspondences); *Mundësi interpretimi,* Prishtinë 1979 (The possibility of interpretation); *Antologji e përrallës shqipe,* Prishtinë 1982 (Anthology of Albanian tales); *Çështje të letërsisë gojore,* Prishtinë 1982 (Questions of oral literature); and *Teksti poetik,* Prishtinë 1985 (The poetic text). He has also written several volumes of poetry for children.

BERISHA, Ibrahim (1955–   ). Kosovo poet and short story writer. He was born in the village of Sllatinë e Madhe near Prishtinë and studied sociology and philosophy at the University of Prishtinë. He now works as a journalist for the daily newspaper *Rilindja* (Rebirth). Berisha has published two volumes of poetry: *Gur që nuk prekesh,* Prishtinë 1983 (The untouchable stone) and *Hardhia e mureve,* Prishtinë 1985 (The wall vine); and a collection of short stories *Fryma e shiut,* Prishtinë 1984 (The spirit of the rain).

BERISHA, Kristë (1922–   ). Kosovo dramatist. He was born in Pejë of a poor family of handicraftsmen and trained as an apprentice in a variety of trades at an early age. After the war he began to write—short stories, poetry, humour, translations, etc.—but has had the most success with drama. Many of his plays, such as *Kryet e hudrës* (The heads of garlic) and *Lugati* (The vampire), have been performed on stage in Kosovo. Three of them have been published in *Tri komedi,* Prishtinë 1973 (Three comedies).

BERISHA, Latif (1931–   ). Kosovo poet. Born in Smrekovnicë near Vuçitërnë, he graduated from secondary school in Pejë in 1950. After studies at the Faculty of Arts of the University of Belgrade, he returned to Vuçitërnë to teach school. Berisha is now professor of Albanian literature at the University of Prishtinë.

His first poetry was published in the Kosovo periodical *Jeta e re* (New life), followed by the collection *Tufa,* Prishtinë 1957 (The crowd).

BERISHA, Rrustem (1938–   ). Kosovo poet and writer. He was born in the village of Godishnjak near Podujevë and studied Albanian language and literature at the University of Prishtinë. Berisha is now on the staff of the

Albanological institute in Prishtinë. Author of: *Bredhje intime*, Prishtinë 1967 (Intimate reflexion); *Qëndresa e emrit*, Prishtinë 1971 (Nominal resistance); *Era e fjetur*, Prishtinë 1974 (The slack wind); *Njeriu dhe kodra*, Prishtinë 1978 (The man and the hill); and *Personifikimi në poezinë popullore shqipe*, Prishtinë 1976 (Personification in Albanian folk verse).

BIDERA, Gjon Emanuel (1784–1858). Arbëresh (q.v.) playwright, poet, prose writer, and folklorist. Born in Palazzo Adriano in Sicily, he lived in Naples, writing among other things libretti for the composer Donizetti. He was also a collector of Albanian folksongs.

BIHIKU, Koço (1927–   ). Literary critic. Head of the section for post-revolutionary literature at the Institute of Linguistics and Literature of the Academy of Sciences in Tiranë.

Among his major publications are *Probleme letrare*, Tiranë 1973 (Literary problems); *Historia e letërsisë shqiptare të realizmit socialist*, Tiranë 1978 (History of the Albanian Literature of Socialist Realism); *Histoire de la littérature albanaise*, Tiranë 1980 (Engl. transl. *History of Albanian literature*, Tiranë 1980); and *Letërsia dhe koha*, Tiranë 1982 (Literature and time).

BILOTA, Bernard (1843–1918). Ital. *Bernardo Bilotta*. Arbëresh (q.v.) poet, linguist, and folklorist from Frascineto. He went to school at the college of Sant' Adriano and entered the Orthodox priesthood in 1866, working thereafter as a teacher. Bilota was a member of the "Consiglio Albanese d'Italia" and promoter of the first Albanian linguistic congress in Corigliano Calabro in 1895.

He is the author of a 6000-word *Dizionario Albanese* containing material from the dialect of Frascineto; a *Monografia di Frascineto*, being a chronicle of his birthplace; and *Zakonet e Frashnitës* (The customs of Frascineto), none of which have been published. He also composed modest poetry, among which are his collection of elegaic sonnets entitled *Versi lugubri*, Castrovillari 1894 (Somber verse); and *Stima agli ottimi, biasimo ai tristi*, Castrovillari 1898 (Homour to the best, disdain to the sad). Bilota is best remembered for his historical *Shpata Skanderbekut ndë Dibrët Poshtë*, Tiranë 1967 (The sword of Scanderbeg in Lower Dibër).

Lit.: GIORDANO, Emanuele, *Bernardo Bilotta, scrittore e poeta albanese di Frascineto*. in Shêjzat 3 (1959), p. 175–181.

BILOTTA, Bernardo. See BILOTA, Bernard.

BITRI, Hysen (fl. 1820). Poet from Krujë. Author of three Bektash (q.v.) religious poems in Albanian, written in Arabic script before 1831.

BITYQI, Ndue. See BYTYÇI, Ndue.

BLANCHUS, Franciscus. See BARDHI, Frang.

BLANCO, Francesco. See BARDHI, Frang.

BLUSHI, Kiço (1943–   ). Prose and film script writer and poet. Born in Korçë, he finished his studies at the University of Tiranë in 1966. He now works for "New Albania" Film Studios and has published a number of works including *Vdekja e një nate*, Tiranë 1971 (One night's death); *Fejesa, televizori, plaku*, Tiranë 1971 (The engagement, the television, the old man); *Beni* *ecën vetë,* Tiranë 1976 (Engl. transl. *Beni walks on his own,* Tiranë 1983); *Sonte dhe nesër në mëngjes,* Tiranë 1977 (Tonight and tomorrow morning); *Mëngjesi i një së hëne,* Tiranë 1980 (One Monday morning); and *Vite mbi supe,* Tiranë 1984 (Years on shoulders).

BOÇARI, Marko (1790–1823). Also known as *Markos Botzaris.* Author of a Greek-Albanian lexicon written in Corfu in 1809 at the instance of François Pouqueville, author himself and French consul in Ioannina. Boçari was a Suliot hero from the Greek wars. The lexicon is of importance for our knowledge of the Suliot dialect.

Lit.: JOCHALAS, Titos, *To ellino-alvanikon lexikon tou Markou Botzari,* Athens 1980.

BOGDANI, Luca. See BOGDANI, Lukë.

BOGDANI, Lukë (fl. 1685). Also known as *Luca Bogdani.* Poet. Cousin of Pjetër Bogdani (q.v.) in whose honour he wrote an eighty-line panegyric poem in Albanian, published in the *Cuneus Prophetarum* (The wedge of the prophets) in 1685.

BOGDANI, Pjetër (ca. 1630–1689). The last and most original writer of early Albanian literature and author of the *Cuneus Prophetarum* (The wedge of the prophets), the first prose work written originally in Albanian (i.e., not a translation).

Born in Guri i Hasit near Prizren about 1630, he was educated in the traditions of the Catholic church to which he devoted all his energies. He studied at Loreto College near Ancona and from 1654 to 1656 at the College of the Propaganda Fide in Rome where he took the title doctor of philosophy and theology. In 1658, he was named Bishop of Shkodër and subsequently made supervisor of the Archdiocese of Bar (Antivari). In 1677, he succeeded his uncle as Archbishop of Skopje. His religious zeal and patriotic fervour kept him in constant conflict with the Turkish authorities who forced him into exile to Dubrovnik, from where he fled to Venice, taking his manuscripts with him.

It was in Padua in 1685 that his vast treatise on theology, in Albanian and Italian, was published with the assistance of Cardinal Barbarigo, whom he had served in Rome. The full title of the work is: *Cuneus prophetarum de Christo salvatore mundi et eius evangelica veritate, italice et epirotice contexta, et in duas partes divisa a Petro Bogdano Macedone, Sacr. Congr. de Prop. Fide alumno, Philosophiae et Sacrae Theologiae Doctore, olim Episcopo Scodrensi et Administratorei Antibarensi; nunc vero Archiepiscopo Scuporum ac totius regni Serviae Administratore.*

Volume 1 of the *Cuneus Prophetarum* deals primarily with the creation of the world and the lives of the prophets and sibyls; volume 2, with the life of the Virgin Mary, the life of Jesus, and visions of the last judgement and paradise. Interspersed, however, are digressions on history, geography, astronomy, and poetry both by Bogdani and other authors, which allow us to assume the presence of a certain literary tradition in northern Albania at the time. The work was reprinted twice under the title *L'infallibile verità della cattolica fede . . .*

(Venice 1691 and 1702) and more recently as volume 24 of the series "Beiträge zur Kenntnis Südosteuropas und des Nahen Orients" (Munich 1977).

Bogdani himself, who is now often considered the father of Albanian prose, returned to Albania in 1685 and died four years later in Prishtinë. His contribution to Albanian literature lies primarily in his lexical enrichment of the language, enabling subsequent authors to express themselves more abstractly.

Lit.: RUGOVA, Ibrahim, *Vepra e Bogdanit 1675–1685*, Prishtinë 1982; SCIAMBRA, Matteo, *Bogdanica—studi di Pietro Bogdani e l'opera sua*, Bologna 1965; ZAMPUTI, Injac, *Shënime mbi kohën dhe jetën e Pjetër Bogdanit*. in: Buletini për Shkencat Shoqërore (1954) 3, p. 39–75.

BOGOMILI, Theodhor (17th century). Possible author of an anonymous manuscript of the Gospels from Elbasan, known as the *Anonimi i Elbasanit* (q.v.). Nothing is known of his life. His name appears on the cover of the work, found in 1949 among the writings of Theodhor Haxhifilipi (q.v.).

BOKSHI, Besim (1934–   ). Kosovo poet and philologist. Born in Gjakovë, he left Kosovo with his family for Albania at an early age and attended school in Dukat near Vlorë and Tiranë. In 1945, he returned to Gjakovë and later studied at the Faculty of Arts of the University of Belgrade. He finished his doctorate in philology at the University of Prishtinë where he now lectures.

His works, known for their pensive, modern sensibilities and richness of expression, have been published in Albanian, Serbo-Croatian, and other languages. He is author of the volume *Në pritje*, Prishtinë 1966 (In expectation).

Lit.: MEKULI, Hasan, *Poezia e Besim Bokshit*. in: Jeta e re (1968) 3, p. 633–644.

BORIÇI, Daut (1825–1896). Writer and nationalist figure of the Rilindja (q.v.) period. He was born in Shkodër and studied from 1850 in Istanbul, where he attended a theological seminary and a teacher training college. After finishing his studies, he returned to Shkodër and worked there as a teacher and school inspector. As a result of his nationalist activities, he was exiled to Turkey in 1880, where he was, however, later able to continue his career as a school inspector. In 1888, we find him back in Albania as a director of school administration for the vilayet of Shkodër.

Boriçi is the author of an Albanian primer, published in Arabic script in Istanbul in 1861. Information as to its size and contents varies. He also wrote a short Albanian grammar and a Turkish-Albanian dictionary which remained unpublished.

Lit.: BUSHATI, Nexhmi, *Të dhana rreth biografisë së Daut Boriçit*. in: Buletin i Universitetit Shtetëror të Tiranës. Seria Shkenc. Shoq. 16 (1962) 2, p. 268–278.

BOSHNJAKU, Tahir (fl. 1835). Also known as *Tahir efendi Jakova* or *Efendiu i Madh* (The Great Efendi). Moslem poet from Kosovo. Born in Gjakovë, he was a student of Islamic theology and later taught at the "Small School" there. He travelled widely throughout Bosnia, whence probably his name.

He is the author of a work entitled *Vehbije*, 1835 (Offering), or *Emni Veh-*

bijje, a collection of disciplined verse in Arabic metre and of prose in the Moslem tradition and highly influenced by Turkish, Persian, and Arabic models. It was printed in the Istanbul alphabet in Sofia in 1907.

BOTASI, Jani (1839–1924). Greek-Albanian politician and writer from the island of Spetsai. After studies in Athens, he emigrated to the United States. In 1874, however, he returned to Greece, took up a career in politics, and became a deputy. In 1889, he was elected president of the Greek society for history and ethnography, a position he was to hold for thirty years. Botasi is also the author of poetry written in Albanian.

BOTZARIS, Markos. See BOÇARI, Marko.

BRAHIMI, Razi (1931–   ). Critic and writer from Delvina, known for his stylistic subtleties. Brahimi teaches at the University of Tiranë. He is the author of the novel *Kthesa të forta,* Prishtinë 1969 (Sharp curves); the short story collections *Tregime,* Tiranë 1959 (Short stories); *Katër vajza—dhe novela të tjera,* Tiranë 1962 (Four girls—and other stories); *Zgjim pranvere,* Tiranë 1969 (Awakening of spring); *Larg familjes,* Tiranë 1972 (Far from home); and the studies *Fjalë për letërsinë,* Tiranë 1960 (A word about literature); *Shënime letrare,* Tiranë 1965 (Literary notes); *Kritika,* Prishtinë 1972 (Criticism); *Kur flasim për poezinë,* Tiranë 1972 (When we speak of poetry); *Kënga popullore e Rilindjes kombëtare,* Tiranë 1979 (Folksongs in the national Renaissance); and *Artet dhe zhvillimi i tyre në RPSSh,* Tiranë 1981 (The arts and their development in Albania).

BRAILE, Maria Antonia (1894–1917). Arbëresh (q.v.) poetess from San Demetrio Corone in Cosenza. Her one volume of verse, entitled *I Canti,* Corigliano Calabro 1917 (Songs), was published by her brother Salvatore Braile (q.v.). This simple, tender, and melancholic collection reflects the sufferings of her short life: war, illness, and the death of her son.

BRAILE, Salvatore (1872–1960). Arbëresh (q.v.) lyric and satirical poet. Brother of Maria Antonia Braile (q.v.). He was born in San Demetrio Corone, Cosenza, and was forced to interrupt his schooling at an early age to work at a post office.

Braile published a collection of youthful verse in Italian, entitled *Fra un telegramma e l'altro,* Corigliano Calabro 1925 (Between one telegramme and another) while working in Shkodër as an Italian teacher at the Franciscan secondary school. He is particularly remembered for his translation of *La commediante, satira ai galantuomini di S. Demetrio Corone* by Konstantin Belluçi (q.v.) (Shkodër 1924). Most of his Albanian poetry, composed between the years 1894 and 1953 remains unpublished. It is contained in a manuscript entitled *Vjersha në dialektin e kolonivet shqiptare të Kalabrís* (Verse in the dialect of the Albanian colony of Calabria).

BRANCATO, G. Nicola. See BRANKATI, Nikollë.

BRANKATI, Nikollë (1675–1741). Ital. *Nicola Brancato.* Arbëresh (q.v.) religious poet. Born in Piana degli Albanesi in Sicily, he became archpriest of the Albanian church in Palermo in 1717, a post he held for the rest of his life.

His metrically refined verse, mostly of a religious nature, was preserved in the Codex Chieuti (1737).

BREDHI, Naum Panajot Haxhi Llazar. See VEQILHARXHI, Naum.

BROCARDUS. See ADAE, Guillelmus.

BROCHARD. See ADAE, Guillelmus.

BROVINA, Flora (1949–   ). Kosovo poetess whose verse has appeared in several periodicals and newspapers in the last few years. She was born in the village of Serbicë in the Drenicë region and studied medicine in Prishtinë. She now works as a pediatrician.

Among her publications are *Verma emrin tim,* Prishtinë 1973 (Call my name); and a collection entitled *Bimë e zë,* Prishtinë 1979 (Plant and voice), expressing a strong commitment to the feminist movement.

BRUTUS. See STAFA, Qemal.

BUBANI, Dionis (1926–   ). Satirical poet and playwright born in Bucharest. Son of Gjergj Bubani (q.v.). Among his plays are *Armiku i grave* (The misogynist); *Sëmundja e rrezikshme* (The serious illness); and *Ilaç i hidhur* (The bitter medicine).

He has published the verse collections: *Yjet nuk shuhen,* Tiranë 1959 (The stars do not die); *Çështje personale,* Tiranë 1962 (A personal matter); *Përtej hundës,* Tiranë 1967 (Beyond the nose); *Zgjidh e merr,* Tiranë 1970 (Pick and choose); *Miku i mikut,* Tiranë 1972 (The friend of a friend); *Poezi të zgjedhura,* Tiranë 1973 (Selected poetry); *Shigjeta,* Tiranë 1975 (The arrow); and *Sekreti i sekretit,* Tiranë 1978 (The secret of the secret).

BUBANI, Gjergj (20th century). Tosk (q.v.) poet and journalist. He grew up with a knowledge of Albanian and Greek, his early verse being in Greek. He studied in Athens and later lived in Bucharest, publishing numerous articles in the periodical *Shqipëria e re* (New Albania), of which he later became editor. Bubani also worked for a time at the Albanian consulate in Constanza and then in Sofia. Upon his return to Albania in 1945, he was arrested on a charge of political collaboration and sentenced to fifteen years imprisonment.

Bubani is primarily known for his satirical poetry but is also the author of plays and translations, especially from Romanian and Russian.

BUBURICKA. See MUSARAJ, Shevqet.

BUCIARELLI, Dari (19th century). Religious writer of the Catholic school of Shkodër. He is the author of *Udha e shejtës kryq,* Rome 1862 (The way of the holy cross), a collection of religious stories based on the lives of the saints.

BUDI, Pjetër (1566–1623). Major figure of early Albanian literature. Budi was born in Guri i Bardhë in the Mati region of the north-central Albanian mountains about 1566. He was a parish priest in Kosovo, vicar general of the Serbian church, and in 1621 became Bishop of Zadrimë. Two years later he drowned, probably by accident, while crossing the River Drin.

In a letter addressed to Cardinal Gozzadini, Budi reported that in order to ease missionary work and strengthen the faith of the Albanian people, he had written several devotional works in their language. Of these we have: *Doktrina e Kërshtenë* or *Dottrina Christiana,* Rome 1618 (Christian doctrine), a translation of the catechism of the Jesuit Roberto Bellarmino; *Rituali Roman* or *Rituale Romanum,* Rome 1621, (Roman ritual), containing Latin prayers and sacraments with comments in Albanian; and *Pasëqyra e t'rrëfyemit* or *Speculum Confessionis,* Rome 1621 (The mirror of confession), a 408-page work including among other things several poems addressed to the Virgin Mary. In all, Budi composed about 3300 lines of religious verse which constitute the earliest poetry in Geg (q.v.) dialect. This and some fifty pages of original prose are particularly important for the study of the language of northern Albania at the beginning of the seventeenth century.

Lit.: ASHTA, Kolë, *Pjetër Budi, prozator e vjershëtar.* in: Shkodra (1966) 1, p. 282–301; DOMI, Mahir, *Pjetër Budi (1566–1622).* in: Studia Albanica (1967) 1, p. 67–73; LACAJ, Henrik, *Pjetër Budi, vjershëtor i parë i letërsisë sonë.* in: Studime Filologjike (1966) 4, p. 151–158; ZAMPUTI, Injac, *Koha dhe veprimtaria e Pjetër Budit.* in: Nëndori (1965) 9, p. 123–142.

BULKA, Nonda (1906–1972). Essayist and satirist. Together with Migjeni (q.v.), Bulka is considered one of the best representatives of progressive literature in the 1930s. Born in Përmet, he studied at the French lycée in Korçë. From there, he went on to study law in Paris. He worked as a barber, photographer, and seller of spirits before becoming a journalist and writer. He also taught French after the war.

His humorous and at times bitterly cynical sketches, published under the pseudonym of *Chri-Chri* in periodicals such as *Bota e re* and *Rilindja* were known for their biting criticism of social and political conditions under the Zog regime. Many of these were collected in the volume *Kur qan e qesh bilbili,* Korçë 1934 (When the nightingale cries and laughs). Among his other publications are *Skica dhe tregime,* Tiranë 1950 (Sketches and tales); *Vargje satirike,* Tiranë 1951 (Satirical verse); *Në dritën e yllit,* Tiranë 1952 (In the starlight); *Soditje,* Tiranë 1957 (Contemplation); *Maska të çjerra,* Tiranë 1966 (Torn masks); *Tregime të zgjedhura,* Tiranë 1972 (Selected short stories); and several translations of nineteenth century French authors (Balzac, Zola, Daudet). His works have been recently reedited in three volumes: *Vepra letrare,* Tiranë 1980 (Literary works).

Lit.: GURAKUQI, Mark, *Disa mendime lidhë me krijimtarinë letrare të Nonda Bulkës.* in: Nëndori (1961) 4, p. 188–214, XHAXHIU, Muzafer, *Veprimtaria letrare e Nonda Bulkës.* in: Studime Filologjike 33 (1979) 1, p. 63–95.

BULO, Jorgo (contemporary). Literary critic. Head of the section of prerevolutionary literature at the Institute of Linguistics and Literature of the Academy of Sciences in Tiranë. He has published *Tradita dhe risi letrare,* Tiranë 1981 (Tradition and literary renewal).

BUSHAKA, Gaqo (1943–   ). Author of children's literature. Born in a mountain village south of Gjirokastër, he was raised in Tiranë. After vocational training at the school of higher technology, he worked first as an electrician.

He continued his education at night school and later went on to study Albanian language and literature at the University of Tiranë. Bushaka is married, has two children, and now works for the Naim Frashëri Publishing Company.

His first collection of short stories appeared in 1967. Since then, he has published over twenty books—short stories and novels for children and young people as well as several plays.

BUTKA, Sali (1852–1938). Nationalist poet from southern Albania. He originated from the village of Butka in Kolonja on the Greek border and was one of the main leaders of Albanian forces against both the Greeks and the Young Turks.

His nationalist and political poetry, inspired in part by Naim Frashëri (q.v.), was published in the collection *Ndjenja për atdhenë*, Korçë 1920 (Patriotic sentiments).

BUXHELI, Qamil (1925–   ). Satirical novelist, short story writer, and dramatist. Born in Sarandë, he took part in the partisan movement of World War II. After the liberation, he studied at the Gorky Institute of World Literature in Moscow and became editor of the periodical *Ylli*. He now teaches in Elbasan at the institute of literature.

Among his collections of short stories are *Një ndodhi në plazh*, Tiranë 1962 (An event at the beach); and *Nihilisti*, Tiranë 1969 (The nihilist). His novel *Karriera e Zotit Maksut*, Tiranë 1971 (The career of Mr Maksut) satirizes the mediocracy and indolence of the civil service. He has also published: *Kali i mbretit dhe kalorës të rinj*, Tiranë 1960 (The king's horse and young knights); *Varka e të dymbëdhjetëve*, Tiranë 1964 (The ship of the twelve); *Rrugë të tërthorta*, Tiranë 1966 (Indirect roads); *Kur qesh tërë qyteti*, Tiranë 1970 (When the whole city laughs); *Pjesë të zgjedhura*, Tiranë 1972 (Selected sketches); and *Perënditë bien nga fiku*, Tiranë 1978 (The gods fall from a fig tree).

BUZËDHELPRI. See JORDANI, Agostin.

BUZUKU, Gjon (fl. 1555). Author of the first Albanian book, usually called the Liturgy or Missal (Alb. *Meshari*). Nothing much is known of his life, although we may assume him to have been a Catholic priest from northern Albania. His Liturgy, of which the title and first sixteen pages are missing, consists of 220 pages of translations from the Bible and a postscript in which the author explains his intentions. It was begun, according to Buzuku himself, on March 20, 1554, and finished on January 5, 1555. The book is thought to have been printed in Venice and survives in one copy only, discovered by Gjon Nikollë Kazazi (q.v.) in 1740 and now preserved in the Vatican Library.

The Liturgy provides us with a unique glimpse into early Albanian including many archaic features not otherwise recorded. It is written in Geg (q.v.) dialect, though at a period of greater linguistic unity than the Geg of subsequent writers such as Budi (q.v.), Bardhi (q.v.), and Bogdani (q.v.).

Lit.: ÇABEJ, Eqrem, *"Meshari" i Gjon Buzukut (1555)*, Tiranë 1968; CAMAJ, Martin, *Il "Messale" di Gjon Buzuku*, Rome 1960, RESSULI, Namik, *Il "Messale" di Giovanni Buzuku*, Vatican City 1958.

BYTYÇI, Ndue (1847–1917). Alternatively *Ndue Bityqi de Marino,* also known as the "Nightingale of Kosovo." Catholic poet and priest. Born near Skopje, he received a Catholic education at the Saverian college in Shkodër which he entered at the age of twelve. Having finished his training, he returned to Kosovo and Macedonia to teach and minister. He was also a close friend of the Arbëresh (q.v.) poet Leonardo de Martino (q.v.).

Bytyçi is the author of religious and some secular poetry, both unpublished for the most part, as well as a number of translations of Italian religious literature. His verse is rich in technique and metrical precision, though permeated with Turkisms which make it difficult for the modern reader. Particularly impressive are his translations of the Psalms of David. His secular, patriotic verse, entitled *Mymleqeti* (The fatherland), was published in 1887.

Lit.: FULLANI, Dhimitër, *Ndue Bytyçi (1847–1917).* in: Nëndori (1962) 6, p. 94–95.

C

ÇABEJ, Eqrem (1908-1980). Albanologist, historical linguist, and lexicographer. Çabej was born in Gjirokastër and studied linguistics and philology in Klagenfurt, Graz, and finally in Vienna, notably under Norbert Jokl. Steeped in the traditions of German philology, he returned to Albania to do pioneer research on the origins and history of the Albanian language.

Among his major publications are: *"Meshari" i Gjon Buzukut*, Tiranë 1968 (The liturgy of Gjon Buzuku); *Hyrje në historinë e gjuhës shqipe*, Tiranë 1958 (Introduction to the history of the Albanian language); *Fonetika historike e shqipes*, Tiranë 1968 (Historical phonology of Albanian); and the unfinished *Studime etimologjike*, Tiranë 1976 (Etymological studies). He is also the author of studies in literature and ethnology. His works have been reprinted in six volumes in *Studime gjuhësore*, Prishtinë 1976 (Linguistic studies).

ÇAÇI, Aleks (1916–   ). Poet. Born in Palasë in the southern Albanian Himarë district, Çaçi studied in Vlorë before joining the then illegal Albanian Communist party, founded in 1941. He took part in the partisan struggle, writing articles and poetry for underground newspapers. After the war, he continued his career in journalism and eventually became editor of the leading Albanian daily newspaper *Zëri i Popullit* (The People's Voice). During the years of the Sino-Albanian alliance, he had an opportunity to visit China and recorded some of his experiences there in the volume *Nëpër komunet popullore*, Tiranë 1963 (Through the people's communes).

Çaçi is perhaps best known for his *Ashtu, Myzeqe*, Tiranë 1947 (That's it, Myzeqe) about the transformation of the backward, swampy Myzeqe district of central Albania, a theme taken up again in his *Ti je, Myzeqe?*, Tiranë 1970 (Is that you, Myzeqe?). Among his other poetry collections are *Me ty, Stalin*, Tiranë 1948 (With you, Stalin); *Këngët e dheut*, Tiranë 1951 (Songs of the earth); *Zarika*, Tiranë 1955 (Zarika); *Na ish një kënetë*, Tiranë 1957 (There was a swamp); *Flamuj të kuq*, Tiranë 1963 (Red flags); *Ëndrat e mia*, Tiranë

1965 (My dreams); *Legjenda e kuqe,* Tiranë 1968 (The red legend); *Fjalë të bardha,* Tiranë 1973 (White words); *Poezi të zgjedhura,* Tiranë 1974 (Selected poetry); *Era e popullit,* Tiranë 1977 (Wind of the people); *Aroma e tokës,* Tiranë 1980 (Aroma of the land); and *Bisedë me diellin,* Tiranë 1983 (Talk with the sun).

ÇAJUPI, Andon Zako (1866–1930). Real name *Andon Çako.* Poet and playwright. Çajupi was born in March 1866 in Sheper, a village in the Gjirokastër district of southern Albania. In 1882, he left for Egypt where his father was a tobacco merchant. After graduating from the French lycée in Alexandria, he went on to study law in Geneva. Upon completion of his degree in 1893, he returned to Cairo, although a dispute with the governor of Egypt soon put an end to his legal career. Çajupi devoted much of his time and energy to organizing the Albanian community in Egypt as part of the nationalist struggle against the Turkish occupation of his homeland and was in close contact with Albanian emigrants in Turkey, Bulgaria, and Romania.

His main work is the collection of poetry *Baba Tomorri,* Cairo 1902 (Father Tomorr), named after Mt. Tomorr, the Parnassus of Albanian mythology, in which he gave expression to his nationalist sentiments. He earned his reputation as a playwright posthumously with *Burri i dheut,* 1937 (The hero), a drama about Scanderbeg (q.v.) and with the one-act comedy *Pas vdekjes,* 1937 (After death). He also found time to write children's verse and to translate La Fontaine, *Perralla,* Heliopolis 1921 (Fables); and a selection of Sanscrit verse, *Lulet e Hindit,* Cairo 1922 (The flowers of India). His writings have been reedited in *Vepra 1–6,* Prishtinë 1983 (Works 1–6).

Lit.: DADO, Floresha, *A. Z. Çajupi, jeta dhe vepra,* Tiranë 1983; SHUTERIQI, Dhimitër, *Autorë dhe tekste,* Tiranë 1977, p. 373–417; ZHEJI, Gjergj, *Andon Zako-Çajupi, jeta dhe vepra,* Tiranë 1966.

ÇAKO, Andon. See ÇAJUPI, Andon Zako.

CAMAJ, Martin (1925–   ). Albanologist and writer. Born in Dukagjin in the northern Albanian alps, he received his schooling in Shkodër and studied Albanology in Belgrade. From there, he went on to do postgraduate research in Italy where he taught Albanian and finished his studies in linguistics at the University of Rome. He is presently professor of Albanology at the University of Munich and lives in the village of Lenggries in Upper Bavaria.

Aside from his extensive linguistic research, including a study of nominal morphology *Albanische Wortbildung,* Wiesbaden 1966, and textbooks for students of the language, *Lehrbuch der albanischen Sprache,* Wiesbaden 1969, and *Albanian Grammar,* Wiesbaden 1984, Camaj has published numerous volumes of prose and poetry. His first volumes of verse *Nji fyell ndër male,* Prishtinë 1953 (A flute in the mountains) and *Kânga e vërrinit,* Prishtinë 1954 (Song of the lowland pastures) were inspired by his native northern Albanian mountains to which he has never lost his attachment, despite long years in exile. These were followed by *Djella,* Rome 1958, a novel, interspersed with verse, about the love of a teacher for a young girl of the lowlands; the poetic works

Legjenda, Rome 1964 (Legends), and *Lirika mes dy moteve,* Munich 1967 (Lyrics between two years), both reprinted in *Poezi 1953-1967,* Munich 1981. Among his other literary publications are the prose works *Rrathë,* Munich 1978; and *Shkundullima,* Munich 1981; a volume of verse entitled *Njeriu më vete e me tjerë,* Munich 1978 (Man by himself and with others); and *Dranja,* Munich 1981, a collection of so-called madrigals. A selection of his poetry has recently been translated into Italian by Francesco Solano (q.v.): *Martin Camaj—Poesie,* Palermo 1985.

CAMARDA, Demetrio. See KAMARDA, Dhimitër.

CAMARDA, Giuseppe. See KAMARDA, Zef.

ÇAMI, Muhamet. See KYÇYKU, Muhamet.

ÇAMI, Qamil I. (1885-1933). Rilindja (q.v.) poet from the Çamëria region (now northern Greece). He took an active part in the nationalist movement leading to Albanian independence. In later years he worked as a teacher.

Çami is the author of popular tales and fables in verse form, published in *Fabula dhe vjersha,* Tiranë 1973 (Fables and verse).

CANDREVA, Carmelo. See KANDREVA, Karmell.

CASTRIOTI, George. See SCANDERBEG.

CATALANO, Nilo (1637-1694). Italian lexicographer. Born in the village of Castania near Messina, Sicily, he became a missionary in Himarë and in 1693 was appointed Archbishop of Durrës. He is also known to have taught Albanian among the Arbëresh.

Catalano is the author of an Albanian-Italian, Italian-Albanian lexicon now said to be preserved in the Royal Library of Copenhagen.

CAVALLIOTI, T. See KAVALIOTI, Theodhor.

ÇEKREZI, Kostantin (fl. 1920). Engl. *Constantine Chekrezi.* Albanian-American writer and editor. Born in the village of Ziçisht in the Korçë area, he emigrated at the outbreak of World War I to the United States where he became editor of the Boston periodical *Dielli* (The sun) until the latter was taken over by Fan Noli (q.v.). He also published the short-lived Boston periodical *Illyria* in 1916 and served as Albanian high commissioner to Washington.

He is the author of the reader *Kendime,* Boston 1910 (Readings); works of history such as *Albania past and present,* New York 1919; *Histori e Shqipërisë,* Boston 1921 (History of Albania); *Histori e vjetër,* Boston 1921 (Ancient history); and of the first English-Albanian dictionary, *Fjalor inglisth-shqip,* Boston 1923.

ÇELA, Zija (1946-   ). Journalist and short story writer. Born in Shkodër, he studied at the Faculty of History and Philology in Tiranë. He is presently secretary of the editing board of the literary weekly *Drita* (The light) and has published the short story collections: *Yje mbi lumë,* Tiranë 1971 (Stars on the river); *Jeta në shtëpinë tonë,* Tiranë 1974 (Life at our house); *Pëllumbat e janarit,* Tiranë 1979 (The January pigeons); and *Buletini i borës,* Tiranë 1984 (The snow bulletin).

CEPA, Kristaq (1908–). Also known as *Kapa*. Satirical poet, whose socially critical verse appeared in the 1930s in the periodicals *Rilindja* and *Bota e re*.

CEPI, Kostandin (fl. 1820). Orthodox writer from southern Albania. Originally from Vithkuq, he is said to have had some sort of function among the Orthodox community in the Korçë area. He is remembered for a codex of religious texts, mostly in Greek, but containing twenty-two pages of Albanian which were obviously used as a teaching aid for the study of the Greek scriptures. The codex, which also contains texts in Aromanian, dates from about 1820–1822.

CERAJA, Jakup (1934–). Kosovo poet from the village of Cerajë in the Shala region of northern Kosovo. He went to school in Mitrovicë and Pejë and studied in Gjakovë and at the University of Prishtinë. He later taught school in the countryside, where he first began writing.

Ceraja is author of the volumes: *Përkushtime*, Prishtinë 1966 (Dedications); *Djersa dhe gjaku*, Prishtinë 1968 (Sweat and blood); *Pranvera po të bëhet verë*, Prishtinë 1971 (May spring turn into summer); *Ngjarje që s'duan shpjegim*, Prishtinë 1973 (Events wanting no explanation); *Kur dhemb zemra*, Tiranë 1976 (When the heart aches); *As duket as humbet*, Prishtinë 1980 (Neither seen nor lost); and *Udhëton me erëra*, Prishtinë 1985 (He travels with the wind). Ceraja has also written poetry for children, satirical verse, prose, and essays.

CERGA, Agim (1935–). Novelist and short story writer. Born in Kukës, he studied at the Faculty of History and Philology of the University of Tiranë. He was the editor of the periodical *Ylli* for several years and is now literary secretary of the Albanian Union of Writers and Artists.

Cerga's novels and short stories deal primarily with young people and the construction of a Communist society. Among his works are *Njeri i zakonshëm*, Tiranë 1962 (The average man); *Dritë në fushë*, Tiranë 1966 (Light on the plain); *Erë e fortë*, Tiranë 1976 (A strong wind); *Bukuria e jetës*, Tiranë 1971 (The beauty of life); *Gjurmë në kohë*, Tiranë 1971 (Traces in time); *Borë e pashkelur*, Tiranë 1972 (Unexplored snow); *Legjenda e vadave*, Tiranë 1974 (Legend of the waterways); *Vëllezërit*, Tiranë 1978 (The brothers); *Fëmijëria*, Tiranë 1983 (Childhood); and *Shtëpia*, Tiranë 1984 (The house).

ÇETTA, Anton (1920–). Kosovo writer and poet. Born in Gjakovë, he was raised in Prizren. At the age of nine, he moved with his family to Tiranë and subsequently to Korçë. He graduated from secondary school in Milan, returning in 1941 to Prizren where he spent the rest of the war years. From 1946 to 1950 he was a student at the University of Belgrade and later taught Albanian at the University of Prishtinë. He is now a folklore researcher at the Albanological Institute in Prishtinë and is one of the editors of the periodical *Gjurmime albanologjike* (Albanological research).

Çetta began to write at a relatively late age and is known for his interest in children's literature, as seen in *Në prehën të gjyshes*, Prishtinë 1955 (On grandfather's knee). He is also the author of many works on folk literature, such as

Tregime popullore, Drenicë, Prishtinë 1963 (Folk tales, Drenicë); *Prozë popullore nga Drenica,* Prishtinë 1972 (Popular prose from Drenicë); *Balada dhe legjenda,* Prishtinë 1974 (Ballads and legends); *Këngë kreshnike I,* Prishtinë 1974 (Heroic songs I); *Kërkime folklorike,* Prishtinë 1981 (Folklore research); *Nga folklori ynë,* Prishtinë 1983 (From our folklore); and of translations from Serbo-Croatian, French, and Italian.

CHAJUP. See ÇAJUPI, Andon Zako.

CHEKREZI, Constantine. See ÇEKREZI, Kostantin.

CHETTA, Nicola. See KETA, Nikollë.

CHIARA, Pietro. See KJARA, Pjetër.

CHRI-CHRI. See BULKA, Nonda.

CIBAJ, Ismet (1935–   ). Short story writer. Born in Vlorë, he finished his studies of Albanian literature at the University of Tiranë in 1958. Cibaj has worked as a teacher and journalist and is now on the staff of the Naim Frashëri Publishing Company. His short stories and sketches have appeared recently in Albanian literary periodicals.

ÇIÇKOJA, Haxhi (19th century). Moslem poet from Korçë. Author of a mevlud (poem on the birth of the prophet Mohammed).

CIKULI, Zisa (contemporary). Dramatist and poetess. Author of *Vjersha,* Tiranë 1955 (Poetry); and *Flakë në shtëpi,* Tiranë 1968 (Flame in the house), a moralistic play about profiteering.

ÇOMORA, Spiro (1918–1973). Satirical poet, humourist, and playwright. Born in Vuno in the Himarë region, he studied law in Rome. He returned to Albania to take part in the liberation of the country and subsequently served as a judge in Elbasan. He later worked for the satirical magazine *Hosteni* (The goad) in Tiranë.

Although he has published in many fields, he is particularly known for his children's poetry and comedies, of which *Karnavalet e Korçës,* Tiranë 1961 (The carnivals of Korçë) and *Dy me zero,* Tiranë 1969 (Two to nothing) were critically acclaimed by Albanian theatrical circles. Çomora is also remembered for his translations of Homer and Aristophanes. His collected works have been republished in a four volume edition: *Vepra letrare,* Tiranë 1980 (Literary works).

CONGRESS OF MONASTIR. See MONASTIR, Congress of.

CONSTANTINE OF BERAT. See BERATI, Kostandin.

CORINALDI, Giuseppe (fl. 1835). Priest from Poreč on the Istrian peninsula. Corinaldi is known for having made, or at least preserved, a translation of the parable of the Prodigal Son (Luke 15:11–32) into the Istrian dialect of Albanian.

A community of Geg (q.v.) speakers emigrated to the Istrian peninsula in the sixteenth or seventeenth century from the Shkodër/Ulcinj area and Albanian was still spoken there in a few villages around Poreč in 1835 at the time of Corinaldi's translation. The dialect became extinct towards the middle of the nineteenth century and the above-mentioned parable constitutes the only text preserved in this dialect.

CORTESE, Danil. See KORTEZE, Daniel.
CRISPI, Giuseppe. See KRISPI, Zef.
CRISPI GLAVIANO, Francesco. See KRISPI GLAVJANO, Frano.
ÇUKA, Pano (1925–). Greco-Albanian poet and prose writer. He was born in the village of Sopik east of Gjirokastër, inhabited primarily by members of the Greek-speaking minority in southern Albania. He attended secondary school in Greece and after the war worked as a journalist for the Greek-language newspaper *Laiko vima.* He is now a professional writer.

Çuka is the author of works in Greek and Albanian. Among his Albanian-language publications are *Çelësat e lumturisë,* Tiranë 1966 (The keys of happiness); *Koka e gjarpërit,* Tiranë 1972 (The snake's head); *Urdhëroni në vendlindjen time,* Tiranë 1973 (Welcome to my native land); and *Soditje nga bedenat,* Tiranë 1982 (Contemplation from the battlements). Many of his Greek-language works have been translated into Albanian. Çuka has also published Greek translations of over thirty works of Albanian literature.

CUKARO, Kate (1955–). Also spelt *Xukaro,* Ital. *Zuccaro.* Arbëresh (q.v.) poetess. Born in Civita, Cosenza, she studied medicine in Florence and Naples. A collection of her verse has been published under the title *Gabim,* Prishtinë 1982 (Mistake). In addition to her poetry which has also appeared in various Arbëresh periodicals, she has published material on Arbëresh folklore.

ÇULI, Diana (1951–). Prose writer. Born in Tiranë, she studied at the Faculty of History and Philology there. She collaborated for several years in the literary weekly *Drita* (The light) and now works for the Albanian French-language periodical *Les lettres albanaises.*

Çuli has published a collection of short stories entitled *Jehonat e jetës,* Tiranë 1982 (The echoes of life); and a novel *Zëri i largët,* Tiranë 1983 (The distant voice).

CUNEUS PROPHETARUM. See BOGDANI, Pjetër.

D

DAKO, Christo A. See DAKO, Kristo A.
DAKO, Kristo A. (–1941). Engl. Christo A. Dako. Journalist and activist. He became involved in the nationalist movement while a student in Bucharest and was imprisoned for a time for his activities. In 1907, he emigrated to the United States, where he vied with Fan Noli for leadership of the Albanian community in Massachusetts, and in 1913 became president of the Vatra Society and editor of the periodical *Dielli* (The sun).

Dako is the author of school texts and works of political history such as *Cilët janë Shqipëtarët,* Monastir 1911 (Who are the Albanians), *Albania, the master key to the Near East,* Boston 1919, and *Liga e Prizrenit,* Bucharest 1922 (The League of Prizren). He was also a promoter of women's education.

DA LECCE, Francesco Maria. See LECCE, Francesco Maria da.
DALLIU, Hafiz Ibrahim (fl. 1930). Religious figure and editor. He was the author of various works, including a 250-page mevlud, and editor of the weekly newspaper *Dajti* in Tiranë from 1923 to 1926. Dalliu was imprisoned after the war by the Communist authorities.
DANIEL, master. See HAXHIU, Dhanil.
DARA, Andrea (1796–1872). Arbëresh (q.v.) folklorist from Palazzo Adriano, Sicily. Son of Gavrill Dara the elder (q.v.) and father of Gavrill Dara the younger (q.v.).

He is the author of an Albanian grammar (1830), a work on village customs among the Arbëresh (1859), an Albanian-Italian, Italian-Albanian dictionary (1867), and a collection of Arbëresh folksongs from Sicily. Most of his works remain unpublished and are preserved in manuscript form in the Royal Library of Copenhagen.

DARA, Gabriele. See DARA, Gavrill
DARA, Gavrill (i ri). See DARA, Gavrill (the younger).
DARA, Gavrill (plaku). See DARA, Gavrill (the elder).
DARA, Gavrill (the elder) (1765–1832). Arbëresh (q.v.) folklorist from Pal-

azzo Adriano in Sicily. Educated in Palermo, he was a doctor of medicine and law.

Dara the elder (Alb. *plaku*) is the author of a manuscript, now lost, of Arbëresh folksongs entitled *Kënkat e plekjërisë* (Songs of old age). He is thought to be the first Albanian writer to have collected folksongs and tales. Only one poem by him has survived: *Shën Llazari* (Saint Lazarus).

DARA, Gavrill (the younger) (1826–1885). Arbëresh (q.v.) poet and man of letters. Son of Andrea Dara (q.v.) and grandson of Gavrill Dara the elder (q.v.). He was born, as were his father and grandfather, in Palazzo Adriano in Sicily of an old Arbëresh family, said to be one of the first to have left Albania after the death of Scanderbeg (q.v.) in 1468. He studied at the Arbëresh seminar in Palermo and later received a degree in law which he practised for a time in Agrigento. Dara became increasingly active in the turbulent political situation during Garibaldi's overthrow of the Kingdom of the Two Sicilies and served in a variety of offices. From 1867 to 1869, he was governor of the city of Trapani; and from 1871 to 1874, director of the periodical *La Riforma* in Rome.

The literary and scholarly interests of Dara the younger (Alb. *i ri*) were wide-ranging: poetry, folklore, philosophy, archeology, and jurisprudence. Aside from one religious poem, dedicated as that of his grandfather to Saint Lazarus, he is remembered primarily for his lengthy romantic ballad *Kënka e sprasme e Balës,* Catanzaro 1906 (Engl. transl. *The last lay of Bala,* Tiranë 1967), first published in installments in the periodical *Arbri i ri* in 1887. Influenced no doubt by Macpherson's Ossian, Dara claimed to have recognized fragments of an old Albanian epic by a mountain bard called Bala in his grandfather's collection of folksongs. Although the work was soon seen to be of Dara the younger's pen, it nevertheless makes quite a successful historical poem, recounting the adventures of Nik Peta and Pal Golemi, Albanian heroes at the time of Scanderbeg.

Lit.: KODRA, Klara, *Mbi artin poetik të Darës*. in: Nëntori 11 (1975); PETROTTA, Gaetano, *Poeti siculo-albanesi* (Palermo 1950), p. 8–24; QOSJA, Rexhep, *Historia e letërsisë shqipe—Romantizmi II,* Prishtinë 1984, p. 349–374.

DARDHA, Llambi (fl. 1920). Author of two patriotic novels: *Dëshmorët e liris* (The martyrs of freedom); and *Kthimi i Skënderbeut në Krujë,* Korçë 1929 (Scanderbeg's return to Krujë).

DEDAI, Salih Nijazi (–1942). Bektash (q.v.) poet from Strajë near Kolonjë. He was raised in Anatolia where in 1908 he became a baba and in 1916 was made an elder *(kryegjysh)* of the Bektash community. He remained in Turkey even after the closure of the tekes and was assassinated in 1942 for reasons unknown. He is the author of Bektash spiritual verse.

DEDAJ, Rrahman (1939–). Kosovo poet and author of children's literature. Born in Penuhë near Podujevë, he is a graduate of the University of Prishtinë and has worked for Radio Prishtinë. He was also executive editor of Rilindja Publishing Company.

Dedaj has published several volumes of poetry for adults and children. His works are characterized by rich, emotive expression and by his search for a balance between tradition and modernity. Among these are *Me sy kange,* Prishtinë 1962 (With song eyes); *Simfonija e fjalës,* Prishtinë 1968 (Word symphony); *Baladë e fshehur,* Prishtinë 1970 (Hidden ballad); *Etje,*Prishtinë 1973 (Thirst); *Nuk e kam thirrë shiun,* Tiranë 1973 (I never called the rain); *Poezi,* Prishtinë 1978 (Poetry), *Koha në unazë,* Prishtinë 1980 (Time in a ring); *Gjërat që s'preken,* Prishtinë 1980 (Intangible things); and *Jeta gabon,* Prishtinë 1983 (Life makes mistakes). A collection of his short stories has appeared in *Tre diejt,* Tiranë 1983 (The three suns).

DEDE, Spiro (1945–   ). Poet from the Zagoria region of southern Albania. He is a graduate of the University of Tiranë and has worked as a journalist for *Zëri i Popullit* (The People's Voice).

His verse, largely political in content, has been published in the collections: *Tranzit,* Tiranë 1972 (Transit); and *Njerëzit për të cilët rroj,* Tiranë 1980 (The people I live for).

DEDJA, Bedri (1930–   ). Critic and author of children's literature. Among his publications are *Përralla popullore mbi kafshët,* Tiranë 1957 (Folk tales about animals); *Letërsia për fëmijë,* Tiranë 1964 (Literature for children); *Burimet e letërsisë shqipe për fëmijë,* Prishtinë 1978 (Source of Albanian children's literature); *Tradita dhe probleme të letërsisë shqipe për fëmijë,* Tiranë 1971 (Tradition and problems of Albanian children's literature); and *Shkrime mbi letërsinë për fëmijë,* Tiranë 1978 (Writing on children's literature.)

DEL GAUDIO, Giuseppe. See GAUDIO, Xhuzepe del.

DEL GAUDIO, Xhuzepe. See GAUDIO, Xhuzepe del.

DELVINA, Dhimitri (fl. 1637). Priest and translator, together with Neofito Rodinò (q.v.), of an unpublished and now lost version of the Christian doctrine.

DELVINA, Namik Selim (–1932?). Author of patriotic lyrics and drama, among which the collection of poetry *Hidhërimet e zemërës,* Salonika 1909 (Pangs of the heart); and the eight-act play *Dashurija e mëmëdheut,* Salonika 1909 (Love of the homeland). He was also editor of the Tiranë journal *Rilindja e Arbënis* (The rebirth of Albania) in 1930.

DEMAÇI, Adem (1936–   ). Kosovo writer. Author of the controversial novel *Gjarpijt e gjakut,* Prishtinë 1958 (The snakes of blood), republished in New York in 1983. Some of his short stories appeared in the journal *Jeta e re* (New life). He was imprisoned in 1959.

DEMAKU, Daut (1944–   ). Kosovo prose writer born in Obri i Epërm in the Drenicë region. He studied in Prishtinë and since 1969 has been a member of the Kosovo Writers' League. He is also editor of the journal *Bujku* (The farmer).

Demaku has published the short story collections *Brigjet e thata,* Prishtinë 1967 (The dry hills); *Plisat e kuq,* Prishtinë 1969 (The red soil); *Kapituj jete,* Prishtinë 1977 (Chapters of life); *Shi e puhi,* Prishtinë 1979 (Rain and wind);

Buka, Prishtinë 1981 (Bread); and the novel *Mote të thata,* Prishtinë 1983 (Dry weather).

DE MARTINO, Leonardo. See MARTINO, Leonardo de.

DEMIR AGA VLONJAKASI. See VLONJATI, Demir.

DEMOLLI, Arif (1949–   ). Kosovo humourist known for his short stories and satirical sketches. He was born in Gllogovicë near Prishtinë and studied Albanian language and literature at the University of Prishtinë. Demolli was arrested and imprisoned in the aftermath of recent turbulence in Kosovo. His sketches have been published in *Ballkonet e një qyteze,* Prishtinë 1979 (The balconies of a little town).

DE RADA, Girolamo. See RADA, Jeronim de.

DE RADA, Jeronim. See RADA, Jeronim de.

DERVISHI, Teki (1943–   ). Also known as *Teki Dërvishi.* Kosovo novelist, poet, and critic, born in Gjakovë. He went to secondary school in Pejë and studied Albanian language and literature at the University of Prishtinë. Dervishi now works as a journalist for the Skopje newspaper *Flaka e vëllazërimit* (The flame of brotherhood). Among his works are *Nimfa,* Prishtinë 1970 (The nymph); *I varun me vargje për drunin e blertë,* Skopje 1971 (Hanging with verses about green wood); *Etje dhe bore,* Skopje 1972 (Thirst and snow); *Pirgu i lartë,* Prishtinë 1972 (The high tower); *Padrona,* Skopje 1973 (Padrona); *Shtëpia e sëmurë,* Skopje 1978 (The sick house); *Zbutësi i njerëzve me sy prej zymrydi,* Skopje 1979 (The tenderness of people with emerald eyes); *Herezia e Dërvish Mallutës,* Prishtinë 1981 (The heresy of Dervish Malluta); and *Thashë,* Skopje 1981 (I said).

DËRVISHI, Teki. See DERVISHI, Teki.

DESHPALI, Shime (1897–1980). Poet from the Dalmatian village of Arbanasi (Borgo Erizzo) near Zadar. He is the author of verse and short stories in the archaic Geg (q.v.) dialect of this Albanian-speaking village founded in 1726 by settlers from Brisk and Shestan west of Lake Shkodër. Deshpali has published the verse collections: *Agimet e parabromjet të Arbëneshit,* Prishtinë 1968 (Albanian dawns and dusks); *E vërteta,* Prishtinë 1972 (The truth); and a volume of short stories entitled *Tregime arbëneshe,* Prishtinë 1966 (Albanian tales).

Lit.: PEROVIQ, Budimir, *Nji vështrim mbi gjuhën e Shime Deshpalit.* in: Jeta e re (1965) 3, p. 470–474.

DESKU, Tahir (1957–   ). Kosovo poet born in Siçevë near Klinë. He attended school in Ujmir and Klinë and studied at the University of Prishtinë. Desku has published: *Prejardhja e dashurisë,* Prishtinë 1982 (The origin of love); and *Nga biografia e pashkruar,* Prishtinë 1984 (From an unwritten biography).

DEVA, Agim (1948–   ). Kosovo poet and critic born in Belgrade. He studied Albanian at the University of Prishtinë and also has a strong interest in children's literature, on which he finished his doctorate and now lectures.

Among his many works are *Romani ynë për fëmijë,* Prishtinë 1977 (Our children's novel); *Antologji e poezisë shqipe për fëmijë,* Prishtinë 1978 (Anthology of Albanian children's poetry); *Vjersha të zgjedhura për fëmijë,* Prishtinë 1980 (Selected children's verse); *Nëpër gurë e valë,* Prishtinë 1982 (Over stones and waves); *Poezia shqipe për fëmijë (1872–1980),* Prishtinë 1982 [Albanian children's poetry (1872–1980)]; *Rrota e historisë,* Prishtinë 1983 (The wheel of history); *Fjala e përjetimi,* Prishtinë 1983 (The word of experience); and *Harta e zemrës,* Skopje 1984 (Map of the heart).

DHANIL mjeshtri. See HAXHIU, Dhanil.

DHASKAL TODHRI. See HAXHIFILIPI, Theodhor.

DHOSI, Mihal (1873–1937). Minor poet of the late Rilindja (q.v.) period. He was born in the village of Kosovë in the southern Albanian Përmet region. After secondary school in Berat, he left Albania, returning in 1906 as a parish priest to his native village.

Dhosi is the author of rather uninspired verse on nationalist themes characteristic of the period. His collection of manuscripts was recently discovered and published in part in *Ç'pate, bilbil, pse pushove,* Tiranë 1973 (What was wrong, nightingale, why did you stop).

DHRËVA, Gjergj. See DHRIVA, Gjergj.

DHRIVA, Gjergj (19th century). Also spelled *Dhrëva* or *Driva*. Greco-Albanian poet from the island of Hydra.

DINE, Spiro Rusto (1846?–1922). Poet and publicist from Vithkuq in the Korçë region. In 1866, he emigrated to Egypt where he met Thimi Mitko (q.v.), an activist of the growing Albanian community there. The two collaborated for a time in collecting Albanian folksongs and tales.

Dine's only publication is *Valët e detit,* Sofia 1908 (The waves of the sea), one of the most important collections of Albanian folklore from the Rilindja (q.v.) period. Aside from his own patriotic verse, it contains poetry by other writers and nationalist leaders of the period such as Koto Hoxhi (q.v.), Thimi Kreji (q.v.), Anastas Kullurioti (q.v.), Loni Logori (q.v.), and Jani Vreto (q.v.), as well as a variety of tales, aphorisms, and rhymes.

DINI, Jonuz (1925–1982). Novelist and playwright from Shkodër. Among his works are *Ditar pa data,* Tiranë 1961 (Undated diary); *Çika me yll në ballë,* Tiranë 1975 (The girl with a star on her forehead); *Elira,* Tiranë 1978 (Elira), *Kështjella mbi Barbanë,* Tiranë 1980 (The castle over Barbanë); and *Shpatë dhe dashuri,* Tiranë 1983 (Sword and love). Dini is also remembered as an actor, theatre director, and author of children's literature.

D'ISTRIA, Dora. See ISTRIA, Dora d'.

DOBRAÇI, Mulla Hysen (fl. 1785). Moslem poet from Shkodër, perhaps identical with Hysen efendi Shkodra (q.v.). Author of anacreontic and historical verse exalting Albanian resistance to Ottoman rule. Zef Jubani (q.v.), who published some of Dobraçi's poetry in his *Raccolta di canti popolari e rapsodie di poemi albanesi,* Trieste 1871 (Collection of folksongs and rhapsodies of Albanian poems), called him indeed the "Albanian Anacreon." His best known poem celebrates the battle of Kara Mahmud Pasha against Turkish forces under Ahmed Pasha in Berat in 1785.

DOCCI, Primo. See DOÇI, Preng.
DOCHI, Primo. See DOÇI, Preng.
DOÇI, Preng (1846–1917). Also known as *Primo Docci* or *Dochi*. Rilindja (q.v.) poet, political and religious figure born in Bulgëri near Lezhë. He studied at the College of the Propaganda Fide in Rome. In 1871 Doçi returned as a priest to the Catholic Mirdita region in northern central Albania, where he took part in the uprising of 1876/77 for which he was exiled to Istanbul. Released and expelled to Rome in 1877, he was sent by the Propaganda Fide to Canada and lived for several years in Saint John, New Brunswick. After many years of petitioning, he finally received permission in 1888 from the Ottoman authorities to return to Albania and in January of the following year was consecrated Abbot of Mirdita, a position which allowed him to exercise considerable political and religious influence in the region for many years. He was also one of the founders of the Bashkimi literary society (q.v.) in Shkodër in 1899 and devised the Bashkimi alphabet.

Doçi is the author of patriotic verse, such as *Shqypnia nën zgjedhë turke* (Albania under the Turkish yoke) and *Shqypnia në robni* (Albania enslaved).

Lit.: BARTL, Peter, *Prenk Doçi (1846–1917)—Zur Bibliographie eines albanischen Patrioten.* in: Serta Balcanica-Orientalia Monacensia in honorem Rudolphi Trofenik (Munich 1981), p. 255–270.

DODA, Xhemil (1915–1976). Kosovo playwright. Born in Prizren of a middle-class family, he went to school in Tiranë and later studied at a military academy in Turin. He returned in 1941 to live in Prizren and has published plays, poetry, and short stories. Many of his prize-winning dramas, such as *Halit Gashi* and *Malësorët* (The mountaineers), have been performed on stage in Kosovo and Macedonia with notable success.

DODANI, Visar (ca. 1857–1939). Rilindja (q.v.) publicist and poet. He finished his studies at the Greek school in Korçë in 1878. Inspired by Thimi Mitko's (q.v.) *Bleta shqiptare* (The Albanian bee), one of the rare Albanian-language books at the time, he resolved to devote his energies to Albanian publications and the nationalist movement. In March 1880, he emigrated to Bucharest, an active centre of Albanian exile politics. There, he joined the Drita society and began a career in journalism, promoting the union of Albanians of all faiths. He later became editor of the fortnightly periodical *Shqipëria* (1897–1899). In 1915, he moved to Geneva to become secretary of the Albanian national committee under Turkan Pasha. He died in Bucharest on March 16, 1939.

Dodani is remembered primarily for his *Mialt' e mbletësë,* Bucharest 1898 (The bee's honey), an anthology of poetry and prose, both by Dodani and other writers of the period. He is also the author of translations of Arabic tales and of Verdi's opera Il Trovatore. Late in life, he published a 200-page *Memorjet e mija—kujtime nga shvillimet e para të rilindjes të kombit shqipëtar ndë Bukuresht,* Constanza 1930 (My Memoirs—memories of initial developments in the rebirth of the Albanian nation in Bucharest).

DODI, Jani (1919–1944). Left-wing writer and poet from the early stages of the Communist movement. He was born in the village of Sinjë near Berat and went to school in Elbasan. At the beginning of the war, he worked as a school teacher in the Fier area and later in Kosovo. In 1943, he became a member of the national liberation council for Berat and was killed the following year.

Dodi wrote poetry, prose, short stories, and literary criticism, little of which was published during his lifetime. A selection of his writings appeared in *Këngë e pambaruar,* Tiranë 1975 (Unfinished song).

DOLCE, Carlo. See DULCI, Carlo.
DOMONICI, Nak. See NIKAJ, Ndoc.
DORSA, Vinçenc (1823–1885). Ital. *Vincenzo Dorsa.* Arbëresh (q.v.) folklorist and writer. Born in Frascineto, he studied at the college of San Demetrio Corone and later at the college of the Propaganda Fide in Rome. For many years, he taught Greek and Latin at a secondary school in his native Cosenza.

Dorsa's work is constituted in a volume of his research and thoughts on the Albanians: *Sugli albanesi, ricerche e pensieri,* Naples 1847 (On the Albanians, research and thoughts). Divided into twenty chapters, it contains a wealth of information about the origins and history of Albania and the Arbëresh as well as on folk poetry, customs, and literature. He also published a *Studi etimologici della lingua albanese,* Cosenza 1862 (Etymological study of the Albanian language), and translated the Gospel of St. Matthew into the dialect of Frascineto (London 1869). Unpublished is his manuscript of about sixty-five Arbëresh folksongs from Cosenza, entitled *Canti popolari albanesi* (Albanian folksongs), which served de Rada (q.v.) in the latter's collection of Arbëresh folk material. It is now preserved in the Royal Library of Copenhagen.

DORSA, Vincenzo. See DORSA, Vinçenc.
DRENOVA, Aleks Stavre. See ASDRENI.
DRINI, Skënder (1935–   ). Novelist and short story writer from Korçë. He studied in Tiranë and has worked as a teacher.

Among his best known novels are *Shembja e idhujve,* Tiranë 1975 (The fall of the idols), which depicts the clash between tradition and progress among the northern mountain tribes in the 1930s; and *Midis dy kohëve,* Tiranë 1978 (Between two epoques), which portrays the same figures and milieu during the Italian occupation. He is also the author of the novels *Kënga e dritës,* Tiranë 1970 (Song of light); *Shqipja e kreshtave tona,* Prishtinë 1971 (The eagle of our mountain peaks); *Njeriu gjigant,* Tiranë 1973 (The giant man); *Vraje tradhtinë,* Tiranë 1980 (Wipe out treachery); and *Kirurgët,* Tiranë 1984 (The surgeons); and of the short story collections *Kumbimet e reja të pyjeve,* Tiranë 1972 (New sounds of the woods); and *Tregimet e veriut,* Tiranë 1977 (The tales of the north).

DRIVA, Gjergj. See DHRIVA, Gjergj.
DUÇI, Milo (–1933). Pseud. *Lulo Malësori.* Journalist and writer of the Albanian community in Egypt. Of Tosk (q.v.) origin, he spent most of his life in Cairo supporting the Albanian cause with his works and publications. In

1897, he became president of the Vllazëria (Brotherhood) society which served as a focal point for Albanians in Cairo and was involved in the publication of a variety of Albanian periodicals, such as *Besa-Besën,* Cairo 1900-1904; the monthly *Toska,* Minya 1901; *Besa,* Cairo 1904, the latter with Thoma Avrami (q.v.), and the weekly *Bisedimet,* Cairo 1925. With the formation of the first independent government in Albania, he returned to the homeland in 1912 where he published the journal *Zâna,* Durrës 1914. The internecine feuding among the various political factions in the newly independent state, however, forced him to flee to Italy in 1914, from where he returned to Egypt, residing there until his death in December 1913.

Under the pseudonym Lulo Malësori, he published patriotic and love poetry in various periodicals. Duçi is also the author of five plays of modest literary value, among which *E thëna,* Cairo 1922 (The saying); and of the novel *Midis dy grash,* 1923 (Between two women).

Lit.: FULLANI, Dhimitër, *Milo Duçi—si patriot dhe si shkrimtar.* in: Buletin i Universitetit Shtetëror të Tiranës, Seria Shkenc. Shoq. 4 (1963), p. 98-115.

DUDESI, Mati (fl. 1635). Lat. *Mattaeus Dudesius.* Dalmatian author of a six-line poem in Latin serving as a dedication to the Latin-Albanian dictionary of Frang Bardhi (q.v.), dated 1635.

DUDESIUS, Mattaeus. See DUDESI, Mati.

DUKAGJINI, Ahmet bej (16th century). Turkish poet of Albanian origin. Author of Turkish mystic poetry.

DUKAGJINI, Jahja bej (16th century). Turkish poet of Albanian origin. One of the leading representatives of classical Turkish poetry in the sixteenth century.

DUKAGJINI, Shpend. See REXHA, Zekeria.

DULCI, Carlo (1765-1850). Also known as *Carlo Dolce* and *Luc Gliqini.* Arbëresh (q.v.) poet from Piana degli Albanesi in Sicily. Author of two or three light-hearted poems first published by Dhimitër Kamarda (q.v.) in 1886.

DURAKU, Nebil (1934-   ). Kosovo prose writer from Brojë e Drenicës. He has taught school, worked as a reporter for the newspaper *Rilindja* (Rebirth), and now works for Prishtinë television. Author of the novels: *Murgesha,* Prishtinë 1966 (The nun); *Shtrojera,* Prishtinë 1969 (Lee side); *Dhengrënësit,* Prishtinë 1971 (The dirt eaters); *Drenusha,* Prishtinë 1980 (The doe); and *I treturi,* Prishtinë 1983 (The dissolved). Duraku is also author of the anthology *Shkrimtarët e Kosovës '43-'83,* Prishtinë 1984 (The writers of Kosovo '43-'83).

DUSHKO VETMO. See Solano, Francesco.

E

EASTER GOSPEL. Alb. *Ungjilli i Pashkëve.* One of the earliest Albanian texts. It consists of fifteen lines based on the Gospel of St. Matthew, found in a Greek manuscript (133) in the Ambrosian Library in Milan. The text is difficult to date, but general consensus of opinion places it at the end of the fifteenth or beginning of the sixteenth century. Author unknown.

Lit.: BORGIA, Nilo, *Pericope evangelica in lingua albanese del secolo XIV,* Grottaferrata 1930.

EFENDIU I MADH. See BOSHNJAKU, Tahir.

EFTHIMIADHI, LI. (fl. 1930). Short story writer. Author of a number of essays which appeared in the newspapers *Illyria* and *Gazeta e re.* Several of his love stories were reprinted in *Lule të veshkura,* Vlorë 1930 (Withered flowers).

EFTIMIU, Viktor (1889–1972). Romanian dramatist, poet, and prose writer of Albanian origin. He was born in Macedonia, the son of an Albanian merchant, and emigrated in 1897 to Romania. In 1905 he began writing and in 1921–1922 worked as a theatre director in Bucharest. In 1948, he became secretary of the Romanian Writers' Society. Eftimiu is the author of fifty-seven plays, some on Albanian subjects, and countless volumes of poetry and prose.

Lit.: BALA, Vehbi, *Viktor Eftimiu, portret monografi,* Tiranë 1978.

ELBASAN, anonymous manuscript of. See ANONIMI I ELBASANIT.

ELBASANI, Ahmet (sheh) (early 19th century). Moslem poet and sheikh from Elbasan. Author of Islamic religious verse.

ELBASANI, Ibrahim (late 18th century?). Moslem poet from Elbasan. He was the author of several pieces of love poetry.

ELBASANI, Sulejman Pasha (late 18th century). Also known as *Sulejman Pasha Vërlaci.* Moslem poet from Elbasan who held the title of vizier. He composed several poems in Albanian.

ENGJËLL, Pal. See ANGELUS, Paulus.

EREBARA, Jashar (early 20th century). Journalist, politician, and patriot from Dibër, now in Macedonia. He studied at the University of Bucharest and later served in the Ottoman administration, until being fired for teaching Albanian. Erebara collaborated in a number of Albanian-language periodicals and in 1905 began publishing the journal *Albanija,* initially in Egypt and later in Belgrade. In 1911, he founded the weekly *Shkupi* in Skopje. After Albanian independence, he became a deputy and lobbied for the unification of Kosovo with Albania.

ETËHEM, Haxhi bej Tirana (1783–1846). Also known as *Etëhem bej Mollai*. Bektash (q.v.) poet and author of mystic verse and a divan in Albanian, of which nothing has survived. He is also the author of four divans in Turkish. Etëhem died in Tiranë and was interred in the mosque bearing his name.

ETËHEM bej Mollai. See ETËHEM, Haxhi bej Tirana.

EUSTRATIOS OF VITHKUQ. See VITHKUQARI, Jani Evstrat.

EVSTRATI NGA VITHKUQI. See VITHKUQARI, Jani Evstrat.

F

FERIZAJ, Thabit Niman (1860–1950). Syrian-Albanian poet. As opposed to his contemporary Mustafa Huluki (q.v.), whose nationalist verse was written in Arabic, Ferizaj chose to write in Albanian using the Arabic alphabet. His verse is often religious and mystic in nature.

FERRARO, Matilda (1950–   ). Arbëresh (q.v.) poetess from Catanzaro. Born in San Nicola del'Alto, she studied at the University of Bari and now works in Melissa as a teacher. Her verse has appeared in various Albanian and Arbëresh periodicals.

FERRI, Rexhep (1937–   ). Kosovo poet born in Kukës in northern Albania. He finished elementary school in Gjakovë and studied applied arts in Pejë and Belgrade. Ferri, who is also well known as a painter, is the author of the volumes: *Punë gjaku,* Prishtinë 1978 (Blood deed); *Qafa e diellit,* Prishtinë 1981 (Neck of the sun); and *Këmisha e bardhë,* Prishtinë 1984 (The white shirt).

FIGLIA, Andrea. See FILJA, Andrea.

FIGLIA, Nicola. See FILJA, Nikolla.

FILJA, Andrea (fl. 1770). Ital. *Andrea Figlia.* Arbëresh (q.v.) priest and poet from Sicily. He served as a parish priest in Chieuti, north of Foggia, and was chaplain of the Imperial Macedonian Regiment. Filja is the author of the last poem in the codex of Chieuti, published by Michele Marchianò (q.v.) in *Canti popolari albanesi delle colonie d'Italia,* Foggia 1908 (Albanian folksongs from the colonies of Italy).

FILJA, Nikolla (1693–1769). Ital. *Nicola Figlia.* Arbëresh (q.v.) poet, folklorist, and writer. Born in Mezzoiuso, Sicily, between 1691 and 1693, he served as an archpriest in the village of Chieuti, north of Foggia. He composed religious verse of no particular literary merit, preserved in the codex of Chieuti, and translated a catechism entitled *I Cristeu i Arbresc,* 1736 (The Albanian Christian) into his native Mezzoiuso dialect. Also in the codex of Chieuti is a collection of eighteen Arbëresh folksongs from Sicily attributed to Filja.

FISHTA, Filip (1904–   ). Author of literary criticism. He was born in Shkodër and worked as a high school teacher. He contributed to the compilation of school anthologies and wrote a series of articles on various Albanian authors of the past in the periodical *Shkëndija,* 1940–1941.

FISHTA, Gjergj (1871–1940). Poet and one of the leading literary figures of prewar Albania. Born on October 23, 1871, in the Zadrimë village of Fishtë between Shkodër and Lezhë, he studied theology and philosophy in Bosnia, being then ordained in 1894 as a Franciscan priest. A versatile public figure and writer, he was the founder of the Illyrian secondary school in Shkodër, the first in the country to teach all subjects in Albanian, cofounder in 1899 of the Bashkimi literary society (q.v.), participant in 1908 at the Congress of Monastir (q.v.) which accepted his proposal for an Albanian alphabet, publisher from 1913 on of the periodical *Hylli i dritës* (The day-star) which finally ceased publication in 1944, delegate in 1919 to the Paris Peace Conference, and deputy for Shkodër in the first Albanian parliament in 1921. The last years of his life were spent in a Franciscan monastery in Shkodër where he died on December 30, 1940.

Politically a conservative, he very easily reconciled himself to Mussolini's absorption of Albania, a fact which helps explain his fall into oblivion. Once acclaimed as the national poet of Albania, Fishta has now all but disappeared from the literary scene. His works are viewed today in Albania among other things as having excessively nationalistic and chauvinistic tendencies, encouraging the incitement of hostilities among the peoples of the Balkans. Given the indivisibility of writing and politics in Marxist literary thinking, it is no doubt more his collaboration with the Italian fascists than the shortcomings of his works that brought about his ostracism from the Albanian Parnassus, although the anti-Slavic and in particular anti-Montenegrin sentiments in his poetry are not to be denied.

His main work is the epic *Lahuta e malcís,* Shkodër 1937, republished in Rome 1958 (The highland lute; German transl. *Die Laute des Hochlandes,* Munich 1958), a 17,838-line historical ballad written between 1899 and 1909. It offers an epic portrayal in thirty cantos of nineteenth century Albanian history from border hostilities between the Albanian Hoti and Gruda tribes and the Montenegrins to the events of the League of Prizren. Fishta also published satirical, lyric, and religious poetry, among which: *Vierrsha t'pershpirtshme,* Shkodër 1905 (Spiritual verse); *Ânzat e Parnasit,* Sarajevo 1907 (The wasps of Parnassus); *Pika voeset,* Durrës 1909 (Dew drops); *Mrizi i zânevet,* Shkodër 1913 (Noontide of the muses); *Gomari i Babatasit,* Shkodër 1923 (Babatasi's donkey); and *Vallja e parrizit,* Shkodër 1925 (Dance of paradise). He is also the author of about thirty other works including plays, translations, and political tracts.

Lit.: Shêjzat 5 (1961), commemorative issue.

FLOQI, Ismail (early 19th century?). Moslem religious poet from the Korçë region. He translated a mevlud (poem on the birth of the prophet Mohammed) into Albanian.

FLOQI, Kristo (1873–194?). Playwright, poet, and political figure. Originally from Korçë, he studied law in Athens, returning then to his native city to practise. However, his involvement in the nationalist movement forced him to keep on the move—Istanbul, back to Korçë, Athens, Vlorë, where he took part in an attempt to declare Albanian independence, and on to the United States. In Boston, he became editor of the Albanian-language weekly *Dielli* (The Sun) in 1911 and was cofounder with Fan Noli (q.v.) and Faik Konica (q.v.) of the Vatra society. After independence, he returned to Albania and pursued a legal and political career, serving as minister of education and counsellor of state. He was also responsible for the first legal documents written in Albanian.

Floqi was a prolific writer. He is the author of four tragedies on nationalist and historical themes, about seventeen comedies and sketches as well as several volumes of poetry, legal, political, and educational texts and translations of Sophocles, Euripides, and Molière. His writings have been republished in *Komedi të zgjedhuna,* Belgrade 1964 (Selected comedies); and in *Vëllazëri e interesë,* Prishtinë 1984 (Brotherhood and interest).

FORMULA E PAGËZIMIT. See ANGELUS, Paulus.

FRAKULLA, Nezim (ca. 1680–1760). Also known as *Nezim Berati* and *Ibrahim Nezimi*. Moslem poet. He was born in the village of Frakull near Fier and lived a good deal of his life in Berat, a flourishing centre of Moslem culture in the eighteenth century. Frakulla studied in Istanbul where he wrote his first poetry in Turkish and Persian. About 1731, he returned to Berat where he is known to have been involved in literary rivalry with other poets of the period. At some point after 1747, he was sent to Khotin in Bessarabia (now in the Ukraine), probably into exile, and died in prison in Istanbul in 1760.

It was after his return to Berat that he composed his first divan in Albanian, which is notable in that it contains the first secular poetry recorded in the language. Aside from traditional themes, it includes nature poetry and interesting references to city life in eighteenth century Albania. Frakulla is also the author of love lyrics dedicated to his nephew.

Lit.: MYDERRIZI, Osman, *Nezim Frakulla.* in: Buletin për Shkencat Shoqërore (1954) 4, p. 56–75; ROSSI, Ettore, *Notizie su un manoscritto del canzionere di Nezim (sec. XVII–XVIII) in caratteri arabi.* in: Rivista degli studi orientali 21 (1945–1946), p. 219–246.

FRANCO, Demetrius. See FRËNGU, Dhimitër.

FRASCINI, Beniamin (fl. 1807). Arbëresh (q.v.) poet and Orthodox priest from Frascineto, Cosenza. He is the author of a long poem of no particular literary merit, though of historical and linguistic interest, which deals with the events of 1807 when French troops ravaged the area. The poem was recopied in 1900 by Professor Domenico Magnelli and discovered in 1960 in one of his manuscripts.

FRASHËRI, Dalip (fl. 1842). Bektash (q.v.) epic poet. Brother of Shahin Frashëri (q.v.). He was born in the prolific village of Frashër and spent most of his life as a Bektash monk in the monasteries of Frashër and Konicë.

Using the pseudonym *Hyxhretiu,* Frashëri wrote a 65,000-line epic entitled *Hadika,* which he finished in 1842. The work is based on another of the same title by the Azerbaijan poet Fuzuli (1498–1556) and deals with the history of Islam. The Albanian version, including poetry and prose, is twice as long as the original and constitutes the first Albanian epic.

FRASHËRI, Mehdi (1874–1963). Writer and political figure. Cousin of Mid'hat Frashëri (q.v.). He was an official in the Ottoman administration, being appointed bey of Jerusalem and governor of Palestine. After independence, he became prefect of the Berat area. In 1914, he went into exile in Lausanne after the departure of Prince Wilhelm of Wied following the latter's inglorious six-month reign as King of Albania. The following years he spent at San Demetrio Corone in southern Italy. After World War I, he returned to Albania, supporting a policy of close ties with Italy. He held various political positions from representative at the League of Nations in Geneva to prime minister in 1935. Despite his italophile sympathies, he spoke out against Mussolini's occupation of the country in 1939 and was imprisoned but in 1943, became chairman of the so-called regency council under German occupation. He left Albania after World War II to live in exile in Italy and died in Rome on May 25, 1963.

In addition to his works on politics, history, and philology, he wrote a romantic novel called *Nevruzi,* Tiranë 1923; and a five-act play entitled *Trathtija,* Tiranë 1926 (Treason), set in the age of Scanderbeg (q.v.).

FRASHËRI, Mid'hat (1880–1949). Pseudonyms *Lumo Skendo* and *Mali Kokojka.* Publicist, politician, and prose writer. Son of Abdyl Frashëri, himself a respected political leader of the Rilindja (q.v.) period. Mid'hat Frashëri is thought to have been born in Ioannina, Greece, and was raised in Istanbul. In 1897, he began publication, together with Kristo Luarasi (q.v.) and Kosta Jani Trebicka (q.v.), of an annual almanac entitled *Kalendari kombiar* (The national calendar) which was designed to spread information about Albanian writing. From 1905 to 1910, he worked for the Ottoman administration in the vilayet of Salonika and took part in the Congress of Monastir (q.v.). He was also publisher of the periodicals *Lirija* (Freedom) and *Diturija* (Knowledge). After independence, Frashëri became Albania's first minister of public works. He subsequently held other ministerial posts and was ambassador to Greece from 1923 to 1926. Under the Zog dictatorship, he left politics temporarily and opened a bookstore in Tiranë. At the end of 1942, he became leader of Balli Kombëtar (The national front), the anti-Communist resistance movement against the German occupation. In the autumn of 1944, he went into exile and died in New York.

Frashëri is the author of a wide variety of educative works, school texts, translations, and didactic short stories, among which: *Istori e shkrimit shqip* (History of Albanian writing), published in 1901 in the journal Diturija, one of the first histories of Albanian literature; *Këndime,* Salonika 1910 (Readings); *Istori e mbretëris otomane,* Istanbul 1912 (History of the Ottoman empire); and *Hi dhe shpuzë,* Sofia 1915 (Ashes and embers), a collection of short stories and reflections.

FRASHËRI, Naim (1846-1900). Poet, prose writer, and nationalist leader, considered by many as the national poet of Albania. Brother of Abdyl and Sami Frashëri (q.v.). Naim was born in the southern Albanian village of Frashër where he studied Turkish, Persian, and Arabic as well as Bektash (q.v.) theology. At the age of nineteen, he followed his distinguished family to Ioannina in northern Greece where he was educated in classical antiquity and modern European civilization, being especially influenced by the French enlightenment. He was also tutored in Moslem literature and developed a particular interest in classical Persian writers, being thus at an early age equally at home in an oriental and occidental culture. After finishing secondary school in 1870, he spent some time in Istanbul where he published a Persian grammar in Turkish. For health reasons, he left Istanbul, hoping in Albania to find relief from tuberculosis which he had contracted as a child. He worked as a civil servant in Berat and from 1874 to 1877 as a customs official in Sarandë. He also spent some time at the Austrian resort of Baden to recuperate from rheumatism and, during a visit to Vienna, had an opportunity to see Scanderbeg's (q.v.) sword and helmet in the Belvedere. In 1881 or 1882, he returned to Istanbul and began organizing the nationalist movement with his brothers. As a member of the board of censorship at the Ministry of Education he was able to a certain extent to circumvent the ban on Albanian-language books imposed by the Sublime Porte.

Naim is the author of twenty-two works: fifteen in Albanian, four in Turkish, two in Greek, and one in Persian. His prose writing in Albanian, mostly educative in character, was of decisive influence to the creation of a literary language. As a poet, the importance of his work lies to a great extent in the impact it had on the nationalist movement rather than in its purely literary qualities. Many of his poems were sung as folksongs during his lifetime and helped unify Albanians of all creeds. Naim had an incalculable influence on early twentieth century Albanian writers. His remains were transferred from Istanbul where he died, to Tiranë for a monument to the three Frashëri brothers, situated in a park outside the city.

Among his major Albanian-language works are *Istori e perghitheshme,* Bucharest 1886 (General history) and *Diturite per mesonjetorët te para,* Bucharest 1888 (Knowledge for elementary schools), both used for teaching purposes in schools; *Bagëti de bujqësija,* Bucharest 1886 (Herds and crops), a poetic collection of bucolics and georgics in Vergilian style depicting the beauties of the Albanian countryside; *Lulete e verese,* Bucharest 1890 (The flowers of spring), a selection of lyric poetry; *Parajsa dhe fjala fluturake,* Bucharest 1894 (Paradise and winged words), a collection of verse embued with Turkish and Persian mystic philosophy; *Fletore e Bektashinjvet,* Bucharest 1896 (Bektash notebook), a prime source for our knowledge of Bektash pantheistic philosophy; *Qerbelaja*, Bucharest 1898 (Kerbela), a religious epic about the battle of A.D. 680 in Kerbela, an Iraqi site of pilgrimage for Shi'ite Moslems, in which Husein, the grandson of the Prophet Mohammed was killed; and *Istori e Skenderbeut*, Bucharest 1898 (History of Scanderbeg), an epic based on Barleti's (q.v.) history of the fifteenth century Albanian hero and one of the most widely read Albanian books of the period. Naim is also the author of fables and translations, including the first book of the Iliad, *Iliadë e Omirit*, Bucharest 1896 (The Iliad of Homer); and together with his brother Sami published the influential periodical *Drita* (The light). He also helped found the first Albanian school in Korçë in 1887.

Lit.: DHIMA, Dodona, *Bibliografi e veprave të Naim Frashërit (1882–1971)*. in: Studime Filologjike 25.8 (1971) 2, p. 171–176; KOKAJKA, Mali, *Naim Be Frashëri*, Sofia 1901; SHUTERIQI, Dhimitër, *Naim Frashëri*, Tiranë 1982; XHOLI, Zija, *Naim Frashëri*, Tiranë 1962.

FRASHËRI, Sami (1850–1904). Known in Turkish as *Şamseddin Sami*. Man of letters, publicist, and ideologist of the nationalist movement. Younger brother of Abdyl and Naim Frashëri (q.v.). Born in the southern Albanian village of Frashër, he studied with his brother Naim at the Zosimea secondary school in Ioannina, Greece, receiving both an occidental education there and an oriental education in Turkish, Persian, and Arabic from private tutors. In 1871, he became a civil servant in the Ottoman administration of the vilayet of Ioannina and transferred in the following year to Istanbul, where he spent most of his life. Although a prime figure in the Albanian nationalist movement, Sami Frashëri made a name both as an Albanian and as a Turkish writer, embodying the unity of the two cultures at the time.

Frashëri is the author of about fifty major works, not to mention his countless newspaper articles. Among his early works in Albanian are school texts such as *Abetare e gjuhësë shqip*, Bucharest 1886 (Albanian language spelling book); *Shkronjetore e ghuhësë shcip*, Bucharest 1886 (Grammar of the Albanian language), the first Albanian school grammar; and *Dheshkronje*, Bucharest 1888 (Geography). Of major significance is his political manifesto *Shqipëria—Ç'ka qenë, ç'është dhe ç'do të bëhetë*, Bucharest 1899, reprinted Sofia 1907 (Albania—What it was, what it is and what will become of it), subtitled "Thoughts about the salvation of the motherland from the dangers it faces," in which he set forth his views of Albania's past and his visions of its future. Together with Naim Frashëri's History of Scanderbeg, it was one of the most widely read Albanian books of the period and has been translated into several languages.

Sami Frashëri is widely regarded as the most talented of the three Frashëri brothers, though he is not a writer of literature per se. His publications in Turkish are no less significant than his Albanian works. He was the chief editor of the Turkish-language daily newspaper *Tercüman-i Şark* (Oriental interpreter) and later founded the periodicals *Sabah* (Morning), *Aile* (The family), and *Hafta*

(The week). With the help of the Armenian newspaperman Mihran, he published a series of cheap books on general knowledge designed for the Turkish public at large, using his series entitled *Cep Kütüphanesi* (Pocket library) to publish fifteen of his own works. As a lexicographer, Frashëri published Turkish-French and French-Turkish dictionaries and was the author of the *Kamus-u Türki,* Istanbul 1901 (Turkish dictionary) which was used by the Turkish Philological Society in 1932 as a guideline for the creation of the modern Turkish literary language. Not to be forgotten is his monumental six-volume Turkish encyclopedia of history and geography *Kamus al-a'lâm,* Istanbul 1889–1899 (Universal dictionary) containing a total of 4830 pages. His works have been republished in *Vepra 1–8,* Prishtinë 1978–1984 (Works 1–8).

Lit.: BAKIU, Zyber, *Vepra letrare e Sami Frashërit.* in: Nëntori 22 (1975) 6, p. 150–154; FRASHËRI, Kristo, *Sami Frashëri (1850–1904).* in: Buletin për Shkencat Shoqërore (1955) 4, p. 56–112; KALESHI, Hasan, *Le rôle de Chemseddin Sami Frachery dans la formation de deux langues littéraires, turc et albanais.* in: Balcanica 1 (1970), p. 197–216; RESO, Esad, *Sami Frashëri. Pikëpamjet filozofike, shoqërore dhe politike,* Tiranë 1962; XHOLI, Zija, *Sami Frashëri. Nga jeta dhe vepra,* Tiranë 1978.

FRASHËRI, Shahin (19th century). Bektash (q.v.) epic poet. Younger brother of Dalip Frashëri (q.v.). He is the author of the verse epic *Myhtarnameja* (The Myhtar Name), a 12,000-line poem dealing with Shi'ite Moslem history. The epic, finished in 1868, was based on a Persian original and served Naim Frashëri (q.v.) as a model for his *Qerbelaja* on a similar theme.

FRËNGU, Dhimitër (1443–1525). Lat. *Demetrius Franco.* Latin historian from Drisht near Shkodër and first cousin of Paulus Angelus (q.v.). He fled Albania in 1478 during the Turkish siege and lived as a priest near Treviso in northern Italy. He is the author of a short history of Scanderbeg (q.v.), known to us only in an imperfect Italian translation: *Gli illustri e gloriosi gesti fatti contra Turchi dal Signor Don Giorgio Castriotto, detto Scanderbeg,* Venice 1545 (The illustrious and glorious deeds accomplished against the Turks by Lord George Castrioti, known as Scanderbeg).

G

GAJTANI, Adem (1935–1982). Kosovo poet. Born in Podujevë, he studied law at the universities of Belgrade and Skopje. Gajtani worked in Skopje as a journalist for Albanian-language newspapers, such as *Rilindja* (Rebirth) and *Flaka e vëllazërimit* (The flame of brotherhood), and in 1955 began contributing regularly to Kosovo literary journals. He has published his pensive lyrics in Albanian, Serbo-Croatian, and Macedonian.

Gajtani published nine volumes of Albanian poetry for adults: *Drita në zemër*, Prishtinë 1961 (The light in the heart); *Dryni i heshtjeve*, Prishtinë 1964 (The lock of silence); *Ti kangë, ti zog i largët*, Prishtinë 1968 (Thou song, thou distant bird); *As dru as zog dashurie*, Skopje 1973 (Neither fear nor bird of love); *Unaza*, Prishtinë 1974 (The ring); *Amfora e fundosur*, Prishtinë 1977 (The sunken amphora); *Kuq*, Prishtinë 1978 (Red); *Poezi*, Skopje 1980 (Poetry); and *Kënga e mjellmës*, Prishtinë 1980 (Swan song). He is also the author of two volumes of verse for children and one play.

GASHI, Mirko (1939–   ). Kosovo poet. Born in Kraljevo, he finished secondary school in Gjilan and studied journalism in Belgrade. He then worked as a reporter for the Skopje newspaper *Flaka e vëllazërimit* (The flame of brotherhood) and later for Radio Prishtinë.

He has published his verse in: *Në vorbullën e ujit*, Prishtinë 1972 (In the whirlpool); *Netët e bardha*, Prishtinë 1975 (The white nights); and *Gjarpëri i shtëpisë*, Prishtinë 1980 (The house snake).

GASPARUS, Stephanus. See GASPRI, Stefan.

GASPRI, Stefan (1604–1672). Lat. *Stephanus Gasparus*. Latin poet. Gaspri was from Durrës and studied at the College of the Propaganda Fide in Rome, as did Frang Bardhi (q.v.). He is the author of two short panegyric poems in Latin dedicated to Bardhi and published in the latter's Latin-Albanian dictionary of 1635.

GAUDIO, Giuseppe del. See GAUDIO, Xhuzepe del.

GAUDIO, Xhuzepe del (1921–). Ital. *Giuseppe del Gaudio*. Arbëresh (q.v.) poet from Catanzaro. He now lives in the town of Melissa and is author of *Zemër arbëreshe*, Tiranë 1984 (Arbëresh heart), a verse collection inspired by a nostalgic reflection on his Albanian origins.

GAVOÇI, Shauket (1918–). Albanian-language poet from Syria. He was born in Shkodër where he attended elementary school. From 1937 to 1944 he lived in Egypt, before moving to Damascus where he organized the first Albanian patriotic society. His verse, little of which has been published, is reminiscent of that of Shiroka (q.v.) and other classical Rilindja (q.v.) poets. He now teaches Albanian in Damascus.

GAZULLI, Gjon (1400–1455). Lat. *Johannes Gazulus*. Mathematician of Albanian origin. He was originally from the Mirdita region and was active in Dubrovnik, both as a scholar and politician.

Lit.: BANFI, F., *Ma i moçmi humanist shqiptar: Johannes Gazulus (sh. XV).* in: Leka 1–2 (1939), p. 17–24; DRANÇOLLI, Jahja, *Gjin Gazulli, astronom dhe diplomat i shekullit XV*, Prishtinë 1984.

GAZULUS, Johannes. See GAZULLI, Gjon.

GEG. Alternatively spelled *Gheg*. Term for the northern Albanians and their dialect group, as opposed to the Tosks (q.v.) of the south. Speakers of Geg dialects are to be found throughout northern Albania, including Kosovo, down to the Shkumbini river south of Elbasan, which marks the traditional dialect border between Geg and Tosk.

GENOVIZZI, Fr. (–1937). Italian Jesuit priest and publicist. He worked actively for the introduction of Albanian in Catholic schools in the Shkodër area. From 1897 to 1920 he was the director of the periodical *Elçija* (The herald).

GENTILE, Cristina (1856–1919). Also known as *Cristina Gentile Mandalà*. Arbëresh (q.v.) folklorist and writer from Piana degli Albanesi in Sicily. She assisted G. Schirò (q.v.) in his collection of Arbëresh folktales and was the author of an unpublished collection herself.

GERMANOS of Crete (–1760). Also known as *Germanos Hieromonakhos*. Greek monk from the monastery of the Holy Trinity at Olympus. He is the author of a grammar of the Albanian language, written about 1750, as well as grammars of Turkish and Italian.

GËRVALLA, Jusuf (1943–1982). Kosovo poet and journalist. Among his collections of poetry are *Kanjushë e verdhë*, Prishtinë 1978 (Yellow stork); *Fluturojnë e bien*, Prishtinë 1975 (They fly and fall); and *Bekimi i nënës*, Tiranë 1983 (The mother's blessing). He is also author of the novel *Rrotull*, Tiranë 1983 (Round).

GHEG. See GEG.

GHICA, Helena. See ISTRIA, Dora d'.

GJAKOVA, Agim (1935–). Prose writer and poet from Kavajë. He studied at the University of Tiranë and has worked as an editor, translator, and teacher. Among his collections of poetry are *Dhe thonë se paqë ka në botë*,

Tiranë 1962 (And they say there's peace on earth); *Kangët e Drinit të Bardhë,* Tiranë 1967 (The songs of the White Drin); *Kjo është Shqipëria,* Tiranë 1970 (That's what Albania is); *Perspektivë,* Tiranë 1972 (Perspective); and the short bilingual volume *Communist,* San Francisco 1984. He has also published the novels *Në kërkim të së vërtetës,* Tiranë 1976 (In search of the truth); *Dritëhijet e një qyteti,* Tiranë 1982 (The silhouette of a city); and the short story collection *Nën hijen e pavdekësisë,* Tiranë 1983 (In the shadow of immortality).

GJAKOVA, Baba Hamza (1882–1952). Bektash (q.v.) poet. Born in Gjakovë, he studied Arabic and travelled throughout the Middle East. Returning to Kosovo, he took the title Baba in 1912 at the teke of Shtipi in Macedonia, where he lived for thirty-eight years. He is the author of much verse of Shi'ite inspiration.

GJAKOVA, Tahir (19th century?). Moslem poet from Kosovo. Author of religious verse in Gjakovë dialect.

GJATA, Fatmir (1922–   ). Prose writer, poet, and dramatist. He was born in Korçë where he studied at the French secondary school before taking part in the partisan movement of World War II. After the war, he studied at the Gorky Institute of World Literature in Moscow and later became editor of the Albanian literary magazine *Nëntori* (November).

Although the author of poetry and some stage works, Gjata is chiefly known as a prose writer. Much of his work deals with the national liberation struggle of World War II, such as the novel *Përmbysja,* Tiranë 1954 (The overthrow), and with the early years of Communist rule, such as the novel *Brezat,* Tiranë 1968 (The generations). His best known novel is no doubt *Këneta,* Tiranë 1959 (The marsh), a moving description of the draining in 1946 of the marsh of Maliq on the plain of Korçë. The partisan theme is taken up once again in his war diary *Me një torbë me fishekë,* Tiranë 1982 (With a bag of cartridges). Among his short stories are *Gruri nuk u doq,* Tiranë 1949 (The wheat did not burn); *Ujët fle, hasmi s'fle,* Tiranë 1951 (Water sleeps, the enemy sleeps not); *Pika gjaku,* Tiranë 1954 (The drop of blood); *Tana,* Tiranë 1955 (Tana) which won the Prize of the Republic; and *Në pragun e jetës,* Tiranë 1960 (On the threshold of life). His volume of poetry *Këngët e maleve,* Tiranë 1954 (The song of the mountains) includes his famous folk ballad *Kënga e partizanit Benko* (The song of partisan Benko). More recently, he has published the verse collection *Kënga e maliherit,* Tiranë 1975 (The song of the rifle).

Lit.: SHAPLLO, Dalan, *50-vjetori i shkrimtarit Fatmir Gjata.* in: Nëndori (1972) 11, p. 91–96.

GJEÇOV, Stefan. See GJEÇOVI, Shtjefën.

GJEÇOVI, Shtjefën (1873–1929). Also known as *Stefan Gjeçov*. Folklorist and scholar. He was born in the village of Janjevë near Prishtinë and studied in Austria before becoming a Franciscan priest in 1895. He spent most of his life in northern Albania and Kosovo, devoting his energies to collecting material on folklore and archeology. He was murdered in the village of Zym near Prizren in a period of ethnic tension between the Albanians and Serbs.

Among Gjeçovi's major works are *Agimi i gjytetnis,* Shkodër 1910 (The dawn of civilization), a collection of articles and aphorisms on Albania and its language; *Kangë popullore gegënishte,* Sarajevo 1911 (Geg folksongs); and *Kanuni i Lekë Dukagjinit,* Shkodër 1933 (The code of Lekë Dukagjini), a unique code of tribal law in the northern Albanian mountains. His verse, under the pseudonym *Lkeni i Hasit,* appeared in Konica's (q.v.) periodical *Albania* at the beginning of the century. He is also the author of translations and religious works such as *Pajtoria e Durzit,* Shkodër 1904 (The patron of Durrës).

Lit.: AJETI, Idriz, *Shtjefën Gjeçovi.* in: Jeta e re (1951) 2–3, p. 158–160; MATA, Ruzhdi, *Shtjefën Gjeçovi, jeta dhe vepra,* Tiranë 1982.

GJERQEKU, Enver (1928–   ). Kosovo poet and master of pensive, elegaic verse. Born in Gjakovë, he studied Albanology at the University of Belgrade and now teaches Albanian literature at the Faculty of Arts of the University of Prishtinë.

His first volume of poetry, entitled *Gjurmat e jetës,* Prishtinë 1957 (The traces of life), was a melancholic reflection on his difficult childhood. This was followed by: *Bebzat e mallit,* Prishtinë 1960 (The pupils of longing); *Tinguj të zgjuem,* Prishtinë 1966 (Awakening sounds); *Blerimi i vonuem,* Prishtinë 1966 (Late verdure); *Ashti ynë,* Prishtinë 1972 (Our bone); *Xixa stralli,* Prishtinë 1976 (Flintstone spark); *Pengu,* Prishtinë 1977 (The pledge); *Pengu i dashurisë,* Prishtinë 1978 (The pledge of love); *Lumi i palodhur,* Prishtinë 1978 (The untiring stream); and *Sogjetar amshimi,* Prishtinë 1982 (Guardian of eternity).

GJETJA, Ndoc (1944–   ). Poet. He was born in Shkodër and studied in Tiranë. Gjetja is a member of the Albanian Union of Writers and Artists and now works in Lezhë.

He is the author of several volumes of poetry, among which: *Rrezatim,* Tiranë 1971 (Radiance); *Shqipja rreh krahet,* Tiranë 1975 (The eagle beats its wings); *Qëndresa,* Tiranë 1977 (The resistance); *E përditshme,* Tiranë 1981 (The daily); and *Çaste,* Tiranë 1984 (Moments), combining reflections on social change and class struggle with an awareness for the beauties of man's natural environment.

GJIKA, Helena. See ISTRIA, Dora d'.

GJIROKASTRITI, Elmaz. (fl. 1820). Poet. Author of a ninety-two-line poem with the Turkish title *Evvel hastallik* (The first pest), dealing with the epidemic which raged in the Gjirokastër area in 1817. It was written in 1820 and is preserved in a manuscript from Gjirokastër.

GJIROKASTRITI, Grigor (fl. 1827). Greek *Grigorios Argyrokastritis*. Bishop of Euboea and from 1827 Archbishop of Athens. He edited an Albanian translation of the New Testament (Corfu 1827), probably translated by Vangjel Meksi (q.v.). The gospel of St. Matthew was published in Albanian in 1824 and the New Testament as a whole in a bilingual Greek-Albanian edition three years later.

GLAVIANO, Francesco Crispi. See KRISPI GLAVJANO, Frano.

GLIQINI, Luc. See DULCI, Carlo.

GODO, Sabri (1924–). Prose writer from Delvinë. As a teenager, he interrupted his studies in Tiranë to take part in the resistance movement of World War II. He is best known for his historical novels such as *Plaku i Butkës,* Tiranë 1964 (The old man from Butkë) about Sali Butka (q.v.); *Ali Pashë Tepelena,* Tiranë 1970 (Ali Pasha Tepelena); and *Skënderbeu,* Tiranë 1975 (Scanderbeg). Among his other works are the partisan novel *Prova e zjarrit,* Tiranë 1977 (Ordeal of fire); and a collection of short stories entitled *Zëra nga burime të nxehta,* Tiranë 1971 (Voices from the hotsprings).

GRAMENO, Mihal (1872–1931). Politician and writer. Born in Korçë of a merchant family, he studied at the Greek secondary school there before emigrating to Romania in 1885. It was in Bucharest that he got involved in the nationalist movement and in 1889 became secretary of the Drita society. In 1907, he joined the Çerçiz Topulli band, an early guerila unit fighting against Turkish troops in southern Albania. He was later editor of the nationalist periodical *Lidhja orthodhokse* (The orthodox league), Korçë 1909–1910, and the weekly *Koha* (Time), the latter originally in Korçë and later in America where he lived from 1915 to 1919. He travelled back to Europe to represent American Albanians at the Paris Peace Conference in 1919 and in the following year returned to Albania. In the 1920s, he carried on his journalistic and literary activities until the Zog dictatorship forced him to retire from public life. Resigned and seriously ill, he died an alcoholic on February 5, 1931, in his native city of Korçë.

As a writer, Grameno first became known in 1903 for his patriotic poem *Vdekja* (Death). He is the author of the comedy *Mallkimi i gjuhës shqipe,* Bucharest 1905 (The curse of the Albanian language); and the historical tragedy *Vdekja e Piros,* Sofia 1906 (The death of Pyrrhus). He also published well-known short stories such as *Oxhaku* (The hearth), *E puthura* (The kiss), and *Varr' i pagëzimit,* (The baptismal font), Korçë 1909; a volume of poetry entitled *Plagët,* Monastir 1912 (The wounds); and memoirs of his experiences as a guerilla, the latter in *Kryengritja shqiptare,* Korçë 1925 (The Albanian uprising). His writings have been republished in *Vepra 1–2,* Prishtinë 1979 (Works 1–2).

Lit.: GJIKA, Thanas, *Mihal Gramenoja publicist demokrat,* Tiranë 1980.

GRIGOR GJIROKASTRITI. See GJIROKASTRITI, Grigor.

GRIGORI I DURRËSIT (–1772). Also known as *Grigor Voskopojari.* He is said to have been the author of a translation of the Old and New Testaments using an alphabet he invented himself. Nothing more is known of the work, now lost. Grigori studied in Voskopojë (Moskhopolis), a centre of religious learning near Korçë and published several religious works in Greek. In 1768, he was appointed Archbishop of Durrës, hence the name.

GRUDA, Lek. See GURAKUQI, Luigj.

GUAGLIATA, Giuseppe. See GUALIATA, Giuseppe.

GUALIATA, Giuseppe (ca. 1814–). Also known as *Guagliata.* Italian Jesuit priest and writer who was sent as a missionary to Albania in 1841. He is the author of an Albanian translation of Bellarmino's Christian Doctrine, entitled *Dottrina e Kerscten,* Rome 1845, and is said to have been the coauthor with Vincenzo Basile (q.v.) of a lost grammar of Albanian written in Italian about 1842.

GUIDERA, Trifon (19th century?). Little known Arbëresh (q.v.) poet from the village of Pallagorio in Catanzaro.

GUNGA, Fahredin (1936–   ). Kosovo poet. Born in Mitrovicë of a poor family, he began his studies at the University of Belgrade in 1957, returning to Kosovo to teach school in his native town. He later worked as a reporter for the daily newspaper *Rilindja* (Rebirth) in Prishtinë and is now on the staff of the Rilindja Publishing Company.

His poetry, which reflects a constant compassion with the struggles and suffering of humanity, has been published in a number of collections: *Pëshpëritjet e mëngjezit,* Prishtinë 1961 (Morning whispers); *Mallkimet e fjetuna,* Prishtinë 1970 (Dormant curses); *Kepi i Shpresës së Mirë,* Prishtinë 1973 (Cape of Good Hope); *Flaka e fjalës,* Tiranë 1975 (Word flames); *Psalmet e gurta,* Prishtinë 1977 (Stone psalms); *Nokturno për Orkidenë,* Prishtinë 1981 (Nocturno for the orchid); and *Mallkimet e zgjuara,* Prishtinë 1985 (Awakened curses).

   Lit.: ALIU, Ali, *Poezi e shpresës dhe e meditimit.* in: Jeta e re (1973) 4, p. 591–597.

GURAKUQI, Luigj (1879–1925). Pseudonyms *Jakin Shkodra* and *Lek Gruda.* Writer and political figure. He was born in Shkodër where he studied Albanian at the Saverian college, one of the best schools in the country at the time. Encouraged by his teachers Anton Xanoni (q.v.) and Gaspër Jakova Merturi, he began writing poetry in Italian, Latin, and Albanian, the latter published in part in the periodical *Elçija* (The herald). In 1897, he left for Italy to study at the college in San Demetrio Corone under Jeronim de Rada (q.v.), who deeply influenced him. He also studied medicine in Naples for a time where he was in contact with Arbëresh (q.v.) literary and political figures. In 1908, Gurakuqi returned to Albania and soon became a leader of the nationalist movement which led to the country's independence in 1912. He served as minister of education in the first Albanian government, minister of the interior in 1921, and minister of finance in 1924 in the democratic government of Fan Noli (q.v.). In the same year, however, the rise of the Zog dictatorship forced him to flee to Italy. He was murdered on March 2, 1925, in Bari by one Baltjon Stambolla, no doubt an agent of Ahmed Zog.

   Among Gurakuqi's didactic works are *Kndime t'para për msojtore filltare të Shqypnisë,* Naples 1905 (First reader for Albanian elementary schools), published under the pseudonym Lek Gruda; *Abetar i vogel shqyp mbas abevet t'Bashkimit e t'Stambollit me tregime n't'dy dhialektet,* Bucharest 1906 (Little Albanian spelling book in the Bashkimi and Istanbul alphabets with tales in both dialects); and *Vargenimi n'gjuhe shcype me gni fjalorth shcyp-frangisht n'marim,* Naples 1906 (Versification of the Albanian language with an Albanian-French glossary at the end). His poetry was published in *Vjersha*, Bari 1941 (Verse); and a selection of his works was republished in *Vepra të zgjedhura*, Tiranë 1961 (Selected works).

Lit.: LACAJ, Henrik, *Luigj Gurakuqi (1879-1925), shënime mbi jetën dhe veprën e tij letrare*. in: Buletin i Universitetit Shtetëror të Tiranës. Seria Shkenc. Shoq. (1959) 4, p. 162-176; TAKO, Piro, *Luigj Gurakuqi. Jeta dhe vepra*, Tiranë 1980.

GURAKUQI, Mark (1922-1977). Poet and critic. Born in Pogradec, he attended school in Elbasan. In 1950, he finished his studies of literature in Bulgaria and returned to Albania to teach.

Gurakuqi is the author of several volumes of poetry dealing mostly with the profound changes which took place in Albania in the first decade after the liberation. Among his works are *Kangë për jetën*, Tiranë 1951 (A song for life); *Miniera nuk u mbyll*, Tiranë 1951 (The mine did not close down); *Pranverë*, Tiranë 1953 (Spring); *Gjeto plaku*, Tiranë 1955 (Old Gjeto); *Kangë për dashurinë*, Tiranë 1957 (A song for love); *Në udhët e jetës*, Tiranë 1960 (On the roads of life); *Në gjurmët e viteve*, Tiranë 1964 (In the traces of years); and *Në rrjedhë të viteve*, Tiranë 1969 (In the course of years). Among his literary studies are *Autorë dhe probleme të letërsisë përparimtare shqipe të viteve '30*, Tiranë 1966 (Authors and problems of progressive Albanian literature of the thirties); and *Mbi veprën poetike të Mjedës*, Tiranë 1980 (On the poetic work of Mjeda).

GURRA, Milto Sotir (1884-1972). Pseudonyms *Nomadhi, Gjon Zeza*, and *D. Toçkas*. Short story writer and journalist. Originally from the village of Opari in the Korçë region, he lived most of his life abroad, first in Odessa, then in Sofia and Constanza. He contributed actively to the literary and nationalist periodicals in exile and was editor of *Lirija e Shqipëris* (The freedom of Albania), Sofia 1911-1915; *Atdheu* (The fatherland), Constanza 1912-1914; and other short-lived nationalist journals.

Gurra was one of the first Albanian short story writers. Among his early works are *Rrëfenja*, Sofia 1911 (Tales); and *Goca e malcis*, Sofia 1912 (The highland girl). A later volume, *Plagët e kurbetit*, Tiranë 1938 (The torments of exile), contains twenty-two short stories dealing largely with the sufferings of Albanian emigrants. His tales are republished in *Tregime*, Prishtinë 1971 (Short stories).

GUSHO, Lazar. See PORADECI, Lasgush.

GUZZETTA, Giorgio (1682-1756). Arbëresh (q.v.) priest and writer from Piana degli Albanesi in Sicily. He was founder of the Arbëresh seminar in Palermo which soon became the intellectual centre of the Albanian community on the island. He was also the author of prose and poetry in Italian, including an etymological study of Albanian, and a historical work entitled *Cronica della Macedonia fino ai tempi di Scanderbeg* (Chronicle of Macedonia up to the age of Scanderbeg).

Lit.: D'ANGELO, Giovanni, *Vita del servo di Dio P. Giorgio Guzzetta greco-abanese della Piana dell'Oratoria di Palermo,* Palermo 1798.

GUZZETTA, Giovan-Chrisostomo (1700–1770). Arbëresh (q.v.) priest and poet from Piana degli Albanesi, Sicily. Nephew of Giorgio Guzzetta (q.v.), he is the author of religious poetry in Albanian.

H

HAKIU, Nexhat (1914–   ). Poet. Born in Vlorë, he is the author of lively, colourful verse published in a variety of prewar periodicals and collected in *Këngët e zambares,* Tiranë 1939 (Songs of the flute); and *Zëri i fyellit,* Tiranë 1959 (The voice of the flute).

HALIL POPOVA, Tahir efendi. See POPOVA, Tahir efendi Halil.

HALIMI, Nexhat (1949–   ). Kosovo poet from the village of Dumnicë near Podujevë. He studied Albanian language and literature at the University of Prishtinë and now works as a journalist for the daily *Rilindja* (Rebirth). He has published the following volumes of poetry: *Parakalimi i etjeve,* Prishtinë 1969 (The parade of thirsts); *Afërsia e largësisë,* Prishtinë 1971 (The proximity of distance); *Hark,* Prishtinë 1973 (Arch); *Dita e daljes,* Prishtinë 1978 (Day of issue); and *Truphija,* Prishtinë 1984 (The shadow), as well as the collections of short stories *Vapë,* Prishtinë 1974 (Heat); and *Unë me unë,* Prishtinë 1983 (I alone).

HAMITI, Sabri (1950–   ). Kosovo poet, prose writer, and critic. Born in the village of Dumnicë near Podujevë. After graduating in Albanian language and literature from the University of Prishtinë in 1972, he continued his studies in Zagreb in 1974–1976 and at the Ecole Pratique des Hautes Etudes in Paris in 1980–1981. He now works for the Rilindja Press in Prishtinë.

Hamiti has published many volumes of poetry, among which: *Njeriu vdes i ri,* Prishtinë 1972 (Man dies young); *Faqe e fund,* Prishtinë 1973 (Page and end); *Thikë harrimi,* Prishtinë 1975 (Knife of oblivion); and *Trungu ilir,* Prishtinë 1979 (The Illyrian stock). He is also the author of literary criticism *Variante,* Prishtinë 1974 (Variants); *Teksti i dramatizuar,* Prishtinë 1978 (The dramatized text); *Kritika letrare* with Ibrahim Rugova (q.v.), Prishtinë 1979 (Literary criticism); *A-Zh, Romanet e Nazmi Rrahmanit,* Prishtinë 1982 (A-Zh, the novels of Nazmi Rrahmani); *Arti i leximit,* Prishtinë 1983 (The art of reading); and a novel *Njëqind vjet vetmi,* Prishtinë 1976 (A hundred years of solitude).

HARALLAMBI, Kristo. See NEGOVANI, Papa Kristo.
HARAPI, Anton. See HARAPI, Ndue.
HARAPI, Ndue (–ca. 1945). Also known as *Anton Harapi*. Franciscan priest and writer from Shkodër. He attended monastic schools in Merano and Hall in Tyrol before studying theology in Rome. His involvement in politics during the German occupation resulted in his arrest and execution in 1944/45. He is remembered for the novel *Valë mbi valë*, (Wave upon wave).
HARAPI, Zef M. (1891–1946). Jesuit priest and prose writer from Shkodër. His works first appeared in literary periodicals. He is the author of two historical plays: *Oso Kuka,* 1921; and *Mustafa Pasha i Shkodrës,* 1923 (Mustafa Pasha of Shkodër); and in particular of the sentimental novel *Pushka e trathtarit,* Shkodër 1914 (The traitor's gun) about vendetta and tribal justice in the northern Albanian mountains.

Lit.: KOLIQI, Ernest, *Zef M. Harapi auktor rromanxash e dramash.* in: Shêjzat 17 (1973), p. 9–45; KONGOLI, Bestar, *Të dhëna për jetën dhe veprimtarinë letrare të Zef M. Harapit.* in: Studime Filologjike 1983. 1, p. 145–158.

HARFF, Arnold von (ca. 1471–1505). German traveller, writer, and author of a short Albanian lexicon. Harff was born of a noble family of the lower Rhineland (Harff on the Erft, northwest of Cologne). In the autumn of 1496 he set out on a journey, ostensibly a pilgrimage to the Holy Land, which took him to Italy, down the Adriatic coast to Greece, Egypt, Arabia, Palestine, Asia Minor, and then back through central Europe to France and Spain. He returned to Cologne in the autumn of 1498 or 1499 and died in 1505.

On his travels, Harff collected material on the languages he encountered. During a stopover in the port of Durrës in the spring of 1497, he noted down twenty-six words, eight phrases, and twelve numbers in Albanian which he recorded with a German translation in his travel narrative. This material constitutes the first substantial, datable text of written Albanian.

Lit.: ELSIE, Robert, *The Albanian lexicon of Arnold von Harff, 1497.* in: Zeitschrift für Vergleichende Sprachforschung 97 (1984), p. 113–122; GROOTE, E. von, *Die Pilgerfahrt des Ritters Arnold von Harff. . . ,* Cologne 1860; LETTS, Malcolm, *The pilgrimage of Arnold von Harff. . . .,* London 1946.

HARXHI, Ramiz (1897–1966). Poet. He was born in Gjirokastër and went to school in Istanbul. He later emigrated to America where he spent six years before returning to Albania. His patriotic poetry first appeared in periodicals in 1914 and was published in the volume *Ndjenjat e zemrës,* 1917 (Feelings of the heart), typical of nationalist verse of the period. He also wrote some sentimental love poetry.

Lit.: VARFI, Andrea, *Një shtatëdhejtëvjetor i nderuar: Ramiz Harxhi.* in: Nëndori (1962) 2, p. 115–116.

HASANI, Hasan (1947–   ). Kosovo poet and prose writer born in Jabllanicë near Gjakovë. He went to school in Gjakovë and studied Albanian language and literature at the University of Prishtinë. He now works as an editor for the fortnightly literary periodical *Fjala* (The word).

Hasani is the author of several volumes of verse, among which: *Krojet e bardha*, Prishtinë 1967 (The white fountains); *Dallgët e verrinit*, Prishtinë 1969 (The waves of winter pastures); *Dy legjenda*, Prishtinë 1969 (Two legends); *Më bekoi pa gjuhë*, Prishtinë 1971 (He blessed me in silence); *Suferinë*, Prishtinë 1977 (Gale); *Emoniana*, Prishtinë 1980; *Shenasa*, Prishtinë 1980; and *Unazëforta*, Prishtinë 1984. He has also published poetry for children and a volume of short stories entitled *Njeriu që grindej me qiellin*, Prishtinë 1979 (The man who argued with the sky).

HASANI, Sinan (1922–). Kosovo novelist. Born in Pozharan near Gjilan of a peasant family, he went to school in Skopje. He joined the partisan movement during the German occupation and was imprisoned several times. After the war, he began writing and took up a career in politics. He served as Yugoslav ambassador to Denmark and has since held a variety of high offices in Yugoslav party and government administration.

Hasani is considered one of the founders of the Albanian novel in Yugoslavia. His first novel *Rrushi ka nisë me u pjekë*, Prishtinë 1957 (The grapes have begun to ripen) is a chronicle of contemporary Albanian life in Yugoslavia. This was followed by *Nji natë e turbullt*, Prishtinë 1960 (A stormy night), dealing with the resistance movement; and *Ku ndahet lumi*, Prishtinë 1963 (Where the river divides), a description of the birth of socialism in Kosovo. Among his other works are *Era dhe lisi*, Prishtinë 1973 (The wind and the oak); *Fëmijëria e Gjon Vatrës*, Prishtinë 1975 (The childhood of Gjon Vatër); *Fëmijëria e dytë e Gjon Vatrës*, Prishtinë 1980 (The second childhood of Gjon Vatër); *Për bukën e bardhë*, Prishtinë 1980 (For white bread); *Djaloshi me dekoratë*, Prishtinë 1980 (The boy with a medal); *Përroi vërshues*, Prishtinë 1980 (The overflowing torrent); and *Udhëpërshkrime*, Prishtinë 1982 (Travel notes).

HASI, Pal (fl. late 16th century). Also known as *Pali prej Hasi*. Franciscan priest and writer. He lived in the second half of the sixteenth century and probably originated from Hasi i Thatë in northeastern Albania. We know of him only from a reference made by Pjetër Budi (q.v.) in the preface to his Christian Doctrine, published in 1618. Budi states: "I earlier wrote down [i.e., copied] in our language two chapters of the Day of Judgment written by the very reverend and pious priest, brother Paul from Hasi." Nothing has survived of Hasi's works. His chapters of the Day of Judgment were no doubt translations into Albanian, perhaps from Bellarmino's Christian Doctrine, also used by Budi.

Lit.: SHUTERIQI, Dhimitër, *Autorë dhe tekste*, Tiranë 1977, p. 63–77.

HATIPI, Tajar (1918–1977). Kosovo prose writer. Born in Elbasan, he moved to Kosovo and worked as a teacher in Prizren, Gjakovë, and later in Prishtinë. In 1962, he became chief editor of the periodical *Pioneri* (The pioneer). He was also editor of the Kosovo literary journal *Jeta e re* (New life) from the start of its publication.

Hatipi is the author of satirical short stories and works for children, among which: *Rrethimi*, Prishtinë 1962 (The siege); *Buni*, Prishtinë 1963 (The cabin); *U bëra trim*, Prishtinë 1973 (I became a hero); and *Vrima thesi*, Prishtinë 1977

(The hole in the bag). His works have been republished in *Vepra 1–4*, Prishtinë 1982? (Works 1–4).

Lit.: MEKULI, Hasan, *Proza humoristike e T. Hatipit.* in: Jeta e re (1963) 2, p. 281–290.

HAXHIADEMI, Etëhem (1907?–   ). Playwright and poet from Elbasan. He studied political science in Berlin and returned to Albania to work in government, becoming head of a department at the Ministry of the Interior in Tiranë. After the war, he was sentenced to life imprisonment.

His classical education finds its expression in his plays based on Greek and Latin models. His trilogy of five-act plays *Ulisi, Akili, Aleksandri,* Tiranë 1931 (Ulysses, Achilles, Alexander) was followed by *Pirrua,* 1934 (Pyrrhus); *Skënderbeu,* 1935 (Scanderbeg); *Diomedi,* 1936 (Diomedes); and *Abeli,* 1939 (Abel). Haxhiademi also published a volume of verse entitled *Lyra* (The lyre) showing classical influence and translated Vergil's Bucolics into Albanian.

HAXHIFILIPI, Theodhor (1730–1805). Also known as *Dhaskal Todhri.* Author of Orthodox religious works. He was born in Elbasan where he received his elementary education. He later studied at the New Academy in the then flourishing city of Voskopojë (Moskhopolis) and returned at the age of twenty to Elbasan to teach at the Greek school there, hence the name Dhaskal (teacher).

The German scholar Johann Georg von Hahn who visited Albania in the first half of the nineteenth century, refers to him as having translated not only the Old Testament but also the New Testament and other religious works. Most of his writings were unfortunately destroyed by fire in 1827. Among the surviving fragments are *Mesha e Sh. Jon Gojarit* (The liturgy of St. John Chrysostom) and a hymn to the Virgin Mary. Todhri used a particular alphabet of fifty-three letters based on Glagolitic, which he appears to have invented himself. Two of Aesop's fables are also preserved in Todhri's alphabet.

Lit.: SHUTERIQI, Dhimitër, *Dhaskal Todhri.* in: Buletin për Shkencat Shoqërore (1954), 4, p. 35–55; *Shkrimet të Dhaskal Todhrit.* in: Buletin për Shkencat Shoqërore (1959) 1, p. 165–198.

HAXHIMIMA, Josif (1882–   ). Pseudonym *Rras'e Bardhë.* Writer from Elbasan. He studied at Monastir and worked as a teacher at the Turkish school in Elbasan. In 1915, he left teaching for a career in legal administration.

Haxhimima is remembered for his poetry and essays which appeared in several periodicals such as *Kalendari Kombiar* (The national calendar) and *Diturija* (Knowledge).

HAXHIU, Dhanil (1754–1825). Also known as *mjeshtri Dhanil* or *master Daniel.* Lexicographer and Orthodox religious teacher from Voskopojë (Moskhopolis) and student of Theodhor Kavalioti (q.v.). He is the author of *Eisagogike didaskalia,* containing a four language lexicon in modern Greek, Aromanian, Bulgarian, and Albanian, published in Venice in 1802. It comprises about 1000 entries, plus 235 phrases of daily life, which although freely translated, are not without interest for the study of Albanian historical morphology and syntax.

Lit.: KRISTOPHSON, J., *Das Lexikon Tetraglosson des Daniil Moschopol-*

itis. in: Zeitschrift für Balkanologie 10 (1974), 1, p. 7–128; LEAKE, William Martin, *Researches in Greece,* London 1814.
HELENAU. See MIRDITA, Kolë.
HIEROMONAKHOS, Germanos. See GERMANOS of Crete.
HIMA, Dervish. See NAXHI, Mehmet.
HOXHA, Mehmet (1908–   ). Kosovo poet and prose writer. Born in Gjakovë of a Moslem family, he finished secondary school in Shkodër. In 1941, he returned to Yugoslavia and took part in the partisan movement.

Hoxha has written articles, poetry, and short stories for leading Kosovo periodicals. Among his works are the short story collections *Për nji grusht kumbulla,* Prishtinë 1967 (For a handful of plums); *Dashunija e mëshehtë,* Prishtinë 1980 (Secret love); and the volume of verse *Kurrë më,* Prishtinë 1978 (Never more). He is also the author of several translations from Serbo-Croatian and French, including Ćosić, Domanović, Andrić, and Stendhal.

HOXHA, Myslim (18th century?). Author of an Albanian translation of the *Tyhfei Shahidi,* a Turkish-Persian dictionary by Ibrahim Dede who died in 1520 and which contains several thousand entries. All we know of Hoxha is that he was from the village of Levan near Fier.

HOXHA, Rexhep (1929–   ). Kosovo author of children's literature. He was born in Gjakovë of a peasant family and studied at the University of Belgrade before returning to Kosovo to teach school in Mitrovicë.

Rexhep Hoxha is one of Kosovo's foremost writers of children's poetry. Among his many collections are *Gjethe të reja,* Prishtinë 1953 (New leaves); *Picimuli,* Prishtinë 1956; *Mbi krahët e fluturës,* Prishtinë 1959 (On butterfly wings); *Vjersha,* Prishtinë 1963 (Poetry); *Micimiri,* Prishtinë 1976; *Tokë trëndafilash,* Prishtinë 1979 (Rose country); *Poezi të zgjedhura,* Prishtinë 1984 (Selected poetry); and *Zogu i qiellit,* Prishtinë 1984 (The sky bird). He is also the author of the children's novel *Lugjet e verdha,* Prishtinë 1959 (The yellow valleys) and of literary criticism.

HOXHI, Kostandin. See HOXHI, Koto.
HOXHI, Koto (1824–1895). Also known as *Kostandin Hoxhi.* Rilindja (q.v.) poet from Qestorat in the Gjirokastër area. He received his education at the Greek school in his native village and later in Istanbul where he met the Frashëri brothers and other leaders of the nationalist movement. It was there that he was inspired to devote himself to the nationalist cause. He died in 1895 in Qestorat while preparing to open an Albanian school in Ioannina for which he had obtained authorization from the Turkish government.

His patriotic verse in a popular vein was published posthumously in Spiro Dine's (q.v.) *Valët e detit* and in Visar Dodani's (q.v.) *Mjalt' e mbletës.*

HULUKI, Ali (1910–   ). Syrian-Arabic writer of Albanian origin. Son of Mustafa Huluki (q.v.). Born in Duma near Damascus, he was educated in the Syrian capital. From 1929 on, he worked as a teacher in various parts of Syria. Huluki is considered the father of the Syrian short story and pioneer of realism in that genre.

Lit.: MUFAKU, Muhamed, *Tregime siriane (1931–1981),* Prishtinë 1981.

HULUKI, Mustafa (1850–1915). Syrian-Arabic poet of Albanian origin, born in Damascus of a family from Kavala in Greece. Father of Ali Huluki (q.v.). He began his studies in Damascus and attended a military college in Istanbul. For a time, he was head of the al-Sultanije school in Beirut and contributed to the compilation of the al-Bustani encyclopaedia. His verse, written in Arabic and Turkish and revealing his nationalist, anti-Ottoman sentiments, appeared in a number of Syrian and Lebanese periodicals at the beginning of the century.

HYSA, Bedri (1935–   ). Kosovo poet born in Mitrovicë. He finished his schooling in Kaçanik and studied Albanology at the Faculty of Arts of the University of Prishtinë. Hysa worked for a time as a teacher in Mitrovicë, Kaçanik, and Ferizaj and later became director of the University Library in Prishtinë. Author of the verse collections: *Duke kërkuar njerinë*, Prishtinë 1973 (Searching for man); *Erë në ere*, Prishtinë 1975 (Wind in the wind); *Myshqe*, Prishtinë 1977 (Mosses); and *Paskajore*, Prishtinë 1980 (Infinitive).

HYXHRETIU. See FRASHËRI, Dalip.

I

IBRAHIMI, Baba (early 20th century). Bektash (q.v.) poet from the teke of Qesarakë near Kolonjë. He was active, like many other Bektash figures, in the distribution of Albanian books and literature. In 1913, he was arrested by the Greek authorities but was subsequently freed by Sali Butka (q.v.). Ibrahimi was the author of both nationalist and religious verse.

IMAMI, Sitki (1912–1983?). Kosovo journalist and short story writer from Gjakovë. He went to school in Albania and worked as a journalist for Radio Belgrade after the war. A collection of his short stories was published under the title *Drejt ditëve të reja,* Prishtinë 1954 (Towards new days). Imami also translated works of Ćosić, the Grimm brothers, and Hans Christian Andersen.

ISAKU, Agim (1955–   ). Poet. He was born in Korçë and studied language and literature at the University of Tiranë. He now teaches in Lezhë. Among his collections of poetry are *Pranvera e lumit tim,* Tiranë 1975 (My river in spring); *Mosha,* Tiranë 1977 (Age); and *Gurët,* Tiranë 1981 (The stones).

ISAKU, Murat (1928–   ). Albanian poet and prose writer from Macedonia. He was born in the village of Gajre near Tetovo and went to school in Prishtinë, Prizren, and Gjakovë. In 1953, he graduated from the University of Belgrade and returned to Tetovo to teach school. He now works for RTV Skopje.

His poetry varies from a melodious symbolism to harsh social criticism. Among his many publications are the verse collections *Zani i malit,* Prishtinë 1960 (The mountain voice); *Buzëqeshjet e mesditës,* Skopje 1963 (Smiles at noon); *Drithma,* Prishtinë 1975 (Trembling); *Blana,* Prishtinë 1982 (Blana); the novels *Dielli e din rrugën e vet,* Prishtinë 1965 (The sun knows its course); *Plagët,* Tiranë 1975 (The wounds); *Rreckajt,* Prishtinë 1979 (The Rreckajs); *Etje,* Prishtinë 1982 (Thirst); and the short story collections *Unaza e djerrinës,* Prishtinë 1971 (The ring of fallow land); and *Gërsheta,* Prishtinë 1978 (The tress).

ISLAMI, Abdylazis (1930–   ). Albanian poet and prose writer from Macedonia. Like Murat Isaku (q.v.), he was born in the village of Gajre near

Tetovo. Islami has published the following collections of often reflective, emotional verse: *Era dhe vargjet,* Prishtinë 1964 (Wind and verse); *Këngët e zgjuara,* Prishtinë 1968 (Awakened songs); *Soditje nga toka,* Prishtinë 1969 (Thoughts from the earth); *Barka ndër valë,* Skopje 1971 (Boats in the waves); *Oaza,* Skopje 1973 (The oasis); *Agullina,* Prishtinë 1978; and *Dritë në sfond,* Prishtinë 1980 (Light in the background). He is also author of the novels: *Gurgurina,* Prishtinë 1974 (Rubble); and *Fatiana,* Prishtinë 1975 (Fatiana).

ISMAJLI, Rexhep (1947–   ). Kosovo scholar and critic born in Preševo. He studied in Prishtinë and Paris and now teaches Albanian language and literature at the University of Prishtinë. Ismajli has published a number of studies in the fields of literary criticism and linguistics. Among his works are *Shenjë dhe ide,* Prishtinë 1974 (Sign and idea); *Shumësia e tekstit,* Prishtinë 1977 (Text plurality); *Rrënjë e fortë,* Prishtinë 1978 (A strong root); *Antologji e poezisë rumune të shekullit XX,* Prishtinë 1979 (Anthology of 20th century Romanian poetry); and *Gramatika e parë e gjuhës shqipe,* Prishtinë 1983 (The first grammar of the Albanian language). He has also translated works of Jacques Prévert, Alain Bosquet, André Martinet, Ferdinand de Saussure, and René Descartes.

ISTANBUL SOCIETY. See SHOQËRI E TË SHTYPURIT SHKRONJA SHQIP.

ISTREFI, Adem (1942–   ). Poet and prose writer. Born in Strellç near Pejë in Kosovo, he moved to Albania in 1956. He studied at the University of Tiranë where he graduated in 1967 and now works for the literary periodical *Nëntori* (November).

Among Istrefi's publications are *Net kosovare,* Tiranë 1967 (Kosovo nights); *Mëngjezi i së nesërmes,* Tiranë 1969 (The next morning); *Dritaret e fjalës,* Tiranë 1972 (The word windows); *Gjerdan lirie,* Tiranë 1977 (Necklace of freedom); *Pasha këtë dhe,* Tiranë 1982 (By this land); and the novel *Lëshoma hisen e diellit,* Tiranë 1984 (Leave me my part of the sun).

ISTRIA, Dora d' (1828–1882). Pseudonym of *Helena Ghica* (Alb. *Gjika*). Romanian writer of Albanian origin. She was born in Bucharest of an aristocratic family originally from Macedonia. Her uncle was Grigore IV, voivode of Wallachia. As a young woman, she travelled with her parents to the courts of Vienna, Dresden, and Berlin and was widely admired for her talents and beauty. In 1849, her marriage to Prince Alexander Masal'sky took her to Russia where she spent almost six years. After her separation from him in 1855, she moved to Switzerland and in 1860 travelled to Greece. The rest of her life was spent in Italy for the most part.

Although she was regarded by some as a dilettante in her various writings, her untiring devotion to the aspirations of national minorities in the Austro-Hungarian Empire, to equality for women, and to popular education made her quite well known all over Europe. Her essay *La nationalité albanaise d'après les chants populaires,* published in Revue des deux mondes 63 (Paris 1866) made an impact on the Albanian nationalist movement in the Rilindja (q.v.) period and was shortly afterwards translated into Albanian and Italian.

Lit.: BALA, Vehbi, *Jeta e Elena Gjikës,* Tiranë 1967.

IVANAJ, Nikolla bej (1879–ca. 1948). Publisher and writer. Born in Montenegro, he studied in Vienna, Zagreb, and Dalmatia. Ivanaj held various positions as a civil servant in Serbia, including that of secretary and interpreter (dragoman) in the Serbian Foreign Ministry. From 1905 to 1908, he published the periodical *Shpnesa e Shqypnise* (The hope of Albania) which appeared in Albanian, Italian, and Serbo-Croatian, firstly in Dubrovnik and later in Trieste. During World War II, he published an autobiography and a volume of verse in Tiranë and was active after the war in the Ministry of Education.

J

JAÇELLARI, Halil (1942–   ). Short story writer. He was born in Lushnjë where he now works as a technician. He is the author of the collections: *Mirëmëngjez, njerëz*, Tiranë 1976 (Good morning, men); and *Hapat e tij*, Tiranë 1981 (His steps).

JAHA, Tahir (1913–   ). Kosovo author of prose, poetry, and drama. He was born in the village of Babaj i Bokës near Gjakovë of a peasant family. In 1942, he joined the Communist movement and contributed actively towards the liberation of the country. Among his works are the plays *Eja, eja . . .*, Prishtinë 1958 (Come on, come on . . .); and *Dialog kohe*, Prishtinë 1968 (Dialogue of time); and the verse collection *Lulet e stinëve*, Prishtinë 1967 (The seasonal flowers).

JAKOVA, Kolë (1916–   ). Playwright, poet, and prose writer. He was born in Shkodër as the son of a silversmith and began writing before World War II in which he fought as a partisan. After the liberation, he studied at the institute of Marxism Leninism in Tiranë and became director of the People's Theatre.

Jakova's works deal primarily with different episodes of Albanian history, ranging from the sixteenth century to the postwar period, all of which he views from a staunchly Marxist perspective. His play *Halili e Hajrija*, Tiranë 1950 (Halili and Hajrija) portrays Albanian resistance to the Turks in the sixteenth century. Better known is his drama *Toka jonë*, Tiranë 1955 (Our land) about the struggle to implement agrarian reform. Scenes from the partisan movement in World War II are dealt with in his epic poem *Herojt e Vigut*, Tiranë 1953 (The heroes of Vig). A recent novel *Kulla buzë liqenit*, Tiranë 1984 (The lakeside fortress) follows the breakdown of traditional patriarchal society in the mountains of the Mirdita region in the 1950s. Among his other works are *Flladi i tetorit*, Tiranë 1956 (October breeze); *Qiriu i fundit*, Tiranë 1963 (The last candle); *Dom Gjoni*, Tiranë 1966 (Dom Gjoni); and the satirical novel *Fshati*

midis ujnave 1-3, Tiranë 1972-1980 (The village between the waters, 1-3).
JAKOVA, Tahir efendi. See BOSHNJAKU, Tahir.
JAKOVA MERTURI, Gaspër (1870-1941). Poet and philologist. He was born in Shkodër where he received a religious education and later became a Jesuit priest. In 1903-1904, he taught Albanian at the Arbëresh college in San Demetrio Corone in southern Italy. It was there that he published a grammar of the language, *Grammatica della lingua albanese,* Frascati 1904, which he supplemented with a collection of historical and legendary folksongs.
JASIQI, Ali D. (1937-   ). Kosovo critic and prose writer from the village of Jasiq near Junik. He studied at the University of Prishtinë and is now editor of the literary periodical *Jeta e re* (New life). He has published: *Josip V. Rela,* Prishtinë 1968 (Josip V. Rela); *Pesha e fjalës,* Prishtinë 1972 (The weight of the word); *Shfletime,* Prishtinë 1973 (Turning pages); the short story collection *Shenjë në lis,* Prishtinë 1974 (Mark on a tree); and *Premtime e realizime,* Prishtinë 1976 (Promises and materializations).
JORDANI, Agostin (1950-   ). Pseudonym *Buzëdhelpri.* Arbëresh (q.v.) poet and editor. He was born in Frascineto in Cosenza and studied at the University of Rome. He is editor of the Arbëresh periodical *Zëri i Arbëreshëve* (The voice of the Arbëresh) in which his first poetry was published. Jordani has since published the collections: *Hroaza,* 1975; and *Hapa mbi kalldrëm,* 1977 (Steps on the pavement).
JORGANXHI, Zhuljana G. (1946-   ). Poetess. She was born in Korçë and studied literature and journalism at the University of Tiranë. She has worked as a journalist for the magazine *Shqiptarja e re* (The new Albanian woman) and in 1975 was appointed literary editor at Albanian radio and television.

Among her collections of verse are *Net provimesh,* Tiranë 1969 (Exam night); *Rritje,* Tiranë 1974 (Growth); and *Lule në pemën e lirisë,* Tiranë 1982 (Flowers on the tree of freedom). She is also the author of a collection of children's stories entitled *Fëmijët e teto Nastës,* Tiranë 1975 (Auntie Nasta's children).
JORGAQI, Nasho (1931-   ). Prose writer, biographer, and critic. Jorgaqi is from Ballësh and now teaches Rilindja (q.v.) literature at the Faculty of History and Philology of the University of Tiranë. His works range from novels and short stories to biographies and film scripts. Best known of these are *Mërgata e qyqeve,* Tiranë 1978 (The migration of the cuckoos), a two-volume novel about the liberation and early postwar period; and a biography of *Qemal Stafa,* Tiranë 1973. Among his works of literary criticism are *Silueta letrare,* Tiranë 1976 (Literary silhouettes); and *Antologji e mendimit estetik shqiptar (1504-1944),* Tiranë 1979 (Anthology of Albanian aesthetic thought).
JORGONI, Perikli (1936-   ). Poet and translator. He was born and raised in Tiranë where he graduated from university in 1963. Jorgoni has worked as a journalist and teacher and is now on the staff of the Naim Frashëri Publishing Company.

He is the author of *Ballada e yjeve të ndezur,* Tiranë 1976 (Ballad of flaming stars); and *Plaku e maleve,* Tiranë 1976 (The old man of the mountains); and has translated Goethe, Heine, Hugo, Lenau, Lorca, Schiller, and Shelley into Albanian.

JUBANI, Giuseppe. See JUBANI, Zef.

JUBANI, Zef (1818–1880). Ital. *Giuseppe Jubany*. Folklorist and writer. Jubani is thought to have been born in Shkodër, where he spent most of his life. He finished his studies in Malta and worked for several years at the English and French missions in Shkodër. His first collection of folklore was lost there in a flood in 1866. He later fled to Italy for a time, for reasons unknown, and was received by de Rada (q.v.).

Jubani is remembered for his *Raccolta di canti popolari e rapsodie di poemi albanesi*, Trieste 1871 (Collection of Albanian folksongs and rhapsodies), which constitutes the first collection of Geg (q.v.) folksongs. He is also the author of a history of George Castrioti (Scanderbeg) (q.v.) which remained unpublished. Of his verse, only two poems have survived: one dedicated to Dora d'Istria (q.v.) and the other about Scanderbeg. His writings have been published in *Vepra të zgjedhuna*, Tiranë 1966 (Selected works).

Lit.: KASTRATI, Jup, *Zef Jubani*. in: Buletin për Shkencat Shoqërore (1955) 1, p. 75–92.

JUBANY, Giuseppe. See JUBANI, Zef.

K

KACALIDHA, Niko (1948–   ). Poet. Born in Vurg, one of the villages inhabited by the Greek minority in southern Albania, he went to school in Sarandë and graduated from the University of Tiranë in 1970.

He has published several volumes of poetry, among which: *Fjalë të thëna në pranverë*, Tiranë 1970 (Words spoken in spring); *Flugeri*, Tiranë 1975 (Windmill); *Shtëpitë tona në jug*, Tiranë 1982 (Our houses in the south); and in Greek *E koite tou potamiou mou*, Tiranë 1983 (The bed of my river).

KADARE, Elena (1943–   ). Prose writer reputed to be the first Albanian woman to publish a novel. She was born in Fier and went to school in Elbasan. After studies at the University of Tiranë, she worked as a journalist and editor. She is the wife of Ismail Kadare (q.v.).

In her works, Kadare has devoted herself, among other things, to the problems of women's emancipation in a Socialist society. Among her publications are the novels *Një lindje e vështirë*, Tiranë 1970 (A difficult birth); and *Bashkëshortët*, Tiranë 1981 (The spouses); and the collections of short stories *Shuajë dritën Vera!*, Tiranë 1965 (Turn off the light, Vera!); and *Nusja dhe shtetrrethimi*, Tiranë 1978 (The bride and the state of siege).

KADARE, Ismail (1936–   ). Prose writer and poet. He was born the son of a post office employee in Gjirokastër and studied at the Faculty of History and Philology of the University of Tiranë and then at the Gorky Institute of World Literature in Moscow until 1960. After returning to Albania, he began a career in journalism and subsequently turned to literature. He is also a member of the People's Assembly and has travelled abroad on several occasions (China, France, Federal Republic of Germany).

Kadare is the only Albanian author to have gained wide international recognition beyond the confines of the Albanian-speaking world. His works have been translated into over twenty languages (especially into French) and during the 1960s, following the publication of his novel *Gjenerali i ushtrisë së vdekur*,

Tiranë 1963 (Engl. transl. *The general of the dead army*, London 1971), he was heralded by Western readers as an Albanian Yevtushenko, a rising meteor on an unknown horizon.

It was as a poet, however, that he first became known to Albanians. Among his collections of verse are *Frymëzimet djaloshare,* Tiranë 1954 (Youthful inspiration); *Ëndërrimet,* Tiranë 1957 (Dreams); *Shekulli im,* Tiranë 1961 (My century); *Përse mendohen këto male,* Tiranë 1964 (What are these mountains thinking about); *Motive me diell,* Tiranë 1968 (Themes with sun); *Koha,* Tiranë 1976 (Time); and *Buzëqeshje mbi botë,* Prishtinë 1980 (Smiles on the world).

His international reputation rests nonetheless primarily in his prose, in particular his historical novels. *The general of the dead army,* a study of postwar Albania as seen through the eyes of an Italian general accompanied by a priest on a mission to Albania to find and repatriate the remains of soldiers fallen in the war, was followed by *Dasma,* Tiranë 1968 (Engl. transl. *The wedding,* New York 1972); *Kështjella,* Tiranë 1970 (Engl. transl. *The castle,* Tiranë 1974); *Kronikë në gur,* Tiranë 1971 (Chronicle in stone); *Dimri i vetmisë së madhe,* Tiranë 1973 (The winter of great solitude); *Nëntori i një kryeqyteti,* Tiranë 1975 (November in a capital). *Dimri i vetmisë së madhe* was to become one of his best novels of recent years under the new title *Dimri i madh,* Tiranë 1977 (The great winter), a six hundred-page panorama of events that led to the Soviet-Albanian rift. In this work, Besnik Struga, a young Albanian journalist accompanying Enver Hoxha to Moscow as an interpreter, sees not only the fate of his country but also his personal life altered by the winter of 1961.

Among Kadare's other prose works are *Qyteti i jugut,* Tiranë 1967 (The southern city); *Autobiografia e popullit në vargje,* Tiranë 1971 (Autobiography of the people in verse); *Emblema e dikurshme,* Tiranë 1977 (Signs of the past); *Ura me tri harqe,* Tiranë 1978 (The bridge with three arches); *Gjakftohtësia,* Tiranë 1980 (Cold-bloodedness); *Prilli i thyer,* Prishtinë 1980 (Broken April); *Komisioni i festës,* Prishtinë 1980 (The festival commission); and *Pashallëqet e mëdha,* Prishtinë 1980 (The great pashalics).

Lit.: BYRON, Janet, *Albanian nationalism and Socialism in the fiction of Ismail Kadare.* in: World Literature Today 53. 3 (Summer 1979), p. 614–616; *Albanian folklore and history in the fiction of Ismail Kadare.* in: World Literature Today 58. 1 (Winter 1984), p. 40–42; ELEZI, Mehmet, *Disa anë të novatorizmit në romanet i I. Kadaresë.* in: Nëndori (1971) 9, p. 34–46.

KADRIU, Ibrahim (1945–   ). Kosovo poet and prose writer. He was born in the village of Zhegër near Gjilan and studied Albanian language and literature at the University of Prishtinë. He now works for the daily newspaper *Rilindja* (Rebirth).

Among his collections of poetry are *Netët e Karadakut,* Prishtinë 1969 (Nights in the Karadaks); *Diçka po ndodh,* Prishtinë 1972 (Something's happening); *Hapësirë,* Prishtinë 1977 (Open spaces); and *Troku,* Prishtinë 1980 (The trot). Of his prose publications are the novels *Kroi i ilaçit,* Prishtinë 1982 (The healing spring); and *Ethet e një dimri,* Prishtinë 1983 (A winter's fever). He also writes poetry for children.

KAJTAZI, Mehmet (1944–   ). Kosovo prose writer from Kllodërnicë in the Drenica region. He studied in Prizren and worked as a teacher before becoming a journalist for the Kosovo daily newspaper *Rilindja* (Rebirth). He has published: *I treti*, Prishtinë 1979 (The third); and *Nata në gur*, Prishtinë 1984 (The night in stone).

KALLAMATA, Miço (contemporary). Prose writer. In his satirical short stories, such as *Kthimi i astronautit* (The return of the astronaut) and *Simfoni e pambaruar* (Unfinished symphony), he has attacked bureaucracy and indifference in Albanian society. Among his works are *I fundit i oxhakut*, Tiranë 1971 (The last of the lineage); *Satirë dhe humor*, Tiranë 1973 (Satire and humour); *Në hijen e dordolecëve*, Tiranë 1973 (In the shadow of the scarecrows); *Shtigjeve të zëna*, Tiranë 1974 (On paths taken); *Sos për mua a për ti*, Tiranë 1977 (Do it for me or for you); *Net gjahtarësh*, Prishtinë 1980 (Nights of the hunters); and *Asnjanësia e zotit Lulo*, Tiranë 1984 (The neutrality of Mr Lulo).

KAMARDA, Dhimitër (1821–1882). Ital. *Demetrio Camarda*. Arbëresh (q.v.) philologist and folklorist. He was born in Piana degli Albanesi in Sicily and studied for the priesthood at the College of the Propaganda Fide in Rome. After being ordained in 1844, he returned to Piana degli Albanesi until he was expelled from the Kingdom of the Two Sicilies in the revolutionary year 1848, having been suspected of collaborating with the liberals. He fled first to Rome and then to the Benedictine monastery of Cesena. In 1852, he was appointed teacher at a secondary school in Leghorn (Livorno) where he spent the rest of his life.

Kamarda was one of the cultural leaders of the Arbëresh in the nineteenth century whose publications on Albanian language and literature gave impetus not only to Albanians in Italy but also to the *Rilindja* (q.v.) movement in the motherland. He is remembered for his *Saggio di grammatologia comparata sulla lingua albanese*, Leghorn 1864 (Essay on the comparative grammar of the Albanian language), one of the first works of Albanian diachronic philology, in which he attempted to derive the language largely from Greek, in contradiction to Franz Bopp who had demonstrated its Indo-European origin in 1854. This was followed by *Appendice al saggio di grammatologia comparata*, Prato 1866 (Appendix to the essay on comparative grammar), a collection of Arbëresh folksongs. Kamarda is also the author of a book of Albanian poetry dedicated to Dora d'Istria (q.v.), entitled *A Dora d'Istria gli albanesi*, Leghorn 1870, containing verse by Doçi (q.v.), Jubani (q.v.), Mitko (q.v.), de Rada (q.v.), Santori (q.v.), Serembe (q.v.), etc. He also translated her essay *La nationalité albanaise d'après les chants populaires* into Albanian in 1867.

KAMARDA, Zef (1831–1878). Ital. *Giuseppe Camarda*. Arbëresh (q.v.) writer and younger brother of Dhimitër Kamarda (q.v.). He is said to have translated the Gospel of St. Matthew into the Albanian of Piana degli Albanesi, which his brother helped have published (London 1868), and was the author of some lyric poetry and a collection of Arbëresh folksongs.

KAMBERI, Hasan Zyko (18th–early 19th century). Moslem poet. He was born in the second half of the eighteenth century in Starje e Kolonjës in southern Albania. Little is known of his life aside from his participation in 1789 in a battle on the Danube between Turkish and Austrian forces. After his death at the beginning of the nineteenth century, his tomb in Starje was turned into a shrine (the turbeh of Baba Hasani).

Kamberi is one of the most eloquent representatives of the Moslem tradition in Albanian literature. He is the author of a mevlud—a religious epic on the life of the Prophet—which was probably one of the first to be composed in Albanian, a number of religious hymns (ilâhi), and about fifty secular poems. The most famous of the latter is his satirical *Paraja* (Money).

Lit.: MYDERRIZI, Osman, *Hasan Zyko Kamberi*. in: Buletin për Shkencat Shoqërore (1955) 1, p. 93–108.

KAMSI, Kolë (1886–   ). Writer from Shkodër. He contributed many articles on folklore, history, language, and literature to Albanian periodicals such as *Diturija* (Knowledge) and *Bota shqiptare* (The Albanian world). Kamsi was the author and coauthor of several school anthologies, among which: *Te praku e jetës*, Tiranë 1941 (On the threshold of life); and *Rreze drite*, Tiranë 1941 (Rays of light). He also published a collection of poetry entitled *Lulet e mendimit*, Vlorë 1919 (The flowers of thought); and an Albanian-language manual, *Manuale pratico della lingua albanese*, Zadar 1930.

KANDREVA, Karmell (1931–1982). Ital. *Carmelo Candreva*. Arbëresh (q.v.) poet from San Giacomo di Cerzeto, Cosenza. He took an active part in the fight against illiteracy in Calabria and encouraged, through his writings, the use of Albanian among the Arbëresh.

Kandreva's verse has been published in Italy, Kosovo, and Albania. Among his publications are *Shpirti i arbërit rron*, Cosenza 1976 (The Albanian spirit lives); *Shpirti i arbërit rron, arbëreshi tregon, II*, Cosenza 1977 (The Albanian spirit lives, the Arbëresh recites, II); *Shpirti i arbërit rron, vuan dega e hershme, III*, Cosenza? 1979 (The Albanian spirit lives, the ancient branch suffers, III); and *Degë e hershme*, Prishtinë 1983 (Ancient branch).

KAPA. See CEPA, Kristaq.

KAPARELI, O. (1852–1940). Arbëresh (q.v.) poet from Acquaformosa in Cosenza.

KASHARI, Haxhi Ymer (18th century). Also known as *Ymer Mustafa Kashari*. Moslem poet from Tiranë. He is the author of religious verse in Albanian and Turkish. His Albanian poetry, though heavily laden with Turkish and Arabic vocabulary, provides us with information on the Tiranë dialect of the mid-eighteenth century.

KASHARI, Ymer Mustafa. See KASHARI, Haxhi Ymer.

KASTRIOTI, Gjergj. See SCANDERBEG.

KAVALIOTI, Theodhor (ca. 1718–1789). Greek *Theodoros Kavalliotis*. Scholar and lexicographer from Voskopojë (Moskhopolis). After elementary schooling there, he studied mathematics, theology, and philosophy in Ioannina between 1732 and 1734, familiarizing himself with the works of Descartes, Malebranche, and Leibniz. He returned to Voskopojë, which was itself beginning to flourish as a centre of learning for Greeks, Albanians, and Aromanians, and in 1746 became director of the school which was to become known as the New Academy.

Kavalioti is the author of several works of philosophy written in Greek, of an elementary grammar of Greek and of a scholarly work entitled *Protopeiria* (Venice 1770) which contains a three-language lexicon in Greek, Aromanian, and Albanian of about 1170 words. This lexicon was republished by the German professor Thunmann from Halle with a Latin translation in 1774 and is of linguistic interest for students of both Albanian and Aromanian.

Lit.: HETZER, Armin, *Das dreisprachige Wörterverzeichnis von Theodoros Anastasiu Kavalliotis aus Moschopolis,* Hamburg 1981; *Neues zu Kavalliotis' "Protopeiria".* in: Balkan-Archiv NF, 8 (1983), p. 97–158; UÇI, Alfred, *T. A. Kavallioti, un représentant albanais des lumières.* in: Studia Albanica 3 (1966), 2, p. 185–196.

KAVALLIOTIS, Theodoros. See KAVALIOTI, Theodhor.

KAZANXHIU, Simon (early 19th century). Lexicographer. Kazanxhiu was a merchant from Elbasan and as such journeyed widely throughout Eastern Europe. In the course of his travels, he recorded bits of vocabulary and compiled them, using the Todhri alphabet, in a lexicon of German, Slovenian, Czech, Hungarian, Italian, and Albanian, written before 1823. A full transcription of the manuscript is preserved at the Institute of Linguistics and Literature in Tiranë.

KAZAZI, Gjon Nikollë (1702–1752). Author of an Albanian compendium of the Christian Doctrine. Kazazi was from Gjakovë and studied theology in Italy. In Rome, he took the title doctor of theology and philosophy. It was there in 1743 that he published this short catechism designed for teaching, which constitutes the first document written in Gjakovë dialect. It was also Kazazi who in 1740 discovered the one surviving copy of Buzuku's (q.v.) Liturgy at the College of the Propaganda Fide in Rome.

Lit.: ASHTA, Kolë, *Gjon Nikollë Kazazi dhe vepra e tij (1743).* in: Buletin i Institutit Pedagogjik Dyvjeçar të Shkodrës (1972) 2, p. 241–265.

KËLLIÇI, Skifter (1938–   ). Prose writer from Tiranë. He studied at the University of Tiranë and has worked as a journalist for Albanian radio and television. He is now on the staff of a publishing company specializing in school texts.

Këlliçi is the author of works for adults and children, including the short story collections *Një tokë të huaj,* Tiranë 1969 (A foreign land); *Zërat e jetës,* Tiranë 1970 (The voices of life); and the novels *Atentat në Paris,* Tiranë 1978 (Assassination in Paris), evoking the assassination of Esat Pasha Toptani by the young student Avni Rustemi on June 13, 1920; *Nën harqet e zjarrta,* Tiranë 1978 (Under the flaming arches); and *Ankthi i ditëve të fundit,* Tiranë 1983 (Engl. transl. *The last days of a Prime Minister,* Ilford 1984).

KELMENDI, Jusuf (1927–   ). Kosovo playwright. He was born in Pejë and worked as a carpenter. After the war, he was able to finish his education and began a career in journalism. He later became active in politics, serving among other things as Yugoslav ambassador to Senegal.

Kelmendi started writing in the 1950s with poetic sketches and short stories, turning them to drama with which he has had the most success. Among his prize-winning plays are *Hakmarrja* (Revenge) and *Rrëmuja* (Confusion).

KELMENDI, Ramiz (1930–   ). Kosovo prose writer. Kelmendi was born in Pejë where he attended elementary school. He studied agriculture in Prishtinë and later lectured at the agricultural college in Gjakovë. He has studied at the University of Belgrade, worked as a journalist and editor, and now teaches Albanian literature at the University of Prishtinë.

Kelmendi is noted for his prose works and criticism. Among his publications are *Vija e vrragë*, Prishtinë 1958 (The rut); *Dy rrëfime*, Prishtinë 1962 (Two confessions); *Letra prej Ulcini*, Prishtinë 1966 (Letters from Ulcinj); *Heshtja e armëve*, Prishtinë 1971 (The silence of weapons); *Ahmet Koshutani*, Tiranë 1973 (Ahmet Koshutani); *Abrakadabra*, Prishtinë 1974 (Abracadabra); *Shtatë persona ndjekin autorin*, Prishtinë 1975 (Seven persons following the author); *Tregimi ynë humoristiko-satirik*, Prishtinë 1975 (Our humorous satirical short story); *Njerëzit dhe kërmijtë*, Prishtinë 1978 (People and snails); *Drama e sotme jugosllave*, Prishtinë 1981 (Contemporary Yugoslav drama); *Kapuç me mëngë*, Prishtinë 1981 (Hood-coat with sleeves); and *Shtegtimet e mia*, Prishtinë 1982 (My wanderings). He has also translated Peter Pan and Hemingway's "The Old Man and the Sea" into Albanian.

Lit.: ALIU, Ali, *Tri fazat krijuese të Ramiz Kelmendit.* in: Jeta e re (1974) 2, p. 310–317.

KËRVESHI, Muhamed (1935–   ). Kosovo poet from Mitrovicë. He studied in Belgrade and Zagreb and now teaches French at the Faculty of Arts of the University of Prishtinë.

His poetry, often of epigrammatic precision, has been published in the following volumes: *Ngjyrat e dashunisë*, Prishtinë 1964 (The colours of love); *Portretë në miniaturë*, Prishtinë 1966 (Portraits in miniature); *Hijet*, Prishtinë 1968 (The shades); *Valët e reja*, Prishtinë 1971 (The new waves); *Rrathët*, Prishtinë 1973 (The circles); *Piramidet*, Prishtinë 1976 (The pyramids); *Ura*, Prishtinë 1978 (The bridge); *Kundruall*, Prishtinë 1980 (Vis-à-vis); *Vazhdimësi*, Prishtinë 1982 (Continuity); and *Zemra ime*, Tiranë 1982 (My heart).

KETA, Nikollë (1740–1803). Ital. *Nicola Chetta*. Arbëresh (q.v.) writer and poet. He was born in 1740 or 1742 in Contessa Entellina, Sicily, and was one of the first students at the Arbëresh seminar in Palermo, where he was taught by Giorgio Guzzetta (q.v.) and Paolo Maria Parrino (q.v.). In 1777, he became rector of the seminar himself.

As a poet, Keta composed both religious and secular verse and has the honour of having written the first Albanian sonnet in 1777. In 1763, he compiled an Italian-Albanian dictionary of 240 pages which was considerably enlarged in 1779 (to 640 pages and about 10,000 words). A copy of this *Vocabolario italiano-albanese* is preserved in the Royal Library of Copenhagen. His *Tesoro di notizie su de' Macedoni*, 1777 (Thesaurus of notes about the Macedonians), published in part in the periodical *La Sicilia* in Palermo 1867, is a historical and ethnographical work written in Italian recounting among other things the history of Albanian emigration to Italy.

Lit.: SHUTERIQI, Dhimitër, *Autorë dhe tekste,* Tiranë 1977, p. 179–204.

KJARA, Pjetër (1840–1915). Ital. *Pietro Chiara.* Arbëresh (q.v.) poet and man of letters. Born in 1840 or 1849 in Palazzo Adriano, Sicily, he is the author of lyric poetry as well as of a number of books in Italian about Albania, including *L'Albania,* Palermo 1869. He was also a political figure and journalist, writing for the periodical *Fjamuri Arbrit* (The flag of Albania).

KOÇA, Vangjel (1900–   ). Writer, critic, and publicist of the Fascist period. He was born in Gjirokastër and published several periodicals. Koça is the author of works of history, philosophy, and literature, including translations of Epictetus, Lucian, and Descartes.

KOÇI, Vito (contemporary). Prose writer and poet. Author of the short stories *Borë në bjeshkë,* Tiranë 1974 (Snow on the alpine meadows) about the living conditions of sawmill workers; and *Dy shokë për një rrugë,* Tiranë 1982 (Two comrades for one road); as well as of the novel *Qëndresa,* Tiranë 1982 (Resistance).

KODRA, Klara (contemporary). Writer, critic, and poetess. Aside from her many works of criticism, she has published: *Era e revolucionit,* Tiranë 1968 (Wind of the revolution); *Buzëqeshje,* Tiranë 1970 (Smiles); *Rrugë të hapura,* Prishtinë 1971 (Open roads); and *Bisedë me vëllezërit,* Tiranë 1984 (A talk with brothers).

KODRA, Lame. See MALËSHOVA, Sejfulla.

KOKALARI, Musine (1920–1982?). Prose writer from Gjirokastër. She finished her studies at the University of Rome in 1942 and returned to Albania, contributing in 1944 to the clandestine social-democratic periodical *Zëri i lirisë* (The voice of freedom). She was arrested at the beginning of 1946 for anti-Communist activities and sentenced to life in prison. She died in Burrel after her release from the prison there.

Kokalari is the author of the folk narrative *Siç më thotë nënua plakë,* 1941 (As my old mother tells me), republished in Livonia, Michigan 1984; and of another work of the same genre, published in 1944.

KOKOJKA, Mali. See FRASHËRI, Mid'hat.

KOKONA, Vedat (1913–   ). Poet, prose writer, critic, and translator. He was born in Izmir (Turkey), grew up in Gjirokastër and attended secondary school in Korçë. He later took a degree in law in Paris before returning to Albania to teach. Kokona has worked as a professional translator and has taught French at the University of Tiranë.

Among his works are the travel narrative *Nga Tirana në Stokholmi,* 1935 (From Tiranë to Stockholm); the volumes of poetry *Dritë dhe hije,* 1939 (Light and shade); and *Shtatë Prilli,* Tiranë 1943 (The seventh of April); the short story collection *Yje të këputura,* 1940 (Falling stars); the two volume novel *Me valët e jetës,* Tiranë 1961, 1965 (With the waves of life); and the play *Hijet e natës,* Tiranë 1966 (The shades of night). He has translated the works of Corneille, Galsworthy, Gorky, Racine, Shakespeare, and Tolstoy, and has also made a notable contribution to the field of lexicography, publishing French-Albanian and Albanian-French dictionaries.

KOKOSHI, Kudret (fl. 1940). Lyric poet from Vlorë. He studied in Italy and became a judge. At the beginning of 1944, he was arrested by the Nazis and sent to Mauthausen. After the war, he tried to leave Albania but was caught by the Yugoslav police, returned to the Albanian authorities, and imprisoned once again, this time in Burrel. Fate unknown.

Kokoshi's poetry shows both elements of classicism and of southern Albanian folk verse in the tradition of Ali Asllani (q.v.).

KOLIQI, Ernest (1903–1975). Poet, prose writer, and one of the leading literary figures of the 1930s and 1940s. He was born in Shkodër and was educated at the Jesuit college of Arice in Brescia, where he first became acquainted with Italian literature and culture. He returned to Albania in 1921 to teach and in 1923, founded the periodical *Ora e maleve*, (The mountain fairy), together with Ndue Harapi (q.v.) and Nush Topalli. In 1924, political circumstances forced him to leave Albania for Yugoslavia where he spent the next five years. From 1930 to 1933, he taught in Vlorë and Shkodër, until forced, once again by political circumstances, to flee the country. He studied and taught at the University of Padua from 1933 to 1937 where his affinity grew for Italian poets, such as Carducci, Pascoli, and D'Annunzio, and for the mounting Fascist movement. After finishing a thesis on the Albanian popular epic, he was appointed in 1937 to the chair of Albanian language and literature at the University of Rome. During Fascist rule in Albania, he served as minister of education and in 1943 as president of the Fascist Grand Council in Tiranë. In 1945, he fled to Italy where he lived, no less active in the field of literature, until his death in 1975.

Koliqi is the author of numerous publications—poetry, short stories, translations, and anthologies. He collaborated in various literary journals of the 1930s, such as the right-wing *Illyria,* and himself founded *Shkëndija* (The spark), 1940–1943, and *Shêjzat,* which he edited in Italy from 1957 to his death. Among his works are the dramatic poem *Kushtrimi i Skanderbeut,* Tiranë 1924 (Scanderbeg's warcry); the short story collections *Hija e maleve,* Zadar 1929 (Mountain shades); and *Tregtar flamujsh,* Tiranë 1935 (Flag merchant); the poetry collections *Gjurmat e stinve,* Tiranë 1933 (The tracks of the seasons); *Symfonia e shqipevet,* Tiranë 1941 (Engl. transl. *The symphony of eagles,* Rome 1972); and *Kangjelet e rilindjes,* Rome 1959 (Songs of rebirth); and the novel *Shija e bukës së mbrûme,* Rome 1960 (The taste of homemade bread). He also translated and published a two-volume anthology *Poetët e mëdhej t'Italis,* Tiranë 1932 and 1936 (The great poets of Italy); and helped in the publication of another two volume anthology, this time of Albanian literature, entitled *Shkrimtarët shqiptarë,* Tiranë 1941 (Albanian writers), edited by Karl Gurakuqi. Later in life, he published the Italian-language works *Poesia popolare albanese,* Florence 1957 (Albanian folk verse); and *Antologia della lirica albanese,* Milan 1963 (Anthology of Albanian poetry).

Lit.: Shêjzat, commemorative issue (1976).

KOLLUMBI, Gaqo (fl. 1956). Prose writer. Author of *Ditar,* Tiranë 1956

(Diary), describing events of the resistance movement in the Korçë area in 1943–1944.

KOLONJA, Shahin (fl. 1900). Publisher and nationalist figure of the Rilindja (q.v.) period. Kolonja graduated from Mülkije, the school of public administration in Istanbul, and taught at several Turkish secondary schools. He was editor of the periodical *Drita* (The light), Sofia 1901–1908, an important organ of the nationalist movement.

KONDO, Anastas (1937–   ). Short story writer, novelist, and political figure. He was born in Kuçovë, now Qyteti Stalin, and studied geology in the Soviet Union, working thereafter as a palaeontologist. He later turned to writing and in 1973, was appointed secretary for literature of the Albanian Union of Writers and Artists. In 1976, he was made deputy minister of education and culture.

Among Kondo's works are *Ura,* Tiranë 1967 (The bridge); *Njerëz dhe gurë,* Tiranë 1970 (People and stones); *Mirupafshim në Saigon,* Tiranë 1972 (Goodbye in Saigon); *Zbulimi,* Tiranë 1972 (The discovery); *Kio,* Prishtinë 1972 (Kio); *Njeriu që propozoj për hero,* Tiranë 1973 (The man I propose as hero); and *Pse e vranë Odisenë,* Tiranë 1982 (Why did they kill Odysseus).

KONICA, Faik (1875–1942). Also known as *Faik Konitza* or *Konitsa.* Political figure and publisher. He was born in the Greek village of Konitsa. After elementary schooling in Turkish, he studied at the Jesuit college in Shkodër and at the French-language Galata secondary school in Istanbul. In 1890, he went to France and graduated in Romance philology from the University of Dijon five years later. In 1897, he moved to Brussels, where he founded the periodical *Albania,* one of the most important organs of the Albanian press at the turn of the century. He moved to London in 1902 and continued to publish the journal there until 1910. His next stop was Boston where he became editor of the newspaper *Dielli* (The sun), a publication of the Vatra (The hearth) society. In 1912, he became head of the Vatra society and represented it in 1913 in London and Trieste. The following years took Konica to Washington as Albanian consul-general, to Vienna, Lausanne, and Sofia. In 1926, he was appointed ambassador to the United States by the Albanian dictator Zog, a post he held until his death.

Konica wrote little in the way of literature, but as a publicist and political figure, he had a tremendous impact on Albanian culture at the time. His periodical *Albania,* written in French and Albanian, helped make the Albanian cause known in Europe and fortified the nationalist movement. Writers like Çajupi (q.v.), Fishta (q.v.), Mitko (q.v.), and Kristoforidhi (q.v.) first became known there. Konica was also one of the first to propagate the idea of editing older Albanian literature and pointed to the necessity of creating a unified literary language. Aside from his numerous articles on politics, language, literature, and history, he is the author of a satirical novel entitled *Dr. Gjëlpëra* (Dr Needle) which appeared as a serial in *Dielli* from 1924; and *Albania, the rock garden of Southeastern Europe and other essays,* Boston 1957.

KONISPOLI, Abdullah Sulejman (fl. 1831). Also known as *Abdullah Sulejman*. Moslem poet from the village of Konispol in the extreme southern corner of Albania. He is the author of a mevlud (poem on the birth of the prophet Mohammed) written about 1831 in Çamërian dialect and of other religious verse translated from Arabic and Turkish.

KONITZA, Faik. See KONICA, Faik.

KONUSHEVCI, Abdullah (1958–). Kosovo poet. He was born in Prishtinë where he attended school and university and is now doing postgraduate research at the University of Zagreb. Konushevci has published three collections of verse: *Pasqyrë dhe diell,* Prishtinë 1979 (Mirror and sun); *Rënia e mollës,* Prishtinë 1981 (The apple's fall); and *Qerrja e diellit,* Prishtinë 1983 (The sun chariot).

KORÇA, Mehmet Iljaz (fl. 1840). Author of a religious prose text translated from Arabic, dated 1840. The manuscript containing the text, originally from Korçë, was discovered in 1953 and is now preserved at the Institute for Linguistics and Literature in Tiranë.

KORESHI, Vath (1936–). Prose writer from Lushnjë. He studied at the University of Tiranë and is now active in publishing. His works include short stories, novels, plays, and film scripts, among which the short story collections *Kur zunë shirat e vjeshtës,* Tiranë 1964 (As the autumn rains began); *Toka nën hijen e shtëpive,* Tiranë 1968 (The land in the shadow of houses); *Ndërrimi i qiejve,* Tiranë 1972 (Change of heavens); *Dasma e Sakos,* Tiranë 1980 (Sako's wedding); and the novels *Dy të shtunat e Suzanës,* Tiranë 1971 (Suzana's two Saturdays); *Mars,* Tiranë 1975 (Mars); and *Mali mbi këneté,* Tiranë 1977 (The hill in the marsh).

KORTEZE, Daniel (1617–16??). Ital. *Danil Cortese*. Arbëresh poet. A native of Lungro in Cosenza, he studied at the college of St. Athanasius in Rome from 1631 to 1639. He is the author of some bits of Albanian poetry published in *Monumentum romanum, Nicolao Claudio Fabriccio Pereschio, senatori acquense doctrinae virtutisque causa factum,* Rome 1638.

KOSTA, Koço (1940–). Prose writer from Gjirokastër. He graduated from the University of Tiranë and now teaches in Gjirokastër. Kosta has published several volumes of sketches and short stories, among which: *Unë dhe komiti,* Tiranë 1969 (The outlaw and I); *Shënime përmes shiut,* Tiranë 1968 (Notes in the rain); *Bisedë në mesnatë,* Tiranë 1971 (Discussion at midnight); *Dademadhja,* Tiranë 1976 (The grandmother); *Era e udhëve,* Tiranë 1982 (Road wind); *Tregime të zgjedhura,* (Selected tales); and the novel *Buka e një stine me borë,* Tiranë 1979 (The bread of a snowy season).

KOTTE, Kostandin (fl. 1929). Dramatist. Author of the three-act play *Shepërblimi i gjaksis,* Zadar 1929 (Punishment for the crime), set in the times of Ali Pasha Tepelena.

KOUPITORIS, Panayotis. See KUPITORI, Panajot.

KRAJA, Fadil (1931–). Poet, dramatist, and short story writer from Shkodër.

He studied at the University of Tiranë and taught at the teacher training college in Shkodër before turning to writing as a profession.

Among his publications are the poetry collections *Kanga ime,* Tiranë 1954 (My song); *Melodi malësore,* Tiranë 1957 (Mountain melody); *Jehonë malesh,* Tiranë 1960 (Echo of the mountains); and the plays *Fisheku në pajë,* Tiranë 1967 (The bullet in the trousseau); *Ditari i një mësuesi,* Tiranë 1969 (A teacher's diary); *Sinjalet e natës,* Tiranë 1972 (The signals of night); *Shpartallimi,* (Destruction); *Luani i shtëpisë,* Tiranë 1977 (The house lion); and *Gjaku i Arbërit,* Tiranë 1983 (The blood of the Albanian). He has also published humorous short stories and tales for children.

KRASNIQI, Mark (1920–   ). Kosovo poet. He was born in the village of Gllavaçicë near Pejë and went to school in Prizren. After graduation, he studied literature at the University of Padua. He followed this by research in geography and ethnology in Belgrade, working from 1950 to 1960 for the Ethnographical Institute of the Academy of Sciences there. He finished his doctorate in Ljubljana in 1960 and was appointed the following year to teach at the Faculty of Law and Economics of the University of Prishtinë. Krasniqi is known as an expert in the folk culture of the Kosovo Albanians.

He is the author of the verse collections *Jehona e kohës,* Prishtinë 1972 (The echo of time); and *Postieri i maleve,* Prishtinë 1984 (The postman of the mountains), of a number of works on ethnography and geography; and of translations from Serbo-Croatian and Russian.

KRASNIQI, Sulejman (1937–   ). Prose writer born of a peasant family in Hoçë near Prizren. Author of the novels *Në shpellën e banditëve,* Tiranë 1973 (In the bandits' cave); *Qielli i përflakur,* Tiranë 1974 (Flaming sky); *Prijësja e komitëve,* Tiranë 1975 (The rebel leaders); *Beteja të nëndheshme,* Tiranë 1976 (Underground oaths); and *Mic Sokoli,* Tiranë 1982 (Mic Sokoli); the short story collection *Tri motra tri histori,* Tiranë 1972 (Three sisters three stories); and of the drama *Besëlidhja shqiptare,* Tiranë 1980 (The Albanian alliance).

KREJI, Thimi Thoma (late 19th century). Also spelled *Krej* and *Krei.* Poet and nationalist figure of the Albanian community in Egypt. He was born in Krushova but spent most of his life in Egypt, where he was a friend of Thimi Mitko (q.v.), Jani Vreto (q.v.), and Spiro Dine (q.v.). In 1882, he was one of the founding members of the patriotic club of Shibin el Kom and became its secretary. He took a great interest in the Albanian alphabet question and wrote a treatise on the subject in Greek.

Kreji is the author of nationalist verse on themes typical of the Rilindja (q.v.) period. His first poem probably dates from 1888, although it is unlikely that any of his poetry was ever published during his lifetime. Some of his verse appeared in Dine's (q.v.) *Valët e detit* in 1908.

Lit.: FULLANI, Dhimitër, *Thimi Krej.* in: Nëndori (1962) 8, p. 166–167.

KRISPI, Zef (1781–1859). Ital. *Giuseppe Crispi.* Arbëresh (q.v.) scholar from Palazzo Adriano in Sicily. He was an Orthodox priest, professor of Greek literature at the University of Palermo, and rector of the Arbëresh seminar in Palermo.

Krispi is remembered for his *Memoria sulla lingua albanese,* Palermo 1831 (Memoir on the Albanian language) in which he attemtped to demonstrate the Pelasgian origins and antiquity of the Albanian people. He is also the author of a collection of Sicilian Arbëresh folksongs with an Italian translation entitled *Canti degli Albanesi di Sicilia* (Songs of the Albanians of Sicily), published in Lionardo Vigo's *Canti popolari siciliani,* Catania 1857 (Sicilian folksongs).

KRISPI GLAVJANO, Frano (1852–1933). Ital. *Francesco Crispi Glaviano.* Arbëresh (q.v.) poet and folklorist from Palazzo Adriano in Sicily. He was a prolific writer, although little of his work was published. Some of his lyric poetry, both nationalist and amorous verse written in the now defunct dialect of Palazzo Adriano, appeared in periodicals of the time. He is the author, among other things, of *Mbi Malin e Truntafilevet,* Palermo 1963 (On Rose Mountain).

Lit.: KAMSI, Kolë, *Frano Krispi Glaviano.* in: Buletin i Universitetit Shetëror të Tiranës. Seria Shkenc. Shoq. (1960) 4, p. 176–191.

KRISTOFORIDHI, Kostandin Nelko (1830–1895). Translator and linguist. He was the son of a silversmith from Elbasan where he went to school. From 1847 to 1850, he attended the Zosimea secondary school in Ioannina and collaborated there with the Austrian vice-consul Johann Georg von Hahn on the latter's monumental *Albanesische Studien,* Vienna 1853 (Albanian Studies). The following years took him to Athens, Durrës, perhaps to London, Izmir, Istanbul, Malta, and Tunis, where he married and taught at a Greek school.

It was during the 1860s that he began working for the "British and Foreign Bible Society" for whom he translated the New Testament into Geg (1872) (q.v.) and Tosk (1879) (q.v.) versions, as well as several books of the Old Testament. These translations helped serve as a basis for the creation of a modern literary language, in the two dialect variants. He also wrote a grammar of the Albanian language in Greek *Grammatiki tis alvanikis glossis,* Istanbul 1882, and compiled an Albanian-Greek dictionary *Lexikon tis alvanikis glossis,* Athens 1904. The latter, regarded as one of the best Albanian dictionaries until recent times, was transliterated and republished by Aleksandër Xhuvani (q.v.) (Tiranë 1961). Kristoforidhi is also the author of children's works, such as *Historia e shentese shkroye per dielmt,* Istanbul 1870 (Bible history for children); and the tale *Gjahu i malësorëvet,* Istanbul 1884 (The hunt of the mountaineers), viewed as one of the first works of modern Albanian literary prose.

Lit.: QOSJA, Rexhep, *Historia e letërsisë shqipe—Romantizmi II,* Prishtinë 1984, p. 375–420; SHUTERIQI, Dhimitër, *Konstandin Nelko-Kristoforidhi (1830–1895). Monografi mbi jetën dhe botimet e tij.* in: Buletin i Institutit të Shkencavet 4 (1950) 1/2, p. 3–37 and 3, p. 3–22; SHUTERIQI, Simon, *Jetëshkrimi i Kostandin Kristoforidhit,* Monastir 1911.

KUKAJ, Rifat (1938–   ). Kosovo author of children's literature. He was born in the village of Tërstenik in the Drenicë region and went to school in Prishtinë.

He now edits children's literature for Rilindja Publishing Company. Among his many publications are the children's novels *Bardha e Mirushja,* Prishtinë 1968 (Bardh and Mirush); *Minaku i përhimtë,* Prishtinë 1973 (The grey mouse); *Lepuri me pesë këmbë,* Prishtinë 1971 (The five-legged rabbit); *Qafa e ujkonjës,* Prishtinë 1977 (The neck of the she-wolf); *Droja,* Prishtinë 1978 (Fear); and the poetry collection *Vjersha të zgjedhura për fëmijë,* Prishtinë 1976 (Selected poems for children). He has also written short stories for children and adults.

KULLURIOTI, Anastas (1822–1887). Greek-Albanian nationalist figure, publisher, and writer. He was born in the Plaka district of Athens, inhabited at the time by Albanians. As a young man, he emigrated to America and made his fortune, although little is known about this period of his life. Upon his return to Greece, he founded the weekly newspaper *I foni tis Alvanias* (The voice of Albania) which lasted from September 1879 to mid 1880. Among the goals of his nationalist activities were the founding of an Albanian political party in Greece, the opening of Albanian-language schools, and the liberation of Albania from the Turkish yoke. His devotion to the Albanian cause inevitably brought him into conflict with both the Turkish and Greek authorities and he is said to have died in prison in Athens at the beginning of 1887.

Kullurioti is the author of *Alvanikon alfavitarion,* Athens 1882 (Albanian primer); and the reader *Klumësht për foshnja,* Athens 1882 (Milk for babies). A didactic poem of his was published in Dine's (q.v.) *Valët e detit.*

Lit.: SHUTERIQI, Dhimitër, *Autorë dhe tekste,* Tiranë 1977, p. 335–356.

KUPITORI, Panajot (1821–1881). Greek *Panayotis Koupitoris.* Greek-Albanian writer from the island of Hydra. He studied literature at the University of Athens and was later principal of several secondary schools. He also apparently organized a night school for Greek-Albanians.

Kupitori is the author of the Greek-language *Meletai peri tis glossis kai tou ethnous Alvanias,* Athens 1879 (Studies on the Albanian language and people). He is also said to have published a primer of Albanian in 1879, although there is no evidence of this, and an Albanian dictionary, now lost.

KUQALI, Gjikë (1921–1944). Poet. He was born in Korçë and studied at the French secondary school there. At an early age, he became involved in the Communist movement and published his first poems in the school newspaper. He was arrested in 1944 and executed at the concentration camp in Prishtinë. Many of his revolutionary poems and sketches were published in the collection *Qiriu, shkrime letrare,* Tiranë 1955 (The candle, literary writing).

KUTELI, Mitrush (1907–1967). Pseudonym of *Dhimitër Pasko.* Short story writer, critic, and poet from Pogradec. He studied in Salonika and Bucharest, returning to Albania in 1934 where he worked first as an economist and then turned to literature and translating.

Kuteli's short stories appeared in the collections: *Netë shqiptare,* Bucharest 1938 (Albanian nights); *Ago Jakupi,* Tiranë 1943 (Ago Jakupi); *Kapllan Aga i Shaban Shpatës* (Kapllan Aga of Shaban Shpata); and *Dashuria e barbarit Artan,* Tiranë 1946 (The barbarian Artan's love). Among his other publications are *Sulm e lotë,* Tiranë 1941 (Assault and tears); *Këngë e britma nga qyteti i djegur* (Songs and cries from a charred city); *Pylli i gështenjave,* Tiranë 1958 (The wood of chestnut trees); *Tregime të moçme shqiptare,* Tiranë 1965 (Ancient Albanian tales); *Tregime të zgjedhura,* Tiranë 1972 (Selected tales); *Baltë nga kjo tokë,* Tiranë 1973 (Mud from this land); and *Në një cep të Ilirisë së poshtme,* Tiranë 1984 (In a corner of lower Illyria). He is also remembered for his translations of the Romanian writers Eminescu and Sadoveanu, and of the Russian writers Fadayev, Gogol, Gorky, Tolstoy, and Turgenev.

Lit.: JASIQI, Ali, *Proza tregimtare e Mitrush Kutelit.* in: Jeta e re (1968) 5, p. 1009–1019; VINCA, Agim, *Profili kritik i Mitrush Kutelit.* in: Jeta e re (1974) 5, p. 969–975.

KYÇYKU, Muhamet (1784–1844). Also known as *Muhamet Çami.* Moslem poet from Konispol in southern Albania. He studied at a theological college in Cairo and returned to his native village as a hodja (Moslem priest) where he lived until his death.

Kyçyku's poetry marks a transition between the classical Moslem verse of Frakulla (q.v.), Naibi (q.v.), and Kamberi (q.v.) and the Rilindja (q.v.) poets of the second half of the nineteenth century. Among his works, most of which were discovered within the last forty years, are a 348-line poem dated 1824 condemning the drinking of wine and raki; a historical poem dated 1826 dealing with the liberation of Missolonghi from the Turks; *Jusufi i Zelihaja,* a long verse tale on a Biblical subject; and *Erveheja* for which he is perhaps best known. *Erveheja,* written about 1820 and based on a Turkish prose original entitled *Revza,* was published in 1888 by Jani Vreto (q.v.), who not only transliterated it but saw fit to purge it of all its Turkish and Arabic vocabulary. The original text, comprising seventeen pages, has since been found in manuscript III F 36 of the National Library in Tiranë. In all, about 200 pages of his works have survived.

Lit.: HETZER, Armin, *Der Wortschatz und die Orthographie der "Erveheja" von Muhamet Kyçyku-Çami.* in: Balkan-Archiv NF, 8 (1983), p. 199–289; *Die "Erveheja" von Muhamet Kyçyku (Çami).* in: Südost-Forschungen 43 (1984), p. 181–239; MYDERRIZI, Osman, *Erveheja e M. Çamit.* in: Buletin i Institutit të Shkencavet (1951) 1, p. 72–82; and *Erveheja.* in: Buletin për Shkencat Shoqërore (1957) 1, p. 253–278; ROSSI, Ettore, *La fonte turca della novella poetica albanese 'Erveheja' di Muhamet Çami (sec. XVIII–XIX), e il tema di 'Florence de Rome' e di 'Crescentia'.* in: Oriente Moderno 28 (1948), p. 143–153.

L

LAÇO, Teodor (1936–   ). Prose writer and dramatist born in Dardhë near Korçë. He finished his studies in agronomy in Tiranë in 1958 and was active for several years as an agronomist. He then turned to literature and has worked recently as a librettist for the theatre of Fier.

Laço has written several historical novels such as *Tokë e ashpër,* Tiranë 1971 (Rough land) about the collectivization of agriculture in mountain regions; *Përballimi,* Tiranë 1975 (Engl. transl. *The face-up,* Tiranë 1980) dealing with the period 1948–1949; *Lëndina e lotëve,* Tiranë 1978 (The meadow of tears) about emigration in the Zog era; and *Korbat mbi mermer,* Tiranë 1981 (Crows on the marble) set in the 1930s. Among his short story collections are *Era e tokës,* Tiranë 1965 (Wind of the land); *Rruga e bardhë,* Tiranë 1967 (The white road); *Një natë shiu,* Tiranë 1969 (A rainy night); *Tregime,* Prishtinë 1971 (Tales); *Ajri i ftohtë i mesnatës,* Tiranë 1972 (The cold air of midnight); *Tregime të zgjedhura,* Tiranë 1974 (Selected tales); *Pylli në vjeshtë,* Tiranë 1976 (The forest in autumn); *Portat e dashurisë,* Tiranë 1980 (The gates of love); and *Një ditë dhe një jetë,* Tiranë 1983 (A day and a life). Laço is also the author of a number of plays such as *Shtëpia në rrugicë,* Tiranë 1971 (The house in the alley); *Një nuse për Stasin,* Tiranë 1971 (A bride for Stasi); *Duke gdhirë viti 1945,* Tiranë 1975 (At the dawn of 1945); *Gjëmimi i atij dimri,* Tiranë 1976 (The rumbling of that winter); and *Vranësirë e shkurtër,* Prishtinë 1979 (Short cloudiness).

LAKO, Natasha (1948–   ). Poet and novelist. She was born in Korçë on May 13, 1948, and studied journalism at the University of Tiranë. She now works for "New Albania" Film Studios.

Lako is one of the most prominent representatives of a rising generation of women writers. She has published the following volumes of poetry: *Marsi brenda nesh,* Tiranë 1972 (March within us); *E para fjalë e botës,* Tiranë 1979 (The world's first word); *Këmisha e pranverës,* Prishtinë 1984 (The spring shirt); and the novel *Stinët e jetës,* Tiranë 1977 (The seasons of life).

LAKO, Nikollë (early 20th century). Publisher and writer. He taught in Korçë in 1897–1898 and lived during the second decade of this century in Paris. Lako contributed various articles, prose, and verse to *Kalendari kombiar* (The national calendar), and himself founded the periodical *Shqipëria* (Albania) in Sofia 1907. He subsequently published a primer and reader for Albanian elementary schools, *Stervitjetore per nxënësit shqipëtarë*, Paris 1909 and *Shkronjëtore e gjuhësë shqip*, Paris 1910, and in 1919 began publishing the political and literary magazine *Opinga* (The sandal), with articles in Albanian and French. After his return to Albania, he collaborated in the periodical *Gazeta e Korçës* (The Korçë gazette). Aside from his nationalist and publishing activities, Lako was also a botanist of note.

LECCE, Francesco Maria da (fl. early 18th century). Italian missionary and linguist. He was sent by the Propaganda Fide to Albania as an apostolic prefect of the missions and learned Albanian there in the course of his missionary work. Twenty years later, he returned to Italy and published his *Osservazioni grammaticali nella lingua albanese*, Rome 1716 (Grammatical observations on the Albanian language), the first Albanian grammar. He is also the author of an Italian-Albanian dictionary written before 1702.

LEKA, Lavdie (1935–   ). Short story writer. She was born in Lushnjë and studied at the Lenin Institute for advanced pedagogical studies in Moscow before returning to Albania to teach. She is chief editor of the periodical *Shqiptarja e re* (The new Albanian woman) and vice-president of the Albanian Union of Women.

Among her collections of short stories are *Mos e këndo atë këngë*, Tiranë 1965 (Don't sing that song); *Erdh një vajzë*, Tiranë 1970 (A girl came by); and *Djemtë e rrugicës me kalldrëm*, Tiranë 1976 (Boys from the paved alley).

LEPAJA, Lutfi (1945–   ). Kosovo prose writer from Bajçinë near Podujevë. He now lives and works in Podujevë. Among his publications are the novels *Tepër serioz*, Prishtinë 1978 (Too serious); and *Parimi i pritjes*, Prishtinë 1982 (The principle of expectation); and the short story collections *Kona*, Prishtinë 1979 (Kona); and *Përqafimi i padukshëm*, Prishtinë 1984 (Invisible embrace).

LERA, Nasi (1944–   ). Prose writer from Korçë. He graduated from the Faculty of History and Philology of the University of Tiranë in 1968 and has worked both as a teacher and as an editor for Albanian radio and television.

He has published the following collections of short stories: *Bora e fundit*, Tiranë 1972 (The last snow); *Era e pishave*, Tiranë 1976 (The smell of the pines); *Nisemi djema*, Tiranë 1977 (Let's go, boys); *Ditë nga ky shekull*, Tiranë 1979 (Days of this century); *Dita e tretë*, Prishtinë 1980 (The third day); and *Sytë e dashurisë*, Tiranë 1982 (The eyes of love). Lera is also author of the novel *Gjaku i prillit*, Tiranë 1981 (The blood of April), about the Italian invasion of Albania in April 1939.

LESHKUQI (contemporary). Arbëresh (q.v.) priest and poet from Lungro in Cosenza. He has published verse in the Arbëresh periodical *Zëri i Arbëreshvet* (The voice of the Arbëresh).

LESKOVIKU, Baba Abidin (2nd half of 19th century). Bektash (q.v.) poet from Leskovik where he founded a teke. Little is known of his life. He was said to have been a talented poet both in Albanian and in Turkish.

LEVONJA, Besim (1922–1968). Playwright. Author of several partisan plays such as the three-act comedy *Prefekti*, Tiranë 1948 (The prefect); and *Cani Hoxhë*, as well as the prose work *Ditari ynë*, Tiranë 1970 (Our journal).

LIPI. See PAPAJANI, Filip.

LKENI I HASIT. See GJEÇOVI, Shtjefën.

LLUKA, Tahir efendi (–1908). Moslem poet. Author of a mevlud (poem on the birth of the prophet Mohammed).

LOGORECI, Mati (1867–1941). Educator. He was born of a Catholic family from Shkodër where he went to school. As a young man, he worked as an apprentice for the Italian trading company Parruca which sent him as an accountant to Monfalcone near Trieste. After his return to Albania, he opened an Albanian school in Prizren on May 1, 1889, the first in Kosovo, and taught there until 1903 when he transferred to Shkodër. In 1907, he founded the fortnightly newspaper *Dashamiri* (The patron) which he had printed in Trieste, and in 1908 represented the Agimi (Dawn) Society (q.v.) at the Congress of Monastir (q.v.), together with Ndre Mjeda (q.v.). In the years that followed, he was active as a teacher and educator in Shkodër, Skopje, and Tiranë.

Logoreci is the author of several school texts and works of history, among which: *Libër leximi*, 1920 (Reader); *Historija e përgjithëshme*, Shkodër 1924 (General history); and *Libër leximi për moshën e njomë*, 1934 (Reader for the young), and *Fjalorth i librit të leximit*, 1934 (Dictionary to the reader).

Lit.: SHPUZA, Halim, *Mati Logoreci*. in: Buletin shkencor i Institutit Pedagogjik Dyvjeçar të Shkodrës 2 (1965), p. 423–431.

LOGORI, Loni (1871–1929). Rilindja (q.v.) poet from Korçë. He emigrated at an early age to Egypt, as did many Albanians of the period, and made his fortune there. Together with Çajupi (q.v.) and Filip Shiroka (q.v.), he was one of the leading figures of the nationalist movement in Egypt. In the early 1920s, he returned to Albania and died in Durrës.

Logori is known for his somewhat elegaic nationalist poetry and sentimental love verse which appeared in periodicals such as *Shqipëtari, Albania,* and *Kalendari kombiar* as well as in Dine's (q.v.) *Valët e detit*.

Lit.: FULLANI, Dhimitër, *Patrioti poet Loni Logori (1871–1929)*. in: Buletin i Universitetit Shtetëror të Tiranës. Seria Shkenc. Shoq. 15 (1961) 3, p. 100–116.

LONDO, Bardhyl (1948–   ). Poet. He was born in Përmet where he graduated from secondary school before studying Albanian language and literature at the Faculty of History and Philology of the University of Tiranë. He now works for the literary periodical *Drita* (The light).

Londo has published several volumes of verse: *Krisma dhe trëndafila*, Tiranë 1975 (Shots and roses); *Hapa në rrugë*, Tiranë 1981 (Steps in the street); and *Emrin e ka dashuri*, Tiranë 1984 (They call it love).

LOPEZ, Rafaele (fl. 1840). Arbëresh (q.v.) folklorist from San Demetrio Corone in Calabria and friend of Luigi Petrassi (q.v.). He taught at the college in San Demetrio Corone with de Rada (q.v.) where the two were arrested for revolutionary activities in 1851. He was still living in San Demetrio Corone in 1885.

Lopez compiled a collection of Arbëresh folksongs which he translated into Italian.

LORECCHIO, Anselmo. See LOREKIO, Anselmo.

LOREKIO, Anselmo (1843–1924). Ital. *Anselmo Lorecchio*. Arbëresh (q.v.) public figure and publisher. He was born in Pallagorio, Catanzaro, and studied law at the University of Naples. He very soon, however, devoted himself to Albanology and took part in the political and cultural movement of the period. He headed the Congress of Lungro in 1897 and was elected president of the Società Nazionale Albanese.

Though a writer and poet himself, he is remembered chiefly as publisher of the influential Arbëresh periodical *La nazione albanese* (The Albanian nation), a fortnightly review of political and cultural affairs which lasted from 1897 until Lorekio's death in 1924.

LUARASI, Kristo (1875–1934). Publisher. He went to school in the village of Hotovë and in 1892 emigrated to Romania where be became a printer. In 1897, he moved to Sofia and founded the "Mbrothësia" (Progress) Press. Together with Kosta Jani Trebicka (q.v.) and Mid'hat Frashëri (q.v.), he published the cultural periodical *Kalendari kombiar* (The national calendar) which appeared, with long interruptions, from 1897 until 1928. He travelled to Corfu, Italy, and Istanbul, coordinating the nationalist movement and encouraging Albanian-language publications. In Sofia, he founded, together with Shahin Kolonja (q.v.), the periodical *Drita* (The light), 1901–1908; and after several years of publishing activity in Salonika, he moved back to Sofia to publish a new weekly newspaper in 1910 called *Liria e Shqipërisë* (The freedom of Albania) which lasted until 1915. In 1921, he returned to Albania and opened in Tiranë what was to be the largest printing press in the country.

It was, however, his press in Sofia which had the greatest impact on the diffusion of Albanian writing. Aside from the influential *Kalendari kombiar*, he printed thirty-seven works of Albanian literature, including those of Kristo Negovani (q.v.), Hilë Mosi (q.v.), Mihal Grameno (q.v.), and Spiro Dine (q.v.), and republished the works of Naim (q.v.) and Sami Frashëri (q.v.), making them available to the public at large.

LUARASI, Petro Nini (1865–1911). Educator and publisher. Together with Kristo Negovani (q.v.), he was one of the first Albanian teachers and in the vanguard of the movement for the creation of Albanian schools. He was born in Luaras in the Kolonjë region and attended Greek schools and a teacher training college. His first posting was as a Greek teacher in the village of Bezhdan in 1882 where he began teaching the children Albanian, using the so-called Istanbul alphabet. Despite the ferocious resistance of the Greek Orthodox church and the Turkish authorities, he managed to found several schools in southern Albania over the next years. In 1903, when the Turkish government began closing down Albanian schools, Luarasi emigrated to America and in 1906 was one of the founding members of the "Malli i mëmëdheut" (Yearning for the homeland) society in Buffalo, New York. In the year of the revolution of the Young Turks, 1908, he returned to Albania and continued his activities, especially in Monastir (Bitola) and died under mysterious circumstances of poisoning in Ersekë in August 1911.

Luarasi's major work is *Mallkim i shkronjavet shqip dhe shpërfolja e shqipëtarit,* Monastir 1911 (Curse of Albanian writing and the scorn of the Albanians), written in Greek and Albanian, in which he defended Albanian education against the Orthodox church which had threatened to excommunicate any Christian recognizing the Albanian alphabet or involved in Albanian language teaching. He also published several nationalist poems in journals of the period.

Lit.: GJIKA, Thanas (ed.), *Petro Luarasi,* Tiranë 1974; LUARASI, Skënder, *Petro Luarasi. Jeta dhe vepra,* Tiranë 1958; and SEVO, G., *Petro Luarasi. Mësonjësi im i shqipës,* Tiranë 1936.

LUARASI, Skënder (1900–   ). Translator and writer from Luaras in the Kolonja region. He took part in the Spanish Civil War in 1936 and now lives and works in Tiranë. For a time, he taught at the English Department of the University of Tiranë. Luarasi began translating before the war (Schiller, Kalidasa, and Walt Whitman's *Leaves of Grass*). More recently, he has done translations of Shakespeare, Goethe, and Byron, written several biographies and published the works of Migjeni, (q.v.) (Tiranë 1961).

LUCA, Ndrekë (contemporary). Playwright. Author of the historical drama *Shtatë shaljanët,* Tiranë 1958 (The seven from Shala) about the struggle for autonomy among the tribes of the northern Albanian mountains at the beginning of the nineteenth century; and the four-act drama *Votra e huej,* Tiranë 1964 (The foreign hearth).

LUMEZI, Lazër (1870–1941). Poet, prose writer, and translator. He is the author of short stories and verse for children, school textbooks, and plays, as well as collections of songs, fables, anecdotes, and popular legends. He also translated the comedies of Molière into Albanian.

Lit.: KRASNIQI, Mark, *Lazër Lumezi.* in: Jeta e re (1958) 4, p. 482.

LUMO SKENDO. See FRASHËRI, Mid'hat.

M

MALA, Agim (1952–). Kosovo writer born in Gjakovë. Author of poetry, prose, and criticism. He has published the following works: *Fjalë e vetmi,* Prishtinë 1978 (Speech and solitude); *Dritarja që s'hapet,* Prishtinë 1981 (The window that doesn't open); and *Pamjet pa ne,* Prishtinë 1984 (Views without us).

MALËSHOVA, Sejfulla (ca. 1900–). Pseudonym *Lame Kodra.* Left-wing poet and major Communist figure until 1946. Originally from southern Albania, Malëshova spent a good deal of his life abroad. He studied in Italy and in 1924, at the age of twenty-three, became the personal secretary of Fan Noli (q.v.) in the latter's democratic government. Inspired by the October Revolution which was to lift Russia out of the feudal conditions which also prevailed in Albania, Malëshova went to Moscow where he was trained by the Comintern as a Marxist ideologist. He took part in the fight to free Albania of Fascism and, after the liberation, was a member of the Central Committee of the Communist party of Albania and organized the first congress of Albanian writers. As minister of education, he followed a relatively liberal course in order to encourage the reintegration of non-Communist forces into the new structures of power. He soon fell into disgrace and was liquidated by Enver Hoxha in the summer of 1946.

Most of the verse of this self-styled rebel poet was written in exile. It was collected in the volume *Vjersha,* Tiranë 1945 (Poetry).

MALËSORI, Lulo. See DUÇI, Milo.

MALIQI, Hilmi (1856–1928). Also known as *Sheh Maliqi.* Moslem poet from Kosovo. Born in Rahovec near Prizren, he received an oriental education, studying Turkish, Arabic, and Persian in addition to Albanian and Serbo-Croatian. His lyric verse in a divan of seventy-seven poems, both descriptive and sentimental, marks a transition from traditional oriental verse to the classical poetry of the late Rilindja (q.v.) period. Maliqi also wrote short stories. His manuscripts are said to be preserved in the teke of Rahovec.

Lit.: AJETI, Idriz, *Mbi gjuhën e 'Divanit' të Sheh-Maliqit.* in Kërkime gjuhësore, Prishtinë 1978; KRASNIQI, Mark, *Sheh Hilmi Maliqi.* in: Jeta e re (1953) 3, p. 260-266.

MALIQI, Sheh. See MALIQI, Hilmi.

MALOKI, Krist (1900-1972). Critic and writer. Born in Prizren, he was sent at the early age of twelve to study in Austria. After finishing two doctorates (in philosophy in 1929 and in law in 1934), he became professor of Albanian at the University of Graz.

Maloki is the author of numerous articles and studies on Albanian literature, many of which were published in the periodical *Hylli i dritës* (The day-star). He was first to introduce psychoanalytic methods to Albanian literary criticism.

MAMAQI, Adelina (contemporary). Poetess, now living in Tiranë. She has published verse for both adults and children. Among her publications are *Ëndrra vashërie,* Tiranë 1963 (Girlhood dreams); and *Poezi të zgjedhura,* Prishtinë 1983 (Selected poetry).

MANASTIR, Congress of. See MONASTIR, Congress of.

MANDALÀ, Cristina Gentile. See GENTILE, Cristina.

MANDIA, Eglantina (1936–). Prose writer from Tiranë. She graduated from university in 1959 and has worked as a journalist and teacher.

Among her publications are the short story collections *Tregime për ty,* Tiranë 1969 (Tales for you); and *Lisa të mëdhenj,* Tiranë 1984 (Great oaks); the novels *Jeta dhe motrat e saj,* Tiranë 1977 (Jeta and her sisters); and *Një pritje e gjatë,* Tiranë 1984 (A long wait); the play *Duke mposhtur vdekjen,* Tiranë 1977 (Conquering death); and the volume of journalistic accounts *Në çdo pëllëmbë të tokës sime,* Tiranë 1981 (On every inch of my land).

MARCHESE, Domenico. See MARKEZE, Domenik.

MARCHIANÒ, Michele (1860-1921). Alb. *Mikel Markianoi.* Arbëresh (q.v.) scholar and folklorist from Macchia Albanese in Cosenza, the birthplace of de Rada (q.v.). He was a teacher in Foggia and later vice-principal of the secondary school in Paola.

Marchianò is the author in Italian of one of the first works on de Rada and of collections of Arbëresh folksongs. Among his publications are *L'Albania e l'opera di Girolamo de Rada,* Trani 1902 (Albania and the work of Jeronim de Rada); *Poemi albanesi di Girolamo de Rada,* Trani 1903 (Albanian poems of Jeronim de Rada); *Canti popolari albanesi delle colonie d'Italia,* Foggia 1908 (Albanian folksongs from the colonies of Italy); *Poesie sacre albanesi,* Naples 1908 (Albanian sacred songs); and *Canti popolari albanesi della Capitanata e del Molise,* Martina Franca 1912 (Albanian folksongs from Capitanata and Molise).

MARGËLLIÇI, Mehmet (19th century?). Moslem poet and author of some didactic verse in Albanian.

MARKAJ, Mirosh (contemporary). Pseudonym of *Misto Marko.* Playwright. Author of the trilogy *Gjergj Kastrioti,* Tiranë 1973, on the life and times of Scanderbeg (q.v.); and of *Besa e madhe,* Tiranë 1978 (The great oath).

MARKEZE, Domenik (1869–). Ital. *Domenico Marchese*. Arbëresh (q.v.) poet from Macchia in Cosenza whose lyric poetry appeared in various Arbëresh journals of the period. He is author of the verse collection *Mërii*, Corigliano Calabro 1898 (Sorrow).

MARKIANOI, Mikel. See MARCHIANÒ, Michele.

MARKO, Misto. See MARKAJ, Mirosh.

MARKO, Petro (1913–). Prose writer and poet from Dhërmi in the Himarë region. He finished his education at the school of commerce in Vlorë in 1932 and fought as a volunteer in the International Brigades during the Spanish civil war. His experiences in Spain were described in his novel *Hasta la vista*, Tiranë 1958, which won the Prize of the Republic. Since the war, he has taught literature and worked as a journalist.

Marko's early poetry, like that of Llazar Siliqi (q.v.), shows the influence of Mayakovsky. Much of his prose writing deals with World War II and the fight to free Albania of Fascism, for example, the novels *Qyteti i fundit*, Tiranë 1960 (The last city) and *Stina e armëve*, Tiranë 1966 (Season of weapons); and the short story collection *Rrugë pa rrugë*, Tiranë 1964 (Impracticable road). Among his other novels are *Ara në mal*, Tiranë 1968 (The field on the mountain); *Halimi*, Tiranë 1969; and *Ultimatum*, Tiranë 1972 (Ultimatum). His works have been republished in the ten-volume edition *Vepra 1–10*, Prishtinë 1972 (Works 1–10).

Lit.: ALIU, Ali, *Koha dhe krijuesi*, Prishtinë 1975; NDOCAJ, Filip, *Petro Marko: poeti, publicisti dhe romancieri ynë*. in: Nëntori (1973) 11, p. 111–115.

MARKU, Rudolf (1950–). Poet. He was born in Lezhë where he went to school. He graduated from the University of Tiranë in 1968 and now teaches in the village of Zejmen south of Lezhë.

His first volume of poetry was entitled *Shokëve të mi*, Tiranë 1974 (My comrades). This was followed by *Rruga*, Tiranë 1977 (The road); and *Sërishmi*, Tiranë 1982 (Once again).

MARTINO, Leonardo de (1830–1923). Arbëresh (q.v.) priest, scholar, and poet from Greci in Apulia. As a Franciscan priest, he was sent in 1865 to Shkodër on missionary work. There, he opened the first Italian school in Albania. He was also for a time secretary to Prenk Pasha, head of the Mirdita tribe. He left Albania at the end of the century and died at the convent of Sarno in Italy at the age of ninety-three.

De Martino is the author of translations and religious poetry in Geg (q.v.) dialect which he learned while in Albania. Best known of his publications is *L'arpa di un Italo-Albanese*, Venice 1881 (The harp of an Italo-Albanian), a volume of 442 pages, divided into Italian and Albanian poetry. His importance as a poet lies primarily in his introduction into Albanian of new metres such as the iambic and his popularization of Sapphic verse. He also wrote a short nativity play entitled *Nata Këshnellavet*, Shkodër 1880 (Christmas night), the first of its kind in Albanian.

MARULI, Mikel (1453–1500). Ital. *Michele Marullò*. Latin humanist and poet of Greco-Albanian origin. He was born perhaps in Constantinople and was raised in Italy, where he is thought to have studied in Venice and Padua. In 1470, he began a military career and served as a soldier in various parts of Italy for ten years. In 1491–1492, he rivalled with Politian in Florence and in 1495, married the poetess Alessandra Scala. He drowned accidentally at la Cecina in 1500. Maruli is the author of four books of Latin epigrammes and four books of "natural hymns."

Lit.: PRENNUSHI, M., *Mikel Maruli—poet e filozof i shquar i shekullit XV*. in: Shqipëria e re, 1, Tiranë 1974, p. 23.

MARULLÒ, Michele. See MARULI, Mikel.
MASCI, Angelo. See MASHI, Engell.
MASERECH, Pietro. See MAZRREKU, Pjetër.
MASHI, Engell (1757–ca.1843). Ital. *Angelo Masci*. Arbëresh (q.v.) scholar from Santa Sofia in Cosenza where he studied under Stefano Baffa (q.v.). He later held important functions in the Kingdom of the Two Sicilies. Mashi is the author of an Italian-language work entitled *Discorso sull'origine, costumi e stato attuale della nazione albanese,* Naples 1807 (Discourse on the origin, customs and present state of the Albanian nation), published in French in Malte Brun's *Annales de voyages,* Paris 1809.

MASTER DANIEL. See HAXHIU, Dhanil.
MATO, Jakup (contemporary). Literary critic. Author of *Risi të letërsisë shqiptare të realizmit socialist,* Tiranë 1983 (Renewal of the Albanian literature of Socialist Realism).

MATO, Sulejman (1941–   ). Poet. Born in Sarandë on the south coast of Albania, he studied at the Faculty of History and Philology of the University of Tiranë. He has worked in the construction industry and for the literary journal *Nëntori* (November).

His first verse appeared in 1964–1965 and he has since published several volumes of lyric poetry: *Shtegu i blertë,* Tiranë 1967 (The green path); *Nën diellin e jugut,* Tiranë 1969 (Under the southern sun); *Mbi glob fryjnë erëra,* Tiranë 1972 (Winds blow around the globe); *Në stinën e poezisë,* Tiranë 1975 (In the poetry season); *Mesi i jetës,* Tiranë 1981 (The middle of life); and *Jeta në dy kohë,* Prishtinë 1983 (Life in two eras). Mato has also produced several plays for the People's Theatre in Tiranë.

MATRANGA, Luca. See MATRËNGA, Lekë.
MATRËNGA, Lekë (1567–1619). Also written *Luca Matranga*. Arbëresh (q.v.) priest and writer from Piana degli Albanesi in Sicily and one of the major authors of early Albanian literature.

He was of an old Arbëresh family which had emigrated to Sicily, probably from the Peloponnese. He studied from 1582 to 1587 at the college of St. Athanasius in Rome, was ordained in 1591, and returned to Sicily. In December 1601, we find him engaged in pastoral duties among the Arbëresh back in Piana degli Albanesi. He died as an archpriest at the age of fifty-two.

Matrënga is the author of *E mbsuame e krështerë,* Rome 1592 (Christian doctrine), a twenty-eight page catechism translated from a Latin work by the Spanish priest Jacob Ledesma (1516–1575). The catechism is the second oldest literary monument of the Albanian language, preceded only by the liturgy of Gjon Buzuku (q.v.). It is also the oldest known Arbëresh text and the first complete work in Tosk (q.v.) dialect. In addition, it contains the first specimen of written verse. The full title of the work, which survives in three versions of one original copy in the Vatican Library, is *Embsúame é chraextérae cciáe prépsn táe díe cghíthae i pistépsm i chraextée. Dotrina christiana che deve saper ogni fedele christiano.*

Lit.: LA PIANA, Marco, *Il catechismo albanese di Luca Matranga (1592), da un manoscritto Vaticano,* Grottaferrata 1912; RROTA, Justin, *Shkrimtari mâ i vjetri i Italo-Shqyptarvet: Lukë Matranga,* Shkodër 1939; SCIAMBRA, Matteo, *La 'Dottrina cristiana' albanese di Luca Matranga. Riproduzione, trascrizione e commento del Codice Barberini Latino 3454,* Vatican City 1964; SULEJMANI, Fadil, *E mbsuame e krështerë e Lekë Matrëngës,* Prishtinë 1979.

MAURI, Domenik (1812–1873). Ital. *Domenico Mauro.* Arbëresh (q.v.) poet from San Demetrio Corone in Cosenza. He was one of the leaders of the 1848 uprising in Calabria and after a long period of exile in Turin became one of Garibaldi's Thousand. Though of Arbëresh origin, he wrote exclusively in Italian. Among his publications are *Versi sciolti in occasione della morte di mio padre in risposta all'amico,* Naples 1835 (Selected verse on the occasion of my father's death in answer to a friend); *Errico, novella calabrese,* Zürich 1845 (Errico, a Calabrian short story); *Poesie varie,* Naples 1862 (Various poetry); and *Errico, poemetto in cinque canti,* Naples 1869 (Errico, a short poem in five cantos).

Lit.: CINGARI, Gaetano, *Romanticismo e democrazia nel Mezzogiorno, Domenico Mauro (1812–1873),* Naples 1965.

MAURO, Domenico. See MAURI, Domenik.

MAZRREKU, Pjetër (fl. 1633). Ital. *Pietro Maserech.* Archbishop of Bar (Antivari). In one of his reports to Rome, dated 1633, he included a list of about thirty Albanian words with Italian etymologies.

Lit.: ROQUES, Mario, *Le dictionnaire albanais de 1635,* Paris 1932; ZAMPUTI, Injac, *Pjetër Mazrreku dhe fjalorthi i tij i vjetit 1633.* in: Studime Filologjike (1964) 2, p. 167–174.

MEÇANI, Baba Abdullah (–1852). Bektash poet. He founded the great teke of Melçani near Korçë and was active in the nationalist movement. Author of much mystic verse in Albanian, of which only one poem dedicated to Sari Salltëk Baba, has survived.

MEHMETI, Din (1932–). Kosovo poet. Born in the village of Gjocaj-Junik near Gjakovë, Mehmeti graduated in Albanology from the University of Belgrade in 1959, lecturing subsequently at the teachers' college in Gjakovë.

Mehmeti's imaginative verse, evoking the spirit and temperament of the people of Kosovo and especially of the Dukagjin highlanders, has always been well received by readers and critics. It is a poetry of passion rather than of diction, embuing a strong attachment to the soil and to the poet's homeland. It has been published in the following collections: *Në krahët e shkrepave,* Prishtinë 1961 (On the wings of cliffs); *Rini diellore,* Prishtinë 1966 (Sunny youth); *Dridhjet e dritës,* Prishtinë 1969 (The trembling of light); *Heshtja e kallur,* Prishtinë 1972 (Burning silence); *Mallkimi i gjakut,* Tiranë 1972 (The blood curse); *Ora,* Prishtinë 1974 (The fairy); *Ikje nga vdekja,* Prishtinë 1978 (Flight from death); *Poezi,* Prishtinë 1978 (Poetry); *Fanar në furtuna,* Prishtinë 1981 (Beacon in the storm); *Zogu i diellit,* Prishtinë 1982 (The sun-bird); and *Fatin tim nuk e nënshkruaj,* Prishtinë 1984 (I do not seal my fate). Mehmeti is also the author of prose, literary criticism, and drama, such as *Agu,* Prishtinë 1983 (The dawn).

Lit.: VINCA, Agim, *Këngë për tokën ujerun dhe qëndresën.* in: Dituria (1983) 2–3, p. 69–75.

MEHZUNI, Baba Muharem (–1867). Bektash (q.v.) poet. He was born in Gjirokastër and lived from 1845 to his death at the famed Bektash teke of Durballi. His verse is permeated with Arabic vocabulary.

MEKSI, Apostol Panajot (mid 19th century). Folklorist. He was from Labovë near Gjirokastër and studied with Kristoforidhi (q.v.) at the Zosimea secondary school in Ioannina. It was there that he helped teach Albanian to the German scholar Johann Georg von Hahn who was Austro-Hungarian consul in Ioannina at the time.

Meksi collected for Hahn four Albanian folktales from his native village which were published in the latter's *Albanesische Studien,* Vienna 1853 (Albanian Studies).

MEKSI, Jorgji (–1942). Journalist and publisher. He studied journalism in Athens and emigrated to Bucharest where, together with Visar Dodani (q.v.), he founded the periodical *Shqipëria* (Albania) which lasted from 1897 to 1899 and to which he contributed numerous articles. For a time, he was also director of the periodical *Demokratia* (Democracy) in Gjirokastër where he died.

MEKSI, Vangjel (–ca. 1823). Translator of the New Testament. Meksi was from Labovë near Gjirokastër. With the help of a letter of recommendation from Ali Pasha Tepelena, he went to Italy in 1803 to study medicine. After finishing his studies in Naples, he returned to Ioannina and served at the court of Ali Pasha. He travelled in Europe and is known to have been in Istanbul and Salonika. He died a bachelor at the age of about sixty in Tripolis, Greece.

Meksi finished his translation of the New Testament for the British and Foreign Bible Society in 1821. He never lived to see the publication of his work, however, which was undertaken by Grigor Gjirokastriti (q.v.) in 1827. Robert Pinkerton, representative of the British and Foreign Bible Society in Istanbul, reported in 1819 that Meksi had also written a grammar of the Albanian language in Albanian. He is, in addition, said to have translated a religious work of Abbé Claude Fleury (1640–1723). Both of these works by Meksi are lost.

MEKULI, Esad (1916–   ). Pseudonym *Sat Nokshiqi*. Kosovo poet, widely considered as the founder of modern Albanian poetry in Yugoslavia. He was born, the son of a hodja, in the Albanian village of Plavë in Montenegro. After secondary schooling in Pejë, he studied veterinary medicine at the University of Belgrade. There, he came into contact with Marxism and subsequently took part in the partisan movement of World War II. He was editor of the Kosovo newspaper *Rilindja* (Rebirth) and of the literary journal *Jeta e re* (New life).

Mekuli began wrriting at an early age. His first collection of poetry *Për ty*, Prishtinë 1955 (For you) was dedicated to his native Kosovo region. This was followed by: *Poetët e 'Bagdallës'*, Prishtinë 1966 (The poets of 'Bagdalla'), an anthology of Serbian poetry; *Avsha ada, vjersha nga ishulli*, Prishtinë 1971 (Avsha ada, verse from an island); *Vjersha*, Prishtinë 1973 (Verse); *Glasovi vremena*, Belgrade 1974 (The voices of time), a selection of his Albanian poetry with a Serbian translation by the author; *Midis dashurisë dhe urrejtjes*, Tiranë 1981 (Between love and hatred); and *Brigjet*, Prishtinë 1981 (The hills). He has also published translations, especially of the nineteenth century Montenegrin poet-prince Njegoš.

Lit.: AGANI, Hilmi, *Mbresa dhe mendime për poezin e Esad Mekulit*. in: Jeta e re (1959) 4, p. 450–464; IVANOVIQ, Radomir, *Poezia e angazhuar e Esad Mekulit*. in: Jeta e re (1971) 1, p. 152–156.

MEKULI, Hasan (1929–   ). Kosovo literary critic. Mekuli was born of a peasant family in the village of Plavë in Montenegro. After schooling in Plavë, Skopje, and Prishtinë, he graduated from secondary school in Ivangrad in Montenegro. From 1950 to 1955, he studied Yugoslav languages and literatures at the University of Belgrade and then took up teaching in Prishtinë. Until 1962, he was a theatre director in Prishtinë and afterwards taught Yugoslav literature at the Faculty of Arts of the university there. Mekuli is now president of the Kosovo Writers' League and head of the University Library in Prishtinë.

MERXHANI, Branko (20th century). Journalist and publisher. Merxhani published the periodical *Përpjekja shqiptare*, 1936–1938 (The Albanian effort), and contributed to the right-wing journal *Illyria* and other periodicals of prewar Albania. His interests were mainly in philosophy and sociology.

MESHARI. See BUZUKU, Gjon.

METO, Memo (1910–1944). Poet from the Labëria region of southern Albania. He is the author of partisan lyrics, both political and satirical, composed during the resistance. He was killed on April 2, 1944. His works were first published after the war in *Këngë për liri*, Tiranë 1955 (Songs for freedom) and have been reedited by Dhimitër Shuteriqi (q.v.) in *Lulet e lirisë*, Tiranë 1976 (The flowers of freedom).

MIGJENI (1911–1938). Acronym of *Millosh Gjergj Nikolla*. Poet and short story writer. Migjeni was born in Shkodër. He studied at the Serbian-language school there and at St. John's Orthodox Seminary in Monastir (Bitola), Macedonia. It was during his studies for the priesthood that he became acquainted with Serbian, Russian, and French authors. On his return to Albania, he gave up his intended career as a priest to become a schoolteacher in Vrakë, a village a few miles from Shkodër, and began to write verse and short stories. Having contracted tuberculosis, then endemic in Albania, he went for treatment to Turin in northern Italy where his sister Olga was studying at the university. After some time in a sanatorium there, he was transferred to the Waldensian Hospital in Torre Pellice, where he died on August 26, 1938, at the age of twenty-six.

Migjeni was one of the first poets to abandon the long-standing tradition of romantic nationalism in Albanian verse. His poetry is characterized by a strong social ethic, not of pity for the poor but of outrage against injustice and oppression. He is thus considered a precursor of Socialist Realism in Albanian literature. His slender volume of poetry entitled *Vargjet e lira* (Free verse) first went to press in 1936 but was immediately confiscated by the Zogist authorities. A second printing in 1944 was more successful. His poetry and short stories have been reedited in *Vepra 1–4*, Prishtinë 1980 (Works 1–4) and have been translated into English, *Migjeni. Selected Albanian songs and sketches,* Tiranë 1962, and into German, French, Italian, Spanish, Russian, Chinese, Ukrainian, Bulgarian, Latvian, and Romanian.

Lit.: BALA, Vehbi, *Migjeni, portret-monografi,* Tiranë 1974; BIHIKU, *Koço, Proza e Migjenit.* in: Studime Filologjike (1971) 4, p. 11–48; EYNTREY, Gertruda Iosifovna, *Tvorchestvo Mid'eni,* Leningrad 1973; FETIU, Sefedin, *Vepra e Migjenit dhe kritika e saj,* Prishtinë 1984; KASTRATI, Jup, *Bibliografia e Migjenit (1934–1961).* in: Nëntori 8 (1961) 10, p. 69–94; PIPA, Arshi, *Albanian literature. Social perspectives,* Munich 1978, p. 126–163; RAIFI, Mensur, *Fan S. Noli dhe Migjeni,* Prishtinë 1975.

MINAROLLI, Hamza (1931–   ). Dramatist and poet. Author of the play *Shënomëni dhe mua,* Tiranë 1976, about the collectivization of agriculture; and of the verse collection *Copëza jete,* Tiranë 1964 (Bits of life).

MIRDITA, Kolë (1900–1936). Pseudonym *Helenau.* Short story writer from Shkodër. He studied at the University of Graz in Austria. His first work was a tragedy on the death of Scanderbeg (q.v.). Mirdita also wrote poetry but is best remembered for his short stories.

Lit.: KASTRATI, Jup, *Kolë Mirdita (Helenau).* in: Nëntori (1956) 12, p. 156–162.

MITKO, Thimi (1820–1890). Nationalist figure and folklorist. Mitko was born in Korçë where he attended the Greek school. His uncle Peti Mitko was the leader of a Christian uprising in Korçë and Tepelenë against the Turkish Tanzimat legislation. Both left Albania in 1850, moving first to Athens, then Plovdiv, and finally to Vienna where Thimi Mitko worked as a tailor. In 1866, he emigrated to Egypt, devoting himself to the nationalist movement, and set up a successful trading business in Beni Suef where he died on March 22, 1890.

From Spiro Dine (q.v.), we know that Mitko had collected folklore material in 1866. He corresponded with de Rada (q.v.), Kamarda (q.v.), Dora d'Istria (q.v.), Jarník, Kristoforidhi (q.v.), and Gustav Meyer and provided Kamarda with folksongs, riddles, and tales for the latter's collection. Mitko's own collection of Albanian folklore, consisting of folksongs, tales, and popular sayings from southern Albania was published in Greek script under the Greek title *Alvaniki melissa,* Alexandria 1878 (The Albanian bee). It was the first folklore collection designed for the Albanian public but was also, according to Mitko himself, meant to provide Europe with information about Albanian customs. The work was reedited by Gjergj Pekmezi (q.v.), using the modern Albanian alphabet, in Vienna in 1924 under the title *Bleta shqypëtare e Thimi Mitkos* (The Albanian bee of Thimi Mitko). Mitko was also the author of numerous articles in European periodicals in support of the Albanian cause and of poetry of modest literary value. His works have been published in *Vepra,* Tiranë 1981 (Works).

Lit.: HAXHIHASANI, Qemal, *Thimi Mitko,* Tiranë 1962; QOSJA, Rexhep, *Historia e letërsisë shqipe—Romantizmi II,* Prishtinë 1984, p. 235–264; SHUTERIQI, Dhimitër, *Mbi Barletin dhe shkrime të tjera,* Tiranë 1979.

MJEDA, Ndre (1866–1937). Classical lyric poet of the late Rilindja (q.v.) period. Mjeda (or Mjedja) was born in Shkodër and received his education, like so many other Geg (q.v.) writers of the period, from the Jesuits. After studies in Spain (1879–1882 at the Porta Coeli college in Valencia), Croatia (1882–1887 at the Jesuit college and the Gregorian university in Kraljevica), and Poland (1891–1895 at the Gregorian theological faculty in Kraków), he finished his training for the priesthood with a doctorate in philosophy and theology. It was during his years in Kraljevica that Mjeda began writing poetry in Albanian, among which his *Vaji i bylbylit,* 1887 (The lament of the nightingale) expressing a longing for his homeland. He was also active as a translator, mostly of religious literature such as *Katekizmi i madh* (The great catechism) in three volumes and *Historia e shejtë* (Sacred history), both published in later years. Mjeda was appointed professor of philosophy and philology at the Gregorian university in Kraljevica where he worked until 1898, when for reasons still unclear, he was expelled from the Jesuit order after a political conflict. In the years following, he was a parish priest in northern Albania and was supported no doubt by his brother Lazar who was bishop of Sapë. Together with Lazar, he founded the *Agimi* (Dawn) cultural society (q.v.) in 1901 which encouraged the use of Albanian in literature and attempted a spelling reform using Croatian as a model. In 1902, he was invited to Hamburg to participate at the Congress of Orientalists and read a paper entitled "De pronunciatione palatalium in diversis albanicae linguae dialectis." He later corresponded with renowned Albanologists such as Gustav Meyer, Norbert Jokl, and Holgar Pedersen. Mjeda's growing interest in the Albanian alphabet question led to his participation at the Congress of Monastir (q.v.) in 1908 at which his "Agimi" alphabet lost out to Fishta's (q.v.) "Bashkimi" alphabet. From 1920 to 1924, Mjeda was a deputy in the National Assembly but withdrew from politics after the defeat of the June revolution and the rise of the Zog dictatorship. From 1930, he taught Albanian language and literature at the Jesuit college in Shkodër.

His poetry, in particular the collection *Juvenalia,* Vienna 1917, is noted for its classical style and purity of language, showing the influence of Albanian folk literature, of the nationalist movement, and of the classical poets of late nineteenth century Italy. His works have been reedited in *Poezi,* Tiranë 1978 (Poetry); and *Vepra 1–3,* Prishtinë 1982 (Works 1–3). Less known are his prose writings included in early school readers he wrote, such as *Këndimet për shkollat e para të Shqypnisë,* 1911 (Reader for Albanian elementary schools) and his many religious works.

Lit.: GRADILONE, Giuseppe, *Studi di letteratura albanese,* Rome 1960, p. 162–206; GURAKUQI, Mark, *Mbi veprën poetike të Mjedës. Studim,* Tiranë 1980; IDRIZI, Rinush, *Ndre Mjedja,* Tiranë 1980; SHUTERIQI, Dhimitër, *Të dhëna të reja mbi jetën dhe krijimtarinë e Ndre Mjedës.* in: Nëndori 10 (1963) 3, p. 98–122.

MJEDJA, Ndre. See MJEDA, Ndre.

MJESHTRI DHANIL. See HAXHIU, Dhanil.

MONASTIR, Congress of. Congress held from November 14–22, 1908 in the Macedonian city of Monastir (now Bitola) to decide upon a definitive alphabet for Albanian. It was convoked upon the initiative of the Bashkimi (The union) literary society (q.v.) under Gjergj Fishta (q.v.) and presided over by Mid'hat Frashëri (q.v.). It was attended by Catholic, Orthodox, and Moslem delegates from Albania and abroad, among whom Gjergj Fishta, Mid'hat Frashëri, Shahin Kolonja (q.v.), Ndre Mjeda (q.v.), Hilë Mosi (q.v.), and Sotir Peci (q.v.). The three main alphabets under discussion were the so-called Istanbul alphabet devised by Sami Frashëri (q.v.), the Bashkimi alphabet supported by Gjergj Fishta and the Bashkimi literary society of Shkodër, and the Agimi alphabet of the Agimi (The dawn) literary society (q.v.) represented by Ndre Mjeda. A committee of eleven delegates headed by Fishta was elected and after three days of deliberations resolved to support two alphabets: a modified form of the Istanbul alphabet which was most widely used at the time and a new Latin alphabet almost identical to the Bashkimi to facilitate printing abroad. With its decision to support two alphabets, the congress helped pave the way for a gradual transition from the Istanbul alphabet to the modern Albanian alphabet based on Latin, without undue controversy or resistance.

MOSI, Hilë (1885–1933). Poet, translator, patriot, and political figure. Mosi was born in Shkodër and trained as a teacher in Klagenfurt, Austria, where he fell under the influence of the German romantics. In 1908, he was a delegate at the Congress of Monastir (q.v.) in Macedonia which was held to establish an Albanian orthography. He collaborated in various journals and was also politically active, taking part in an uprising in northern Albania in 1911. He later became Albania's representative at the League of Nations and minister of education.

Mosi is the author of patriotic and love lyrics and was the first poet to adapt hexametre to Albanian verse. He published several collections of poetry, among which: *Këngat shqipe,* Salonika 1909 (Albanian songs); *Zân' i atdheut,* Trieste 1913 (The voice of the homeland); *Lotët e dashnís,* Shkodër 1916 (Tears of love); and *Lule prendvere*, Tiranë 1927 (Flowers of spring). These have been reedited in part in *Vepra të zgjedhura, 1–3*, Prishtinë 1972 (Selected works, 1–3). He is also known for his translations, especially from the German and Italian, of Goethe, Schiller, Lessing, Uhland, Körner, Heine, and Goldoni.

Lit.: LACAJ, Henrik, *Hilë Mosi (1885–1933), shënime mbi jetën dhe veprën e tij letrare*. in: Buletin i Universitetit Shtetëror të Tiranës. Seria Shkenc. Shoq. (1961) 3, p. 88–99.

MUÇO, Betim (1947–). Poet and prose writer from Tiranë. He studied physics at the Institute of Natural Sciences and now works for the Institute of Seismology. Muço has published several books of prose and poetry, among which: *Rrugëve të atdheut*, Tiranë 1967 (The homeland roads); *Etydë*, Tiranë 1970 (Study); *Kokra gruri*, Tiranë 1978 (Wheat); *Tregime*, Tiranë 1978 (Tales); *Ditë që vështrojnë larg*, Tiranë 1982 (The far-seeing days); and *Ditëlindja e këngës*, Tiranë 1984 (The birthday of a song).

MULAJ, Avni R. (1947–). Poet from Tropojë in the northern Albanian mountains. He studied commerce at the University of Tiranë in 1970–1971 and now works for Albkontroll in Durrës. He has published two collections of poetry: *Valbona e kaltër*, Tiranë 1974? (The blue Valbonë); and *Orët e mia*, Tiranë 1976 (My fairies). Mulaj is also the author of the drama *Gërsheti i luftërave*, Tiranë 1979 (The warriors' plaited hair).

MURIQI, Nebih (1943–). Kosovo poet and painter born in Novosellë near Pejë. He studied applied and figurative arts in Pejë and Belgrade and now teaches art at the Academy of Arts in Prishtinë. His first collection of verse appeared under the title *Në synin e pranverës*, Prishtinë 1965 (First glimpse of spring). He is also author of the volumes: *Kariatidet*, Prishtinë 1973 (The caryatids); and *Yll në gur*, Prishtinë 1980 (Star in stone).

MUSACHI, Giovanni. See MUZAKA, Gjon.

MUSAJ, Ali (1933–). Kosovo poet. He was born in Tiranë where he went to school until his family returned to Kosovo in 1943. He graduated from secondary school in Gjakovë where he now lives.

Musaj began writing in 1953. He has published several volumes of verse for adults and children, among which: *Vetëm jehona*, Prishtinë 1963 (Only the echo); *Shkallëzimet e frigës*, Prishtinë 1972 (The degrees of fear); *Katarzë*, Prishtinë 1978 (Catharsis); and *Zëri i vetmisë*, Prishtinë 1982 (The voice of solitude).

MUSARAJ, Shevqet (1914–). Prose writer, poet, and journalist. He was born of a peasant family in the village of Matogjin, near Vlorë. During World War II, he took part in the resistance movement, writing articles, poetry, and satire for the clandestine Communist press using the pseudonym *Buburicka*. After the war, he was a party cadre and worked as a correspondent for the daily newspaper *Zëri i Popullit* (The People's Voice).

Musaraj's best known work is the satirical epic poem *Epopeja e Ballit Kombëtar*, Tiranë 1944 (The epic of the National Front) about the conservative resistance movement which vied with the Communists for power during the war. His prose writing, such as the two-volume novels *Para agimit*, Tiranë 1965-1966 (Engl. transl. *Before the dawn*, 2 vol., Tiranë 1981, 1982) and *Belxhiku që këndon vënçe*, Tiranë 1979 (The Belgian rifle that sings at its leisure) also deal for the most part with the war. Musaraj's works have been republished in a six-volume edition *Vepra letrare 1–6*, Tiranë 1979 (Literary works 1–6).

Lit.: BRAHIMI, Razi, *Vepra letrare e Shevqet Musaraj.* in: Studime Filologjike 32 (1978) 3, p. 55–89.

MUSLIU, Beqir (1945–   ). Kosovo poet and prose writer from Gjilan. He went to school there and studied Albanian language and literature at the University of Prishtinë. He has published the following volumes of poetry: *Rima të shqetsueme*, Prishtinë 1965 (Anxious rhymes); *Lulekuqet e gjakut*, Prishtinë 1966 (The blood poppies); *Kunorë sonetesh*, Prishtinë 1968 (Crown of sonnets); *Bukurija e zezë*, Prishtinë 1968 (Black beauty); *Sezamet*, Prishtinë 1972 (Open sesame); *Parabola*, Prishtinë 1976 (The parabola); and *Darka e magjisë*, Prishtinë 1978 (The magic supper). He has also written the novel *Vegullia*, Prishtinë 1979 (The hallucination); and the short story collection *Mbledhësit e purpurit*, Prishtinë 1982 (The collectors of purple).

Lit.: KAMBERI, Alush, *Në vështrim mbi poezinë e B. Musliut.* in: Jehona (1970) 7–8, p. 73–77.

MUSLIU, Ramadan (1954–   ). Kosovo poet from the village of Beguncë near Viti. He studied Albanian language and literature at the University of Prishtinë and now works as a journalist for the Kosovo daily newspaper *Rilindja* (Rebirth). He has published two verse collections: *Parodia e trupit*, Prishtinë 1981 (Bodily parody); and *Shqisa e gjashtë*, Prishtinë 1983 (The sixth sense).

MUZAKA, Gjon (fl. 1510). Ital. *Giovanni Musachi*. Italian-language author of Albanian origin. He was of a noble family from the Myzeqe region about whom in 1510 he wrote a *Breve memoria de li discendenti de nostra casa Musachi* (Short memoir on the descendents of our Myzeqe lineage). The work was published in Ch. Hopf, *Chroniques gréco-romanes*, Paris 1873, p. 270–340.

N

NAIBI, Sulejman (-1772). Also known as *Sulejman Ramazani*. Bektash-Moslem poet and contemporary of Nezim Frakulla (q.v.). He was born in Berat where he spent a good deal of his life.

Naibi is the author of an Albanian-language divan (verse collection), a copy of which survived in Fier until 1944. Among the little of his verse which has been published, we find delicate lyrics describing the joys of love and the beauty of women. His Albanian, refined in metrical precision, is purer and less imbued with oriental vocabulary than that of Frakulla or Kyçyku (q.v.).

Lit.: MYDERRIZI, Osman, *Një dorëshkrim shqip i panjohur i Gjirokastrës*. in: Buletin i Universitetit Shtetëror të Tiranës. Seria Shkenc. Shoq. (1957), 1, p. 177–200.

NAPOLETANO, Pietro (1931–). Arbëresh (q.v.) poet. He was born in Firmo in Cosenza and now works as a teacher in the village of Saracena near Castrovillari. He has published several volumes of verse in Italian and Albanian, among which: *Nderim Fermës*, Corigliano Calabro 1976 (In honour of Firmo).

NASIBIU, Tahir (-1835). Poet. He was founder of the Bektash teke (monastery) of Frashër in 1825 and is said to have written poetry in Albanian, Persian, and Turkish, nothing of which has survived.

NAXHI, Mehmet (1873–1928). Also known as *Dervish Hima*. Publicist and nationalist figure. He was born in Struga on Lake Ohrid in 1873 or 1875 and went to school in Monastir (Bitola) and Salonika. He studied medicine for two years in Istanbul where he at first joined the Young Turk movement and began to reflect on the Albanian question. From 1895 until World War I, he wandered indefatigably from country to country, often pursued by the Ottoman authorities, and propagated the Albanian cause with articles and pamphlets. In Bucharest, he edited the periodical *Pavarësia e Shqipërisë,* 1898 (The independence of Albania) and in Rome, together with Mehmed bey Frashëri, *Zëri i Shqipërisë* (The voice of Albania). At the beginning of the century, he published the periodical *L'Albanie* in Geneva, in 1909 the weekly *Shqiptari-Arnavud* (The Albanian) in Istanbul with Hilë Mosi (q.v.) and in 1911 the newspaper *Shkumbi* (The nation). In the autumn of 1917, he was appointed school inspector for the Tiranë district by the Austro-Hungarian authorities and later became the first director of the Albanian press office.

NEGOVANI, Papa Kristo (1875–1905). Also known as *Kristo Harallambi*. Nationalist figure, religious leader, and writer. Born in the village of Negovan, near Florina in northern Greece, he went to school in Athens and later emigrated to Brăila in Romania. There, he first came into contact with the nationalist movement and learned to write Albanian (in the Istanbul alphabet). In 1897, he returned to his native village and worked as a teacher and parish priest. Negovani transformed his house into a school and taught over one hundred children and adults to read and write Albanian. He also preached and said mass in Albanian, much to the displeasure of the Greek Orthodox hierarchy. On February 12, 1905, he was murdered by bandits.

Negovani is the author of prose and poetry, including school texts, translations and fables. Among his publications are *Istori e Dhiatës së Vjetërë*, Bucharest 1899 (History of the Old Testament); *Vjershë shkresëtoreja*, Sofia 1899 (Poetic writings); *Prishija e Hormovese*, Sofia 1904 (The destruction of Hormova); *I vogeli Dhonat Arghendi*, Constanza 1904 (Little Donat Argendi); *Benate te shentorevët dhergimetare*, Sofia 1906 (Works of the holy apostles); *I drugneti kryc*, Sofia 1906 (The wooden cross); and *Istori shkronje e Plikatit*, Salonika 1909 (Written history of Plikat).

Lit.: FULLANI, Dhimitër, *Papa Kristo Negovani*. in: Buletin i Universitetit Shtetëror të Tiranës. Seria Shkenc. Shoq. 16 (1960) 2, p. 188–221.

NEZIMI, Ibrahim. See FRAKULLA, Nezim.

NIKAJ, Ndoc (1864–1951). Prose writer and publisher from northern Albania. He studied at the seminary in Shkodër and worked as a parish priest in the Shkreli mountains. Nikaj devoted all his energy to the nationalist movement. Together with Preng Doçi (q.v.), he founded Lidhja e mshehët (The secret league) which prepared the way for the revolt of 1910. He was a member of the Bashkimi (The union) literary society (q.v.) and founded the newspaper *Koha* (The time), later called *Bashkimi* (The union), Shkodër 1910–1913, and *Besa Shqyptare* (The Albanian word of honour), Shkodër 1913–1921. He also collaborated actively, using the pseudonym *Nak Domonici*, in Faik Konica's (q.v.) periodical *Albania* published in Brussels. Arrested by the Communist authorities in 1946 at the age of eighty-two, he died in prison five years later.

Nikaj is considered by some to be the father of the Albanian novel. Among his publications of note are *Vakinat e sceites kisc*, Rome 1888 (History of the holy church); *Marzia e ksctenimi n'filles t'vet*, Shkodër 1892 (Foolishness and the origins of Christianity); *Shkodra e rrethueme*, Shkodër 1892 (Shkodër under siege); *Historia e Shqypnis*, Brussels 1902 (History of Albania); *Lulet në thes*, Shkodër 1913 (The flowers in a bag); *Bukurusha*, Shkodër 1918 (The beautiful girl); and *Bërbuqja*, Shkodër 1920 (The little girl).

Lit.: LACAJ, Henrik, *Dom Ndoc Nikaj (1864–1951), shënime mbi jetën dhe veprat.* in: Buletin i Universitetit Shtetëror të Tiranës. Seria Shkenc. Shoq. (1963) 1, p. 184–197.

NIKOLLA, Millosh Gjergj. See MIGJENI.

NOKSHIQI, Sat. See MEKULI, Esad.

NOLI, Fan Stylian (1882–1965). Statesman, religious leader, writer, and translator. Noli was born in the village of Ibrik Tepe (Alb. Qytezë), south of Edirne in Turkey. He attended the Greek secondary school in Edirne until 1900, moving then to Istanbul and Athens. From 1903 to 1906, he lived in Egypt where he was in contact with leaders of the Albanian community such as Spiro Dine (q.v.), Jani Vruho (q.v.), and Thanas Tashko. In 1906, he emigrated to America, arriving in New York on May 10. He worked as deputy editor of the Boston newspaper *Kombi* (The nation) founded by Sotir Peci (q.v.) and founded the Besa-besën (The oath) society of Boston in 1907. The following year, he was ordained as a deacon in Brooklyn and held services in Albanian, the first step towards the organization of an Albanian Autocephalic Orthodox church, whose head he was to become. From 1909 to 1911, he edited the newspaper *Dielli* (The sun). Together with Faik Konica (q.v.), he founded the Panalbanian Vatra (The hearth) Federation on April 28, 1912, which was destined to become the most significant Albanian organization in America. In the same year, after graduating from Harvard University, he returned to Albania and took part in the congress of Trieste in 1913. Back in the United States in 1915, he founded the periodical *Adriatic review,* financed by the Vatra Federation. On July 27, 1919, he was appointed bishop of the Albanian Orthodox church in the United States and later headed an Albanian delegation to Geneva where he was successful in having Albania admitted to the League of Nations in 1920. From Geneva, he returned to Albania and represented the Vatra Federation in parliament there. In 1922, he became foreign minister in the government of Xhafer Ypi and in 1924, himself prime minister of Albania, leading a short lived but democratic government which tried desperately to cope with the catastrophic economic and political problems facing the young Albanian state. With the overthrow of his government by Zogist forces, Noli went back into exile to Boston. He died in Fort Lauderdale, Florida, on March 13, 1965.

Noli's first literary work was a three-act drama entitled *Israilitë dhe Filistinë,* Boston 1907 (Israelites and Philistines). He was also a noted historian, publishing a *Historia e Skënderbeut,* Boston 1921 (Engl. version *George Castrioti Scanderbeg,* New York 1947); and *Beethoven and the French revolution,* New York 1947. His poetry was first published in *Albumi,* Boston 1948 (The album). In addition, Noli is the author of a number of religious works published in the United States, and of translations into Albanian of Shakespeare, Longfellow, Ibsen, Poe, Blasco Ibañez, Cervantes, and Molière as well as of the Rubaiyat of Omar Khayyam (Edward Fitzgerald). His works have been republished in seven volumes in *Vepra të plota 1–7,* Prishtinë 1968 (Complete works 1–7) and are widely read in Albania.

Lit.: ARAPI, Fatos, *Mbi evolucionin krijues në poezinë e Fan Nolit.* in: Nëntori (1980) 3, p. 161–184; BALA, Vehbi, *Jeta e Fan S. Nolit,* Tiranë 1972; NOLI, Fan S. *Fiftieth anniversary book of the Albanian Orthodox Church in America 1908–1958,* Boston 1960; PIPA, Arshi, *Fan Noli as a national and international Albanian figure.* in: Südost-Forschungen 43 (1984), p. 241–270; RAIFI, Mensur, *Fan S. Noli dhe Migjeni,* Prishtinë 1975; TAKO, Piro, *Fan Noli në fushën politike dhe publicistike,* Tiranë 1975.
NOMADHI. See GURRA, Milto Sotir.

P

PAÇARIZI, Haxhi Ymer Lutfi (1869–1929). Moslem poet and mystic born in Prizren between 1869 and 1871. He studied at the Fatih medresa in Istanbul. Though imbued in Islamic tradition, he welcomed the October Revolution and supported the fledgling Communist party in Skopje as early as 1920, which brought him into conflict with the Serbian police.

Lit.: KALESHI, Hasan, in: Gjurmime Albanologjike 1 (1962), p. 113; KRASNIQI, Mark, *Haxhi Ymer Lutfi Paçarizi*. in: Jeta e re (1955) 5, p. 418–426.

PAÇRAMI, Fadil (1922–   ). Dramatist and political figure. Paçrami was born in Shkodër and although of Moslem origin, was educated by the Franciscans who sent him to Italy where he studied medicine. In 1942, he interrupted his studies to join the partisan movement back in Albania. After the war, he worked in the Communist youth movement, became chief editor of the daily newspaper *Zëri i Popullit* (The People's Voice), president of the Albanian union of journalists, and head of the Albanian-Soviet friendship society. Until 1973, he served as president of the People's Assembly. At the fourth Plenary Session of the Central Committee that year he was condemned as a deviationist and an enemy of the people.

Paçrami's plays, in the tradition of Socialist Realism, are devoted for the most part to an analysis of the relations between the individual and a Socialist society. Among them are *Çështja e inxhinierit Saimirit* (The case of the engineer Saimiri); *E bardha dhe e zeza* (The white and the black); *Lagja e varfër* (The poor neighbourhood); *Ngjarje në fabrikë* (Incident in a factory); *Njëzet ditë* (Twenty days); *Rrugëve të pashkelura* (On untrodden roads); *Shtëpia në bulevard* (The house on the boulevard); and *Viti 61* (The year 61).

PALAJ, Bernardin (1897–194?). Franciscan priest, poet, and folklorist. He was born in the Dukagjin region and studied in Austria before returning as a parish priest to the mountains of northern Albania. There, he collected folksongs and wrote articles on Geg (q.v.) folklore and tribal customs. His conservative politics, similar to the position of Gjergj Fishta (q.v.), led to his arrest after the war. He died in prison in the late 1940s.

Aside from his articles on folklore and oral literature, Palaj is the author of lyric and epic poetry, much of which was published in Shkodër in the Franciscan periodical *Hylli i dritës* (The day-star). He is remembered in particular for *Nata e vetme* (The solitary night), an ode composed on the death of Gjergj Fishta, and for his long ballad *Ndërmjet Shën Gjergjave* (Between the two Saint Georges).

Lit.: KOLIQI, Ernest, *Bernardin Palaj dhe nji poemth i tij i pakryem.* in: Shêjzat 16 (1972), p. 152–184.

PALI, Gaspër (1916–1942). Poet. He was born of a family of merchants in Shkodër and studied literature at the University of Florence. Pali died at an early age, leaving but one cycle of verse entitled *Hyjt mbi greminë*, Tiranë 1959 (Stars over the precipice).

Lit.: JORGAQI, Nasho, *Përkujtojmë poetin Gaspër Pali.* in: Nëndori (1956) 9, p. 138–142.

PALI prej Hasi. See HASI, Pal.

PAPA, Loni (1932–   ). Dramatist. Best known of his publications is the play *Cuca e maleve,* Tiranë 1967 (The mountain lass) about a woman's fight for equality among the feudal mountain tribes of northern Albania. Among his other works are *Fillo këngën çifteli,* Tiranë 1956 (Begin your song mandolin), an early volume of verse; *Një copë rrugë,* Tiranë 1976 (Down the road a bit); *Zbatharakët,* Tiranë 1976 (The barefooted ones); and *Marga,* Tiranë 1971 (Marga).

PAPAJANI, Filip (1878–1945). Pseudonym *Lipi.* Poet, prose writer, and dramatist active in the 1930s. He is the author of five historical novels: *Pelazgë, qytetnim, vllazni!* (Pelasgians, civilization, brotherhood!); *Fatbardhi* (The lucky one); *Ndreka* (Ndreka); *Bardhushi* (Bardhushi); and *Moisi Golemi* (Moisi Golemi). His works were republished in *Tregime,* Prishtinë 1971 (Tales).

PAPLEKA, Ndoc (1945–   ). Poet. Papleka was born in Tropojë and studied language and literature at the University of Tiranë. He now works as a teacher. Among his publications are *Zëri im,* Tiranë 1971 (My voice); *Ecim,* Tiranë 1974 (We're off); *Njatjeta diell,* Tiranë 1976 (Hello, sun); *Arkitektura e dritës,* Tiranë 1981 (The architecture of light); *Djepi i klithmave,* Prishtinë 1982 (The cradle of lamentation); and *Rrathët e lisit,* Tiranë 1984 (The circles of the oak).

PARRINO, Demetrio (mid 18th century). Arbëresh (q.v.) priest from Piana degli Albanesi in Sicily and father of Francesco Parrino (q.v.). He is said to have made an Albanian translation of several parts of the liturgy, some of which in verse. None of these have survived.

PARRINO, Francesco (1754–1831). Arbëresh (q.v.) priest from Piana degli Albanesi in Sicily and son of Demetrio Parrino (q.v.). He is the author of two Albanian-language poems on Saint Lazarus.

PARRINO, Paolo Maria (1710–1765). Arbëresh (q.v.) scholar born in Palazzo Adriano, Sicily. He was a student of Giorgio Guzzetta (q.v.) and later became rector of the Arbëresh seminar in Palermo, founded by the latter. Parrino is the author of a Latin work on the Albanian church and people, the full title of which is *In septem perpetuae consensionis libros albanensis ecclesia cum romana omnium matre et magistra*. Much of his work, still unpublished, deals with the origins and history of the Albanians, their customs and language (macedono-albana lingua). It served, no doubt, as a model for Nikollë Keta's (q.v.) *Tesoro di notizie su de' Macedoni*, 1777. We know Parrino to have been familiar with most Albanian-language authors of the period, such as Buzuku (q.v.), Budi (q.v.), Bardhi (q.v.), and Matrënga (q.v.).

Lit.: SCIAMBRA, Matteo, *Paolo Maria Parrino, scrittore siculo-albanese*. in: Shêjzat, 1967.

PASHA, Vaso. See VASA, Pashko.

PASHKU, Anton (1938–   ). Kosovo prose writer and dramatist. He was born in the village of Grazhdanik near Prizren and started writing while at secondary school in Prishtinë, contributing short stories to Kosovo periodicals. He now edits prose and drama for Rilindja Publishing Company in Prishtinë.

Among his works are *Tregime*, Prishtinë 1961 (Short stories); *Nji pjesë e lindjes*, Prishtinë 1965 (A part of birth); *Kulla*, Prishtinë 1968 (The tower); *Oh*, Prishtinë 1971 (Oh); *Kjasina;* Prishtinë 1973; *Lutjet e mbrëmjes*, Prishtinë 1978 (Evening prayers); and *Tragjedi moderne*, Prishtinë 1982 (Modern tragedy).

Lit.: QOSJA, Rexhep, *Proza e Anton Pashkut*. in: Jeta e re (1968) 4, p. 821–836.

PASKO, Dhimitër. See KUTELI, Mitrush.

PATA, Mulla Sali (2nd half of 18th century). Moslem poet from Shkodër. He was a contemporary of Mulla Hysen Dobraçi (q.v.) and poet at the court of the Bushatis. Pata is the author of satirical "bejts," two of which are dedicated to Karamahmud Pasha. His verse appeared in the periodicals *Dielli* (The sun) and *Albania*.

PEÇI, Shefqet (contemporary). Poet and prose writer. Among his works, dealing primarily with the partisan movement of World War II, are *Shqipëri vënd i bekuar*, Tiranë 1964 (Albania blessed country); *Kujtime dhe dokumenta nga Lufta Nacional-Çlirimtare*, Tiranë 1959, 1961 (Memoirs and documents from the National Liberation War); and *Ngjarje të ditëve të veshtira*, Tiranë 1973 (Incident of difficult times). His verse has been published in the collections: *Gjerdan këngësh*, Tiranë 1978 (Necklace of songs); *Erë malesh*, Tiranë 1981 (Mountain wind); and *Poezi*, Tiranë 1982 (Poetry).

PECI, Sotir (20th century). Publicist and political figure from Dardhë near Korçë. He studied physics and mathematics at the University of Athens before emigrating to the United States. In 1906, he founded the weekly *Kombi* (The nation) in Boston, the first Albanian-language newspaper in the United States. Peci represented Albanian-Americans at the Congress of Monastir (q.v.) in 1908 and later taught school in Elbasan and Korçë. In 1920, he became Albanian minister of education and was elected to a seat in parliament to represent Korçë. He is also the author of a grammar of Albanian and other school texts.

PEKMEZI, Gjergj (1872–1938). Scholar and linguist. Pekmezi was born in Ohrid and studied at the Greek secondary school in Monastir (Bitola) before going on to Belgrade and Vienna to finish his education. He lived most of his life in Vienna where he was appointed Albanian consul in 1924. He is remembered for his *Grammatik der albanesischen Sprache,* Vienna 1908 (Grammar of the Albanian language), one of the first scientifically written grammars of the language and the first of such written by a native speaker.

PERONE, Lluka (1920–   ). Ital. *Luca Perrone.* Arbëresh (q.v.) poet and folklorist from Eianina near Castrovillari in Calabria. He studied French and law and now teaches French language and literature.

Perone has written several collections of verse: *Lule shkëmbi,* Spezzano 1969 (Rock flowers); *Hjea e ariut,* Castrovillari 1969 (The shadow of the bear); and *Vjershe lirije,* Castrovillari 1971 (Free verse). He has also published a bilingual collection of Arbëresh tales and fables entitled *Novellistica italo-albanese,* Florence 1967.

PERRONE, Luca. See PERONE, Lluka.

PETRASSI, Luigi (–ca. 1843). Arbëresh (q.v.) scholar from the village of Cerzeto in Cosenza. He studied at the college of Sant' Adriano in San Demetrio Corone and was a close friend of Rafaele Lopez (q.v.) and Jeronim de Rada (q.v.).

Petrassi is known to have made a collection of Arbëresh folksongs from Calabria. He also translated the first canto of Byron's *Childe Harold* and Foscolo's *Dei sepolcri.* These constitute the first known translations of European romantic poetry into Albanian.

Lit.: SHUTERIQI, Dhimitër, *Autorë dhe tekste,* Tiranë 1977, p. 234–250.

PETRELA, Hasan (1927–   ). Novelist from Tiranë. He studied history and geography at the university there and took up a career in journalism. Petrela worked in China as a correspondent for the Albanian daily *Zëri i Popullit* (The People's Voice) during the Sino-Albanian alliance.

Among his works are *Të munduarit,* Tiranë 1961 (The tormented ones); a family chronicle set in a central Albanian village in the period 1906–1911; *Kronikë e viteve të paharruara,* Tiranë 1965 (Chronicle of unforgettable years); *Nisemi për në Hanoi,* Tiranë 1968 (Let's go to Hanoi); *Lindja është e kuqe,* Tiranë 1971 (The East is red); *Kurthi i gjelbër,* Tiranë 1976 (The green trap); and *Luginat,* Tiranë 1979 (The valleys).

PETRITI, Koçi (1941–   ). Poet from Korçë. He studied at the Faculty of History and Philology of the University of Tiranë and is now in the teaching profession.

Petriti has published several volumes of verse, among which: *Lirikat e majit,* Tiranë 1962 (The poetry of May); *Përsëri në udhë,* Tiranë 1967 (On the road again); *Firma e popullit tim,* Tiranë 1974 (My people's signature); and *Prush nëpër shekuj,* Tiranë 1979 (Embers over the centuries).

PETTA, Eugenio (fl. 1807). Arbëresh (q.v.) priest and poet from Sicily. He is known to have served in Chieuti, northern Apulia, in 1804 and 1807. Two Albanian-language distichs are attributed to him. They were found in the church of San Mercurio a Serracapriola and were published by Marchianò (q.v.) in 1906.

PEZA, Murteza (1919–). Albanian dramatist and prose writer from Macedonia. He was born in Elbasan where he went to school. In 1941, he moved to Yugoslavia and took part in the partisan movement in Macedonia. After the war, he worked as a journalist for the periodicals *Flaka e vëllazërimit,* Skopje (The flame of brotherhood), and *Jehona* (The echo). Peza is the author of plays, short stories, and film scenarios.

PIPA, Arshi (1920–). Albanian–American scholar and writer. Pipa was born in Shkodër where he went to school until 1938. He studied philosophy at the University of Florence from which he received the degree "dottore in filosofia" in 1942. After working as a teacher in Tiranë during the war, he was arrested in April 1946 and sent to prison for ten years. In 1957, he escaped to Yugoslavia and emigrated to the United States the following year. Pipa has since held teaching posts at various American universities and is presently professor of Italian at the University of Minnesota.

As a writer, Pipa has published works on literary criticism (esp. Albanian and Italian), aesthetics, philosophy, and several volumes of poetry. Among his major publications are *Trilogia albanica,* Munich 1978 [1) Albanian folk verse—structure and genre, 2) Hieronymus de Rada, 3) Albanian literature—social perspectives]; *Montale and Dante,* Minneapolis 1968; and four collections of Albanian verse: *Lundërtarë,* Tiranë 1944 (Sailors); *Libri i burgut,* Rome 1959 (The prison book), an account of his experiences in Albanian prisons and labour camps; *Rusha,* Munich 1968 (Rusha); and *Meridiana,* Munich 1969 (Meridiana).

PITARKA, Sulejman (contemporary). Dramatist. Pitarka is the author of plays such as *Familja e peshkatarit,* Tiranë 1955 (Engl. transl. *The fisherman's family,* Tiranë 1980); *Trimi i mirë me shokë shumë,* Tiranë 1958 (The good hero with many friends); *Heronjtë e Linasit,* Tiranë 1970 (The heroes of Linas).

PLATONICUS. See STAFA, Veli.

PODRIMJA, Ali (1942–). Kosovo poet of innovative talent. He was born in Gjakovë where he went to school. In 1961, he studied Albanology at the University of Belgrade and now writes for major Kosovo newspapers and journals. He also works as an editor for Rilindja Publishing Company.

Podrimja's verse, preoccupied with man and his destiny, is rich in unusual metaphors and similies. Among his collections of poetry are *Thirrje,* Prishtinë 1961 (The calls); *Shamija e përshëndetjeve,* Prishtinë 1963 (The handkerchiefs of greeting); *Dhimbë e bukur,* Prishtinë 1967 (Sweet pain); *Loja nën diell,*

Prishtinë 1967 (The game in the sun); *Lili dhe lirija jonë,* Skopje 1968 (The lily and our liberty); *Sampo,* Prishtinë 1969 (Sampo); *Torzo,* Prishtinë 1971 (Torso); *Hija e tokës,* Prishtinë 1971 (The shadow of the land); *Folja,* Prishtinë 1973 (The verb); *Credo,* Prishtinë 1976 (Credo); *Poezi,* Prishtinë 1978 (Poetry); *Sampo 2,* Prishtinë 1980 (Sampo 2); *Drejtpeshimi,* Prishtinë 1981 (Balance); and *Lum Lumi,* Prishtinë 1982 (Lum Lumi).

Lit.: HAMITI, Sabri, *Poezia e Ali Podrimjes.* in: Jeta e re (1973) 3, p. 461–472.

POPOVA, Tahir efendi Halil (1856?–1949). Moslem poet from Vuçitërnë in Kosovo. Author of a mevlud (poem on the birth of the prophet Mohammed) printed in Istanbul in 1876 and still widely read in Kosovo. Popova's mevlud is a translation of that of Suleyman Chelebi.

Lit.: KALEŠI, Hasan, *Mevludi kod Arbanasa.* in: Zbornik Filozofskog Fakulteta u Univerziteta Beogradu 4 (1958) p. 349–358.

PORADECI, Lasgush (1899–   ). Pseudonym of *Lazar Gusho.* Poet. Poradeci was born in the town of Pogradec on Lake Ohrid. He studied at the Romanian school in Monastir (Bitola), Macedonia, the French college in Athens, the Academy of Fine Arts in Bucharest, and finally at the University of Graz in Austria. From 1936 on, he taught secondary school in Tiranë and after the war worked for the state publishing company, doing excellent translations of Burns, Pushkin, Lermontov, Mayakovsky, Goethe, Heine, and Brecht. He now lives in retirement, spending the winter in Tiranë and the summer working in his garden in Pogradec.

His verse, much influenced by the Romanian poet Eminescu, shows a high degree of aesthetic sensitivity and elements of pantheistic mysticism. It was originally published in two collections: *Vallja e yjve,* Bucharest 1933 (The dance of the stars); and *Ylli i zemrës,* Bucharest 1937 (The star of the heart). Hardly affected by the subsequently all-pervasive influence of Socialist Realism in Albanian literature, Poradeci is widely considered one of the great Albanian poets of the twentieth century. His works have been republished in the series *Poezia shqipe 10,* Tiranë 1973 (Albanian poetry, no. 10); and in *Vdekja e nositit,* Prishtinë 1978 (The death of the pelican).

Lit.: ARAPI, Fatos, *Shënime mbi lirikën e Lasgush Poradecit.* in: Studime Filologjike 32 (1978) 4, p. 127–150; JASIQI, Ali, *Ndikimi i poezisë popullore në lirikën e Lasgush Poradecit.* in: Jehona (1966) 7, p. 74–89; QOSJA, Rexhep, *Vallet poetike të Lasgush Poradecit.* in: Jeta e re (1967) 2, p. 214–229 and 3, p. 445–468.

POSTENANI, Nikolla Ikonom (ca. 1748–1838). Scholar from the southern Albanian village of Postenan near Leskovik (hence the name). He taught school there and in Ioannina as did his brother Stefan (q.v.). Jani Vreto (q.v.) notes that it was Nikolla Postenani who first taught him to write Albanian.

Postenani is the author of translations of a grammar by the Byzantine humanist Manuel Chrysolaras and of other religious works. His Albanian translations, none of which have survived, were written in Greek script with some additional Latin letters.

POSTENANI, Stefan (early 19th century). Scholar. He was born in Postenan near Leskovik and taught school in Ioannina during the reign of Ali Pasha Tepelena. He is also said to have founded a Greek-language school in his native village. At some point before 1822, he emigrated to Russia.

Postenani is the author of a grammar of Greek, written in Albanian, mentioned by Jani Vreto (q.v.) in 1895. Like the translations of his brother Nikolla (q.v.), he used Greek script with some additional Latin letters.

POSTOLI, Foqion (1889–1927). Novelist and playwright. He was born in Korçë and studied economics in Istanbul. After returning to Korçë, he emigrated with his family to the United States and set up home in Hanson, Massachusetts. Postoli became secretary of the Vatra Federation and collaborated in the Boston newspaper *Dielli* (The sun) where much of his writing was first published. In 1921, after a fourteen-year absence, he returned to Albania to help found the Albanian Autocephalic Orthodox church.

Postoli is remembered for his sentimental novels: *Për mbrojtjen e atdheut,* 1921, 1926 (In defence of the homeland); and *Lulja e kujtimit,* 1924 (The flower of remembrance); as well as the drama *Detrya e mëmës,* Boston 1925 (A mother's duty).

POSTRIPA, Gegë. See SHIROKA, Filip.

PRENNUSHI, Vinçenc (1885–1949?). Poet, folklorist, and translator from Shkodër. Prennushi studied in Austria and was ordained as a Franciscan priest in 1908. He collected folksongs in northern Albania and contributed articles to the Catholic press—*Elçija* (The herald), *Hylli i dritës* (The day-star), and *Zani i Sh'Nout* (The voice of Saint Anthony). In 1936, he was appointed Bishop of Sapa and in 1940 Archbishop of Durrës, figuring at the same time as one of the major Catholic authors of prewar Albania. He was arrested after the war and died in prison some time between 1946 and 1954.

Prennushi's collection of folklore material was published in *Kangë popullore gegnishte,* Sarajevo 1911 (Geg folksongs). His lyric poetry, mostly on nationalist themes, appeared in *Gjeth e lule,* Shkodër 1924 (Leaves and flowers). He is also the author of religious publications and translations of works such as Silvio Pellico's *Le mie prigione* and Henryk Sienkiewicz's *Quo vadis*.

PRIFTI, Naum (1932–   ). Prose writer from Kolonjë in the Korçë region. He studied at the Faculty of History and Philology of the University of Tiranë and was editor of the periodical *Ylli* (The star).

Known primarily for his short stories, Prifti has also written plays and children's literature. Among his publications are *Tregime të fshatit,* Tiranë 1956 (Village tales); *Çezma e floririt,* Tiranë 1960 (The golden fountain); *Tregime,* Tiranë 1962 (Tales); *Një pushkë më shumë,* Tiranë 1966 (One more rifle); *Litar i zjarrtë,* Tiranë 1970 (Burning rope); *Tregime të zgjedhura,* Tiranë 1972 (Selected short stories); *Tre vetë kapërcejnë malin,* Prishtinë 1972 (Three people cross the mountain); *Njëqind vjet,* Tiranë 1983 (One hundred years); and the plays *Dasmë pa nuse,* Tiranë 1969 (Marriage without a bride); and *Mulliri e Kostë Bardhit,* Tiranë 1970 (The mill of Kostë Bardhi).

PRISHTINA, Mesihi (15th century). Turkish poet of Albanian origin. Author of a "divan."

PRUCHER, Bonaventura (fl. 1752). Italian priest and missionary in Albania. Prucher is the author of an Italian-Albanian catechism to which was apparently appendixed an Italian-Albanian lexicon. Both works, in a manuscript dated 1752, are now lost.

PULAHA, Ruzhdi (1942–   ). Short story writer and dramatist. He was born in Korçë and graduated from the University of Tiranë in 1964. Since then, he has worked as a journalist, editor, and writer. Among his publications are *Ndodhi të ditës,* Tiranë 1968 (It happened one day); *Zjarret e Shkurtit,* Tiranë 1970 (February fires); *Një vajzë në vagonin tonë,* Tiranë 1971 (A girl in our carriage); *Rruga Budi 723,* Tiranë 1975 (723 Budi St.); *Nusja e humbëtirës,* Tiranë 1975 (The bride from the sticks); *Zonja nga qyteti,* Tiranë 1976 (The lady from the city); *Shoqja nga fshati,* Tiranë 1980 (The village comrade); and *Drama,* Tiranë 1981 (Drama).

Q

QAFËZEZI, Ilo Mitkë (1889–1964). Historian, scholar, poet, and translator. Qafëzezi was from Korçë where he served as director of the Romanian school. In the 1920s, he emigrated to Bucharest and published the newspaper *Shqipëria e re* (New Albania).

Qafëzezi is the author of a volume of satirical poetry entitled *Vjersha,* 1910 (Verse); a collection of short stories *Rreshku arbëror,* Salonika 1910 (The Albanian way); and a satirical play *Dhaskall Gjoka,* 1936 (Gjoka the teacher). He also published a number of translations of note including the *Koran,* 1921, 1927, and Oscar Wilde's *Salome,* Korçë 1926. It is, however, as an historian that he is primarily remembered. Among his publications in this field are *Historia e Ali Pashës Tepelenës,* Bucharest 1917 (History of Ali Pasha Tepelena); *Histori e Napoleon Bonapartit,* Bucharest 1921 (History of Napoleon Bonaparte); and *Qysh u gjënd Amerika,* 1923 (How America was discovered).

QAFËZEZI, Luan (1922–   ). Poet and prose writer from Gjirokastër. Qafëzezi began writing during the war and worked in later years for the most part as a journalist. He has published numerous volumes of poetry, including: *Vjersha,* Tiranë 1949 (Verse); *Komunisti,* Tiranë 1953 (The Communist); *Miqësija e madhe,* Tiranë 1955 (The great friendship); *Lulja e maleve,* Tiranë 1959 (Mountain flowers); *Proletarët,* Tiranë 1960 (The proletarians); *Faqe e revolucionit,* Tiranë 1972 (Pages of the revolution); *Pa malet nuk ka maja,* Tiranë 1975 (No peaks without mountains); *Malet e Skënderbeut,* Tiranë 1980 (Scanderbeg's mountains); and *Internacionale, bota jonë e re,* Tiranë 1981 (The International, our new world). He is also the author of novels such as: *Dielli u duk përsëri,* Tiranë 1972 (The sun came out again); and *Yje dhe helmeta,* Tiranë 1977 (Stars and helmets).

QENA, Muharrem (1930–   ). Kosovo playwright and actor from Mitrovicë. He went to school in Prishtinë and studied acting in Belgrade. Qena is now a well-known actor and film director in Kosovo. He is author of the prize-winning drama *Bashkëshortët* (The spouses) as well as of verse, short stories, and song lyrics.

QIRIAZI, Dhori (1933–   ). Poet. Born in Kolonjë, Qiriazi studied at the Faculty of History and Philology of the University of Tiranë and then turned to teaching.

His early poetry appeared in the Albanian literary journal *Nëntori* (November); and he has subsequently published several verse collections: *Kur zemra rreh së pari,* Tiranë 1958 (When the heart first beats); *Ballada intime,* Tiranë 1963 (Intimate ballad); *Poema e ushtarit,* Tiranë 1968 (A soldier's poems); *Pisha me kristale,* Tiranë 1971 (The crystal torch); and *Vitet,* Tiranë 1982 (The years).

Lit.: ZIKO, Vangjush, *Biografia poetike.* in: Nëndori (1973) 6, p. 156–163.

QIRIAZI, Gjerasim (1861–1894). Writer and educator, Qiriazi attended the Greek school in his native Monastir (Bitola) in Macedonia and an American college in Samokov, Bulgaria. On finishing his studies, he was offered a job by the British and Foreign Bible Society for whom he worked in Korçë. He also began writing an Albanian grammar and is known to have preached in Albanian. In 1883, while travelling near Lake Ohrid, he was attacked by bandits who held him for ransom for over a year. In 1891, he and his sister Sevastia Qiriazi opened the first Albanian girls' school in Korçë. He died at an early age of pleurisy contracted during his period of captivity.

Qiriazi is the author of poetry, songs, and school textbooks. A selection of his writings was published by his brother Gjergj (q.v.) in the collection *Hristomathi a udëheçës për ç'do shtëpi shqiptari,* Sofia 1902 (Chrestomathy and guide for every Albanian home).

Lit.: LUARASI, Skënder, *Gjerasim Qirjazi, jeta dhe vepra,* Tiranë 1962

QIRIAZI, Gjergj (1868–1912). Publisher and writer. He was born in Monastir (Bitola) in Macedonia where he attended the Greek school. Like his brother Gjerasim (q.v.), he studied at an American college in Samokov, Bulgaria, and was hired by the British and Foreign Bible Society. He took over the direction of the first Albanian girls' school in Korçë upon the death of his brother. In 1908, he was a delegate at the Congress of Monastir (q.v.).

Qiriazi was one of the founders of an Albanian-language printing press known as "Bashkimi i kombit" (National unity). He published two volumes of literature entitled *Hristomathi a udëheçes për ç'do shtëpi shqiptari,* Sofia 1902 (Chrestomathy and guide for every Albanian home); and a collection of religious verse *Kënkë të shenjtëruara,* Sofia 1906 (Sacred songs).

QOSJA, Rexhep (1936–   ). Kosovo literary critic and writer. He studied Albanian language and literature in Prishtinë and Belgrade and is now one of Kosovo's leading critics. Among his many works are *Epizode letrare,* Prishtinë 1967 (Literary episodes); *Dialogje me shkrimtarët,* Prishtinë 1968 (Dialogues with writers); *Kritika letrare,* Prishtinë 1969 (Literary criticism); *Antologjia e lirikës shqipe,* Prishtinë 1970 (Anthology of Albanian lyrics); *Kontinuitete,* Prishtinë 1972 (Continuities); *Asdreni, jeta dhe vepra e tij,* Prishtinë 1972 (Asdreni, his life and works); *Panteoni i rralluar,* Prishtinë 1973 (The rarified Pantheon); *Vdekja më vjen prej syve të tillë,* Prishtinë 1974 (Death comes with such eyes); *Shkrimtarë dhe periudha,* Prishtinë 1975 (Writers and periods); *Anatomia e kulturës,* Prishtinë 1976 (Anatomy of culture); *Mite të zhveshura,* Prishtinë 1978 (Unclothed myths); *Prej tipologjisë deri te periodizmi,* Prishtinë 1979 (From typology to periodism); *Nocione të reja albanologjike,* Prishtinë 1983 (New notions in Albanology); and *Historia e letërsisë shqipe—Romantizmi, I, II,* Prishtinë 1984 (History of Albanian literature—Romanticism, I, II).

QULLI, Muço (–1915). Publisher. In 1911–1912, he published a journal called *Drita* (The light) and in 1914–1915 the periodical *Populli* (The people), which appeared initially in Vlorë and later in Shkodër.

QURKU, Viktor (1941–1983). Journalist and poet. Author of three collections of verse: *Midis jush,* Tiranë 1966 (Among you); *Stinë pas stine,* Tiranë 1971 (One season after another); and *Mos harroni,* Tiranë 1976 (Don't forget); a volume of essays, *Maska e humanizmit,* Tiranë 1972 (The mask of humanism); and one short story collection *Bijtë e nënave,* Tiranë 1976 (The sons of mothers).

R

RADA, Camillo de (fl. 1847). Arbëresh (q.v.) writer. Brother of Jeronim de Rada (q.v.). He was an Orthodox priest from Lecce and is reported by his brother to have written a grammar of Albanian, part of which was published by the latter.

RADA, Girolamo de. See de RADA, Jeronim.

RADA, Jeronim de (1814–1903). Ital. *Girolamo de Rada*. Arbëresh (q.v.) poet and writer. Foremost figure of the Albanian nationalist movement in nineteenth century Italy. Born the son of an Orthodox priest in Macchia Albanese, Cosenza, he attended the college of Sant' Adriano in San Demetrio Corone. Already imbued with a passion for his Albanian heritage, he began collecting folklore material. In 1834, he registered at the Faculty of Law of the University of Naples but continued his studies of literature and began writing. His first and best known Albanian-language work, under the Italian title *Poesie albanesi del secolo XV. Canti de Milosao, figlio del despota di Scutari* was published in Naples in 1836. A second poem, *Canti storici albanesi di Serafina Thopia* (Naples 1839), was seized by the Bourbon authorities because of de Rada's alleged affiliation with conspirative groups. The work was later republished by de Rada under the title *Canti di Serafina Thopia, principessa di Zadrina nel secolo XV* (Naples 1843). In 1844, de Rada got to know the French romantic poet Lamartine, whom he visited in Ischia. In the revolutionary year 1848, he founded the newspaper *L'Albanese d'Italia* (The Albanian of Italy) which included articles in Albanian. Discouraged by the events of that year, however, he left Naples and returned to San Demetrio Corone to teach school. There he managed to have Albanian included in the curriculum but was fired in 1853 for his liberal political views. In 1868, he became director of the secondary school in Corigliano Calabro, a position he held for ten years. He corresponded with leading figures of the Rilindja (q.v.) movement [Thimi Mitko (q.v.), Zef Jubani (q.v.), Dora d'Istria (q.v.)] and devoted himself to writing and publishing.

In 1883, he founded the bilingual monthly periodical *Fiamuri i Arbërit—La bandiera dell'Albania* (The Albanian flag) which lasted until 1888 and which was widely read by Albanians in the Balkans despite Turkish and Greek censorship. In 1892, he was appointed to teach Albanian language and literature at the college in San Demetrio Corone and in 1895 organized the first Albanological congress in Corigliano Calabro.

De Rada's journalistic, literary, and political activities were instrumental in creating an Albanian national literature and in fostering an awareness for the Arbëresh minority in Italy. The most popular of his literary works is the abovementioned *Canti di Milosao,* Alb. *Këngët e Milosaos* (The songs of Milosao), a long romantic ballad portraying the love of a noble youth of fifteenth century Shkodër for the shepherd's daughter Kollogre. De Rada is also the author of the epic *Skanderbeccu i paa faan,* Corigliano Calabro 1873 (Unlucky Scanderbeg) which he considered to be his masterpiece. His works have been reedited in *Vepra 1–5,* Prishtinë 1980–1983 (Works 1–5).

Lit.: DOUGLAS, Norman, *Old Calabria,* London 1930; *Jeronim De Rada. Me rastin e 150-vjetorit të lindjes,* Tiranë 1965; GUALTIERI, Vittorio G., *Girolamo de Rada, poeta albanese,* Palermo 1930; KASTRATI, Jup, *Jeronim de Rada, jeta dhe veprat,* Tiranë 1979; MARCHIANÒ, Michele, *L'Albania e l'opera di Girolamo De Rada,* Trani 1902; PIPA, Arshi, *Hieronymus de Rada,* Munich 1978; QOSJA, Rexhep, *Historia e letërsisë shqipe—Romantizmi II,* Prishtinë 1984, p. 35–184.

RADOJA, Engjëll (1820–1880). Catholic author from Shkodër. He published religious works and translations among which: *Jesu Criscti n'semer t'mesctaarit,* Rome 1862 (Jesus Christ in the sacristan's heart); and *Dotrina e kerscten me msime e me spieghime,* Shkodër 1876 (Christian doctrine with lessons and explanations).

RAMADANI, Musa (1944–   ). Kosovo poet, prose writer, and theatre critic from Gjilan. He studied Albanian language and literature in Prizren and now works for the daily newspaper *Rilindja* (Rebirth).

Ramadani has published the following works: *Mëkatet e Adamit,* Prishtinë 1967 (Adam's sins); *Thirravaje,* Prishtinë 1971 (Laments); *Neurosis,* Prishtinë 1973 (Neurosis); *Muzat nuk flejnë,* Prishtinë 1976 (The muses do not sleep); *Fluroma,* Prishtinë 1978 (Bubbles); *Zezona,* Prishtinë 1978 (The misfortunes); *Fjala në skenë,* Prishtinë 1980 (Words on the stage); and *Ligatina,* Prishtinë 1983 (The swamp).

RAMAZANI, Sulejman. See NAIBI, Sulejman.

RAMI, Ahmad (1892–   ). Egyptian-Arabic poet of Albanian origin. He was born in Cairo of a family from Crete. He finished school in Egypt and studied librarianship in France from 1922 to 1929. Returning to Cairo, he worked for the next thirty years at the National Library, Dar al-Kutub. Rami is the author of romantic verse in the style of Alfred de Musset, collections of which were first published in 1917, 1920, and 1925. He is also known in the Arabic world as the translator of the Rubaiyat of Omar Khayyam.

REKAS, Josef Bageri. See BAGERI, Josef.

RELA, Josip (1895–1966). Also known as *Josif Vlladoviq-Rela*. Playwright from the Dalmatian village of Arbanasi (Borgo Erizzo) near Zadar. He worked as a teacher and after the war as a theatre manager and school principal in Zadar. Rela is the author of dramas and comedies dealing mostly with peasant problems, which he wrote in the archaic Geg (q.v.) dialect of this Albanian-speaking village founded in 1726 by settlers from Brisk and Shestan west of Lake Shkodër. Thirteen of these plays were published in the volume *Vepra, dramat*, Prishtinë 1968 (Works, the dramas).

Lit.: JASIQI, Ali D., *Josip V. Rela,* Prishtinë 1968; QOSJA, Rexhep, *Josif Vlladoviq-Rela (1895–1966).* in: Gjurmime albanologjike (1968) 2, p. 71–101.

REM VOGLI. See ARANITI, Midhat.

RESSULI, Namik (1908–). Scholar. Originally from Berat, he contributed to the anthology *Shkrimtarët shqiptarë*, Tiranë 1941 (Albanian writers). After the death of Ernest Koliqi (q.v.) in 1975, he took over the position of professor of Albanology at the University of Rome. His monographs include *Il 'Messale' di Giovanni Buzuku*, Vatican City 1958 (The 'Missal' of Gjon Buzuku); and *I piu antichi testi albanesi*, Turin 1978 (The oldest Albanian texts).

REXHA, Zekeria (1910–1972). Pseudonyms *Ramë Zuka, Azi,* and *Shpend Dukagjini.* Prose writer from Gjakovë. Rexha attended elementary school in his native Gjakovë and Tiranë and the French secondary school in Korçë. He later went on to study philosophy in Montpellier and graduated from the University of Belgrade. Active in education both in Kosovo and in Albania itself, he taught French, Latin, and philosophy in Prishtinë and was a staff member of the University of Tiranë, where he died.

He is remembered for his satirical and humorous short stories and as one of the founders of the literary periodical *Jeta e re* (New life) in 1949. Best known of his publications is *Talush Efendia*, Prishtinë 1973 (Talush Efendia). Rexha also compiled a volume of Albanian folk songs and translated Balzac and Flaubert into Albanian.

REXHA-BALA, Kosovë (1929–). Poet. He was born in Gjirokastër and grew up in Kosovo. After studies in Belgrade, he worked for a time as a teacher and journalist in Kosovo. In 1964, he emigrated to Sweden, working at first in industry and then as a teacher in Gothenburg where he now lives.

His early works appeared in Kosovo literary journals such as *Jeta e re* (New life). He is the author of two collections of Albanian poetry: *Belbëzime poetike*, Gothenburg 1972 (Poetic stammering); and *Kronika poetike*, Gothenburg 1974 (Poetic chronicles). He has also published two volumes of verse in Swedish: *Poetiskt mummel,* Gothenburg 1980 (Poetic mumbling); and *Viskningar och slammer,* Gothenburg 1980 (Whispers and cries). Rexha-Bala now edits the Albanian-language cultural review *Stinët e jetës,* Västra Frölunda, Sweden 1981– (The seasons of life).

Lit.: HILUSHI, *Poezija e Kosovë Rexha-Balës.* in: Shêjzat 17 (1973), p. 76–82.

RIBECCO, Agostino (1867–1928). Alb. *Agostin Ribeko.* Arbëresh (q.v.) poet

and nationalist figure from Spezzano Albanese in Cosenza. He published two collections of love and patriotic poetry: *Vjersha malli,* Sofia 1902 (Poems of longing); and *Shpirt e zemër,* 1917 (Soul and heart).
RIBEKO, Agostin. See RIBECCO, Agostino.
RILINDJA. Term signifying "rebirth" and denoting the period of so-called Albanian national renaissance in the nineteenth century or, more specifically, the literary activity of the ideologists of the nationalist movement from 1878 or earlier, up to independence in 1912.

Lit.: BARTL, Peter, *Die albanischen Muslime zur Zeit der nationalen Unabhängigkeitsbewegung (1878–1912),* Wiesbaden 1968; FAENSEN, Johannes, *Die albanische Nationalbewegung,* Berlin 1980; FRASHËRI, K., *Rilindja kombëtare shqiptare,* Tiranë 1962; SKENDI, Stavro, *The Albanian national awakening 1878–1912,* Princeton 1967.

RODINÒ, Neofito (1576–1659). Cypriot missionary and writer. He spent a number of years in Arbëresh (q.v.) settlements in southern Italy (Mezzoiuso in Sicily and Barile in Potenza). From 1628 to 1643, he lived and worked in the Himarë district of southern Albania. Together with his student Dhimitri Delvina (q.v.), an Albanian priest, he translated the Christian doctrine [probably that of Ledesma, also translated by Matrënga (q.v.)] into Albanian before 1637. The Propaganda Fide in Rome, however, declined to publish the work, arguing that the Christian doctrine was already available in Albanian—a second edition of Budi's (q.v.) translation. Rodinò's work thus remained in manuscript form and is now lost.

RODOTÀ, Pompilio (fl. 1758). Italian writer of Arbëresh (q.v.) origin. Born in San Benedetto Ullano in Cosenza, he was educated at the Greek college in Rome and later appointed translator of Greek at the Vatican Library. He is the author of an Italian-language work (in three versions) dealing with the history of the church in Italy and Albania. It is entitled *Dell'origine, progresso e stato presente del rito greco in Italia,* Rome 1758, 1760, and 1763 (reprint Cosenza 1961). The second version contains a good deal of material on the Arbëresh.

ROKO, Kosmo (1925–   ). Arbëresh (q.v.) poet from San Cosmo Albanese in Cosenza. He is a handicraftsman and has been active in the organization of Arbëresh folklore groups.

RRAHMANI, Nazmi (1941–   ). Kosovo novelist from the village of Ballovc near Podujevë. He studied at the Faculty of Arts of the University of Prishtinë and now works for Rilindja Publishing Company. Rrahmani made an unexpected arrival on the literary scene in Kosovo with several very successful novels. Among his works are *Malsorja,* Prishtinë 1965 (The mountain girl); *Tymi i votrës së fikun,* Prishtinë 1969 (The smoke of an extinguished hearth); *Toka e përgjakur (1–2),* Prishtinë 1973 [The bloodstained earth (1–2)]; *Mbas vdekjes,* Prishtinë 1975 (After death); *Rruga e shtëpisë simë,* Prishtinë 1978 (The road to my house); and *Kthimi i njeriut të vdekur,* (The return of the dead man).

Lit.: HAMITI, Sabri, *A-Zh, Romanet e Nazmi Rrahmanit,* Prishtinë 1982.

RRAHMANI, Zejnullah (1952–   ). Kosovo novelist and short story writer from Ballovc near Podujevë. He studied Albanology at the Faculty of Arts of the University of Prishtinë where he now lectures. Author of *Zanoret e humbura,* Prishtinë 1974 (The lost vowels); *Udhëtimi i një pikë-uji,* Prishtinë 1976 (The journey of a drop of water); *E Bukura e Dheut,* Prishtinë 1977 (The terrestrial beauty); and *Sheshi i Unazës,* Prishtinë 1978 (Ring Square).

RRAS'E BARDHË. See HAXHIMIMA, Josif.

RROTA, Justin (1889–1964). Scholar from Shkodër. He was educated at the Franciscan school in Shkodër and at a theological seminary in Austria. Rrota is the author of various articles which appeared in Shkodër in the Franciscan press of the period. Of note are his monographs on Albanian philology and literary history, such as: *Monumenti mâ i vjetri i gjuhës shqype—D. Gjon Buzuku,* Shkodër 1930 (The oldest monument of the Albanian language—Gjon Buzuku); *Letratyra shqype,* Shkodër 1934 (Albanian literature); *Për historín e alfabetit shqyp,* Shkodër 1936, reprint Prishtinë 1968 (On the history of the Albanian alphabet); and *Shkrimtari mâ i vjetri i Italo-Shqyptarvet. Lukë Matranga,* Shkodër 1939 (The oldest Italo-Albanian writer, Lekë Matrënga).

RUCI, Llambro (1946–   ). Poet. Born in the village of Dhërmi near Vlorë, he finished his studies at the "November 7" Polytechnic in Tiranë. Until 1971, he worked at the Stalin hydroelectric power station in Bistricë. He later studied journalism at the University of Tiranë and worked for the literary periodical *Nëntori* (November).

Ruci is the author of several volumes of poetry. Among his publications are *Jam elektricist,* Tiranë 1967 (I am an electrician); *Vij nga bregdeti,* Tiranë 1970 (I come from the coast); *Gërma dashurie,* Tiranë 1973 (Letters of love); *Shpërthim prilli,* Tiranë 1976 (April awakening); *Motive të ditës,* Tiranë 1978 (Day themes); *Mes njerëzve,* Tiranë 1982 (In people's midst); and *Fletë nga fëmijëria,* Tiranë 1983 (Pages from childhood).

RUGOVA, Ibrahim (1945–   ). Kosovo critic and writer from the village of Cerrcë near Istog. He studied at the University of Prishtinë and at the Ecole Pratique des Hautes Etudes in Paris under Roland Barthes and is now on the staff of the Albanological Institute in Prishtinë.

Rugova has helped introduce structuralist methods to Albanian literary criticism. He is author of *Prekje lirike,* Prishtinë 1971 (Lyric encounters); *Kah teoria,* Prishtinë 1978 (Towards theory); *Kritika letrare* (with Sabri Hamiti), Prishtinë 1979 (Literary criticism); *Strategjia e kuptimit,* Prishtinë 1980 (The strategy of meaning); and *Vepra e Bogdanit 1675–1685,* Prishtinë 1982 (The work of Bogdani 1675–1685).

RUHI, Baba Selim (1863–1944). Bektash (q.v.) poet from Elbasan. He was educated in his native Elbasan and in Gjirokastër, taking the title Baba in 1907. He is indeed considered one of the best educated Bektash writers of the period.

Ruhi is the author of three divans in Arabic, Turkish, and Persian. Towards the end of his life, he also wrote in Albanian. The German oriental scholar Franz Babinger, who visited him at his teke, described Baba Selim's verse as being exceptionally beautiful.

RUKA, Petrit (1955–   ). Poet. He was born in Tepelenë and studied at the teacher training college in Shkodër. He now teaches school in his native Tepelenë. Ruka has published two volumes of poetry: *Rinia ime,* Tiranë 1978 (My youth); and *Atdheu fillon tek zemrat,* Tiranë 1983 (The fatherland begins where the hearts are).

S

SABRIU, Jonuz efendi (early 19th century). Moslem poet.

SADEDDIN, Omer efendi (18th century?). Moslem poet. Author of love lyrics.

SAKO, Zihni (1912–1981). Prose writer, poet, and folklorist from Gjirokastër. He was director of the Folklore Institute in Tiranë until 1979. He is best known for his short stories and sketches for adults and children, many of which deal with the partisan movement of World War II. Among his publications are *Ditë të gëzuara,* Tiranë 1953 (Happy days); *Vjersha,* Tiranë 1955 (Poetry); *Njerëz dhe ngjarje,* Tiranë 1961 (People and events); *Buka jonë e përbashkët,* Tiranë 1965 (Our common bread); *Populli dhe feja,* Tiranë 1967 (The people and religion); *Tregime të zgjedhura,* Tiranë 1973? (Selected tales); and *Studime për folklorin,* Tiranë 1984 (Studies on folklore).

Lit.: GJERGO, Edor, *Zihni Sako tregimtar.* in: Nëndori (1973) 9, p. 92–96.

SALIHU, Baba (early 20th century). Bektash (q.v.) poet from Matohasanaj near Tepelenë. He took the title of Baba at the time of the League of Prizren and opened a clandestine Albanian-language school. He was involved in the distribution of Albanian books until his arrest by the Turks in 1902. In prison, he wrote poetry and translated Arabic and Persian literature into Albanian.

ŞAMSEDDIN, Sami. See FRASHËRI, Sami.

SANTORI, Francesco Antonio (1819–1894). Arbëresh (q.v.) priest and writer. Santori was born in Santa Caterina (Pizziglia) in Cosenza. At the age of sixteen, he began his studies for the priesthood in a seminary and from 1842 to 1860 lived in a monastery of the Reformed Order of San Marco Argentano. In 1848, the year of the Neapolitan constitution, he composed a hymn entitled *Vale garees madhe* (Dance of great joy) which was published in de Rada's (q.v.) periodical *L'Albanese d'Italia.*

Santori is the author of poetry, plays, an unfinished novel entitled *Sofia Kom-*

iniate, adaptations of 112 of Aesop's fables, and an Albanian grammar written in verse. Much of his writing, in an original and rather difficult orthography, remained unpublished until recently. Of the works which were printed at the time are *Rozhaari i S. Myriis Virgkiyry,* Cosenza 1849 (Rosary of the Virgin Mary); *Il prigionero politico,* Naples 1850 (The political prisoner), containing Italian and Albanian verse; *Cryshteu i shyityruory,* Naples 1855 (The sanctified Christian), religious songs, most of which translations; and the play *E Mira* which appeared in part in de Rada's (q.v.) journal *Fiamuri i Arbërit* in 1886–1887 and which is considered the first original Albanian drama. *E Mira* has been republished (Grottaferrata 1984) by Francesco Solano (q.v.) who has also published what is considered Santori's main collection of poetry, *Il canzoniere albanese,* Corigliano Calabro 1975 (The Albanian song collection). Karmell Kandreva (q.v.) and Gj. Shkurtaj have also edited his *Satirat* (The Satires) in Studime Filologjike (1982) 1, p. 173–208.

Lit.: ALTIMARI, Francesco, *Un saggio inedito di F. A. Santori sulla lingua albanese e i suoi alfabeti,* Cosenza 1982; QOSJA, Rexhep, *Historia e letërsisë shqipe—Romantizmi II,* Prishtinë 1984, p. 185–234.

SCANDERBEG (1405–1468). Alternatively spelled *Skanderbeg,* Alb. *Skënderbeu.* Real name *George Castrioti,* Alb. *Gjergj Kastrioti.* Albanian prince and national hero.

Sent by his father as a hostage to Sultan Murad II, he converted to Islam, and after education in Edirne, was given the name Iskender and the rank of bey (hence Scanderbeg). In 1443, after the Turkish defeat at Nish at the hands of John Hunyadi, Scanderbeg abandoned the Ottoman army, returned to Albania and reembraced Christianity. He took over the fortress of Krujë and was proclaimed commander-in-chief of an independent Albanian army. In the following years, he successfully repulsed thirteen Ottoman invasions and was widely admired in the Christian world for his resistance to the Turks, being titled "Atleta Christi" by Pope Calixtus III. Albanian resistance held out until after Scanderbeg's death on January 17, 1468, at Lezhë (Alessio). In 1478, however, his fortress at Krujë was taken and Albania was to return to over four centuries of Turkish rule. For Albanians today, Scanderbeg is the symbol and quintessence of resistance to foreign domination and as such is a source of much literary inspiration.

Lit.: FRASHËRI, Kristo, *Georges Kastriote-Scanderbeg, héros national des Albanais (1405–1468),* Tiranë 1962; KOKONA, Luan, *Skanderbeg dans la littérature albanaise contemporaine.* in: Studia Albanica (1967) 2, p. 193–205; KOSTALLARI, Androkli, *La figure de Scanderbeg dans la littérature mondiale.* in: Studia Albanica (1968) 1, p. 191–216; NOLI, Fan S., *George Castrioti Scanderbeg,* New York 1947; PETROVITCH, Georges, *Scanderbeg (Georges Castriota), essai de bibliographie raisonnée,* Paris 1881 (reprint Munich 1967); *Sympoziumi për Skënderbeun,* Prishtinë 1969.

SCHIRÒ, Giovanni (19th century). Alb. *Gjon Skiroi.* Arbëresh (q.v.) writer from Piana degli Albanesi in Sicily. He is the author of an Italian-language

work of history entitled *Rapporti tra l'Epiro e il Regno delle Due Sicilie,* 1834 (Relations between Epirus and the Kingdom of the Two Sicilies).
SCHIRÒ, Giuseppe (1865–1927). Alb. *Zef Skiroi.* Arbëresh (q.v.) poet and prose writer from Piana degli Albanesi in Sicily. He studied at the Arbëresh college in Palermo where he developed an interest in Albanian literature and folklore. In 1887, together with Francesco Petta, he founded the periodical *Arbëri i ri* (New Albania) in Palermo. From 1888 to 1894, he taught classics at the Garibaldi secondary school in Palermo and in 1901 was appointed to the chair of Albanian at the Oriental Institute in Naples.

Schirò was the author of many works in Albanian and Italian, among which: *Rapsodie albanesi,* Palermo 1887 (Albanian rhapsodies); *Mili e Haidhia,* Palermo 1890 (Mili and Haidhia), an idyllic, Odyssean poem in eighteen cantos; *Këngat e luftës,* Palermo 1897 (The battle songs), a selection of poems on nationalist themes written in Shkodër; *Te dheu i huaj,* Palermo 1900 (In a foreign land), a long idyllic poem on the epic flight of the fifteenth century Albanians from their homeland and the colonization of Sicily; *Canti popolari dell'Albania,* Palermo 1901 (Folksongs from Albania); *Canti sacri delle colonie albanesi di Sicilia,* Naples 1907 (Sacred songs of the Albanian colonies of Sicily); *Canti tradizionali ed altri saggi delle colonie albanesi di Sicila,* Naples 1923 (Traditional songs and other essays of the Albanian colonies of Sicily); *Këngat e litorit,* Palermo 1926 (The songs of the littoral) inspired by the rise of the Italian Fascist movement; and *Këthimi,* Florence 1965 (The return), an epic poem about Albanian independence.

Lit.: PETROTTA, Gaetano, *Poeti siculo-albanesi* (Palermo 1950), p. 25–36.
SCHIRÒ, Paolo (1866–1941). Alb. *Pal Skiroi.* Arbëresh (q.v.) scholar. He was born in Piana degli Albanesi in Sicily and, like his brother Giuseppe Schirò (q.v.), studied at the Arbëresh college in Palermo, of which he later became rector. Aside from numerous religious publications, which appeared in particular in his weekly periodical *Fiala e t'in' Zoti* (The word of our Lord) in 1912–1913, he is remembered for having brought to light the Liturgy of Gjon Buzuku (q.v.) (1555).
SCHIRÒ DI MAGGIO, Giuseppe (1944–   ). Alb. *Xhusepe Skiro di Maxho.* Arbëresh (q.v.) poet and translator from Piana degli Albanesi in Sicily. He studied literature and now teaches in Settimo Torinese near Turin. Among his verse collections are *Nëpër udhat e parrajsit shqipëtarë e t'arbreshë,* 1974 (On the roads of Albanian and Arbëresh paradise); *Sunata,* 1976 (Sonnets); *Trima të rinj arbëreshë apo arsyeja e gjëravet,* 1976 (New Arbëresh heroes or the origins of things); and *Gjuha e bukës,* Prishtinë 1981 (The language of bread). He has also translated Leopardi's *Paralipomeni della batracomiomachia* into Albanian: *Lufta e mivet me brethqit,* 1975.
SCHIRÒ DI MODICA, Giuseppe (contemporary). Alb. *Xhusepe Skiro di Modika.* Arbëresh (q.v.) poet from Sicily. His verse has appeared in a number of Arbëresh literary periodicals.

SELIMI, Fehime (1954–   ). Kosovo poetess. She was born in Preševo and attended school in Skopje and Prishtinë. After studies at the Faculty of Arts of the University of Prishtinë, she took up journalism and now works for the Kosovo regional council. Selimi has published two volumes of verse: *Fjala ime ka etje*, Skopje 1980 (My speech is thirsty); and *Lule në ethe*, Prishtinë 1982 (Flowers in heat).

SEREMBE, Cosmo (1879–1938). Arbëresh (q.v.) poet from San Cosmo Albanese in Cosenza. The grandson of Zef Serembe (q.v.), he worked as a lawyer and devoted himself to the study of Albania. In addition to various articles in Italian, he is the author of a volume of Albanian verse entitled *Kënka lirie*, Bucharest 1898 (Songs of freedom). His *Kënkat e Krujës* (The songs of Krujë), an epic poem in twenty-five cantos, remained unpublished.

SEREMBE, Giuseppe. See SEREMBE, Zef.

SEREMBE, Zef (1843–1901). Ital. *Giuseppe Serembe*. Arbëresh (q.v.) romantic poet. He was born in San Cosmo Albanese (Alb. Strigari) in Cosenza and, though of a poor family, travelled widely through Italy and France trying to win support for the Albanian cause. In 1875, he sailed for Brazil, where with the help of a letter of recommendation from Dora d'Istria (q.v.), he was received by Emperor Dom Pedro II. He soon returned to Europe, however, disappointed and dejected. Landing in Cadiz, he made his way on foot back to Italy, losing most of his manuscripts (poetry, drama, and a translation of the Psalms of David) on the way. Only thirty-nine poems survived and were published by his grandson Cosmo Serembe (q.v.). Towards the end of his life, he emigrated a second time to South America. In 1897, he managed to start a new life in Buenos Aires, but four years later, mentally exhausted, he died in São Paolo.

Serembe's verse, despondent and pessimistic in character, though often idealistic and patriotic in inspiration, ranks among the best lyric poetry in Albanian. Some of his early poems appeared in journals of the period such as Schirò's (q.v.) *Arbëri i ri* (New Albania) and in the bilingual collection *Poesie italiane e canti originali tradotti dall'albanese*, Cosenza 1883 (Italian poetry and original songs translated from the Albanian). His remaining verse was published in *Vjersha*, Milan 1926 (Verse).

Lit.: KODRA, Klara, *Vepra poetike e Zef Serembes*, Tiranë 1975; SHUTERIQI, Dhimitër, *Mbi jetën e krijimtarinë e Zef Serembes*. in: Buletin i Universitetit Shetëror të Tiranës. Seria Shkenc. Shoq. (1961) 4, p. 69–105; and *Autorë dhe tekste*, Tiranë 1977, p. 251–309.

SHANTOJA, Lazër (1892–1945). Poet, essayist, and translator from Shkodër. He studied for the priesthood in his native city and in Austria. In the spring of 1945, he was executed for collaboration with the Fascists. His works appeared in the Catholic press of prewar Shkodër.

Shantoja is remembered primarily for his translations from the German: Schiller's *Wilhelm Tell* and *Das Lied von der Glocke;* and Goethe's *Hermann und Dorothea* and parts of *Faust*.

SHAPLLO, Dalan (1928–   ). Critic, essayist, and short story writer. Shapllo was born in Gjirokastër and attended secondary school in Tiranë. After the war, he studied at the Faculty of Arts of Lomonosov University in Moscow and is now a professor of literature at the University of Tiranë and editor of the literary periodical *Nëntori* (November).

Among Shapllo's works are *Përtëritje,* Tiranë 1960 (Renewal); *Në bregun e hijes,* Tiranë 1965 (On the shady bank); *Letërsia dhe realiteti ynë,* Tiranë 1968 (Literature and our reality); *Kohë lufte,* Tiranë 1971 (Wartime); *Dukuri dhe vepra letrare,* Tiranë 1974 (Phenomena and literary works); *Vështrime teoriko-letrare,* Tiranë 1978 (Theoretical and literary reflections); and *Vepra dhe probleme të realizmit socialist,* Tiranë 1982 (Works and problems of Socialist Realism).

SHEH MALIQI. See MALIQI, Hilmi.

SHEHU, Agim (1934–   ). Poet and essayist. He was born in Kurvelesh near Vlorë and finished his studies at the teacher training college in Tiranë in 1957. He has since worked as a teacher and journalist in various parts of Albania.

Shehu has published the following volumes of poetry: *Horizont i kaltërt,* Tiranë 1959 (Blue horizon); *Vite pa thinja,* Tiranë 1970 (Years without grey hair); *Lirikë,* Prishtinë 1972 (Lyrics); *Vallja e kalldrëmeve,* Tiranë 1977 (Street dance); *Çeliku dhe liria,* Tiranë 1978 (Steel and freedom); and *Gurra e fjalës,* Tiranë 1980 (The source of words). His essays and literary sketches have appeared in *Fjalë nga zemra,* Tiranë 1977 (Words from the heart); and *Me buzën në gaz,* Tiranë 1979 (Smile at the lips).

SHEHU, Bashkim (1955–   ). Prose writer from Tiranë. He studied at the University of Tiranë and now works for "New Albania" Film Studios. A collection of his short stories was published in *Një kohë tjetër,* Tiranë 1977 (Another age).

SHEHU, Maksut (1930–   ). Kosovo poet from Prishtinë. He studied biology in Belgrade and worked for twenty years as journalist for the Kosovo newspaper *Rilindja* (Rebirth), serving among other things as New York correspondent, before joining RTV Belgrade. Shehu has published nineteen books, including verse for adults and children. Among his publications are *Kunora e kuqe,* Prishtinë 1960 (The red crown); *Flamujt e zemrës,* Prishtinë 1964 (The flags of the heart); *Gruni dhe ari,* Prishtinë 1967 (Wheat and acre); *Nipi i minatorit,* Prishtinë 1969 (The miner's grandson); *Dielli lind në jug,* Prishtinë 1971 (The sun is born in the south); *Numra,* Prishtinë 1973 (Numbers); *Ylli në zemër,* Prishtinë 1976 (Star in the heart); and *Bardh e zi,* Prishtinë 1985 (White and black).

SHËMBËRDHENJI, Baba Meleq (fl. 1914). Bektash (q.v.) poet. He was from the Skrapar region and was educated at a Bektash teke in Cairo, where he became a dervish. He returned to Albania and took part in the nationalist movement. Shëmbërdhenji held the title Baba at the teke of the same name until 1914 when the latter was destroyed. Author of both nationalist and religious verse, he is reputed to have been one of the best Bektash poets of the period.

SHEMIMIU. See SHKODRA, Shemimi.

SHIROKA, Filip (1859–1935). Pseudonym *Gegë Postripa*. Lyric poet from Shkodër. Like many other Albanian intellectuals of the period, he spent most of his life in exile. Though devoted to the nationalist cause, he was forced in 1880 to emigrate to the Middle East, living in Egypt and Lebanon where he worked as an engineer in railway construction.

Shiroka's poetry is characterized by a lyric nostalgia for his homeland. Some of his early verse appeared in periodicals such as *Elçija* (The herald) and Faik Konica's (q.v.) *Albania*. The collection *Zâni i zêmrës*, Shkodër 1933 (The voice of the heart) was published two years before his death in Beirut. Perhaps best known of his poems is the wistful *Shko dallndryshë* (Fly away, swallow).

SHIROKA, Gjon (–1914). Translator and publicist from Shkodër. Born of a well-to-do family, he dedicated himself to the nationalist cause. He translated and published Silvio Pellico's moral treatise *Dei doveri degli uomini* in *Ligjiratë mbi detyrat e trimit*, Shkodër 1912 (Discourse on the duties of man). Shiroka was murdered on August 30, 1914.

SHITA, Vehap (1924–). Kosovo drama critic, publicist, and translator. He was born in Gjakovë and went to secondary school in Skopje and Prishtinë. Since the war, he has worked for various newspapers and periodicals and for Radio Prishtinë, contributing reviews of literature and drama. Among his publications are *Skena shqipe*, Prishtinë 1964 (The Albanian stage); *Gjurmave të letërsisë*, Prishtinë 1970 (In the traces of literature); and *Kur ndizen dritat*, Prishtinë 1977 (When the lights go on).

SHKODRA, Hysen efendi (18th century?). Poet, perhaps identical with Mulla Hysen Dobraçi (q.v.). Author of two poems in a nineteenth century manuscript, no. III F 36, preserved in the National Library in Tiranë. Nothing is known of the author.

SHKODRA, Jakin. See GURAKUQI, Luigj.

SHKODRA, Shemimi (fl. 1835). Lexicographer from Shkodër. He is the author of an Albanian-Turkish dictionary of about 1000 words. The work, entitled *Nytkë* (Speech), was written in 1835 in an Arabic script of forty-five letters and according to its author was to serve the needs of Turkish soldiers in Albania and of Albanians who knew no Turkish. The Albanian is that of Shkodër mixed with elements of Berat dialect, which leads us to the assumption that the author must have lived in Berat for some time.

Lit.: MYDERRIZI, Osman, *Nji fjalor i vjetër shqip-tyrqisht*. in: Buletini i Institutit të Shkencave 1 (1951); ROSSI, Ettore, *Un lessico rimanto turco-albanese composto a Scutari nel 1835*. in: Rivista degli studi orientali (1951).

SHKODRANI, Vasa Pasha. See VASA, Pashko.

SHKRELI, Adem (1936–). Kosovo dramatist and poet from the village of Shkrel in the mountainous Rugovo area near Pejë. He attended school in

Pejë, Prishtinë, and Belgrade and now works as a journalist for the Kosovo daily newspaper *Rilindja* (Rebirth). His verse has been published in the collection *Zemra e verbët,* Prishtinë 1971 (The blind heart.)

SHKRELI, Azem (1938–). Kosovo poet and prose writer. He was born in the village of Shkrel near Pejë and studied Albanology in Prishtinë. He was president of the Writers' Union, a theatre director in Prishtinë, and head of "Kosova Film" studios.

Both his prose and his highly expressive poetry deal among other things with life in the Rugovo mountains and the conflict between traditional ways and a modern Socialist society. His early publications include the verse collections *Bulzat,* Prishtinë 1960 (The buds); *Engjujt e rrugëve,* Prishtinë 1963 (The angels of the roads); *E di një fjalë prej guri,* Prishtinë 1969 (I know a word of stone); the short story collection *Sytë e Evës,* Prishtinë 1965 (Eve's eyes); the novel *Karvani i bardhë,* Prishtinë 1960 (The white caravan); and a four act dramatization of it *Fosilet,* Prishtinë 1968 (The fossils). Among his more recent works are *Lotët e maleve,* Prishtinë 1974 (The mountain tears); *Nga bibla e heshtjes,* Prishtinë 1975 (From the Bible of silence); *Vjersha,* Prishtinë 1977 (Verse); *Pagëzimi i fjalës,* Prishtinë 1981 (The baptism of speech); and the drama *Varri i qyqes,* Prishtinë 1983 (The cuckoo's grave).

Lit.: ALIU, Ali, *Shtresat artistike në prozën e Azem Shkrelit.* in: Jeta e re (1973) 3, p. 453–460; MEKULI, Hasan, *Koordinatat jetësore në poezinë e Azem Shkrelit.* in: Jeta e re (1970) 3, p. 435–460; VINCA, Agim, *Poet i ideve dhe i giykimit të thellë.* in: Jeta e re (1983) 4, p. 662–679.

SHKRELI, Ymer (1945–). Kosovo writer from the Rugova region near Pejë. He attended school and university in Prishtinë. Ymer Shkreli is among the most prolific of the modern Kosovo writers, with a multitude of prose works and poetry for adults and for children. He has also written plays and film scripts. Among his publications are the poetry collections *Ditari i Hajnit,* Prishtinë 1971 (Heine's diary); *Romanella,* Prishtinë 1974 (Romanella); *Febris,* Prishtinë 1975 (Febris); *Kërkoj dënim me vdekje,* Prishtinë 1978 (I demand punishment by death); *Balcanica,* Prishtinë 1980 (Balcanica); *Poezi të zgjedhura,* Prishtinë 1983 (Selected poetry); the novels *Njeriu në bisht,* Prishtinë 1975 (The squatter); *Vdekja në ajër të pastër,* Prishtinë 1976 (Death in clean air); *Nata nyjë,* Prishtinë 1982 (Knot night); *Pikëpjekja,* Prishtinë 1982 (The meeting); short stories *Bima e dreqit,* Prishtinë 1981 (The devil's plant); and drama *Trilogji ilire,* Prishtinë 1977 (Illyrian trilogy).

SHLLAKU, Gjon (–1946). Catholic priest and publicist. He finished his studies at the University of Louvain in Belgium and became director of the Franciscan periodical *Hylli i dritës* (The day-star) after the Italian invasion of Albania in 1939. As the main organizer of the anti-Communist "Bashkimi Kombtar" (The national union), he was arrested and executed at the beginning of 1946.

SHOQËRI E TË SHTYPURIT SHKRONJA SHQIP. "Society for the publication of Albanian writing," also known as the Istanbul Society, founded in Istanbul in the autumn of 1879. The aims of the society included the publication and distribution of books and writing in Albanian, the founding of a printing press, a newspaper, and national schools in Albania. Among its members were Sami Frashëri (q.v.) who was elected its president, Abdyl Frashëri, Koto Hoxhi (q.v.), Pandeli Sotiri (q.v.), Pashko Vasa (q.v.), Jani Vreto (q.v.), and Mehmed Ali Vrioni.

SHUKRIU, Edi. See SHUKRIU-HOTI, Edi.

SHUKRIU-HOTI, Edi (1950–   ). Kosovo poetess from Prizren. She studied archeology in Belgrade and now lectures at the University of Prishtinë. Author of the collections: *Sonte zemra ime feston,* Prishtinë 1972 (Tonight my heart rejoices); *Gjakim,* Prishtinë 1979 (Yearning); and *Legjenda e Hasit,* Tiranë 1980 (The legend of Has).

SHUNDI, Stefan (1906–   ). Playwright and publicist from Tiranë. He contributed articles and reviews to Tiranë periodicals such as *Gazeta e Tiranës* (The Tiranë gazette) and *Drita* (The light). He is also the author of the lyrical tragedy *Kalorësi i vdekjes* (The rider of death).

SHUTERIQI, Dhimitër S. (1915–   ). Poet, prose writer, critic, and scholar. Born in Elbasan, Shuteriqi finished secondary school at the French lycée in Korçë before continuing his studies in philosophy and law in France in 1936. He returned to Albania and took part in the partisan movement of World War II. From 1946 to 1973, he was president of the Albanian League of Writers and Artists and is now a member of the Albanian Academy of Sciences.

Shuteriqi is one of the most influential literary historians and theoreticians in Albania. As such, he is noted not only for his short stories and poetry but for his research in the fields of history, folklore, literature, and language. Among his literary works are the poetry collections *Kangët e rinisë së parë,* 1935 (The songs of first youth); *Kangë,* 1936 (Songs); *O Ptoleme,* Elbasan 1945 (O Ptolemy); *Mbi krahn e praruar të paqës,* Tiranë 1950 (On the gilded wings of peace); *Poemë e pambaruar,* Tiranë 1972 (Unfinished poem); *Vargje të zgjedhura,* Tiranë 1974 (Selected verse); the short story collections *Pesë tregime,* Tiranë 1953 (Five stories); *Rruga e rinisë,* Tiranë 1963 (Engl. transl. *The lute and the rifle,* Tiranë 1965); *Këngë në minierë,* Tiranë 1965 (Song in the mines); *Tregime të zgjedhura,* Tiranë 1972 (Selected short stories); *Maratonomaku ynë,* Tiranë 1977 (Our soldier of Marathon); and the novel *Çlirimtarët,* Tiranë 1952, 1955 (The liberators) which set the pace for postwar Albanian prose. Much of his writing has been republished in the eight volume edition *Vepra letrare,* Tiranë 1982 (Literary works).

Of his scholarly monographs of note are *Metrika shqipe,* Tiranë 1947 (Albanian metrics); *Letërsia shqipe e rilindjes kombëtare,* Tiranë 1947 (Albanian literature of the national renaissance); *Folklora shqipe,* Tiranë 1947 (Albanian folklore); *Letërsia e re shqipe,* Tiranë 1950 (New Albanian literature); *Antologji e letërsisë shqipe,* Tiranë 1955 (Anthology of Albanian literature); *Histori e letërsisë shqipe,* Tiranë 1955 (History of Albanian literature); *Nëpër shekujt letrarë,* Tiranë 1972 (Over the centuries in literature); *Gjurmime letrare,* Tiranë 1974 (Literary research); *Shkrimet shqipe në vitet 1332–1850,* Tiranë 1976 (Albanian writing in the years 1332–1850); *Autorë dhe tekste,* Tiranë 1977 (Authors and texts); and *Mbi Barletin dhe shkrime të tjera,* Tiranë 1979 (On Barleti and other writers).

SHUTERIQI, Simon (1883–   ). Writer and journalist from Elbasan. He is the author of *Abetare shqipe,* 1911 (Albanian spelling book); *Varri i dashnorëvet,* Monastir 1911 (The lovers' grave); and *Jetëshkrimi i Kostandin Kristoforidhit,* Monastir 1911 (Biography of Kostandin Kristoforidhi).

SILIQI, Drago (1930–1963). Meditative lyricist and critic from Tiranë. Siliqi took part in World War II as a partisan and studied literature in Moscow. He returned to Albania to teach and work as a journalist and was later appointed director of the Naim Frashëri Publishing Company.

His poetry has appeared in the collections: *Zgjimi i pranverës,* Tiranë 1951 (The awakening of spring); *Këngë e re për dashurinë e vjetër,* Tiranë 1959 (A new song for an old love); *Kur zemra flet,* Tiranë 1970 (When the heart speaks); and *Poezi,* Tiranë 1980 (Poetry). He is also the author of the study *Në kërkim të së resë,* Tiranë 1969 (In search of something new).

SILIQI, Llazar (1924–   ). Poet. Son of the poet Risto Siliqi (q.v.), he was born in Shkodër. Llazar Siliqi was early to join the Communist movement. For his activities he was interned in 1944 in the Nazi concentration camp at Prishtinë, an ordeal he later described in verse of Mayakovskian passion: *Prishtina,* Tiranë 1949 (Prishtina). After the war, he studied at the Gorky Institute of World Literature in Moscow. Following graduation, he returned to Albania and became editor of the literary periodical *Nëndori* (November).

Siliqi has written not only poetry of note but also film and opera scenarios. Among his verse collections are *Rruga e lumtunis,* Tiranë 1950 (The road of happiness); *Vjersha dhe poema,* Tiranë 1953 (Verses and poems); *Mësuesi,* Tiranë 1955 (The teacher); *Thirrja e zemrës,* Tiranë 1957 (The call of the heart); *Kangët nuk mbeten kurr të pakëndueme,* Tiranë 1959 (The songs never remain unsung); *Ringjalle,* Tiranë 1960 (Resurrection); *Kangë entuziaste,* Tiranë 1966 (The great spring); *Nga porti i ri deri ku vlon malësia,* Tiranë 1967 (From the great port to where the mountains teem); *Festë,* Tiranë 1970 (Festival); *Poema e dritës,* Tiranë 1972 (Poem of light); *Heshtja që flet,* Prishtinë 1972 (The silence that speaks); *Ju flet Tirana,* Tiranë 1974 (This is Tirana calling); and *Përpara historisë,* Tiranë 1979 (Before history).

SILIQI, Risto (1882–1936). Writer, poet, and nationalist figure. Father of the poet Llazar Siliqi (q.v.), he was born in Shkodër where he attended a Serbian elementary school and a Turkish secondary school. He later moved to Montenegro and began to take an active part in the Albanian nationalist movement. In 1911, he participated in the armed insurrection against Turkish rule in the northern Albanian Malësia region. The events of this revolt he recorded in his chronicle *Pasqyra e ditëve të pergjakëshme,* Trieste 1912 (Mirror of bloody days). Together with Hilë Mosi (q.v.), he published the periodical *Shqypnia e re* (New

Albania) in 1913–1914. In later years, he worked as a lawyer in Shkodër where he died.

Siliqi's literary and publishing activities cover the years 1905–1915. He is the author of about 4000 lines of mostly patriotic verse, some of which appeared in journals of the period such as *Kalendari kombiar* (The national calendar) and *Liri e Shqipërisë* (Freedom of Albania). Much of his work was republished in *Vepra të zgjedhura,* Tiranë 1956 (Selected works).

Lit.: FULLANI, Dhimitër, *Risto Siliqi (1882–1936).* in: Buletin i Shkencave Shoqërore (1956) 2, p. 58–100.

SIRDANI, Aleksander (20th century). Folklorist from Bogë in northern Albania. Sirdani studied for the priesthood in Shkodër and returned to work in his native Bogë. He wrote a number of articles in the periodical *Hylli i dritës* (The day-star) and the monograph *Fjalë ari,* Shkodër 1928 (Folk sayings).

SIRDANI, Marin (1887–   ). Franciscan priest and historian from northern Albania. He is the author of several articles in *Hylli i dritës* (The day-star) and the work *Skanderbegu mbas gojdhanash,* Shkodër 1926 (Scanderbeg according to legend).

SKANDERBEG . See SCANDERBEG.

SKËNDERBEU. See SCANDERBEG.

SKENDO, Lumo. See FRASHËRI, Mid'hat.

SKIRO DI MAXHO, Xhusepe. See SCHIRÒ DI MAGGIO, Giuseppe.

SKIRO DI MODIKA, Xhusepe. See SCHIRÒ DI MODICA, Giuseppe.

SKIROI, Gjon. See SCHIRÒ, Giovanni.

SKIROI, Pal. See SCHIRÒ, Paolo.

SKIROI, Zef. See SCHIRÒ, Giuseppe.

SOLANO, Francesco (1914–   ). Pseudonym *Dushko Vetmo.* Arbëresh (q.v.) poet, prose writer, and scholar. He was born in Frascineto in Calabria of a family of Çamërian origin and moved in 1934 to Buenos Aires where he studied theology and foreign languages and later worked as a teacher and priest. He returned to Italy and is presently professor of Albanian at the University of Cosenza.

Solano is the author of works in a wide variety of genres. Among his publications are *Bubuqe t'egra,* Buenos Aires 1946 (Wild buds); *Tregimet e lëronit,* Trebisacce 1975 (Ploughing tales); and *Te praku,* Trebisacce 1977 (At the threshold); and the textbook *Manuale di lingua albanese,* Corigliano Calabro 1972 (Albanian language manual).

SOTIRI, Pandeli (1852–1890). Publicist and nationalist figure. Little is known of his early life. In 1879, he was living in Istanbul and was among the founding members of the society for the publication of Albanian writing. In 1884, he published the periodical *Dituria* (Knowledge), the first Albanian-language journal in Turkey. Sotiri was also responsible for the establishment in Korçë of the first Albanian school in 1887. As a result of political intrigues, though, he was soon forced to leave Korçë and returned to Istanbul where he died under mysterious circumstances in 1890 or 1891.

SPAHIU, Xhevahir (1945–   ). Poet. Born in Skrapar, he studied at the

University of Tiranë before taking up a career as a journalist. He now works for the literary periodical *Nëndori* (November).

Among Spahiu's publications are the verse collections *Mëngjes sirenash,* Tiranë 1970 (Siren morning); *Vdekje perëndive,* Tiranë 1977 (Death of the gods); *Agime shqiptare,* Tiranë 1981 (Albanian dawns); and the collection of essays *Dyer dhe zemra të hapura,* Tiranë 1977 (Open doors and hearts).

SPASSE, Sterjo (1914–   ). Novelist and short story writer. He was born, the son of poor parents, in the village of Gllomboç on Lake Prespa and went to school in Elbasan. In 1932, he worked as a teacher initially in the village of Derviçan south of Gjirokastër, studied in Italy, and after the war, continued his studies in Tiranë and at the Gorky Institute of World Literature in Moscow.

Spasse has had a major impact on the development of modern Albanian prose. His first work, the novel *Pse,* 1935 (Why), portrays the dilemma of a young intellectual in a backward rural society. Written in diary form, this nihilistic classic of prewar Albanian literature is based largely on Spasse's own experiences as a village teacher. A second novel *Afërdita,* 1944 (Afërdita) is similar in theme, though more influenced by Socialist Realism, which the author was later to adopt and develop. His *Ata nuk ishin vetëm,* Tiranë 1952 (They were not alone), a description of struggle and the first awakening of class conscience among the pre-war Albanian peasantry, was honoured with the Prize of the Republic. *Afërdita përsëri në fshat,* Tiranë 1955 (Afërdita in the countryside again) once more takes up the theme of the village teacher from a more consciously Socialist perspective. In *Buzë liqenit,* Tiranë 1961 (At the lakeside) and *Zjarret,* Tiranë 1972 (The fires), Spasse analyzes the psychological impact and ideological problems of collectivization. Among his further novels are *Zgjimi,* Tiranë 1974 (Engl. transl. *The awakening,* Tiranë 1980); *Pishtarë,* Tiranë 1975 (Torches); *Ja vdekje, ja liri,* Tiranë 1978 (Liberty or death) which deal with the Rilindja (q.v.) period leading to Albanian independence; and *Kryengritësit,* Tiranë 1983 (The rebels). Spasse is also the author of several collections of short stories and of translations of Victor Hugo, Harriet Beecher-Stowe, and the Bulgarian writer Ivan Vazov. His works have been republished in the eight volume edition *Vepra letrare,* Tiranë 1981 (Literary works).

Lit.: GJATA, Fatmir, *Shkrimtari Sterjo Spasse.* in: Nëndori (1964) 12, p. 33–42.

SPIRU, Nako (20th century). Pamphleteer and journalist. Secretary of the Central Committee of the Communist youth movement. He was the author of articles and editorials in World War II attacking Fascism and *Balli Kombëtar* (The national front), the anti-Communist resistance movement which for a time rivalled the Communists.

STAFA, Felice (fl. 1845). Ital. *Felice Staffa.* Arbëresh (q.v.) writer from Falconara in Cosenza. Little is known of his life. In 1820–1821, he studied in Naples under the poet Gabriele Rossetti, father of the English Pre-Raphaelites Christina and Dante Rossetti. He is said to have taken part in the revolution of 1848 and was sentenced to three years in prison.

Stafa published the first collection of Albanian folksongs, entitled *Canti al-*

banesi, Naples 1845 (Albanian songs). A copy of the now rare edition is preserved at the National Library in Tiranë.

Lit.: SHUTERIQI, Dhimitër, *Autore dhe tekstë,* Tiranë 1977 p. 219–233.

STAFA, Qemal (1921–1942). Pseudonym *Brutus.* Revolutionary figure and poet. Born in Elbasan, he attended school in Shkodër and Tiranë. He collaborated, together with his brother Veli (q.v.) in the journal *Bota e re* (New World), which was closely associated with the founding of the Albanian Communist party. Stafa is said to have studied in Italy and returned to Albania to become founder and first political secretary of the Communist youth movement. He died on May 5, 1942, in Tiranë in a shootout with the police.

Stafa is the author of poetry, sketches, and tales showing similarities with the work of Migjeni (q.v.). His elegaic poem *Hijes së tim vlla* (In my brother's shadow) was written soon after Veli's death. His works are collected in the volume *Qortimet e vjeshtës,* Tiranë 1962 (Autumn accusations).

STAFA, Veli (1914–1939). Pseudonym *Platonicus.* Revolutionary figure and poet. Born in Elbasan, he went to school in Shkodër and studied medicine in Bologna. He died of an illness shortly after graduation in March 1939. His writings have been published in *Vepra letrare,* Tiranë 1982 (Literary works).

STAFFA, Felice. See STAFA, Felice.

STAVRE, Aleks. See ASDRENI.

STËRMILLI, Haki (1895–1953). Prose writer and dramatist from Dibër, now in Macedonia. He went to school in Salonika and Monastir (Bitola) before emigrating, during a wave of political turbulence, to Albania at the age of eighteen. He was a member of the "Bashkimi" (The union) Society (q.v.) and became its secretary after the death of Avni Rustemi. With the fall of the democratic government of 1924, Stërmilli went into exile, living in Italy, France, Austria, Germany, the Soviet Union, and Yugoslavia. In 1929, he was extradited by the Serbian authorities to Zogist-ruled Albania and sentenced to five years in prison. During World War II, he led the resistance movement in his native Dibër region. In later years, he was appointed director of the National Library and of the Museum of the National Liberation War and was elected as a member of the People's Assembly.

Stërmilli is the author of novels, plays, short stories, and translations. He is remembered in particular for his nationalist dramas: *Dibraneja e mjerueme,* 1923 (The Dibër woman in distress); *Dashuri e besnikëri,* 1923 (Love and fidelity); and *Agimi i lumnuëshem,* 1924 (Joyful dawn). His diary *Burgu,* 1935 (Prison) is an account of his years in prison (1929–1935). Most widely read of his works is the sentimental novel in diary form *Sikur t'isha djalë,* 1936 (If I were a boy), which recounts the struggles of a young girl named Dija (Knowledge) for emancipation in an oppressive patriarchal society. Among his other works are *Shtigjet e lirisë,* Tiranë 1967 (The paths of freedom); and *Kalorësi e Skënderbeut,* Tiranë 1967 (The knight of Scanderbeg). His writings have been republished in *Vepra letrare 1–3,* Tiranë 1983 (Literary works 1–3).

Lit.: JORGAQI, Nasho, *Rruga e një shkrimtari patriot.* in: Nëndori (1966)

4, p. 90–107; RRECAJ, Kajtaz, *Krijimtaria letrare e Haki Stërmillit*. Doctoral dissertation, Prishtinë 1984.

STRATICÒ, Alberto (fl. 1896). Arbëresh (q.v.) scholar. Author of one of the first histories of Albanian literature *Manuale di letteratura albanese*, Milan 1896.

STRATICÒ, Vincenzo (1822–1886). Alb. *Vinçenc Stratigo*. Arbëresh (q.v.) poet from Lungro in Calabria. He was taught at the college of Sant' Adriano in San Demetrio Corone by de Rada (q.v.). In 1848, he took an active part in the revolution and in 1859 headed an uprising against the corrupt Kingdom of the Two Sicilies. The following year, he joined Garibaldi's Red Shirts and participated in the battle for Naples.

Author of political, satirical, and love verse, Straticò is considered the first Socialist poet of the Arbëresh. His works were never published during his lifetime but circulated in manuscript form.

Lit.: KAMSI, Kolë, *Vinçenc Stratigo, poet arbëresh*. in: Buletin i Universitetit Shtetëror të Tiranës. Seria Shkenc. Shoq. (1959) 1, p. 80–94; KODRA, Ziaudin, *Vinçenc Stratigo (1822–1885)*. in: Studime Filologjike (1965) 4, p. 71–89.

STRATIGO, Vinçenc. See STRATICÒ, Vincenzo.

SULEJMAN, Abdullah. See KONISPOLI, Abdullah Sulejman.

SULEJMANI, Hivzi (1912–1975). Kosovo prose writer, playwright, and poet from Mitrovicë. He went to school in Skopje and studied electromechanics at the University of Belgrade. After World War II, he held various positions in the Kosovo regional administration and retired in 1963.

Among Sulejmani's publications are the short story collection *Era dhe kolona*, Prishtinë 1965 (The wind and the column); the autobiographical novel *Njerëzit*, Prishtinë 1966 (The men); *Ëndrra e korbit*, Prishtinë 1968 (The crow's dream); the novel *Fëmijët e lumit tim*, Prishtinë 1969 (The children of my river); and the collection *Poezi, drama*, Prishtinë 1981 (Poetry, drama).

Lit.: QOSJA, Rexhep, *Një shkrimtar i preokupuar me probleme morale*. in: Jeta e re (1969) 3, p. 428–451.

SULI, Vincenzo (early 19th century). Arbëresh (q.v.) poet from Palazzo Adriano in Sicily. He is the author of a poem on wine.

SULLI, Nicolai Athanasi (–1785). Arbëresh (q.v.) poet from Palazzo Adriano in Sicily. He was vice-rector of the Arbëresh seminary in Palermo and author of a poem in a 1757 manuscript now preserved in the library of the Arbëresh Seminary in Piana degli Albanesi.

SUMA, Lukë (fl. 1685). Also known as *Luca Summa*. Poet from Shkodër. Author of an eight-line poem in Albanian composed on August 30, 1685, in honour of Pjetër Bogdani (q.v.) and published in the latter's *Cuneus prophetarum*.

SUMMA, Luca. See SUMA, Lukë.

SURROI, Rexhai (1929–   ). Kosovo prose writer. He was born in Prizren and studied in Prishtinë and Belgrade. After working as a journalist and editor, he took up a career in politics and served as Yugoslav ambassador to Bolivia and Mexico. Surroi is the author of novels and short stories, among which: *Besniku,* Prishtinë 1959 (Besnik); *Dashunija e urrejtja,* Prishtinë 1961 (Love and hatred); *Pranvera e tretë,* Prishtinë 1970 (The third spring); and *Orteku,* Prishtinë 1974 (The avalanche).

T

TAHIR efendi Halil Popova. See POPOVA, Tahir efendi Halil.
TAHIR efendi Jakova. See BOSHNJAKU, Tahir.
TAHIR efendi Lluka. See LLUKA, Tahir efendi.
TAMBURI, Francesco Saverio (fl. 1834). Arbëresh (q.v.) author of an Albanian catechism in the dialect of San Basile in Cosenza.
TEMANI, Sulejman (18th century). Moslem poet and sheikh from Berat. He is the author of several pieces of religious verse.
TËRPO, Nektar (fl. 1731). Abbot of Ardenica near Lushnjë, to whom a sentence in Albanian, dated 1731, is attributed. It reads *Virgjin ë Mame eperëntis uro prë nee faj torëte* (Virgin, mother of God, pray for us sinners). Written originally in Greek script together with text in Aromanian, Latin, and Greek, the sentence is preserved at the Academy of Sciences in Tiranë on a folio with an engraving of St. Mary of Ardenica.
THAÇI, Kolë (1886–1941). Translator and poet from Shkodër. He studied at the Jesuit college where he was himself to teach from 1905 to 1911. He was elected to Parliament in 1921 and later became minister of finance and a senator.

Thaçi is the author of patriotic poetry and articles but is chiefly remembered for his translation of two plays by the eighteenth century Italian writer Pietro Metastasio: *Sh. Eustaki,* Shkodër 1909 (S. Eustazio); and *Zefi i njoftun,* Shkodër 1910 (Giuseppe riconosciuto).

TIGANI, Shefqet (1945–   ). Short story writer born in Pejë. He finished his studies at the University of Tiranë in 1970 and now works as a teacher in Vlorë.

Tigani has published several volumes of short stories, including *Mrekullia e diellit,* Tiranë 1968 (The miracle of the sun); *Mjegulla e çarë,* Tiranë 1971 (The torn fog); *Burimi i Valit,* Tiranë 1977 (The source of the Vali); and *Jeta nën diell,* Tiranë 1979 (Life under the sun).

TOÇKAS, D. See GURRA, Milto Sotir.
TODHRI, Dhaskal. See HAXHIFILIPI, Theodhor.
TOMEU, Leonik (1456–1531). Latin man of letters of Albanian origin. He was born in Venice and studied ancient Greek and Latin there and in Padua. He was a noted classical scholar, much appreciated by Erasmus, and translator of the works of Aristotle and other ancient Greek philosophers.
TOMORI, Baba Ali (–1947). Bektash (q.v.) poet and translator. Born towards the end of the nineteenth century near Tepelenë, he studied at the secondary school in Ioannina. After the burning of the tekes in 1913–1915, he left for Cairo, returning to Albania after the end of World War I. In 1921, he helped organize the First Bektash Congress.

Tomori is the author of four books of Bektash literature and history, including poetry translations and original verse. He opposed all religious fanaticism in his writings and endeavoured to combine Christian and Bektash elements. Some of his verse appeared in newspapers and journals of the period.

TOPTANI, Murat (1866–1917). Nationalist figure, sculptor, and poet. He was born in Istanbul where he grew up with the Frashëri family to whom he was related. For his nationalist activities, he was imprisoned by the Ottoman authorities and exiled to Anatolia. Later in Albania, he was present in Vlorë when Ismail Qemali declared Albania independent in 1912 and was involved in the establishment of Tiranë's first Albanian school.

Toptani is the author of patriotic poetry characteristic of the Rilindja (q.v.) period which was published in the volume *Vjershat e Murat Toptanit,* 1924 (Verse of Murat Toptani).

TOSK. Term for the southern Albanians and their dialect group, as opposed to the Gegs (q.v.) of the north. Speakers of Tosk dialects are to be found in Albania south of the Shkumbini river which marks the traditional dialect border between Geg and Tosk, in Greece, and in most Arbëresh (q.v.) settlements in Italy.

TOTASI, Papa (17th century). Possible author of an anonymous manuscript of the Gospels from Elbasan, known as the *Anonimi i Elbasanit* (q.v.). He is thought to have originated from the Shpati region between Elbasan and Librazhd. Nothing is known of his life. His name appears in Greek letters on the inside cover of the manuscript which contains parts of the Gospels in Elbasan dialect, written in an original alphabet.

TOTO, Ismet (1908–1937). Prose writer and poet from the village of Progonat in Labëria. He was editor of the periodical *Arbënia,* 1935–1937. His writings also appeared in various other Tiranë periodicals of the 1930s, such as *Ora* and *Illyria.*

TOZAJ, Nexhat (1943–). Prose writer from Vlorë. He studied at the Faculty of Political Science of the University of Tiranë and began publishing in 1961.

Tozaj is the author of detective and spy stories and of film scenarios. Among his works are *Hapa të matura,* Tiranë 1972 (Sure-footed); *Në gjurmë të të tretit,* Tiranë 1973 (Tracing the third man); *Dëshmi nga varri,* Tiranë 1974 (Testimony from the grave); *Takimi i fundit,* Tiranë 1976 (The last meeting); *Rrëmbimi i arkivit,* Tiranë 1977 (The theft of the archives); *Gëzhoja e vjetër,* Tiranë 1981 (The old shell); and *Dora e ngrohtë,* Tiranë 1983 (The warm hand).

TREBICKA, Kosta Jani (fl. 1897). Publisher and poet. He was cofounder of the "Mbrothësia" (Progress) Press in Sofia in 1897 and together with Kristo Luarasi (q.v.) and Mid'hat Frashëri (q.v.) published the literary and cultural periodical *Kalendari kombiar* (The national calendar). His poetry appeared both there and in the contemporary periodical *Albania.* Trebicka is also the author of a three-part novel entitled *Fushatë e vdekura të Sibirit,* Bucharest 1896 (The fatal campaign of Siberia).

TROIANO, Mosè (early 19th century). Arbëresh (q.v.) writer from Plataci in Cosenza. He is known to have translated two Italian poems into Albanian using the alphabet made popular by de Rada (q.v.). They are found in a manuscript dating from the first half of the nineteenth century.

TURANI, Baba Ahmed (–1928). Bektash (q.v.) poet. He was born in Turan near Tepelenë at the end of the nineteenth century and travelled to the Middle East in his youth. He took the title Baba in 1908 at Turan. In 1914, his teke was burned down by the Greeks and he was forced to move to Vlorë. He is said to have been a talented poet.

TUTULANI, Kristaq (1919–1943). Writer and Communist activist. He was born in Berat and went to school in Korçë and Shkodër. His studies of medicine in Italy were interrupted by the war during which he returned to Albania and took an active part in the fight against fascism. In 1942, he was a delegate to the first party conference in Berat and was elected as a member of the local central committee. On July 6, 1943, he was killed with his sister Margarita (q.v.) in the village of Gosë, south of Kavajë.

Tutulani is the author of patriotic and left-wing poetry, short stories, and sketches, some of which appeared in the periodical *Bota e re* (New World). His works have been published in the volume *Shkrime të zgjedhura,* Tiranë 1966 (Selected writings).

TUTULANI, Margarita (1924–1943). Author of articles and poetry and Communist activist. She was born in Berat and studied at the Tiranë Women's Institute in 1938. During World War II, she was a party activist responsible for youth education and was elected to the central committee in 1943. She was killed on July 6, 1943, in Gosë, near Kavajë.

U

UÇI, Alfred (contemporary). Scholar and critic. Among his works are *Jani Vreto*, Tiranë 1965 (Jani Vreto); *Estetika, jeta, arti*, Tiranë 1970 (Aesthetics, life, art); *Labirintet e modernizmit*, Tiranë 1978 (The labyrinths of modernism); *Probleme të estetikës*, Prishtinë 1980 (Problems of aesthetics); and *Mitologjia, folklori, letërsia*, Tiranë 1982 (Mythology, folklore, literature).

UJKANI, Qerim (1937–). Kosovo poet. He was born and raised in Pejë and studied at the Faculty of Law of the University of Belgrade, later working for Radio Prishtinë. Among his verse collections are *Hullinat*, Prishtinë 1963 (The furrows); *Prralla e votrës*, Prishtinë 1967 (The sea or the uneasy poem); *Pagëzimet*, Prishtinë 1969 (The baptisms); *Antisonete*, Prishtinë 1972 (Antisonnets); *Pasthirrmë*, Prishtinë 1975 (Interjection); *Lartësi toke*, Prishtinë 1979 (The elevation); *Gjaku im*, Tiranë 1980 (My blood); *Hije e këputur*, Prishtinë 1982 (Torn shadow); and *Dielli që po e krijoj*, Prishtinë 1983 (The sun which I'm discovering).

UJKO, Vorea (contemporary). Pseudonym of *Domenico Bellizzi*. One of the best known contemporary Arbëresh (q.v.) poets. He was born in Frascineto, Cosenza, (his birthdate is given variously as 1918 or 1931) and now teaches modern literature in Firmo.

Ujko's verse has been published in Italy, Albania, and Kosovo. Among his recent works are the collections: *Zgjimet e gjakut*, Castrovillari 1973 (The awakening of the blood); *Kosovë*, Cosenza 1973 (Kosovo); *Mote moderne*, Ventura Schiavonea 1976 (Modern times); *Ankth*, Prishtinë 1979 (Anguish); *Stinët e mia*, Corigliano Stazione 1980 (My seasons); and *Këngë arbëreshe*, Tiranë 1982 (Arbëresh songs).

ULQINAKU, Hafëz Ali (1853–1913). One of the last in a long tradition of Moslem writers. He was from Ulcinj (as his surname denotes), now on the Montenegrin coast. Ulqinaku is the author of a large Turkish-Albanian, Albanian-Turkish dictionary in Arabic script (1897) and of a mevlud published in Istanbul about 1878, which is a translation of the famous mevlud of Suleyman Chelebi.

Lit.: KALEŠI, Hasan, *Mevludi kod Arbanasa*. in: Zbornik Filozofskog Fakulteta u Univerziteta Beogradu 4 (1958), p. 349–358; MYDERRIZI, Osman, *Fjalori shqip-turqisht i H. Ali Ulqinakut*. in: Buletin i Universitetit Shtetëror të Tiranës. Seria Shkenc. Shoq. (1961) 3, p. 117–146.

UNGJILLI I PASHKËVE. See EASTER GOSPEL.

V

VANÇI, Ali (early 20th century). Prose writer. He is the author of the novels *Varri i mallkuar*, (The cursed grave); and *Nga dallgët e jetës*, (From the waves of life); the short story collection *Katua*, (The cellar); and the comedy *Ngjelka faqesimite*, (Bun-faced Angela).

VARFI, Andrea (1914–   ). Poet, critic, and essayist. He was born in Vlorë and studied agronomy in Italy. His literary activity began in the 1930s and carried on through the postwar period. Varfi has published the following volumes of poetry: *Në tingujt e revolucionit*, Tiranë 1951 (At the sounds of the revolution); *Dielli i jetës sonë*, Tiranë 1957 (The sun of our life); *Në zgjim*, Tiranë 1962 (At reveille); and *Blerim Nëndori*, Tiranë 1966 (November greenery). Many of his poems were popularized in well-known partisan songs and marches. Among his other works are the play *Në shpellën e kuqe*, Tiranë 1959 (The red grotto) and translations.

VARIBOBA, Giulio. See VARIBOBA, Jul.

VARIBOBA, Jul (1724–ca.1788). Ital. *Giulio Variboba*. Arbëresh (q.v.) poet and no doubt the most original of the eighteenth century Arbëresh authors. Variboba was born in San Giorgio Albanese in Cosenza and studied in San Benedetto Ullano. He returned to his native village to teach and later worked in Rome as secretary of a religious order.

It was there that he published what is widely considered the first work of notable artistic value in Arbëresh literature, the *Ghiella e Shën Mëriis Virghiër*, Rome 1762 (Life of the Virgin Mary), a loosely structured narrative poem dealing mostly with the nativity, using the poet's native Calabria as a background.

Lit.: DEMIRAJ, Shaban, '*Gjella e Shën Mëriis Virgjër*' *e Jul Varibobës*. in: Buletin për Shkencat Shoqërore (1956) 3, p. 262–270; FERRARI, Giuseppe, *Giulio Variboba e la sua opera poetica albanese*, Bari 1963; LAMBERTZ, Maximilian, *Giulio Variboba*. in: Zeitschrift für Vergleichende Sprachforschung

74 (1956), p. 47–122, 185–224; LIBRANDI, V., *Grammatica albanese con le poesie rare di Variboba*, Milan 1897.

VASA, Pashko (1825–1892). Also known as *Vaso Pasha, Vasa Pasha Shkodrani*, and *Wassa Effendi*. Statesman, scholar, writer, poet, and patriot. He was born in Shkodër where he learned Italian, French, and Serbo-Croatian. In 1849, he took part in a Venetian uprising against the Austrians and was subsequently forced to flee to Turkey. There, after a period of initial hardship, he rose to a position of power in the Ottoman administration. In 1879, he acquired the title of Pasha and in 1883, became governor of the Lebanon. Despite his functions, he never forgot his homeland and through his contacts in Istanbul, took part in the organization of the Albanian nationalist movement which led to the creation of the League of Prizren in 1878. Together with other nationalist figures in Istanbul, such as Hoxha Tahsin, Jani Vreto (q.v.), and Sami Frashëri (q.v.), he devoted himself to the creation of an alphabet for Albanian, the so-called Istanbul alphabet, and to the foundation of a society for the publication of Albanian writing, the "Shoqëri e të shtypurit shkronja shqip" (q.v.).

Vasa is the author of *La vérité sur l'Albanie et les Albanais*, Paris 1879 (The truth about Albania and the Albanians), a widely translated brochure designed to inform the Western reader about the plight of his people. To make the Albanian language better known, he published a *Grammaire albanaise à l'usage de ceux qui désirent apprendre cette langue sans l'aide d'un maître*, London 1887 (Albanian grammar for those wishing to learn this language without the aid of a teacher). He also dabbled in literature, publishing a volume of sensitive Italian verse entitled *Rose e spine*, Istanbul 1873 (Roses and thorns) and, under the pseudonym Albanus Albano, a French-language novel of rather excessive sentimentality *Bardha de Témal, scènes de la vie albanaise*, Paris 1890 (Bardha of Temal, scenes from Albanian life). He is best known in Albania, however, for his poem *O moj Shqipni* (Oh Albania, poor Albania) which circulated among Albanian patriots in 1878–1880. Among his historical publications are *La mia prigionia, episodio storico dell'assedio di Venezia*, Istanbul 1850 (My prisons, historical episode from the siege of Venice); *La Bosnie et l'Herzegovine pendant la mission de Djevdet Efendi*, Istanbul 1865 (Bosnia and Hercegovina during the mission of Jevdet Efendi); and *Esquisse historique sur le Monténégro d'après les traditions de l'Albanie*, Istanbul 1872 (Historical sketch of Montenegro according to Albanian traditions).

Lit.: BALA, Vehbi, *Pashko Vasa, portret monografi*, Tiranë 1979; KASTRATI, Jup, *Pashko Vasa*. in: Nëntori 22 (1975) 9, p. 164–180; KHAIR, Antoine A., *Wassa Pacha (1883–1892), le moutaçarrifat du Mont*, Beirut 1973; QOSJA, Rexhep, *Historia e letërsisë shqipe—Romantizmi II*, Prishtinë 1984, p. 306–348.

VELABISHTI, Ismail Pasha (–1764). Moslem poet, ruler of Berat, and patron of Nezim Frakulla (q.v.). He was sent to guard the Turkish fortress of Lepanto in Greece and later returned to Albania, dying in Vlorë in August 1764. Only one of his poems, written in Arabic script, has survived.

VELLARAI, Jan (1771–1823). Mod. Greek *Ioannis Vilaras*. Author of Modern Greek-Albanian grammatical notes. The son of a doctor, Vellarai studied medicine in Padua in 1789 and later lived in Venice. In 1801, he became the physician of Veli, son of Ali Pasha Tepelena. His exact nationality, whether Greek, Aromanian, or Albanian, is not known, but he is remembered primarily as a modern Greek poet.

His forty-nine pages of grammatical notes, dated 1801, were written in the dialect of Çamëria in an original alphabet of thirty letters based on Latin and to a lesser extent on Greek and are preserved at the Bibliothèque Nationale in Paris (Supplément grec 251, f. 138–187).

Lit.: SHUTERIQI, Dhimitër, *Nëpër shekujt letrare*, Tiranë 1972.

VEQILHARXHI, Naum (1797–1846). Real name *Naum Panajot Haxhi Llazar Bredhi*. Nationalist figure of the early Rilindja (q.v.) period and inventor of an Albanian alphabet. The exact place of his birth is not known. His family originated from Bredhi, a little village near Vithkuq in the Korçë region. It was probably after the destruction of Vithkuq in 1819 that Veqilharxhi emigrated, like many others in the region, to Romania. In 1821, he took part in a Wallachian uprising against the Turks, in which he acquired the name Veqilharxhi, from the Turkish "vekilharc" (chamberlain). He spent most of his life, apparently as a lawyer, in the port of Brăila on the Danube and died of poisoning in Istanbul, allegedly by Greek Orthodox fanatics.

Veqilharxhi was first to formulate the ideals and objectives of the Albanian nationalist movement. In an encyclical which he circulated, he pointed to the backwardness and misery of the Albanians due to long centuries of Turkish rule, stressing in particular the need for a new Albanian alphabet as a means of overcoming the situation and uniting the country. He had already begun working on a thirty-two-letter alphabet in 1824 or 1825 which he printed in his eight-page *Ëvetar shqip* (Albanian spelling book) in 1844. The work was augmented to forty-eight pages in a second edition of 1845.

Lit.: ISLAMI, Myslim, *Naum Veqilharxhi,* Tiranë 1967; QOSJA, Rexhep, *Historia e letërsisë shqipe—Romantizmi II,* Prishtinë 1984, p. 7–34; SHUTERIQI, Dhimitër, *Autorë dhe tekste,* Tiranë 1977, p. 310–334.

VËRLACI, Sulejman Pasha. See ELBASANI, Sulejman Pasha.

VETMO, Dushko. See SOLANO, Francesco.

VEXH-HI, Baba Adem (1841–1927). Bektash (q.v.) poet born in Gjakovë. He travelled widely, in particular on pilgrimages to Mecca, Medina, and Kerbela. In 1877, he was sent as a baba to Prizren where he opened a teke. From 1922 to his death, he headed a teke in Gjakovë. Author of much mystical verse.

VILARAS, Ioannis. See VELLARAI, Jan.

VINCA, Agim (1947–   ). Kosovo poet and critic from Veleshtë near Struga in Macedonia. He finished school in Struga and studied Albanian language and literature at the University of Prishtinë where he now teaches contemporary literature.

Vinca has published the verse collections: *Feniksi,* Skopje 1972 (The phoenix); *Shtegu i mallit,* Prishtinë 1975 (The path of nostalgia); *Në vend të biografisë,* Tiranë 1977 (In lieu of a biography); and *Buzëdrinas,* Prishtinë 1984 (Inhabitant of the lower Drin). Among his other works are *Aspekte të kritikës sonë,* Prishtinë 1977 (Aspects of our criticism); *Qasje,* Prishtinë 1980 (Approach); and *Struktura e poezisë së sotme shqipe (1945–1980),* Prishtinë 1985 [The structure of contemporary Albanian poetry (1945–1980)].

VITHKUQARI, Jani Evstrat (–1822). Also known as *Eustratios of Vithkuq.* Priest and teacher from Vithkuq, as the name denotes. He studied at the Academy in Voskopojë (Moskhopolis) and in Ioannina. A scholar well versed in both Greek and Albanian culture, he is known to have taught in Arta, Voskopojë, Përmet, and Ioannina and was a school director in Gjirokastër.

Vithkuqari is the coauthor of material on the Albanian language which appeared in William Martin Leake's *Researches in Greece,* London 1814. In a preface to his section on Albanian grammar, Leake writes, "The greater part of the information upon which the following remarks are founded, was derived from Evstratio of Viskuki, who holds the rank of Hieroceryx in the Greek church, and had been many years school-master at Moskhopoli." The section includes a 2000 word Greek-English-Albanian dictionary.

VLLADOVIQ-RELA, Josif. See RELA, Josip.

VLONJAKASI, Demir aga. See VLONJATI, Demir.

VLONJATI, Demir (–1845). Also known as *Demir aga Vlonjakasi.* Moslem poet. Author of a historical poem dealing with the Tanzimat legislation and the Turkish massacre in Vlorë in 1845.

VLORA, Eqrem bey (1885–1964). Political figure and publicist. Born of an aristocratic family of beys in Vlorë, he was educated in Basle and Vienna. At an early age he acquired a knowledge of Italian, German, French, Arabic, and Turkish. In 1904, with the influence of his uncle, the Grand Vizier Ferid Pasha, he was given a position at the Turkish Foreign Ministry and travelled widely for the Porte. After the revolution of the Young Turks, he was a cofounder of the Bashkimi (The union) Society (q.v.) and was involved in the publication of the bilingual periodical *Shqiptari-Arnavud* (The Albanian). Following Albanian independence, he was appointed a senator and elected as a member of Parliament representing a conservative faction later headed by Ahmed Zogu. In 1928, he was appointed Albanian ambassador to London and subsequently held various offices during the Zogu dictatorship and Italian occupation. He emigrated to Italy in 1944 and died in Vienna.

On the whole, Vlora was more successful as a writer than as a political figure. Among his early works are *Abeceja pelasgjike,* Istanbul 1909 (Pelasgian spelling book); *Aus Berat und vom Tomor,* Sarajevo 1911 (From Berat and Tomor); and *Le dolanze del popolo albanese,* Rome 1913 (The sufferings of the Albanian people). His memoirs, published in German under the title *Lebenserinnerungen,* Munich 1968, 1973, though written from the subjective stance of the aristocracy of the period, are of interest both from a literary and historical point of view.

VOKA, Rexhep (fl. 1910). Moslem scholar and publicist from Tetovo in Macedonia. He studied in Istanbul and was a mufti in Monastir (Bitola) during the revolution of the Young Turks. An active member of the Bashkimi (The union) Society (q.v.), he died in Istanbul.

Voka invented an Albanian alphabet using Arabic script, which comprised forty-four letters, both consonants and vowels. He published it in his *Elifbaja shqip,* Istanbul 1910 (Albanian spelling book). He is also the author of three other works: *Kujtimet e Kongresit Dibresë,* Monastir 1909 (Memories of the Congress of Dibër); *Mendime,* Istanbul 1911 (Thoughts); and *Arnavudçe müfessal ilmihal,* Istanbul 1911 (Primer of religion in Albanian).

VOSKOPOJARI, Grigor. See GRIGORI I DURRËSIT.

VRETO, Jani (1822–1900). Publicist and nationalist figure of the Rilindja (q.v.) period. Vreto was born in the village of Postenan near Leskovik near the Greek border. Though of a poor family, he studied at the famous Zosimea secondary school in Ioannina where he first began to take an interest in his native language. Using Greek script, he composed a poem on Scanderbeg (q.v.) and collected Albanian sayings and folksongs. In Istanbul, he came into contact with leading figures of the Rilindja movement and was a member of the commission set up to create an alphabet for Albanian, the so-called Istanbul alphabet proposed by Sami Frashëri (q.v.). In 1879, the commission published an *Alfabetare e gluhësë shqip* (Spelling book of the Albanian language), several parts of which were written by Vreto. He also took part in the founding of the "Shoqëri e të shtypurit shkronja shqip" (q.v.) (Society for the publication of Albanian writing) the same year and in the publication of the periodical *Drita* (The light) which began publishing Albanian-language books in 1886, includ-to Bucharest and later visited Egypt, organizing and collecting funds for the nationalist movement. In Bucharest, he founded a new society called "Drita" (The light) which began publishing Albanian-language books in 1886, including two of Vreto's own works: *Mirëvetija,* Bucharest 1886 (Ethics); and *Numeratoreja,* Bucharest 1886 (Arithmetic). Vreto was also responsible for the transliteration and publication of Muhamet Kyçyku's (q.v.) *Erveheja* (Bucharest 1888) and Tahir Boshnjaku's (q.v.) *Vehbije*. His own writings have been republished by Alfred Uçi (q.v.) in *Vepra të zgjedhura,* Tiranë 1973 (Selected works).

Lit.: QOSJA, Rexhep, *Historia e letërsisë shqipe—Romantizmi II,* Prishtinë 1984, p. 265–305; UÇI, Alfred, *Jani Vreto,* Tiranë 1965.

VRUHO, Jani (ca. 1871–1931). Publicist and nationalist figure of the Rilindja (q.v.) period. He was born in the Berat region and emigrated to Egypt where he devoted himself to the nationalist movement. His articles and verse appeared in periodicals such as *Kalendari kombiar* (The national calendar) and *Liria e Shqipërisë* (The freedom of Albania).

W

WASSA EFFENDI. See VASA, Pashko.

X

XANONI, Anton (1863–1915). Writer and poet. He was born in Durrës and received a Catholic education in Shkodër, being later sent by the Jesuits to study in France, Spain, Austria, Italy, and Poland where he graduated in philosophy and theology. In 1892, he was ordained as a priest and returned to Shkodër to teach.

Xanoni is the author of poetry, fables, translations, a grammar, school texts, a novel, and a play as well as numerous religious works. Among his publications are *Gramatika shqyp*, Shkodër 1909 (Albanian grammar); *Shkurtorja e historis së moçme*, 1910 (Outline of ancient history); the translation *Muzhiktari i verbët*, Shkodër 1911 (The blind musician); and *Llagoret e mullîjve*, 1915 (The millraces).

Lit.: KASTRATI, Jup, *Anton Xanoni.* in: Shkodra (1962) 1, p. 84–111.

XHUVANI, Aleksandër (1880–1961). Scholar, educator, and linguist. Born in Elbasan, he taught for three years in the Arbëresh (q.v.) settlement of San Demetrio Corone in southern Italy (1906–1909). From 1909 to 1920, he was director of the teacher training college in his native Elbasan and later worked as secretary to the minister of education. In 1950, he was elected a deputy of the People's Assembly.

Xhuvani is particularly remembered for his linguistic research. Among his major publications in this field are *Për pastërinë e gjuhës shqipe*, Tiranë 1956 (For the purity of the Albanian language); *Studime gjuhësore*, Tiranë 1959 (Linguistics studies); and *Prapashtesat e gjuhës shqipe*, Tiranë 1962 (The suffixes of the Albanian language).

Lit.: GRACENI, Bardhyl, *Aleksandër Xhuvani. Jeta dhe veprat*, Tiranë 1980.

XHUVANI, Dhimitër (1934–   ). Novelist, short story writer, dramatist, and film script writer. He was born in Pogradec on Lake Ohrid and studied at the Gorky Institute of World Literature in Moscow. Xhuvani worked in agricultural co-operatives, at the Bistrica hydroelectric plant and in the chemical industry in Fier before turning to teaching and journalism. He is now a professional writer.

Among Xhuvani's works are *Këmbanat e fundit,* Tiranë 1958 (The last bells); *Midis dy netëve,* Tiranë 1962 (Between two nights); *Tuneli,* Tiranë 1966? (The tunnel); *Përsëri në këmbë,* Tiranë 1970 (Standing again); *Fan Smajli,* Tiranë 1971 (Fan Smajli); *Rrugëve të kantiereve,* Tiranë 1971 (In the streets of construction sites); *Zgjimi i Nebi Surrelit,* Tiranë 1976 (The awakening of Nebi Surreli); *Do të jetojmë ndryshe,* Tiranë 1979 (We'll live differently); *Vdekja e zotit Kaloti,* Tiranë 1981 (The death of Mr Kaloti); and *Bota ime,* Tiranë 1984 (My world). He has also written plays and film scripts.

XOXA, Jakov (1923–1979). Novelist of Socialist Realism. He was born in Fier and studied French language and literature at the University of Sofia in 1952. He returned to Albania and was active as a journalist, university teacher, and professional writer.

Xoxa is the author of two widely read and translated novels situated in his native Myzeqe area. The first, *Lumi i vdekur,* Tiranë 1965 (The dead river), portrays the exploitation of the peasantry by the beys in this backward, swampy region of prewar Albania. Xoxa's second novel, *Juga e bardhë,* Tiranë 1971 (The white south), deals with the collectivization of agriculture in the same region after the war. He also published the novel *Lulja e kripës,* Tiranë 1981 (The salt flower) and a collection of short stories entitled *Novela,* Tiranë 1949 (Short stories). His works have been reedited in *Vepra 1–8,* Prishtinë 1971 (Works 1–8) and *Vepra letrare 1–6,* Tiranë 1983 (Literary works 1–6).

XUKARO, Kate. See CUKARO, Kate.

Z

ZADE, Muçi (fl. 1725). Moslem poet from southern Albania. Author of a light-hearted poem in praise of coffee. Found in a manuscript from Korçë and now preserved in Tiranë, it constitutes the earliest known Albanian poem written in Arabic script and the oldest Tosk (q.v.) verse written in Albania.

ZADEJA, Ndre (1890–ca.1945). Playwright and poet. Zadeja was a priest from Shkodër and is the author of several historical plays: *Ora e Shqipnis* (Albania's hour); *Hijet e zeza* (The dark shadows); *Rrethimi i Shkodrës* (The siege of Shkodër); *Ruba e kuqe* (The red kerchief); and *Rozafa* (Rozafa). Some of his poetry appeared in prewar periodicals. Most of his writing, however, remains unpublished.

ZAKO, Andon. See ÇAJUPI, Andon Zako.

ZALOSHNJA, Moisi (1919–   ). Poet and prose writer. Born in Zaloshnja in the southern Albanian Skrapar region, he went to school in Elbasan and took part in the resistance movement during World War II.

Among his publications are the short story collections: *Rreth zjarrit partizan*, Tiranë 1954 (Around the partisan fire); *Kohët ndryshuan*, Tiranë 1957 (Times change); *Nën hijen e Tomorit*, Tiranë 1961 (In Tomorr's shadow); *Lëndohet një plagë e vjetër*, Tiranë 1965 (An old wound inflames); *Zëra të fuqishëm*, Tiranë 1969 (Strong voices); *Tregime të zgjedhura*, Tiranë 1973 (Selected tales); *Gurë stralli*, Tiranë 1978 (Flintstone); *Tregim për tokën*, Tiranë 1982 (Tale for the land); and the novel *Kur malet kërkonin diellin*, Tiranë 1976 (When the mountains look for the sun); as well as the poetry *Misioni*, Tiranë 1952 (The mission); and *Në zemër të popullit*, Tiranë 1953 (In the heart of the people).

ZARISHI, Pjetër (1806–1866). Poet. He was born in Blinisht in the Zadrima region and studied for the priesthood in Rome, returning to Albania by 1831 to work as a village priest. He later became an abbot in the Mirdita area and died in Kallmet in his native Zadrima.

Zarishi is the author of religious and, to a lesser extent, secular poetry in a harmonious blend of foreign influence (Italian, Latin, and Turkish) and native northern Albanian elements. He also introduced and popularized a number of metres, e.g., hendecasyllabic and Sapphic, as yet foreign to Albanian poetry. Some of his verse appeared in the prewar periodical *Hylli i dritës* (The daystar), though much remained unpublished.

ZEQO, Moikom (1949–   ). Poet. He was born in Durrës and studied at the Faculty of History and Philology of the University of Tiranë. He now works for the Museum of Archeology in Durrës.

He has published several volumes of verse, among which: *Vegime të vendlindjes,* Tiranë 1968 (Visions of my native land); *Qyteti Feniks,* Tiranë 1970 (Phoenix city); and *Brenda vetes,* Prishtinë 1974 (Inside oneself). He is also the author of children's literature and of the short story collections *Kalorësit dardanë,* Tiranë 1977 (The Dardanian knights); and *Dialogë në levizje,* Tiranë 1981 (Dialogue in movement); as well as of the biography *Mujo Ulqinaku,* Tiranë 1975 (Mujo Ulqinaku).

ZEZA, Gjon. See GURRA, Milto Sotir.

ZHEJI, Gjergj (1926–   ). Novelist, critic, and poet from Tiranë. Author of: *Kullat,* Tiranë 1969 (The towers), a novel about the struggle for women's emancipation in Albania; *Murat e Krujës,* Tiranë 1968 (The walls of Krujë) which deals with the Scanderbeg (q.v.) period; *Rusha,* Tiranë 1971 (Rusha); and the monographs *Fjalorth termash letrare,* Tiranë 1965 (Short dictionary of literary terms); *Andon Zako-Çajupi, jeta dhe vepra,* Tiranë 1966 (Andon Zako-Çajupi, life and works); *Artisti dhe jeta,* Tiranë 1973 (The artist and life); and *Vëzhgime metrike,* Tiranë 1980 (Metrical observations). Zheji has also translated Mark Twain, William Saroyan, Ibsen, Pushkin, Krylov, and Chekhov into Albanian.

ZIKO, Vangjush (1931–   ). Poet and dramatist from Korçë. He studied in the Soviet Union and now works as a teacher in Korçë. Ziko began writing in 1950. Among his publications are the verse collections *Takim me malet,* Tiranë 1970 (Meeting with the mountains); *Këngët e grurit,* Tiranë 1976 (Wheat songs); *Galeritë e nëntokës,* Tiranë 1980 (The underground galleries); and the plays *Motra Katerinë,* Tiranë 1959 (Sister Catherine); *Rruga e madhe,* Tiranë 1976 (The highway); and *Provimi,* (The test).

ZUCCARO, Kate. See CUKARO, Kate.

ZUKA, Ramë. See REXHA, Zekeria.

ZURNAXHIU, Shaip (1884–1951). Kosovo poet from Rahovec. He was a Moslem priest and student of Hilmi Maliqi (q.v.). Zurnaxhiu is the author of translations and of poetry in Albanian, Turkish, and Serbo-Croatian. Most of his Albanian verse is of a religious nature.

   Lit.: KRASNIQI, Mark, *Shaip Zurnaxhiu.* in: Jeta e re (1954) 2, p. 96–100.

ZYKO, Hasan. See KAMBERI, Hasan Zyko.

✥ BIBLIOGRAPHY ✥

Anthologie de la poésie albanaise (Tiranë 1983).
Anthologie de la prose albanaise (Tiranë 1983).
Anthologie du récit albanais (Tiranë 1982).
Antologjia e letërsisë shqiptare (letërsi e realizmit socialist) për shkollat e mesme 2 (Tiranë 1979).
Armao, Ermanno. *Catalogo ragionato della mia biblioteca* (Florence 1953).
Balotă, Anton. *Albanica. Introducere in studiul filologiei albaneze* (Bucharest 1936).
Bartl, Peter. *Die albanischen Muslime zur Zeit der nationalen Unabhängigkeitsbewegung* (Wiesbaden 1968).
Bernath, Mathias (ed.). *Bibliographisches Lexikon zur Geschichte Südosteuropas* (Munich 1974–).
———. *Bibliografia e librit shqip për vitet 1945–1957* (Tiranë 1959).
———. *Bibliografia kombëtare e Republikës Popullore Socialiste të Shqipërisë, Libri shqip* (Tiranë 1960–).
Bihiku, Koço. *An outline of Albanian literature* (Tiranë 1964).
———. *A history of Albanian literature* (Tiranë 1980).
Bihiku, Koço (ed.). *Historia e letërsisë shqiptare të realizmit socialist* (Tiranë 1978).
———. *Buletini i Universitetit Shtetëror të Tiranës* (Tiranë).
Çabej, Eqrem. *Për gjenezën e literaturës shqipe* (Prishtinë 1970).
Çoba, A., and Zef Prela. *Albanica. Vepra të botuara në shek. XVI–XVIII* (Tiranë 1965).
Drita. E përjavshme letrare-artistike (Tiranë 1961–).
Duraku, Nebil. *Shkrimtarët e Kosovës '43–'83* (Tiranë 1984).
Dutsch, Mikolaj. *Die albanische Gegenwartsliteratur.* in: *Südosteuropa-Jahrbuch 11* (Munich 1978).
Faensen, Johannes. *Die albanische Nationalbewegung* (Berlin 1980).
Fjala. E përdyjavshme kulture arti e letërsie (Prishtinë).
Fullani, Dhimitër. *Poetë të Rilindjes* (Tiranë 1973).
Gjerqeku, Enver (ed.). *Panoramë e letërsisë bashkëkohore shqipe në Jugosllavi* (Belgrade 1964).
Gradilone, Giuseppe. *Studi di letteratura albanese* (Rome 1960).
———. *Altri studi di letteratura albanese* (Rome 1974).

Guys, Henri. *Bibliographie albanaise. Description raisonnée des ouvrages publiés en albanais ou relatifs à l'Albanie de 1900 à 1910* (Tiranë 1938).
Hahn, Johann Georg von. *Albanesische Studien, 1–3* (Vienna 1853).
Hamiti, Sabri. *Arti i leximit* (Prishtinë 1983).
Hetzer, Armin. *Geschichte des Buchhandels in Albanien* (Berlin 1985).
Hetzer, Armin, and Viorel S. Roman. *Albanien. Ein bibliographischer Forschungsbericht* (Munich 1983).
———. *Historia e letërsisë shqiptare për shkollën e mesme të përgjithshme 1* (Tiranë 1975)
Horecki, Paul (ed.). *Southern Europe. A guide to basic publications* (Chicago 1969).
Ismajli, Rexhep. *Rrënjë e fortë. Poezia arbëreshe e ditëve tona* (Prishtinë 1978).
Jeta e re. Revistë letrare (Prishtinë 1949–).
Jorgaqi, Nasho, and Hysen Sinani. *Degë e blertë. Antologji e poezisë së sotme arbëreshe* (Tiranë 1980).
Kaleši, Hasan. *Arbanaska knjizevnost na arapskom alfabet. in: Godišnjak Balkanološkog Instituta 1* (Sarajevo 1957).
———. *Albanska Aljamiado književnost. in: Prilozi za orijentalnu filologiju, 16/17,* (Sarajevo 1966–1967), p. 49–76.
Kastrati, Jup. *Bibliografi shqipe 29.XI.1944–31.XII.1958* (Tiranë 1959).
Kersopoulos, Jean. *Albanie. Ouvrages et articles de revues parus de 1555 à 1934* (Athens 1934).
Kodra, Klara. *Poetë arbëreshë* (Tiranë 1974).
Kodra, Ziaudin. *Letërsia e vjetër shqipe dhe arbëreshe* (Tiranë 1954).
Koliqi, Ernest. *Antologia della lirica albanese* (Milan 1963).
———. *Saggi di letteratura albanese* (Florence 1972).
Körner, Christine. *Entwicklung und Konzeption der Presse in Albanien und der albanischen Exilpresse* (Munich 1982).
Körner, Christine, and Peter Bartl. *Katalog der Bibliothek des Albanien-Instituts e.V. München* (Munich 1977).
Legrand, Emile. *Bibliographie albanaise. Description raisonée des ouvrages publiés en albanais ou relatifs à l'Albanie du XVe siècle à l'année 1900* (Paris 1912, reprint Leipzig 1973).
Les Lettres Albanaises. Revue littéraire et artistique (Tiranë 1978–).
Lussu, Joyce. *La poesia degli albanesi* (Turin 1977).
Manek, Franz, Georg, Pekmezi, and A. Stotz. *Albanesische Bibliographie. Bibliographija shqype* (Vienna 1909).
Mann, Stuart. *Albanian literature. An outline of prose, poetry and drama* (London 1955).
Metais, Michel. *Ismail Kadaré et la nouvelle poésie albanaise* (Paris 1973).
Mufaku, Muhamed. *Prapa natës. Poezi e shqiptarëve të Sirisë* (Prishtinë 1980).
———. *Lidhjet letrare shqiptare-arabe* (Doctoral dissertation) (Prishtinë 1981).
Myderrizi, Osman. *Letërsia shqipe në alfabetin arab. in: Buletin për Shkencat Shoqërore 9,* (Tiranë 1955) p. 148–154.
Nëntori (Nëndori) (Tiranë 1954–).
Pano, Nicholas C. *The People's Republic of Albania* (Baltimore 1968).
Petrotta, Gaetano. *Popolo, lingua e letteratura albanese* (Palermo 1931).
———. *Saggio di bibliografia albanese 1500–1930* (Palermo 1931).
———. *Poeti siculo-albanesi* (Palermo 1950).
———. *Svoglimento storico della cultura e della letteratura albanese* (Palermo 1950).

Pipa, Arshi. *Calabro-Albanian romanticism. in: Zeitschrift für Balkanologie* 13 (1977).
———. *Trilogia albanica* (Munich 1978).
Podrimja, Ali, and Sabri Hamiti. *Dega e pikëlluar. Poezi shqipe në Jugosllavi* (Prishtinë 1979).
Qosja, Rexhep. *Epizode letrare* (Prishtinë 1967).
———. *Dialogje me shkrimtarët* (Prishtinë 1968).
———. *Kritika letrare* (Prishtinë 1969).
———. *Antologjia e lirikës shqipe* (Prishtinë 1970).
———. *Historia e letërsisë shqipe—Romantizmi 1–2* (Prishtinë 1984).
Qvick, Ullmar. *Örnarna och bergen. Albansk poesi* (Gävle 1979).
Ressuli, Namik. *I piu antichi testi albanesi* (Turin 1978).
Roques, Mario. *Recherches sur les anciens textes albanais* (Paris 1932).
Rrota, Justin. *Letratyra shqype* (Shkodër 1934).
Rugova, Ibrahim, and Sabri Hamiti. *Kritika letrare* (Prishtinë 1979).
Savadjian, Léon. *Bibliographie balkanique 1920–1938, 1–8* (Paris 1931–1939).
Schirò, Giuseppe, Jr. *Storia della letteratura albanese* (Milan 1959).
Serkova, T. *Albanskaja klassičeskaja poezija* (Moscow 1981).
Shêjzat, Le Pleiadi. *Rivista culturale, sociale ed artistica* (Rome 1957–1974).
Shema, Isak, and Ibrahim Rugova. *Bibliografi e kritikës letrare shqiptare 1944–1974* (Prishtinë 1976).
Shita, Vehap, and Hasan Mekuli. *Drama Shqipe* (Belgrade 1966).
Shuteriqi, Dhimitër. *Letërsia shqipe e rilindjes kombëtare* (Tiranë 1947).
———. *Antologji e letërsisë shqipe* (Tiranë 1955).
———. *Bibliografi e letërsisë së vjetër shqipe. in: Buletin i Universitetit Shtetëror të Tiranës. Ser. Shkenc. Shoq.* (1962) 1, p. 121–160; 2, p. 137–168; 3, p. 107–147.
———. *Antologjia e letërsisë shqipe për shkollat e mesme* (Tiranë 1966).
———. *Nëpër shekujt letrarë* (Tiranë 1972).
———. *Gjurmime letrare* (Tiranë 1974).
———. *Shkrimet shqipe në vitet 1322–1850* (Tiranë 1976).
———. *Autorë dhe tekste* (Tiranë 1977).
———. *Mbi Barletin dhe shkrime të tjera* (Tiranë 1979).
Shuteriqi, Dhimitër (ed.). *Historia e letërsisë shqiptare* (Tiranë 1983).
Shuteriqi, Dhimitër, Koço Bihiku, and Mahir Domi (ed.). *Historia e letërsisë shqipe 1–2* (Tiranë 1959–1960).
Skendi, Stavro. *Albanian and south Slavic oral epic poetry* (Philadelphia 1954).
———. *Albania* (New York 1956).
———. *The Albanian national awakening (1878–1912)* (Princeton 1967).
Straticò, Alberto. *Manuale di letteratura albanese* (Milan 1896).
———. *Studia albanica* (Tiranë 1964–).
———. *Studime filologjike* (Tiranë 1964–).
———. *Studime dhe kritikë letrare. Nga autorë shqiptarë të Kosovës, Maqedonisë e të Malit të Zi* (Tiranë 1983).
———. *Südosteuropa-Bibliographie* (Munich 1945–).
Tönnes, Bernhard. *Sonderfall Albanien* (Munich 1980).
Xhiku, A., D. Dilaveri, and V. Librazhdi. *Historia e letërsisë shqiptare për shkollat e mesme profesionale 1* (Tiranë 1978).
Żajmi, Yii. *Antologji e letërsisë së vjetër shqipe* (Prishtinë 1972).

INDEX

Numbers in italics indicate main entry.

Abdalli, Mulla Fejzo, 1
Abdihoxha, Ali, 1
Abrami, Thoma. *See* Avrami, Thoma
Adae, Guillelmus, 1
Agimi Society, *2*, 87, 99, 100
Agolli, Dritëro, *2*, 6
Albano, Albanus. *See* Vasa, Pashko
Aliaj, Hamit, 2
Aliaj, Tasim T., 2
Ali Pasha Tepelena, 7, 96, 113, 115, 147
Aliu, Ali, 3
Aliu, Mulla, 3
Aliu, Sylejman, 3
Aljamiado Literature, 3
Altimari, Francesco, 3
Andoni, Sotir, 3
Angelus, Paulus, *4*, 47
Anonimi I Elabasanit, *4*, 18, 140
Anonymous manuscript of Elbasan. *See* Anonimi I Elbasanit.
Araniti, Midhat, 4
Arapi, Fatos, 4
Arbëresh, 3, *5*, 7, 8, 9, 10, 11, 12, 13, 14, 16, 19, 23, 30, 31, 32, 37, 38, 41, 43, 44, 50, 54, 55, 56, 68, 73, 74, 76, 77, 81, 82, 86, 88, 92, 93, 94, 95, 103, 108, 109, 110, 111, 119, 121, 122, 125, 126, 127, 128, 134, 135, 137, 139, 140, 141, 143, 145, 153

Argondica, Anton, 5
Argondizza, Antonio. *See* Argondica, Anton
Argyrokastritis, Grigorios. *See* Gjirokastriti, Grigor
Arnauti, Abdylatif, *5*, 6
Arnauti, Abdylkader, 5, *6*
Arnauti, Ajshe, 5, *6*
Arnauti, Hatixhe, 5, *6*
Arnauti, Maruf, 6
Arnauti, Muhamed Barakat Latif, 6
Arnauti, Raxha, 7
Artioti, Maksim, 7
Ascuri, Costantino, 7
Asdreni, 7
Ashkiu, Mehmet, 7
Asllan bej Puçe, 7
Asllani, Ali, *7*, 78
Avati, Francesco, 8
Avrami, Thoma, *8*, 38
Azi. *See* Rexha, Zekeria
Azzopardus, Franciscus, 8

Babi, Pashko, 9
Baffa, Pasquale, 9
Baffa, Stefano, *9*, 94
Bageri, Josef, 9
Bala, Muhamet, 9
Bala, Vehbi, 9
Balashi, Adelina, 10

INDEX

Ballaci, Sinan, 10
Ballanca, Faik, 10
Ballauri, Elsa, 10
Balliu, Fahri, 10
Banushi, Aleksandër, 10
Baptismal Formula. *See* Angelus, Paulus
Barbaci, Giovanni Tommaso. *See* Barbaçi, Gjon Thoma
Barbaçi, Gjon Thoma, 10
Barça, Zef, 11
Barcia, Giuseppe. *See* Barça, Zef
Bardhi, Frang, 8, *11*, 22, 38, 49, 109
Bardhi, Pashko, 11
Barleti, Marin, 11
Barletius, Marinus. *See* Barleti, Marin
Basha, Eqrem, 12
Bashkimi Society, *12*, 36, 42, 100, 104, 136, 148, 149
Basile, Angelo, 12
Basile, Vincenzo, *12*, 54
Bastari, Zenel, 12
Bazhdari, Gjon, 13
Becichemus, Marinus. *See* Beçikemi, Marin
Beçikemi, Marin, 13
Bedo, Resul, 13
Bejtexhi, 13
Bektashi, 12, *13*, 16, 32, 40, 44, 45, 47, 51, 63, 87, 96, 103, 123, 125, 129, 140, 141, 147
Beliçi, Domeniko. *See* Ujko, Vorea
Bellizzi, Domenico. *See* Ujko, Vorea
Belluçi, Konstantin, 13
Bellusci, Michele. *See* Bellushi, Miqel
Bellushi, Miqel, 14
Belmonte, Vincenzo, 14
Benusi, Gasper, 14
Benussi Skodrani, Casper. *See* Benusi, Gasper
Beqiri, Shaip, 114
Berati, Kostandin, 14
Berati, Kostë. *See* Berati, Kostandin
Berati, Nezi, 15
Berati, Nezim. *See* Frakulla, Nezim
Berisha, Anton, 15
Berisha, Ibrahim, 15
Berisha, Kristë, 15
Berisha, Latif, 15

Berisha, Rrustem, 15
Bidera, Gjon Emanuel, 16
Bihiku, Koço, 16
Bilota, Bernard, 16
Bilotta, Bernardo. *See* Bilota, Bernard
Bitri, Hysen, 16
Bityqi, Ndue. *See* Bytyçi, Ndue
Blanchus, Franciscus. *See* Bardhi, Frang
Blanco, Francesco. *See* Bardhi, Frang
Blushi, Kiço, 16
Boçari, Marko, 17
Bogdani, Luca. *See* Bogdani, Lukë
Bogdani, Lukë, 17
Bogdani, Pjetër, *17*, 22, 137
Bogomili, Theodhor, 4, *18*
Bokshi, Besim, 18
Boriçi, Daut, 18
Boshnjaku, Tahir, 3, *18*, 149
Botasi, Jani, 19
Botzaris, Markos. *See* Boçari, Marko
Brahimi, Razi, 19
Braile, Maria Antonia, 19
Braile, Salvatore, 14, *19*
Brancato, G. Nicola. *See* Brankati, Nikollë
Brankati, Nikollë, 19
Bredhi, Naum Panajot Haxhi Llazar. *See* Veqilharxhi, Naum
British and Foreign Bible Society, 82, 96, 116
Brocardus. *See* Adae, Guillelmus
Brochard. *See* Adae, Guillelmus
Brovina, Flora, 20
Brutus. *See* Stafa, Qemal
Bubani, Dionis, 20
Bubani, Gjergj, 20
Buburicka. *See* Musaraj, Shevqet
Buciarelli, Dari, 20
Budi, Pjetër, *20*, 22, 59, 109, 122
Bulka, Nonda, 21
Bulo, Jorgo, 21
Bushaka, Gaqo, 21
Butka, Sali, *22*, 53, 63
Buxheli, Qamil, 22
Buzëdhelpri. *See* Jordani, Agostin
Buzuku, Gjon, *22*, 75, 95, 109, 127
Bytyçi, Ndue, 23

INDEX

Çabej, Eqrem, 25
Çaçi, Aleks, 25
Çajupi, Andon Zako, 26, 79, 87
Çako, Andon. See Çajupi, Andon Zako
Camaj, Martin, 26
Camarda, Demetrio. See Kamarda, Dhimitër
Camarda, Giuseppe. See Kamarda, Zef
Çami, Muhamet. See Kyçyku, Muhamet
Çami, Qamil I., 27
Candreva, Carmelo. See Kandreva, Karmell
Castrioti, George. See Scanderbeg
Catalano, Nilo, 27
Cavallioti, T. See Kavalioti, Theodor
Çekrezi, Kostantin, 27
Çela, Zija, 27
Cepa, Kristaq, 28
Cepi, Kostandin, 28
Ceraja, Jakup, 28
Cerga, Agim, 28
Çetta, Anton, 28
Chajup. See Çajupi, Andon Zako
Chekrezi, Constantine. See Çekrezi, Kostantin
Chetta, Nicola. See Keta, Nikollë
Chiara, Pietro. See Kjara Pjetër
Chri-Chri. See Bulka, Nonda
Cibaj, Ismet, 29
Çiçkoja, Haxhi, 29
Cikuli, Zisa, 29
Çomora, Spiro, 29
Congress of Monastir. See Monastir, Congress of
Constantine of Berat. See Berati, Kostandin
Corinaldi, Giuseppe, 29
Cortese, Danil. See Korteze, Daniel
Crispi, Giuseppe. See Krispi, Zef
Crispi Glaviano, Francesco. See Krispi Glavjano, Frano
Çuka, Pano, 30
Cukaro, Kate, 30
Çuli, Diana, 30
Cuneus Prophetarum. See Bogdani, Pjetër

Dako, Christo A. See Dako, Kristo A.
Dako, Kristo A., 31

Da Lecce, Francesco Maria. See Lecce, Francesco Maria da
Dalliu, Hafiz Ibrahim, 31
Daniel, master. See Haxhiu, Dhanil
Dara, Andrea, 31, 32
Dara, Gabriele. See Dara, Gavrill
Dara, Gavrill (i ri). See Dara, Gavrill (the younger)
Dara, Gavrill (plaku). See Dara, Gavrill (the elder)
Dara, Gavrill (the elder), 31, 32
Dara, Gavrill (the younger), 31, 32
Dardha, Llambi, 32
Dedai, Salih Nijazi, 32
Dedaj, Rrahman, 32
Dede, Spiro, 33
Dedja, Bedri, 33
Del Gaudio, Giuseppe. See Gaudio, Xhuzepe del
Del Gaudio, Xhuzepe. See Gaudio, Xhuzepe del
Delvina, Dhimitri, 33, 122
Delvina, Namik Selim, 33
Demaçi, Adem, 33
Demaku, Daut, 33
De Martino, Leonardo. See Martino, Leonardo de
Demir Aga Vlonjakasi. See Vlonjati, Demir
Demolli, Arif, 34
De Rada, Girolamo. See Rada, Jeronim de
De Rada, Jeronim. See Rada, Jeronim de
Dervishi, Teki, 34
Dërvishi, Teki. See Dervishi, Teki
Deshpali, Shime, 34
Desku, Tahir, 34
Deva, Agim, 34
Dhanil, mjeshtri. See Haxhiu, Dhanil
Dhaskal Todhri. See Haxhifilipi, Theodhor
Dhosi, Mihal, 35
Dhrëva, Gjergj. See Dhriva, Gjergj
Dhriva, Gergj, 35
Dine, Spiro Rusto, 35, 61, 81, 83, 87, 88, 98, 105
Dini, Jonuz, 35
D'istria, Dora. See Istria, Dora d'

Dobraçi, Mulla Hysen, *35*, 109, 130
Docci, Primo. *See* Doçi, Preng
Dochi, Primo. *See* Doçi, Preng
Doçi, Preng, 12, *36*, 104
Doda, Xhemil, 36
Dodani, Visar, *36*, 61, 96
Dodi, Jani, 37
Dolce, Carlo. *See* Dulci, Carlo
Domonici, Nak. *See* Nikaj, Ndoc
Dorsa, Vinçenc, 37
Dorsa, Vincenzo. *See* Dorsa, Vinçenc
Drenova, Aleks Stavre. *See* Asdreni
Drini, Skënder, 37
Driva, Gjergh. *See* Dhriva, Gjergj
Duçi, Milo, 37
Dudesi, Mati, 38
Dudesius, Mattaeus. *See* Dudesi, Mati
Dukagjini, Ahmet bej, 38
Dukagjini, Jahja bej, 38
Dukagjini, Shpend. *See* Rexha, Zekeria
Dulci, Carlo, 38
Duraku, Nebil, 38
Dushko Vetmo. *See* Solano, Francesco

Easter Gospel, 39
Efendiu i Madh. *See* Boshnjaku, Tahir
Efthimiadhi, Li., 39
Eftimiu, Viktor, 39
Elbasan, anonymous manuscript of. *See* Anonimi I Elbasanit
Elbasani, Ahmet (sheh), 39
Elbasani, Ibrahim, 39
Elbasani, Sulejman Pasha, 39
Engjëll, Pal. *See* Angelus, Paulus
Erebara, Jashar, 40
Etëhem, Haxhi bej Tirana, 40
Etëhem bej Mollai. *See* Etëhem, Haxhi bej Tirana
Eustratios of Vithkuq. *See* Vithkuqari, Jani Evstrat
Evstrati Nga Vithkuqi. *See* Vithkuqari, Jani Evstrat

Ferizaj, Thabit Niman, 41
Ferraro, Matilda, 41
Ferri, Rexhep, 41
Figlia, Andrea. *See* Filja, Andrea
Figlia, Nicola. *See* Filja, Nikolla

Filja, Andrea, 41
Filja, Nikolla, 41
Fishta, Filip, 42
Fishta, Gjergj, 12, *42*, 79, 99, 100, 108
Floqi, Ismail, 42
Floqi, Kristo, 43
Formula e Pagëzimit. *See* Angelus, Paulus
Frakulla, Nezim, 3, 7, *43*, 84, 103, 146
Franco, Demetrius. *See* Frëngu, Dhimitër
Frascini, Beniamin, 43
Frashëri, Dalip, 3, *44*, 47
Frashëri, Mehdi, 44
Frashëri, Mid'hat, *44*, 88, 100, 141
Frashëri, Naim, 13, 22, *45*, 46, 47, 88
Frashëri, Sami, 45, *46*, 88, 100, 146, 149
Frashëri, Shahin, 3, 44, *47*
Frëngu, Dhimitër, 47

Gajtani, Adem, 49
Gashi, Mirko, 49
Gasparus, Stephanus. *See* Gaspri, Stefan
Gaspri, Stefan, 49
Gaudio, Giuseppe del. *See* Gaudio, Xhuzepe del
Gaudio, Xhuzepe del, 50
Gavoçi, Shauket, 50
Gazulli, Gjon, 50
Gazulus, Johannes. *See* Gazulli, Gjon
Geg, 21, 22, 29, 34, *50*, 82, 93, 99, 108, 121
Genovizzi, Fr., 50
Gentile, Cristina, 50
Germanos of Crete, 50
Gërvalla, Jusuf, 50
Gheg. *See* GEG
Ghica, Helena. *See* Istria, Dora d'
Gjakova, Agim, 50
Gjakova, Baba Hamza, 51
Gjakova, Tahir, 51
Gjata, Fatmir, 51
Gjeçov, Stefan. *See* Gjeçovi, Shtjefën
Gjeçovi, Shtjefën, 51
Gjerqeku, Enver, 52
Gjetja, Ndoc, 52
Gjika, Helena. *See* Istria, Dora d'
Gjirokastriti, Elmaz, 52, 96

INDEX

Gjirokastriti, Grigor, *52*, 96
Glaviano, Francesco Crispi. *See* Krispi Glavjano, Frano
Gliqini, Luc. *See* Dulci, Carlo
Godo, Sabri, 53
Grameno, Mihal, *53*, 88
Greek, ethnic minority, 30, 71
Grigor Gjirokastriti. *See* Gjirokastriti, Grigor
Grigori i Durrësit, 53
Gruda, Lek. *See* Gurakuqi, Luigj
Guagliata, Giuseppe. *See* Gualiata, Giuseppe
Gualiata, Giuseppe, 12, *53*
Guidera, Trifon, 54
Gunga, Fahredin, 54
Gurakuqi, Luigj, 12, *54*
Gurakuqi, Mark, 55
Gurra, Milto Sotir, 55
Gusho, Lazar. *See* Poradeci, Lasgush
Guzzetta, Giorgio, *55*, 56, 76, 109
Guzzetta, Giovan-Chrisostomo, 56

Hahn, Johann Georg von, 60, 82, 96
Hakiu, Nexhat, 57
Halil Popova, Tahir efendi. *See* Popova, Tahir efendi Halil
Halimi, Nexhat, 57
Hamiti, Sabri, 57
Harallambi, Kristo. *See* Negovani, Papa Kristo
Harapi, Anton. *See* Harapi, Ndue
Harapi, Ndue, *58*, 78
Harapi, Zef M., 58
Harff, Arnold von, 58
Harxhi, Ramiz, 58
Hasani, Hasan, 58
Hasani, Sinan, 59
Hasi, Pal, 59
Hatipi, Tajar, 59
Haxhiademi, Etëhem, 60
Haxhifilipi, Theodhor, 4, 18, *60*
Haxhimima, Josif, 60
Haxhiu, Dhanil, 60
Helenau. *See* Mirdita, Kolë
Hieromonakhos, Germanos. *See* Germanos of Crete
Hima, Dervish. *See* Naxhi, Mehmet

Hoxha, Mehmet, 61
Hoxha, Myslim, 61
Hoxha, Rexhep, 61
Hoxhi, Kostandin. *See* Hoxhi, Koto
Hoxhi, Koto, 35, 61, 132
Huluki, Ali, *61*, 62
Huluki, Mustafa, 41, 61, *62*
Hysa, Bedri, 62
Hyxhretiu. *See* Frashëri, Dalip

Ibrahimi, Baba, 63
Imami, Sitki, 63
Isaku, Agim, 63
Isaku, Murat, 63
Islami, Abdylazis, 63
Ismajli, Rexhep, 64
Istanbul Society. *See* Shoqëri e Të Shtypurit Shkronja Shqip
Istrefi, Adem, 64
Istria, Dora d', 9, *64*, 69, 73, 98, 119, 128
Ivanaj, Nikolla bej, 65

Jaçellari, Halil, 67
Jaha, Tahir, 67
Jakova, Kolë, 67
Jakova, Tahir efendi. *See* Boshnjaku, Tahir
Jakova Merturi, Gaspër, 54, *68*
Jasiqi, Ali D., 68
Jordani, Agostin, 68
Jorganxhi, Zhuljana G., 68
Jorgaqi, Nasho, 68
Jorgoni, Perikli, 68
Jubani, Giuseppe. *See* Jubani, Zef
Jubani, Zef, 35, *69*, 73, 119
Jubany, Giuseppe. *See* Jubani, Zef

Kacalidha, Niko, 71
Kadare, Elena, 71
Kadare, Ismail, 6, *71*
Kadriu, Ibrahim, 72
Kajtazi, Mehmet, 73
Kallamata, Miço, 73
Kamarda, Dhimitër, *73*, 98
Kamarda, Zef, 73
Kamberi, Hasan Zyko, 3, *73*, 84
Kamsi, Kolë, 74

INDEX

Kandreva, Karmell, 74, 126
Kapa. See Cepa, Kristaq
Kapareli, O., 74
Kashari, Haxhi Ymer, 74
Kashari, Ymer Mustafa. See Kashari, Haxhi Ymer
Kastrioti, Gjergj. See Scanderbeg
Kavalioti, Theodhor, 60, 74
Kavalliotis, Theodoros. See Kavalioti, Theodhor
Kazanxhiu, Simon, 75
Kazazi, Gjon Nikollë, 22, 75
Këlliçi, Skifter, 75
Kelmendi, Jusuf, 75
Kelmendi, Ramiz, 76
Kërveshi, Muhamed, 76
Keta, Nikollë, 76, 109
Kjara, Pjetër, 77
Koça, Vangjel, 77
Koçi, Vito, 77
Kodra, Klara, 77
Kodra, Lame. See Malëshova, Sejfulla
Kokalari, Musine, 77
Kokojka, Mali. See Frashëri, Mid'hat
Kokona, Vedat, 77
Kokoshi, Kudret, 78
Koliqi, Ernest, 78, 121
Kollumbi, Gaqo, 78
Kolonja, Shahin, 79, 88, 100
Kondo, Anastas, 79
Konica, Faik, 43, 52, 79, 104, 105, 130
Konispoli, Abdullah Sulejman, 80
Konitza, Faik. See Konica, Faik
Konushevci, Abdullah, 80
Korça, Mehment Iljaz, 80
Koreshi, Vath, 80
Korteze, Daniel, 80
Kosta, Koço, 80
Kotte, Kostandin, 80
Koupitoris, Panayotis. See Kupitori, Panajot
Kraja, Fadil, 80
Krasniqi, Mark, 81
Krasniqi, Sulejman, 81
Kreji, Thimi Thoma, 35, 81
Krispi, Zef, 81
Krispi Glavjano, Frano, 82
Kristoforidhi, Kostandin Nelko, 79, 82, 96, 98

Kukaj, Rifat, 82
Kullurioti, Anastas, 35, 83
Kupitori, Panajot, 83
Kuqali, Gjikë, 83
Kuteli, Mitrush, 83
Kyçyku, Muhamet, 3, 84, 103, 149

Laço, Teodor, 85
Lako, Natasha, 85
Lako, Nikollë, 86
Lecce, Francesco Maria da, 86
Leka, Lavdie, 86
Lepaja, Lutfi, 86
Lera, Nasi, 86
Leshkuqi, 86
Leskoviku, Baba Abidin, 87
Levonja, Besim, 87
Lipi. See Papajani, Filip
Lkeni i Hasit. See Gjeçovi, Shtjefën
Lluka, Tahir efendi, 87
Logoreci, Mati, 87
Logori, Loni, 35, 87
Londo, Bardhyl, 87
Lopez, Rafaele, 88, 110
Lorecchio, Anselmo. See Lorekio, Anselmo
Lorekio, Anselmo, 88
Luarasi, Kristo, 44, 88, 141
Luarasi, Petro Nini, 88
Luarasi, Skënder, 89
Luca, Ndrekë, 89
Lumezi, Lazër, 89
Lumo Skendo. See Frashëri, Mid'hat

Mala, Agim, 91
Malëshova, Sejfulla, 91
Malësori, Lulo. See Duçi, Milo
Maliqi, Hilmi, 91, 156
Maliqi, Sheh. See Maliqi, Hilmi
Maloki, Krist, 92
Mamaqi, Adelina, 92
Manastir, Congress of. See Monastir, Congress of
Mandalà, Cristina Gentile. See Gentile, Cristina
Mandia, Eglantina, 92
Marchese, Domenico. See Markeze, Domenik
Marchianò, Michele, 41, 92, 111

INDEX

Margëlliçi, Mehmet, 92
Markaj, Mirosh, 92
Markeze, Domenik, 93
Markianoi, Mikel. *See* Marchianò, Michele
Marko, Misto. *See* Markaj, Mirosh
Marko, Petro, 93
Marku, Rudolf, 93
Martino, Leonardo de, 23, *93*
Maruli, Mikel, 94
Marullò, Michele. *See* Maruli, Mikel
Maserech, Pietro. *See* Mazrreku, Pjetër
Mashi, Engell, 94
Master Daniel. *See* Haxhiu, Dhanil
Mato, Jakup, 94
Mato, Sulejman, 94
Matranga, Luca. *See* Matrënga, Lekë
Matrënga, Lekë, *94*, 109, 122
Mauri, Domenik, 95
Mauro, Domenico. *See* Mauri, Domenik
Mazrreku, Pjetër, 95
Meçani, Baba Abdullah, 95
Mehmeti, Din, 95
Mehzuni, Baba Muharem, 96
Meksi, Apostol Panajot, 96
Meksi, Jorgji, 96
Meksi, Vangjel, 52, *96*
Mekuli, Esad, 97
Mekuli, Hasan, 97
Merxhani, Branko, 97
Meshari. *See* Buzuku, Gjon
Meto, Memo, 97
Migjeni, 21, 89, *97*, 136
Minarolli, Hamza, 98
Mirdita, Kolë, 98
Mitko, Thimi, 35, 36, 73, 79, 81, *98*, 119
Mjeda, Ndre, 2, 12, 87, *99*, 100
Mjedja, Ndre. *See* Mjeda, Ndre
Mjeshtri Dhanil. *See* Haxhiu, Dhanil
Monastir, Congress of, 42, 44, 87, 99, *100*, 109, 116
Mosi, Hilë, 88, *100*, 104, 133
Moskhopolis. *See* Voskopojë
Muço, Betim, 101
Mulaj, Avni R., 101
Muriqi, Nebih, 101
Musachi, Giovanni. *See* Muzaka, Gjon
Musaj, Ali, 101

Musaraj, Shevqet, 101
Musliu, Beqir, 102
Musliu, Ramadan, 102
Muzaka, Gjon, 102

Naibi, Sulejman, 3, 84, *103*
Napoletano, Pietro, 103
Nasibiu, Tahir, 103
Naxhi, Mehmet, 103
Negovani, Papa Kristo, 88, *104*
Nezimi, Ibrahim. *See* Frakulla, Nezim
Nikaj, Ndoc, 104
Nikolla, Millosh Gjergj. *See* Migjeni
Nokshiqi, Sat. *See* Mekuli, Esad
Noli, Fan Stylian, 9, 27, 43, 54, 91, *105*
Nomadhi. *See* Gurra, Milto Sotir

Paçarizi, Haxhi Ymer Lutfi, 107
Paçrami, Fadil, 107
Palaj, Bernardin, 107
Pali, Gaspër, 108
Pali prej Hasi. *See* Hasi, Pal
Papa, Loni, 108
Papajani, Filip, 108
Papleka, Ndoc, 108
Parrino, Demetrio, 108
Parrino, Francesco, 108
Parrino, Paolo Maria, 77, *109*
Pasha, Vaso. *See* Vasa, Pashko
Pashku, Anton, 109
Pasko, Dhimitër. *See* Kuteli, Mitrush
Pata, Mulla Sali, 109
Peçi, Shefqet, 109
Peci, Sotir, 100, 105, *109*
Pekmezi, Gjergj, 99, *110*
Perone, Lluka, 110
Perrone, Luca. *See* Perone, Lluka
Petrassi, Luigi, 88, *110*
Petrela, Hasan, 110
Petriti, Koçi, 110
Petta, Eugenio, 111
Peza, Murteza, 111
Pipa, Arshi, 111
Pitarka, Sulejman, 111
Platonkicus. *See* Stafa, Veli
Podrimja, Ali, 111
Popova, Tahir efendi Halil, 112
Poradeci, Lasgushm, 112
Postenani, Nikolla Ikonom, *112*, 113

Postenani, Stefan, 112, *113*
Postoli, Foqion, 113
Postripa, Gegë. *See* Shiroka, Filip
Prennushi, Vinçenc, 113
Prifti, Naum, 113
Prishtina, Mesihi, 114
Propaganda Fide, College of, 8, 11, 17, 36, 37, 49, 73, 75, 86, 122
Prucher, Bonaventura, 114
Pulaha, Ruzhdi, 114

Qafëzezi, Ilo Mitkë, 115
Qafëzezi, Luan, 115
Qena, Muharrem, 115
Qiriazi, Dhori, 116
Qiriazi, Gjerasim, 116
Qiriazi, Gjergj, 116
Qosja, Rexhep, 116
Qulli, Muço, 117
Qurku, Viktor, 117

Rada, Camillo de, 119
Rada, Girolamo de. *See* Rada, Jeronim de
Rada, Jeronim de, 8, 14, 54, 69, 73, 88, 92, 98, 110, *119*, 126, 137, 141
Radoja, Engjëll, 120
Ramadani, Musa, 120
Ramazani, Sulejman. *See* Naibi, Sulejman
Rami, Ahmad, 120
Rekas, Josef Bageri. *See* Bageri, Josef
Rela, Josip, 121
Rem Vogli. *See* Araniti, Midhat
Ressuli, Namik, 121
Rexha, Zekeria, 121
Rexha-Bala, Kosovë, 121
Ribecco, Agostino, 121
Ribeko, Agostin. *See* Ribecco, Agostino
Rilindja, 14, 27, 35, 36, 44, 50, 61, 65, 68, 73, 79, 81, 84, 87, 91, 99, 119, *122*, 135, 140, 147, 149
Rodinò, Neofito, 33, *122*
Rodotà, Pompilio, 122
Roko, Kosmo, 122
Rrahmani, Nazmi, 122
Rrahmani, Zejnullah, 122
Rras'e Bardhë. *See* Haxhimima, Josif

Rrota, Justin, 123
Ruci, Llambro, 123
Rugova, Ibrahim, 123
Ruhi, Baba Selim, 123
Ruka, Petrit, 123

Sabriu, Jonuz efendi, 125
Sadeddin, Omer efendi, 125
Sako, Zihni, 125
Salihu, Baba, 125
Şamseddin, Sami. *See* Frashëri, Sami
San Benedetto Ullano, College of, 8, 14
Sant' Adriano, College of (San Demetrio Corone), 5, 7, 9, 13, 16, 37, 54, 68, 88, 110, 119, 120, 137
Santori, Francesco Antonio, 73, *125*
Scanderbeg, 4, 5, 11, 26, 32, 44, 45, 47, 69, 92, 98, *126*, 149, 156
Schirò, Giovanni, 126
Schirò, Giuseppe, 50, *127*, 128
Schirò, Paolo, 127
Schirò Di Maggio, Giuseppe, 127
Schirò Di Modica, Giuseppe, 127
Selimi, Fehime, 128
Serembe, Cosmo, 128
Serembe, Giuseppe. *See* Serembe, Zef
Serembe, Zef, 73, *128*
Shantoja, Lazër, 129
Shapllo, Dalan, 129
Sheh Maliqi. *See* Maliqi, Hilmi
Shehu, Agim, 129
Shehu, Bashkim, 129
Shehu, Maksut, 129
Shëmbërdhenji, Baba Meleq, 129
Shemimiu. *See* Shkodra, Shemimi
Shiroka, Filip, 50, 87, *130*
Shiroka, Gjon, 130
Shita, Vehap, 130
Shkodra, Hysen efendi, 35, *130*
Shkodra, Jakin. *See* Gurakuqi, Luigj
Shkodra, Shemimi, 130
Shkodrani, Vasa Pasha. *See* Vasa, Pashko
Shkreli, Adem, 130
Shkreli, Azem, 131
Shkreli, Ymer, 131
Shllaku, Gjon, 131

Shoqëri e Të Shtypurit Shkronja Shqip, *131*, 146, 149
Shukriu, Edi. *See* Shukriu-Hoti, Edi
Shukriu-Hoti, Edi, 132
Shundi, Stefan, 132
Shuteriqi, Dhimitër S., 97, *132*
Shuteriqi, Simon, 133
Siliqi, Drago, 133
Siliqi, Llazar, 93, *133*
Siliqi, Risto, 133
Sirdani, Aleksander, 134
Sirdani, Marin, 134
Skanderbeg. *See* Scanderbeg
Skënderbeu. *See* Scanderbeg
Skendo, Lumo. *See* Frashëri, Mid'hat
Skiro Di Maxho, Xhusepe. *See* Schirò Di Maggio, Giuseppe
Skiro Di Modika, Xhusepe. *See* Schirò Di Modica, Giuseppe
Skiroi, Gjon. *See* Schirò, Giovanni
Skiroi, Pal. *See* Schirò, Paolo
Skiroi, Zef. *See* Schirò, Giuseppe
Solano, Francesco, 27, 126, *134*
Sotiri, Pandeli, 132, *134*
Spahiu, Xhevahir, 134
Spasse, Sterjo, 135
Spiru, Nako, 135
Stafa, Felice, 135
Stafa, Qemal, 136
Stafa, Veli, 136
Staffa, Felice. *See* Stafa, Felice
Stavre, Aleks. *See* Asdreni
Stërmilli, Haki, 136
Straticò, Alberto, 137
Straticò, Vincenzo, 137
Stratigo, Vinçenc. *See* Straticò, Vincenzo
Sulejman, Abdullah. *See* Konispoli, Abdullah Sulejman
Sulejmani, Hivzi, 137
Suli, Vincenzo, 137
Sulli, Nicolai Athanasi, 137
Suma, Lukë, 137
Summa, Luca. *See* Suma, Lukë
Surroi, Rexhai, 137

Tahir efendi Halil Popova. *See* Popova, Tahir efendi Halil

Tahir efendi Jakova. *See* Boshnjaku, Tahir
Tahir efendi Lluka. *See* Lluka, Tahir efendi
Tamburi, Francesco Saverio, 139
Temani, Sulejman, 139
Tërpo, Nektar, 139
Thaçi, Kolë, 139
Tigani, Shefqet, 139
Toçkas, D. *See* Gurra, Milto Sotir
Todhri, Dhaskal. *See* Haxhifilipi, Theodhor
Tomeu, Leonik, 140
Tomori, Baba Ali, 140
Toptani, Murat, 140
Tosk, 20, 37, 50, 82, 95, *140*, 155
Totasi, Papa, 4, *140*
Toto, Ismet, 140
Tozaj, Nexhat, 140
Trebicka, Kosta Jani, 44, 88, *141*
Troiano, Mosè, 141
Turani, Baba Ahmed, 141
Tutulani, Kristaq, 141
Tutulani, Margarita, 141

Uçi, Alfred, *143*, 149
Ujkani, Qerim, 143
Ujko, Vorea, 143
Ulqinaku, Hafëz Ali, 3, *143*
Ungjilli i Pashkëve. *See* Easter Gospel

Vançi, Ali, 145
Varfi, Andrea, 145
Variboba, Giulio. *See* Variboba, Jul
Variboba, Jul, 145
Vasa, Pashko, 9, 132, *146*
Vatra Society, 31, 43, 79, 105, 113
Velabishti, Ismail Pasha, 146
Vellarai, Jan, 147
Veqilharxhi, Naum, 147
Vërlaci, Sulejman Pasha. *See* Elbasani, Sulejman Pasha
Vetmo, Dushko. *See* Solano, Francesco
Vexh-hi, Baba Adem, 147
Vilaras, Ioannis. *See* Vellarai, Jan
Vinca, Agim, 147
Vithkuqari, Jani Evstrat, 148
Vlladoviq-Rela, Josif. *See* Rela, Josip

Vlonjakasi, Demir aga. *See* Vlonjati, Demir
Vlonjati, Demir, 148
Vlora, Eqrem bey, 148
Voka, Rexhep, 149
Voskopojari, Grigor. *See* Grigori i Durrësit
Voskopojë, 53, 60, 74, 148
Vreto, Jani, 35, 81, 84, 112, 113, 132, 146, *149*
Vruho, Jani, 105, *149*

Wassa Effendi. *See* Vasa, Pashko

Xanoni, Anton, 54, *153*
Xhuvani, Aleksandër, 82, *153*
Xhuvani, Dhimiter, 153

Xoxa, Jakov, 154
Xukaro, Kate. *See* Cukaro, Kate

Zade, Muçi, 155
Zadeja, Ndre, 155
Zako, Andon. *See* Çajupi, Andon Zako
Zaloshnja, Moisi, 155
Zarishi, Pjetër, 155
Zeqo, Moikom, 156
Zeza, Gjon. *See* Gurra, Milto Sotir
Zheji, Gjergj, 156
Ziko, Vangjush, 156
Zuccaro, Kate. *See* Cukaro, Kate
Zuka, Ramë. *See* Rexha, Zekeria
Zurnaxhiu, Shaip, 156
Zyko, Hasan. *See* Kamberi, Hasan Zyko

About the Author

ROBERT ELSIE is a Translator for the Government of the Federal Republic of Germany. Born in Canada, he received his Ph.D. from the University of Bonn, and has traveled extensively in Albania and Kosovo. He has previously published an *Anthology of Albanian Poetry*.

INDEXED IN Balay # BE 1093

R0156035003 HUM SR ✓
                      891.
    35.00   99103
                      E49

ELSIE, ROBERT
    DICTIONARY OF
ALBANIAN LITERATURE

Houston Public Libraries
FOR LIBRARY USE ONLY

JAN 88
  JAN 88

This Book is Dedicated To My:

Family, Readers and Supporters.
I LOVE you guys so much. Please believe that!!

—Joy Deja King

"I've been in this game for years, it made me an animal, there's rules to this shit so I wrote me a manual..."

—Notorious BIG

A KING PRODUCTION

Nico Carter

Men Of The Bitch Series

Joy Deja King

Chapter 1

I Got A Story To Tell

I came into this world wanting one thing... love. I couldn't get that love from my mother so I stole it from the streets. Eventually, I did get the love, respect, and money I craved, but it came at a very high price. As I stand here today, I can't help but ask myself, was it worth it? But before I can answer that question and move forward, I have to go back to what brought me here.

"Nico, get yo' ass in this house," my mother yelled out the window.

"I'm coming!" I yelled back for the third time, running with the ball in my hands, knowing I was lying again. We were playing the hood version of football and my team was winning so I didn't want to stop. See, the older boys in the neighborhood thought they could kick our ass 'cause we were young.

My boy Lance and I were only 10, but we were both tall for our age, fast, and already had a lil' muscle tone. My best friend, Ritchie, and the other boys on our team were either below average or average at best. But with Lance and my skills and the other boys just following our lead, we would constantly beat the older boys. It would drive them crazy and I loved it.

"Touch down!" I hollered and started doing my signature two-step dance move before throwing the ball down. "Peace out motherfuckers!" I grinned, before running towards my apartment.

"We see you tomorrow!" I heard Ritchie and the other boys yell back.

"Boy, you see what time it is?" my mother popped as soon as I closed the door. "You know you ain't supposed to be outside when it get this dark."

"Sorry. I was playing football and didn't realize it was so late."

"Well go in there and get yo'self cleaned up. Yo' daddy will be over here in a little bit," my mom said, fixing her hair in the mirror.

"Now it makes sense," I mumbled.

"What you say, boy?" my mother said, shooting me one of her evil looks.

"I just said I was hungry," I lied.

"I'm sure yo' daddy will take us out to eat when he gets here. So hurry up! I want you to be clean, dressed, and ready when he walk through that door."

I was wondering why my mom was so concerned about me coming in the house. Normally, I could come home at any time of the night and she wouldn't notice or care. She would assume I was at Ritchie's house or another kid in the building and it almost felt like she preferred I stayed there. The only time she wanted me around was if my father was coming over to visit. She would always put on this big show as if she was the Mother Of The Year. I would play along because part of me was always hoping that maybe one day her pretending would rub off and become a reality.

After taking a bath, I decided to put on the New York Knicks jersey my dad had gotten me. I smiled looking at myself in the mirror. I was the spitting image of my father and that made me feel proud.

"Where my lil' man Nico at!" I heard my father call out.

"What up, Dad!" I said, running up to him. He wrapped his strong arms around me giving me a hug like only he could.

"I just saw you a couple days ago and you already grew a few inches. Damn, you a handsome kid, if I say so myself." My dad smiled proudly.

"You only saying that 'cause he look just like you." My mother laughed.

"But of course. Nico know where he get them good looks from, don't you boy," my dad teased, putting his huge hand on top of my head and playfully shaking it. "You ready to go?"

"Yes, sir. Where we going?"

"I got us tickets to go see the Yankees play."

"No way!"

"Do I ever lie to you?"

"Nope, you sure don't, Daddy."

"And I never will. Now let's get outta here."

"Nico said he was hungry. I thought the three of us would go get something to eat," my mother said, folding her arms.

"Maybe next time, Shaniece. Tonight it's just me and my son," my dad said, taking my hand. When I turned to tell my mother bye, she was rolling her eyes.

"What you mean maybe next time? Don't you see me dressed? You think I got all jazzed up to sit in this apartment?"

"Here, go out and have a good time wit' your girlfriends. Nico can stay with me for the night," my dad said, giving my mother a bunch of money. She balled it up in her fist tightly, but I could tell she was steaming mad.

"Fine, you keep him, but you still owe me dinner," she snapped, putting her other hand on her hip.

"See you tomorrow, Mom," I said about to go give her a hug goodbye, but she walked away. I took my dad's hand and we left.

My dad had recently bought a new gold, two door Mercedes Benz sedan and this was the first time I was going for a ride in it. Last week when he stopped by so I could see it, everybody went crazy on the block. My dad was the man and when I grew up I wanted to be just like him. After we got in the car and settled in my dad turned on the radio. But before I could start jamming to the beat, he turned the music down and looked at me.

"Nico, I want you to know something," he said with a stone face. My dad was always smiling and joking so it was weird seeing him so serious.

"What is it, Dad?"

"You're my son, my only child and I love you no matter what."

"I know and I love you, too."

"You might not be seeing me around at your mother's place that much anymore, but I want you to come stay at my house on the weekends. Is that okay with you?"

"Yes! I just wanna spend time with you. I don't care where."

"That's my boy. Now let's go see these Yankees." My dad smiled and drove off.

Although I was young, I knew exactly what was going on. Ever since I could remember my mother and father were on and off. They never lived together and half the time they were arguing and the other half they were in the bedroom with the door locked. I guess they were about to be off again. My dad had never told me he wasn't going to be coming around, so something had changed, I just didn't know what.

Chapter 2

Family Ties

"Motherfucker, you think 'cause you got a new bitch that shit done change! Please, yo' ass will be back like always! But in the meantime don't think you gon' be gettin' my son on the weekends!" I heard my mom scream to my dad. I closed my bedroom door not wanting to hear the arguing, but my mom was being extra loud tonight so I had no choice, but to hear every word. My dad, who was normally so chill, was even amped up.

"Shaniece, that's our son and yes the fuck I will be getting him every weekend. Try to keep Nico away from me and see how real shit get for you."

"Is that a threat, motherfucker? Is you threatening me? Let me pick up the gotdamn phone right now and call the fuckin' police so I can let them know my baby daddy is threatening me."

"Put that phone down!" I heard my father holler. Then I heard what sounded like a small tussle. "Give me the phone, Shaniece!"

"I ain't giving you shit!" I heard what sounded like some more scuffling, so I ran out my room to see what was going on. When I got in the living room I saw my mother slam the telephone on the side of my father's head.

"Fuuuuuuck!" my dad yelled out in pain as he held his head. "You lucky I don't put my hands on no woman," he said, wiping away some blood that was dripping down the side of his face.

"Go 'head hit me! You supposed to be so big and bad. Give it yo' best shot," my mother cracked trying to provoke my father into a fight. As if feeling my presence my mother turned in my direction. "Nico, go back in yo' room!"

"Daddy, are you okay?" I asked, concerned about my father.

"I'm fine, son."

"Don't worry 'bout yo' daddy. He a grown man. Now get yo' ass back in yo' room."

I heard what my mother said, but I couldn't move. I felt like my dad needed me. I didn't know what I could do to help, but I thought standing here, where he could see me, somehow let him know that I was on his side.

"I ain't gon' tell you again, Nico. Go to your

room!" my mother screamed like she had lost her mind.

"Go 'head son. Go to your room. I'm fine. I'll come check on you before I leave," my father said, trying to console me. I put my head down and went back to my room. I didn't close my door though because I had now become fixated on wanting to hear every single word.

"Royce, don't make this get ugly. You go 'head and have fun wit' yo' new bitch and when you ready to get yo' shit together, you can come back to your family. But Nico will not be spending the weekends at your house. If you want to see him, you can come over here."

"If you want to keep a roof over your head, food on the table, a car parked outside, and clothes on your back you will let me have my son on the weekends. Do you understand me?" my father warned.

"You saying you would cut me off? If I don't eat then yo' son don't eat."

"My son is going to eat just fine. He ain't gon' neva starve, but you won't have nothing. If you do have something, it won't be coming from me. The choice is yours, but either way, I will have my son. I don't have to lay a finger on you to let you know that I mean every single word."

"Fuck you, Royce! You gon' pay for this shit!!" my mother yelled, but instead of responding to her, he came to my bedroom.

"I'm sorry you had to hear all that, son," my

father said, giving me a hug.

"It's not your fault."

"It's not your mother's fault either. She just can't help herself," my dad said jokingly and then laughed, trying to put a smile on my face. "I'll be here on Friday to pick you up so be ready."

"I will! You promise?" My eyes lit up, excited by the idea of spending the entire weekend at my dad's house for the first time.

"Yes, I promise. See you soon. Love you, lil' man."

"I love you too, Daddy." I hugged my dad one more time, extra tight and watched him walk out the door.

♛ ♛ ♛

Like my father always did, he kept his promise. He came to get me that weekend and every weekend after that. When he arrived my mom would be standing at the front door with a frown on her face, her arms folded and hand out. It was as if she was selling me off to my dad every weekend. It was then that I realized all women had a price, including mothers.

"Nico, do you want me to make you some more spaghetti?" Chrissy, my dad's girlfriend, asked.

"No, thanks, I'm good."

"Okay, but if you need anything let me know.

I'll be in the kitchen."

"I will. Thanks." I smiled when Chrissy walked away. Although she was a lot older than me, that woman was fine. She had the smoothest chocolate-colored skin I had ever seen which made her perfectly-white, straight teeth sparkle even more. Not only was she fine, but she was nice. She treated my father like a king and me like a little prince. I now understood why my dad had moved on from my mom and kept Chrissy around permanently... she was what I would hear old heads call, a keeper.

As the years passed, I began to think of Chrissy as a mother figure. Honestly, she seemed to love me more than my own mother. She gave me that affection I never got from my mother and it seemed genuine. I wanted to move in with them full time, but my mother wasn't having it. I don't think it was so much that my mother wanted me around, but because she didn't want the cash to stop coming in from my father. I had become a steady paycheck for her and she had no intentions of letting that go.

"How you like Chrissy?" my dad asked out the blue while we were riding in his car, on our way to Marvin's house, who was like a brother to my dad and I called uncle. I loved when my dad would let me hang out with him when he had running around to do. I would listen to all the small talk him and his friends would make and learned so much about the streets. I was fascinated and wanted to be them, although my father was adamant I would go to college.

"You know I like Chrissy. She makes the best sweet potato pie, too." I grinned, nodding my head, thinking about how good that last slice I had tasted.

"Boy, I know she can cook, but do you like her? I mean, really like her?"

"I more than like her, I love her, Dad." I noticed my dad's eyes get a little glassy. "Dad, are you okay?"

"I'm better than okay. I'm just so happy you said that, because I didn't want to ask her to be my wife unless you approved. We partners you know." He smiled before shaking my hand.

"You're finally going to get married?"

"If Chrissy accepts my proposal."

"You know she will. Chrissy has wanted to be your wife for a long time."

"How you know that?"

"That day she had to pick me up from school early because I had gotten sick and I couldn't get in touch with Mom. Well, when I was leaving one of the kids asked me was that my mother and I said no, she's my dad's wife. I thought you all were already married."

"You did?"

"Yep. I mean you been living together for the last few years. But when I said that, Chrissy smiled and told me she wasn't your wife yet, but hopefully one day soon. That's how I know she'll accept your proposal."

"Good, because after we stop by Marvin's place

we're going to go pick up the ring. I'm popping the question tonight."

"Does that mean I can live with you all the time now?" I wanted to know.

"I would love that, son, but convincing your mother is another story."

"If anybody can convince her, it's you."

"I'll work on it."

"You promise?" I knew if I made my dad promise that meant he would do his best because my father never liked to make a promise and not keep it.

"I promise," he said and winked his eye. After my dad said that I sat back in my seat and relaxed for the rest of the car ride. He was like a superhero to me and now that he made a promise I knew he would make my wish come true.

♛ ♛ ♛

"Shaniece, listen, I wanted to talk to you about something," my dad said when he brought me home after one of my weekend visitations. Instead of going to my bedroom, I sat down on the living room couch and started rumbling through my overnight bag like I was looking for something. I was hoping he was finally going to ask her about me living with him full time, since it had been weeks since I asked him to.

"What is it?" my mom replied with her arms

folded tightly, giving off major attitude. I already knew this wasn't going to go well, but I didn't care because I wanted out.

"I was thinking that maybe it would be best if Nico come live with me. I mean, he just turned 13 so he's a teenager now. I think I'll be a good influence for him."

"A good influence... what you gon' teach him? How to sell drugs?" she smacked. "You gon' teach my son how to make money by being a street hustler like you?"

"You don't seem to have a problem taking my money. Since it's good enough for you, I think we need to leave the subject of me selling drugs alone. Nico will be well taken care of in my home."

"Who gon' take care of him? That little bitch you got engaged to? Yeah, I heard you asked that heffa to marry you. So the woman that pushed out your first-born son wasn't good enough for you to put a ring on, but you married some gold-digging hussy. If you think you gon' take my son and my money, you must be motherfuckin' crazy."

"First off, leave my fiancé out of this. Secondly, our son is not a paycheck. But because he will be coming to see you I don't have a problem still giving you money. It may not be as much, but we can work out something."

"We ain't working out shit! Nico ain't going nowhere. I'll see yo' ass in court first. Ain't no judge gonna take a son away from their mother, and give custody to a drug dealer. So you and yo' fiancé go have yo' own baby, 'cause this one right here," my mother turned and pointed to me, "ain't going nowhere."

"Well, I guess I'll be seeing you in court, Shaniece. But I advise you to get your own house in order, 'cause I ain't the only one with skeletons. I'll see you Friday, Nico."

"Okay, Dad... love you."

"Love you, too," he said before closing the door behind him.

I could feel my mother staring at me, but I refused to look up. I kept going through my bag until she walked away. I had never seen her so angry, but inside I was smiling. I got absolutely no happiness living with her. I loved my mother because I thought it was the right thing to do. I believed that you were supposed to love the woman that brought you into this world even if there wasn't a nurturing bone in her body. I wanted to live with my father and I was positive that one way or another my dad would make that my reality.

Chapter 3

The Moment I Feared

"I'm so sick of this shit," I said to Ritchie as we were walking home from school.

"You always complaining. What you sick about now?"

"Living with my mom, going to school, doing homework. That same shit over and over again."

"Man, you don't even do no homework. You be letting Kecia or one of your other lil' girlfriends do it for you."

"'Cause that homework shit is a waste of time. When we go out in these streets and make money ain't nobody gon' be asking us about science, history, and that other crap. All we need to know is math so we can count our fuckin' money."

"Whatever, Nico. Yo' pops already said you wouldn't be hustling in them streets. We supposed to go to college, remember."

"Fuck that. College ain't for me. I'm in 8th grade and already tryna come up with a way to get out of it, so you know college is out the question."

"Yo' pops will kick yo' ass. And you know yo' moms ain't having it."

"Like my mom would care. As long as I don't bother her and interrupt her flow she don't give a fuck what I do. I'm just a way of her getting money from my dad."

"That ain't true," Ritchie said half-heartedly.

"All my mom do is run the streets with yo' mom. My mom only pretend like she give a fuck when my pops come around so she can keep getting money from him."

Ritchie tried to pretend not hear what I said because he was in denial. He knew his mom was the same way, but he only wanted to see the best in her. That was a major difference between the two of us. I looked at the world for what it was, the good, bad, and ugly. Ritchie, on the other hand, wanted to remain a kid forever and view the world from the eyes of a child.

"So are we hooping this weekend or what," Ritchie said, changing the subject. Sometimes on the weekends Ritchie would come stay at my dad's with me, but I wasn't sure if I wanted him to come this time.

"I might, but nah if I can get in on this dice game that kid Manny have going on."

"Dice? You mean like gambling?"

"Yes, you square ass nigga, gambling. I need to get my money up. If only my pops would let me work one of his corners I wouldn't have to play no dice."

"You bet not let yo' dad find out you playing dice," Ritchie said, shaking his head.

"And you bet not open yo' big ass mouth and say nothing," I warned, tossing a rock at his back.

"Ouch, that hurt." Ritchie sighed.

"Stop whining before I throw another one and hit you in the head." I laughed.

"You betta not!"

"I betta not what?" I yelled, as I started chasing him home. We both laughed as Ritchie almost tripped and fell, but we kept running. Right when I got up on Ritchie to throw him to the ground, we stopped in our tracks noticing a bunch of cops surrounding our apartment complex.

"What's going on?" I asked a crack head who was standing off to the side, watching everything.

"Somebody got killed. That's all I know. The cops questioning everybody," he said, seeming antsy.

"Come on, let's find out what's going on," Ritchie said, grabbing my arm. I picked up my backpack and followed him over to the large crowd that was gathered in a circle.

"Yo, that kid just rolled up and shot him and

rolled out," I heard a local neighborhood man say.

"I know, the shit happened so fast, I don't even remember what he looked like," another dude said.

"Look, that must be the body over there," Ritchie said, nudging my arm. He pointed towards the yellow tape where the man's body was covered. "I've never seen a dead body before, let's get closer," Ritchie urged.

"Okay," I agreed as we headed closer to the dead body that was sprawled out near a parked car. I heard of a few people getting killed in our projects, but like Ritchie I had never seen a dead body with my own eyes. The cops were talking amongst each other and to some residents. I figured they were trying to find witnesses, but I doubted anybody in our hood would say shit. I then noticed another man come up, but I figured he must've been a detective because he was wearing a suit. He went over to the body, bent down and lifted the sheet.

"Noooooooooooooo!" Is all I remember screaming out before running towards my dad's dead body.

"Nico, come back," I heard Ritchie yell out, but I was gone.

"He can't be dead! My dad can't be dead," I kept screaming trying to reach him, but was held back by one of the officers. "Let me go! Let me go! I have to get to my father!"

I could hear voices talking to me, but I couldn't understand their words. I had zoned out. My mind was in another place. The man that I had looked up to and wanted to be like, was gone. Someone had put a bullet through his head and left him bloodied on the concrete like he was trash. My father was dead.

♛ ♛ ♛

For the next few weeks after my father died, I refused to come out of my room. The only place I went was to his funeral. The pain I was in seemed almost unbearable. I was full of rage. I wasn't sure if I was angry because I blamed my father for leaving me. Although I knew somebody shot and killed him, I still felt like it was his fault.

"Nico, unlock the door!" I heard my mother scream, interrupting my thoughts.

I got up from the bed and took my time unlocking the door, not wanting to be bothered.

"Boy, you need to get yo' shit together. You can't just stay in this damn room every day all day. You need to take yo' ass back to school," she belted, looking around my bedroom.

"I don't feel like going to school. I just want to stay in my room," I said, lying back down on my bed.

"I don't give a damn what you feel like doing. Yo' father is dead, now get over it," she said and slammed the door.

I wanted to bury my face in the pillow and cry, but I was tired of crying. It wasn't going to bring my father back. So instead of crying I started punching my pillow. I needed to release all this anger I had balled up. I kept punching until I heard my mom calling my name.

"Nico, come here. Somebody is here to see you."

At first I wasn't going to come out my room because I figured it was Ritchie or one of the other kids in the neighborhood, but I decided to see; because honestly my frustrations were getting the best of me and I felt like I was suffocating. I needed to breathe.

"There's my guy," I heard a cheerful voice say when I walked out of my bedroom.

"Uncle Marvin, it's good to see you," I said with a slight smile when I saw his tall slim body, dressed in his standard attire of a suit, standing by the door.

"It's good to see you, too," he said, giving me a hug. "Listen, I wanted you to go for a ride with me. That is if your mother doesn't mind," he said, looking over at my mom.

"Go 'head. If you can get him out his room and this apartment then by all means take him," she said huffing.

"How 'bout it, Nico?" Marvin questioned.

"Sure," I said somewhat reluctantly. "Give me a minute. I need to get dressed."

"Take your time. I'll be right here waiting for you."

By the time I took a shower and got dressed I was actually ready to go and looked forward to spending some time with Uncle Marvin. He was almost like the closest person I could get to that was like my dad. They had known each other since before I was born and were so tight that they had a lot of the same body gestures and similar word usage.

"I heard you weren't doing too well," Uncle Marvin said when we got in his car. "I miss your dad, too," he added.

"Why did God have to take my dad from me? I just don't understand. He was the only person that loved me," I said, putting my head down.

"That's not true, Nico. I love you, your mom love you, and so does Chrissy."

I looked up at Uncle Marvin and could see the sincerity in his eyes, but I wasn't all the way convinced about my mother. I didn't tell him that though. I knew he meant well and I figured that's what really mattered.

"I don't know what to do now that he's not here anymore," I confided.

"You stand up and be the young man he taught you to be. Your father was strong and he raised you to be the same way. I can't never replace your father, but I'll step in where he left off, if you want me to."

"You mean I can still come hang out at your store and stuff?"

"All that. We can go to the games, you can help me run errands, I'll get your school clothes or whatever you need, I got you. Your father looked out and came through for me more times than I can count and I know he would want me to come through for you."

'Thank you, Uncle Marvin," I said, genuinely grateful that I still had him in my life.

"You don't have to thank me. I feel honored. You know you've always been like the son I never had. You will get through this. We both will. There is somebody who wants to see you if you're up to it."

"Who?" I wanted to know.

"Chrissy. She's been asking about you, but she didn't feel comfortable calling over to your mother's house."

"Yes, I do miss Chrissy."

"Great. She gonna be happy to see you. Don't ever think you're alone in this. We're here for you Nico," Uncle Marvin reassured me as we headed to Chrissy's place.

I sat back in the car and for the first time since my father died, I felt a glimpse of hope. I would never get over losing my dad, but I didn't feel so alone anymore. Being around my mother, she didn't seem to understand or care about my pain, but now I felt like I had other people I could share my sadness with. I finally believed that I would get through the darkest days of my life.

Chapter 4

It's My Time

It had been over a year since my father was murdered and not a day went by that I didn't think about him. There had been no arrest, but I continued to keep my ears to the street believing that one day I would find out exactly who was responsible for his death. In the meantime, I continued to become more immersed in learning the game and the more time I spent with Uncle Marvin, the more that became true. Unlike my father, Uncle Marvin wasn't constantly preaching to me about doing well in school and going to college. He seemed to actually enjoy the act of hustling unlike my dad.

See, my dad looked at selling drugs as a way to make money and take care of himself and his family.

He didn't have a high school degree and felt there wasn't a legitimate way of making enough money to provide for his family sufficiently. That's why my dad always stressed the importance of me going to school because he didn't want me to have to hustle like he did. The thing was, I honestly got some sort of excitement from learning how the drug game worked. To me, it equated to being your own boss and running a corporation if you played your cards right. Uncle Marvin saw that hunger in me and fed it every chance he got.

"Uncle Marvin, I was thinking," I said casually as we were in his store unpacking boxes of cigarettes.

"Should I be worried? I know what happens when you get to thinking," he joked.

"Nah, you don't have to be worried. I think it will help you out."

"Then get to talkin'," he said enthusiastically.

"I'm always hearing you complain about how Corey is running the project across from where I live."

"Yeah... and?"

"Well, the only reason you keep him is because you don't have anybody else you trust that knows them blocks."

"True, so what's your point?"

"I can oversee that project. I know those blocks like the back of my hand."

"Boy, I ain't got time to be entertaining your

jokes right now." Uncle Marvin chuckled brushing me off.

"I'm not joking. Like I said, I know the blocks, you can trust me and I'll bust my ass to make sure that project turns into a goldmine for you," I said confidently.

"You serious?" He said, stopping in the middle of lifting a box and staring at me.

"You know I don't joke when it comes to business."

"You sounded just like your father when you said that." Uncle Marvin grinned.

"So does that mean yes?"

"Nope."

"Why?"

"You not ready yet plus you got school."

"We get out next week. That would be the perfect time for me to grind and really get my hands dirty. Think of it as my job for the summer."

"I tell you what. I'll tell Corey that I want you to work for him for the summer."

"Why I gotta work for that chump?" I questioned, feeling like working for Corey was beneath me. From what I heard he was lazy and did a half ass job when it came to running those corners. Instead of bringing in the profits it had the potential to make, he would basically break even.

"Hold up. Let me finish," Uncle Marvin said, putting up his hand. "One thing you'll learn about running a business is: A) never get rid of a worker until you've gotten everything you need from them and they're no longer a benefit, and B) if at all possible don't let a worker become an enemy unless you prepared to kill him."

"How is Corey's lazy ass a benefit?" I was curious to know.

"Mainly because if he sees you as working for him, he'll say and do things that can enhance your skills if you take over. Meaning that, the bullshit he does that hinders his ability to make money, you'll see it and you'll know not to do that same dumb shit. And the decisions he makes that are profitable, I don't care if it's only a handful, you take those business skills and you apply them to make sure you run your operation even tighter."

"I get what you're saying. I only have one thing to add."

"What's that?"

"It's not *if* I take over it's *when* I take over, because you will want me to take over. These streets will be mine. You wait and see." I smiled.

"You too much, Nico. All I can say is I'm glad you on my side." Uncle Marvin laughed.

♛ ♛ ♛

For the last few weeks I felt like I had become Corey's personal do boy. That nigga was bossing me around like I was on his payroll although he wasn't giving me a dime; my money came straight from Uncle Marvin. I played my position though. Corey had no idea that everyday I was waiting and plotting on taking over his spot.

"Corey, after I drop this package off, I'ma head home. I'll be back first thing in the morning," I said, before jumping off the top of the stairs.

"That ain't gon' work. I need you to come right back. I have somewhere I need to go so I need you to hold shit down while I'm gone."

"But you just got back from being gone for like two hours," I said, frowning at his clown ass.

"What, you clockin' my time now? You work for me, not the other way around, motherfucker." I walked back over to Corey and we were standing eye to eye. Although he was five years older than me I was tall for my age so we were the same height. I started to ball up my fist because I was about to punch him dead in his mouth, but I caught myself. My father had always told me the importance of keeping your emotions in check, especially when you were anger, so I stepped back.

"My fault, Corey. You right… I work for you."

"Exactly," he shot back like he was the boss of some shit. But that's what I wanted him to think.

"No disrespect. I'll drop this off and I'll come right back. You go and handle whatever you need to and I'll hold it down this way."

"Now that's the attitude I'm talkin' 'bout. You

act right I might let you leave the block a little early tomorrow. Now hurry up 'cause I got a piece of ass waitin' on me," Corey boasted.

I simply nodded my head like the obedient motherfucker Corey wanted me to be. As I walked to my destination I kept replaying the bullshit conversation I had with my so-called boss. It had only been a few short weeks since Uncle Marvin sent me in to prove myself and business had already improved drastically and it had nothing to do with Corey. He was even a lazier fuck than I thought he was. Not only that, he got off on treating me like a minion. Letting me do all the work but he take all the credit. But Corey would get his and never see it coming.

♛ ♛ ♛

"I don't ever see you no more," Ritchie said while we sat in my room watching television.

"I'm out here hustlin' man. If I'm hangin' wit' you that mean I ain't makin' no money." I chuckled.

"What about school? Once the summer break ended, you came for the first couple weeks and then you started disappearing. It seems like you coming less and less. Your mother cool with that?"

"She don't know. I be intercepting the letters from the school and deleting the messages they leave on the answering machine. Plus, it ain't like I've completely dropped out." I shrugged.

"At the rate you going, it's close to it."

"School ain't for everybody. We all have a gift and mine can't be found between the pages of a book. My gift is knowing how to make money on these streets. Uncle Marvin said at my age now, I'm just as sharp as my dad was when he was running the blocks. Can you believe that," I said wide eyed.

"Foreal!" Ritchie said as if he was impressed by what I said.

"Yep. But I'ma be even sharper than my dad. He got caught slippin' in these streets and it cost him his life. After all this time we still ain't found his killer," I said, shaking my head. "But one thing I've learned is you can't trust nobody. It's a jungle out here. These niggas are animals."

"You can trust me," Ritchie replied with his puppy dog eyes staring up at me.

"I know man," I said rubbing his head playfully. "You haven't been corrupted by this game so you don't count. You still green." I laughed.

"Stop making fun of me. I bet I could be a good worker, too."

I kept laughing at Ritchie until I realized he was serious. "What, you want to join me on the block... is that what you saying?"

"Yeah, why not?"

"Ummm, weren't you screaming books and shit, schoolboy. You can't be on the corner hustlin' if you stuck in school."

"I can work after school and on the weekends."

"Ritchie, I don't think you cut out for this shit."

"You forget my dad used to hustle with your dad, so I bet I would be good at it, too. Just give me a chance," Ritchie said.

"Why, the sudden interest?"

"Because I miss hanging out with my best friend," Ritchie said sincerely.

"Listen, some things are about to change soon. The dude Corey who is overseeing things is on his way out and I'll be taking over."

"Foreal? You gonna be the man over them projects?" Ritchie asked with excitement.

"Sure am. And when that happens, I'ma need some trustworthy soldiers under me and you'll be my first recruit."

"You mean that, Nico?"

"I said it didn't I? I give you my word on that. Just be patient and give me a little time," I said nodding my head. I was serious, too. My conversation with Ritchie got my hustlin' juices flowing. I had been focusing so much on knocking Corey out the picture that I hadn't thought about what I would do once I did. I needed to start compiling my team of who would follow me and Ritchie was first on my list. He was leaned more on the soft side, but Ritchie was loyal, followed directions and was a good listener. Those were key qualities to be a suitable member of my team. If everything continued to come together correctly, I would be able to take-over even sooner than I had anticipated.

Chapter 5

The Devil Is A Lie

"I thought you said you were staying over Ritchie's house tonight?" my mom said when I walked through the door.

"It's good to see you too, Ma," I shot back, not up for a conversation after working the block all damn day.

"What you came to get something before you leave?" she continued.

"No. I'm not staying at Ritchie's tonight. I'm tired. All I want to do is go to sleep in my own bed," I explained.

"Well, if you staying here you gon' have to stay in your room because I'm tired too and I don't want to be disturbed. That means none of yo' friends can come over either," my mom added.

"Whatever," I mumbled under my breath before going in my room and closing the door. I was exhausted and didn't even care why my mom was running her mouth. I was used to her talking crazy so I didn't even ask her any questions. Plus, I had no desire to have company or come out my room. The block was on fire all day and night so the only thing I wanted was some sleep. Before my head even hit the pillow it was lights out for me. I fell into a deep sleep and didn't awake until the middle of the night when I needed to use the bathroom. I was sleeping so good that at first I fought off the urge to get up, but eventually I gave in.

When I opened my bedroom door I stopped in my tracks because I heard arguing. But it wasn't the loud voices that made me pause, it was who they were arguing about that made me take a closer listen. I stepped in the hallway making sure not to make a sound. I quietly walked towards the living room so I could hear even better. I was tempted to peep my head around the corner so I could see who my mother was arguing with, but I decided not to take the chance, because I definitely didn't want to be seen. I was able to catch all the dialogue and that's what mattered most at this point.

"I ain't heard nothing from you in over a year and you call me out the blue yesterday saying you want to see me. I'm thinking you finally got some money for me, but you show up here empty handed. What type of shit is that!"

"Shaniece, calm yo' ass down. You know shit was hot for me after Royce got killed. I had to get outta town."

"Oh please! Didn't nobody know you had anything to do with his murder. You just didn't keep yo' end of the bargain that's why yo' ass bounced. I did my part now it's time for you to pay up."

"I told you he didn't have no money on him."

"Tyrone, you a lie! I know for a fact he had just dropped off a package to Jerome and picked up a lot of money."

"Well, like I told you that day he ain't have it on him. I don't know who got the money, but it wasn't me."

"After all this time you still sticking to that damn story?"

"Cause it ain't no story, it's the truth."

"So basically you saying that I set up Royce to be killed for nothing. Ain't that some bullshit!"

It felt as if someone had pounded me in the head with a hammer and wouldn't stop. I leaned up against the wall to regain my composure. I couldn't wrap my mind around what I had just overheard. My mother was responsible for my father's death. My emotions were on overdrive and I felt at any moment I might explode, but I knew that would be the wrong move. I had to keep my cool, but I also had to see the person that pulled the trigger and killed my father.

"Nico, what are you doing up?" my mother snapped when I came walking in the living room

"I wanted to get some juice from the kitchen," I mumbled, rubbing my eyes as if I had just woken up.

"Well hurry up!" she snarled with her arms folded.

I walked slowly, trying to pretend that I wasn't paying attention to the man sitting on the couch. He had his head tilted down as I strolled passed him. There was an eerie silence while I poured some juice. Neither my mother nor the man said a word the entire time I was in the kitchen. When I finished drinking the juice I put the glass in the sink before coming out. That's when it happened. It was as if I caught the man off guard and our eyes met. They locked for what felt like an eternity. I could tell my glare was making the man uneasy, but I didn't care. I wanted to remember every detail, from his haircut, the shape of his eyes, the color of his skin and every feature on his smug face.

"Is there a problem lil' homey?" the man finally said, tired of me burning a hole through him with my glare.

"Nah, just wanted to see who was keeping my mom company in the middle of the night."

"That ain't none of yo' business, Nico. Now take yo' ass back to bed!" my mom shouted.

I simply nodded my head and went to my room. I locked the door and for a few minutes I stood there with my fist balled up. My breathing became rapid and I wasn't sure what to do to calm myself, but the thing was I didn't want to get calm. I wanted to stay angry and enraged so that's what I did. I sat on the edge of my bed and remained up for the rest of the night plotting and planning my next move.

♛ ♛ ♛

The next day after I overheard the conversation between my mother and Tyrone I began asking around to see if anybody knew who he was. Luckily, he was a local dude that had been a low level dealer in the neighborhood. I found out where he hung out and for the next few weeks I began tracking his moves. I had become consumed with clocking every step he made that I had to tell Uncle Marvin I needed to take a break from working the blocks. I lied and told him my mother found out I wasn't going to school and so I needed to buckle down on my studies before I flunked out. He understood and said my job would be waiting for me whenever I was ready to come back. I did plan on going back to the block, but for now Tyrone was my top priority.

    I watched from a short distance as Tyrone kicked it with a few guys in front of a corner store. After smoking a cigarette, he headed up the street and I figured he was on his way to see this chick I found out he was fucking with. He seemed to go visit her almost every other day, but tonight's visit would end much different.

Like clockwork, Tyrone came sauntering out of the chick's crib a couple hours later and then took the same backstreet shortcut he always used. He was so busy smoking that Tyrone didn't notice I was on his ass until he felt the tip of cold metal against the back of his head.

"Yo… yo… yo… what the fuck!" Tyrone said, putting his hands up. "I ain't got shit on me."

"Nigga, don't nobody wanna rob you. That's what yo' pussy ass like to do. Now keep walking," I directed, nudging the gun even harder against his head, leading him towards a back alley.

"Where we going?" he asked nervously.

"Just move!" I yelled. Tyrone was actually a little nigga so I was tempted to pick his ass up and throw him in the alley, but I started pushing him instead. I had replayed this moment so many times in my head that I was eager to see it through once and for all.

Once we reached the alley, I shoved Tyrone down causing him to knock over one of the trash-cans. I could have easily killed Tyrone when I first walked up on him from behind, but I wanted him to see my face before he died. "Remember me, motherfucker," I said aiming the gun at his face.

Tyrone frowned at me with a raised eyebrow

not saying a word. He kept staring at me as if trying to place where he recognized me. "Am I supposed to?"

"So you wanna act like you don't know. Let me help..."

"Wait, you Shaniece son," he said cutting me off. "Hold up. Did yo' mom put you up to this? Let me explain," he stuttered.

"I don't need you to explain shit. I already know everything. I heard the conversation between you and my mom. I know it was you that killed my father."

"You got it all wrong. It was all your mother's idea. I was only tryna help her out. She said he was beatin' her and shit," he rambled.

"Shut the fuck up!" I barked, anxious to pull the trigger. "I know my mother had you rob and kill my father and you gon' die for that shit."

"Wait... wait... wait. I got some money at my crib. I can give it to you," he tried to reason.

"I don't want nothing from you but yo' life. You killed my father and the only thing that gives me a little peace of mind is that your blood is on my hands. Now die nigga." Before Tyrone could say another word I lit his body up emptying the entire chamber in his face and chest. His brain splatter covered the brick wall as Tyrone's body slumped down to the ground. At the age of 14, I could now add killer to my resume.

Chapter 6

On My Own

"Nico, where do you think you going?" my mother questioned, as I stood in front of the door with a large duffel bag in my hand.

"I'm leaving. I can't stay here no more."

"Boy, what is you talkin' 'bout."

"I can't stay in the same place with you for one more day. Having to look at your face right now is making me sick."

"Who in the hell do you think you talkin' to! You betta watch yo' mouth before I knock yo' teeth out," my mother threatened, stepping towards me.

"I'm talkin' to you and I advise you not to step any closer," I warned. My mother's eyes widened in rage and her nose began to flare like it would when she was about to lose it. She lounged at me and I grabbed her wrist midair. Her anger had now switched to being stunned. "You will never put your hands on me again," I stated still holding on to her wrist.

"You done lost your motherfuckin' mind!" she screamed before lounging her other arm at me, but I dropped my duffel bag and held her other wrist too. I was tall and towered over my mother. I could've easily broken both her wrist and she knew it.

"Step away from me," I said coldly, before releasing her from my grasp. The look in my mother's eyes was a combination of shock, fury, and confusion.

"I don't know what the hell has gotten into you but..."

"Don't say another word," I said, putting my hand up. "I know what you did. It was you that set my father up to be killed. You!" I shouted so loudly I thought every piece of glass in the apartment would break. My mother began backing away from me as terror engulfed her face.

"Nico," she said in almost a whisper.

"You have never been a mother to me, but you had to take my father. If you hadn't given birth to me, you would be a dead woman right now."

"Son, you don't mean that."

"I'm not your son. You're nothing to me. I don't have a mother. Stay out my life. I don't ever want to see your face again."

"Nico, you don't mean that. You angry right now, but you have to understand. Your father wanted to take you away from me and raise you with his fiancé like she was yo' mother. I couldn't let that happen. I gave that man everything. I was good to yo' father, but instead of him appreciating it, he tossed me aside and wanted to take my only child. You have to understand, he left me no choice. I did it for you. Please forgive me," she pleaded.

"You didn't do it for me. You did it for yourself. It killed you that Daddy was happy and that even though he didn't want you, he loved me. You were jealous that I had a father that gave a fuck when you didn't. You gon' have to live wit' this shit for the rest of your pathetic life. But I won't be here to see it," I said, turning to leave.

"Nico, wait! Where will you go?"

"It don't matter. I'm dead to you," I said, shutting the door behind me.

♛ ♛ ♛

When I showed up at Uncle Marvin's house with my duffel bag, instead of him grilling me, he showed me to his guest bedroom and told me I was welcome to stay for however long I wanted. He knew something was wrong and part of me wanted to tell him what had happened, but this other part of me wanted to protect my mother. I wanted nothing to do with her, but I also didn't want to be responsible for her death. I knew that Uncle Marvin would kill my mother himself if I told him the role she played in my father's death. I decided to let sleeping dogs lie as long as she stayed the hell out of my life.

"Uncle Marvin, listen I think I'm ready to take over for Corey," I said casually as we sat in the kitchen eating breakfast.

"Really now," he replied, not looking up from the newspaper.

"Yep. I've been working with him for months and I'm basically maintaining the blocks. I know what to do to keep the money flowing," I said confidently.

"Umm hmm," he mumbled, taking a sip of his orange juice, but still not making eye contact with me.

"I've even began gathering my team to work the blocks with me." That got my uncle's attention because he finally looked giving me a curious glare.

"And who is going to be a part of your so-called team?"

"Ritchie is on board."

"You talking about Ricardo's son?"

"Yep, and my man Alton and Lance. I want to recruit two more guys, but I think that's enough to start with," I said, nodding my head like I had everything figured out.

"I see. I know Ritchie still in school what about Lance and Alton?"

"Lance is, but Alton graduated last year and right now he just working at this warehouse stocking boxes and stuff. He ready to get on these streets and make this money."

"I tell you what. If you get two more solid recruits then I'll let you take over for Corey."

"Foreal!" I couldn't contain my excitement. "You mean that, Uncle Marvin?"

"I do. But remember, you're vouching for your team so you're responsible for them. You get all the credit good or bad. So be wise with your decision-making process because your team will either make you or break you."

"Got you. But I promise I won't let you down. I'm gonna be the best that ever did it in these streets.

"So listen, I wanted us to meet up 'cause I had a conversation with my uncle earlier today and it's official."

"What's official?" Ritchie questioned like he was lost or some shit.

"I'm 'bout to take over them blocks and you all are gonna help me," I said without hesitation.

"Stop playing!"

"I ain't playin', Ritchie. I'm serious. I'm vouching for each of you so ya bet not let me down neither."

"We won't," Ritchie, Lance, and Alton said in unison.

"So when we start? I'm tired of stacking boxes for chump change. I need to make some real money," Alton huffed.

"There is only one... no, make that two hold-ups." I sighed.

"What's that?" Lance asked.

"I have to get two more solid guys to join our team before my uncle will let me take over for Corey."

"Nico, I got a cousin who would be perfect. He hungry like me, but he way smarter. I mean that nigga a math genius."

"Is he in school?"

"Nah."

"What he got a job... where he work?"

"That's the thing, he can't really keep a job. He was in school, but dropped out 'cause he was bored. Then he always get hired, but then he think he know more than his bosses, which he does, but they end up firing him 'cause he be telling them how they should do they job."

"I see," I said not feeling Alton's suggestion. The last thing I needed was a know-it-all telling me how to run my shit.

"It's like my auntie always saying, he too smart for his own good, but I do know he got nothing, but time on his hand and he will grind hard for you."

"I don't know, Alton. That motherfucker can't

be tryna tell me what the fuck to do. We a team, but I'm the leader of this team. He got to do what I tell him to do not the other way around."

"I feel you. At least meet him. I promise he's worth a meeting," Alton insisted.

"Okay, I'll meet him. Get him here tomorrow. I'm ready to get this shit rolling," I said, anxious to be rid of Corey. If Alton's cousin did work out then all I needed was one more person to set this shit off.

Chapter 7

Clique

"So you Reese," I said, sizing Alton's cousin up. "Alton, tells me you interested in being a part of the team."

"From what my cousin told me, it sounds like something I want to be a part of."

"Did Alton explain how this situation would work?" I wanted to know.

"What you mean?"

"Meaning, that although you would be a member of the team you would take orders from me. I heard you had a problem taking orders," I said, staring directly in his eyes. Reese shot a mean glare over to his cousin and Alton quickly put his head down like he got busted or something.

"I know how to take orders," Reese replied.

"I didn't say you don't know how to take orders, I said you have a problem taking orders, there's a difference. So will you have a problem taking orders from me?"

"Nah, I don't think I will."

"I don't need you to think, I need you to know. I'm a few years younger than you and Alton, but my father ran these streets. My uncle runs these streets and it's only right that I do it better than both of them. I say that so you understand that this is my shit. Nobody has ever or will ever do it better than what I'm about to do. Brooklyn and the surrounding boroughs will not only love me, but they'll respect me. That starts with my team. I don't need no on the fence niggas representing me."

"I wanna be a part of this and you the boss. I respect that," Reese said, standing up to shake my hand.

"Then you in my man," I said, shaking his hand. "We 'bout to do big things." I grinned, as Ritchie, Lance, Alton, and Reese all smiled. The excitement almost seemed contagious. I could feel the energy and it was getting me so hyped. All I needed was one more piece to the puzzle. I wanted it so bad I could almost taste the shit and it tasted even better than the sweet potato pie that Chrissy would bake. I just hoped to get my slice sooner rather than later.

Nico Carter

♔ ♔ ♔

As I stood on the corner watching Corey not doing shit, but laughing and joking, I wanted to smack that nigga. It had been a few weeks and I hit a snag in my operation. I couldn't find my fifth recruit for nothing. The other team members had brought person after person for me to meet, but none of them felt like the missing link instead more like dead weight. They didn't have that hunger in their eyes that for me was mandatory. My frustration level had reached a boiling point, but I had to keep my game face on while dealing with Corey. I didn't want him to have any idea that I was gunning for his position. But I couldn't front, the shit was working my patience. The nigga was a complete loser and taking orders from him was like a nonstop sucker punch.

"Nico, what you doing just standing there?" Corey barked, shaking me out of my thoughts. "We got work to do."

"I been working. All you gotta do is count that big knot in yo' pocket." I smirked.

"Well, you need to work harder. It's too much money out here to get. I gotta make a run so don't be slackin' off 'cause I won't be around to patrol you," Corey stated.

"You ain't neva around no way, so I'm good," I said under my breath.

"Speak up, I didn't hear you," Corey's punk ass said walking towards me.

"I said, I got you covered... you good."

"That's my nigga. I'll see you in a couple hours," he said, patting me on my shoulders like I was his pet dog or some shit.

Two hours passed and of course Corey was nowhere in sight. He was probably running up in some dirty pussy since a fat ass always came before money with him. It began snowing and shit slowed all the way down. I was about to go inside one of the buildings when I saw a girl walking towards me. At first, I thought maybe it was a customer, but her eyes seemed too clear and alert to be an addict. *Maybe she making a buy for someone else,* I thought to myself.

"Are you Nico?" the cutie asked me. I didn't care how cute she was, I wasn't about to answer that question with a yes. This might be some type of set up.

"Nope."

"Do you know where I can find him?"

"Nope."

"Oh, well Lance told me he would be over here and I needed to speak to him."

"How you know Lance and what you need to speak to Nico about?"

"Lance dates my little cousin, Cheryl, and he said I might be able to get a job from Nico."

"A job? You wanna work for Nico?"

"Yep, why do you work for him?"

"I guess you can say that."

"How you like it?"

"It's cool, but he works the shit outta you. I mean, you see it's snowing out here and I'm still grinding. If you ain't willing to bust yo' ass then I would suggest you not even consider working for him. Just 'cause you a female he ain't gon' go no easier on you either."

"I wouldn't want him to. I would bust my ass just like a nigga would. I work at an after hours spot now and I bring in more money and work harder than any man in there."

"Then why you want to work for Nico?" I asked.

"'Cause they don't wanna pay me like they pay the men. Most of the time they don't want to pay me at all. They just use the women as eye candy to draw in customers, but I need money."

"Why, you got kids or something to take care of?"

"No. I'm just ready to get out of my mom's crib. She got a boyfriend and he always tryna have sex wit' me. I'm sick of fighting his ass off."

"Have you told your moms what's going on?"

"I'm too scared she'll throw me out if I tell her so I just wanna get my money up so I can leave on my own," she said shaking her head.

"What's your name?"

"Tracy... Tracy Taylor."

"So type of work you want to do for Nico?"

"As long as it don't require me to sell no pussy then I'll do whatever he wants," she said. And there it was, that hunger I was itching for. Even the snow couldn't hide the hunger in her eyes. Never did I think about recruiting a female to the team, but Tracy might be just what my clique needed.

"You got the job. Welcome to the team." I smiled.

"Don't I need to meet Nico first?"

"I am Nico."

"You're Nico! You had me running my mouth this entire time, thinking I was talking to one of Nico's workers and it was you. I feel like such a dumbass," Tracy said, putting her head down.

"You passed the test and you're in, so don't feel like a dumbass. You see how empty these streets are right now, but you out here in the snow begging for a job. That's the type of people I need out here representing me. You just might end up being my best worker."

"I will be your best worker. Thank you so much for the opportunity, you will not regret it."

"I know I won't. I'll have Lance get in touch with you when it's time to get started."

"When will that be because I really need to get to work."

"Sooner than you think." I smiled realizing that all of our lives were about to change forever.

Like the good do boy Corey thought I was, I waited for him to get back to the block five hours later and I handed him the rest of the money I earned. I gave him a fake ass smile and walked the fuck off. I knew his time was officially up so it was easy to play the bullshit game. I couldn't wait to get home and speak to Uncle Marvin. On the low, I think he started wondering if I was really going to be able to deliver and I wanted him to know that I had.

"Uncle Marvin, I'm so glad you here," I said as soon as I walked through the door.

"Where else would I be?" he laughed. "If I didn't know better, I would think you ran all the way home the way you huffing and puffing," he commented.

"Basically, I wanted to tell you the good news."

"What's that?"

"I found my fifth and final person. I finally got my team together," I announced proudly.

"Really? I know you were having some problems with that. It's been a few weeks now. So who is he?"

"It's not a he, it's a she."

"A she, meaning a female?"

"Yeah, her name is Tracy Taylor. But before you go passing judgment thinking a woman can't do the job, trust this one can," I said without hesitation.

"No judgment from me. Like I said, this is your team. You get the credit good or bad so if you want to vouch for this woman then that's on you."

"Thank you 'cause my instincts tell me she is going to be a great secret weapon in more ways than one."

"I see. Well, since you've held up to your end of the agreement then I'll deliver on mine. Just give me a week to handle the Corey situation."

"Uncle Marvin, let me handle it."

"I don't think you ready for that." Uncle Marvin grinned as if he found what I said funny.

"Trust me, I can handle it. Those are gonna be my blocks so let me deal with Corey."

"You sure?" Uncle Marvin questioned with caution.

"Positive. I'm about to be the boss of my team so I need to be able to make executive decisions, why not start with Corey?"

"Lead the way my boy. But if you change your mind and need my help just ask."

"I got this, but thanks." I smiled before heading to my bedroom.

I stayed up for the rest of the night getting my thoughts together. I was going to meet with my clique tomorrow and set shit in motion. There was no turning back now and I was ready for everything that would come my way.

Chapter 8

Crew Love

"This is our first official meeting as a crew. I believe each of you are going to play a vital role and I'm pleased to have you as a member of my team," I said, standing in front of Tracy, Ritchie, Alton, Lance, and Reese. They each sat looking up at me like they were war ready even Ritchie scary ass. I was impressed and excited at the same time.

"So, when we start working the blocks?" Alton was the first to ask.

"Yeah, cause I need to start making some coins, ASAP," Reese chimed in.

"Me too," Tracy added.

"I feel you. We all trying to get rich and I promise if each of you follow my lead, we will all make more money than we ever imagined," I promised.

"Foreal?" Ritchie asked, in his normal wide-eyed way.

"Yes, foreal, Ritchie, but we have to take care of one thing first."

"What is it? Let's get it done so we can start making that money," Lance said, as everyone nodded their head in agreement.

"I need to get rid of Corey and Tracy I need your help to do it."

"Tell me what I need to do."

"I need you to put on your tightest best fitting jeans and take a walk down the block where we hustle at."

"Wait, you don't want me to fuck this nigga do you?" she questioned.

"Nope, you won't have to. I just need you to be the perfect bait. No disrespect, you have a fat ass and a pretty face so you are the perfect bait," I explained.

"So, what's the rest of the plan?" Tracy wanted to know.

"After you come walking down the block, when he approaches you, give him your digits. Wait for him to call and when he does I'll tell you what to do next because I'll take it from there."

"What if he doesn't try to holla?" Tracy asked.

"Ass is Corey's weakness so best believe he will try to holla. Just make sure you don't have on a coat that's covering yo' ass up when you take that walk." I smiled.

"Got you. So when do you want me to do it?"

"Tomorrow. I'll call you in the morning to let you know the exact time, so be waiting by your phone."

"Nico, man what you gon' do to Corey?" Lance asked.

"What you think... I'ma get rid of his motherfuckin' ass."

"Like kill him?" Ritchie questioned, looking scared.

"Yeah, nigga. He's a problem that needs to be erased. If I let him live, trust he'll come back for retaliation. We can't leave no loose ends."

"Nico, you the man!" Lance jumped up and said, shaking my hand.

"I'm not the man yet, but I will be," I said, nodding my head confidently. "A'ight ya, this meeting is over. We'll start working on Friday if everything goes as planned and I have no doubt that it will."

♛ ♛ ♛

It was cold as a motherfucker outside but the sun was shining bright, just the way I liked. I stood on the stool kicking shit with Corey, something I normally didn't do, but I needed to hype his ass up for what was about to go down.

"Damn, look at shorty coming up the street," I commented as if I was about to holla at a girl. "She pretty as hell," I said as Tracy made her approach right on cue.

"Yeah, she cute, but what that ass looking like?" Corey huffed, nonchalantly.

"I don't know, but she bad and I'm 'bout to get them digits," I said, standing up as if I was about to walk off.

"Hold up youngin'," Corey said, placing his hand on my coat right as Tracy was slowly walking past us. She was on point with the shit too. Them jeans were gripping her ass and she was wearing a cropped jacket that was accentuating every curve she had. Even in the freezing cold I could tell Corey was like a dog in heat. "That's way too much woman for you, young homey. You sit yo' ass down and let a real man handle this," Corey boasted.

I pretended to feel some kinda way as he pimp walked over to Tracy. I could tell that at first she tried to act like she wasn't interested and let Corey continue to spit game. A few minutes later he was grinning and I knew that meant he got the number. Shortly after, Corey came back over to the stool where I was grinning from ear to ear.

"See, that's how you handle business. Watch, I'll be all up in that pussy by tomorrow," Corey bragged.

"You think so? Homegirl bad. She might try to play hard to get."

"Fuck that, I buy her a meal, spit a lil' game, and them panties coming off."
"You sound awfully sure."
"'Cause I am. Don't no chick tell me no."
"So sure you wanna place a bet?" I said, getting Corey hyped up.
"Oh, so just wanna giveaway yo' money. Sure, I'll be more than happy to take yo' chump change. I'll use it to pay for the next bitch meal I buy."
"Let's put a hundred on it then."
"Have my money first thing Thursday, 'cause like I said I'll be all up in them ovaries tomorrow night." Corey laughed. "But enough of all this bullshitting. Get back on them blocks and make me some money," he ordered.
"Whatever you say, boss." I gave a sly smile and went to work.
I spent the rest of the day laughing to myself about Corey. His arrogance would be the death of him literally.

"I'm a little nervous," Tracy said when I met her at her house that night. "I wasn't expecting him to call so soon."
"I did place a bet with him to make sure there were no delays," I admitted.
"A bet... like for money?"
"Yeah, I had to speed shit up. Aren't you ready to get to work?"

"You know I am, but I've never set nobody up to be killed before," Tracy said, seeming uneasy.

"Before I hired you, you said you were willing to do anything for the job except sell pussy. Are you backing out now?"

"Hell no! I said I was nervous, I didn't say I wouldn't do it. I'm a woman of my word and I need this job."

"Then you betta put on your best poker face. You can't be acting nervous and shit around Corey. You don't want to raise any suspicions," I said.

"I'll be ready for tomorrow, I promise," Tracy said.

"Remember, during dinner you have to drop subtle hints that you down to drop them panties for him. If he ask to come to your place tell him he can't 'cause yo' mom is home and she don't allow you to have guys over. That's when he should invite you to this apartment he keeps in Brooklyn where he take all his chicks to fuck."

"Then what?"

"I'll be waiting. You just keep your cool. That's the most important thing."

"You don't have any sort of fear about killing someone or that the table can turn and Corey can end up killing you?" Tracy asked me with a confused looked on her face.

"I used to fear my father, but he's no longer here. So now, I fear nobody, but God. Only He can judge me and when my time comes I'll take whatever punishment He sees fit. But while I'm here in these streets I'ma do whatever I need to survive and for me, survive means to win. Everyday I'm taking a chance with my life, but I'll take the risk," I said matter of factly.

"Nico, I don't understand how you are so young, but so focused and driven. Where does that come from?"

"Pain. It can either break you or make you. I use my pain as ammunition to become unstoppable."

"I'm just happy you letting me come along for the ride." Tracy smiled. "Because there is no doubt that whatever you put your mind to, you will make happen."

"Long as you know. So be ready 'cause this ride is gon' have a lot of twist and turns. Don't say I didn't warn you. But let me get outta here. You have a big day ahead of you tomorrow so I want you to get your mind right," I said before opening the front door.

"Don't worry, Nico, I won't let you down. I wanna see you become the King of New York." Tracy winked her eye.

"Have a goodnight," I said and closed the door. I stood in the hallway for a second thinking about the King of New York statement Tracy made. I wanted that too and was willing to do just about anything to make it happen.

Chapter 9

Takeover

The apartment Corey kept was a walkup in a seedy part of Brooklyn. The front door entrance lock didn't even work properly, so it was nothing for me to get inside and post up. The rent was stabilized and most of the tenants were older and had been living there the majority of their lives. For that reason, I didn't have to worry about being seen because there wasn't any heavy foot traffic coming in and out. It was the perfect spot for a cheap, dirty nigga like Corey to do his shit.

I got to the location early because I wanted to have plenty of time to get my own mind right. Although I had told Tracy to do that, I needed to do the same thing. Yeah, I had already killed one person, but that was different. I was driven by rage and revenge for my father. Corey's death was more of a business decision. Nah, I didn't like the silly fuck, but I didn't dislike him enough to want him dead. But from a business standpoint, I knew if I let him live I would always be looking over my shoulders, wondering not if, but when he would come back to take what he felt was stolen from him... his blocks. The time, energy and work it would take for me to become a boss would bring enough headaches; I could not let Corey be an unnecessary one.

As I began thinking about all the moves me and my crew would make and the plans I had for us I heard the entrance door open. I had already scoped out the area ahead of time and knew Corey's apartment was on the second floor. I told Tracy when they walked through the door for her to start laughing and talking a little loud so I would know it was them and get into position. At first I didn't hear anything, but when I stepped closer to the stairwell I heard a female giggling.

"Corey, you so silly," Tracy said extra loud and giggled some more.

"Shhh, shhh, keep yo' voice down, baby. Ain't nothing, but senior citizens up in here. We don't wanna wake them up." Corey's corny ass chuckled.

"You right." Tracy giggled again. "I can't wait for us to get some alone time," I heard Tracy say as they began to walk up the stairs.

"Me too, wit' yo' fine self," I heard Corey say

then it sounded like he smacked Tracy's ass.

"Boy, you so silly," Tracy said making eye contact with me as they were about to turn the corner. Corey hadn't noticed me yet because his eyes were still glued to Tracey's ass, but once they reached the hallway midway I stepped out of the darkness.

"Nigga, what the fuck is you doing here," Corey barked, but kept walking towards me.

"Baby, who is this?" Tracy questioned, pretending to be as shocked as Corey was by my presence.

"Nobody. He just a lil' nigga that work for me. He must got some money for me or something," Corey said to Tracy before turning his attention back to me. "Is that why you here, to bring me some damn money? It better be a lot since you decided to interrupt my evening wit' my baby," Corey said, trying to show off in front of his date.

"My man, Corey. I just wanted to come over and tell you bye." I gave him a half smile and he raised his eyebrow with a puzzled look on his face. Before any more words could be spoken, I fired off three bullets in his chest and one in his face just to make sure he was dead. Tracy covered her mouth to stop from screaming. I quickly grabbed her arm so we could get the fuck outta there before someone decided to open their door to see where the noise was coming from. But more than likely, they slept right through the shit and wouldn't notice Corey's dead body until the morning.

"Damn, Nico! You said we would start work on Friday and here we are. I wasn't sure if you would be able to make that happen, but now I know not to ever doubt you again," Alton said, cheesing extra hard.

"I try to be a man of my word." Although I had just turned 16, I did feel like a man. As I began my rise to the top, I did want a reputation as being a man of my word and that started with my own team. I planned to lead by example.

Friday came around fast so I created a preliminary schedule to see who worked best together. Since Alton and Reese were out of school they both worked the morning shift. I started them off together to see if they would develop a healthy competition since they were cousins. Or if it would have the opposite effect and they would be too lax because they spent the majority of the time kicking it instead of working. Since Tracy was also not in school I planned on having her switch up and work with Alton and Reese separately to see how she vibed with each of them and also with Lance and Ritchie. Since Lance and Ritchie were both still in school they would work mostly on the weekends and in the evening time after school. Adjustments would be made accordingly, but I thought this was a decent start.

"So listen, I'ma spend this weekend working with both of you. I want you to watch and learn. Monday, you'll work the blocks without me, so I can see what you can do. Got it?" I asked looking Alton and Reese in their eyes.

"Yep," they said in unison nodding their heads.

"When Tracy, Lance, and Ritchie come later on then the two of you will be dismissed from your shift. So let's get started," I said ready to get to work.

"I'm ready," Alton spoke up extra giddy.

"Me too," Reese added.

The day seemed to go by quick as hell, mainly because the blocks were on fire. The cold weather was starting to break so the fiends were out like cockroaches. Alton and Reese was on it too. They didn't let a customer get away. When their shift was over and Tracy, Lance, and Ritchie came they still didn't leave. Although I told them they wouldn't get paid for the overtime they still stayed because they said they wanted to continue to watch and learn. That was their first test and they passed it. If Alton and Reese were anxious to get off the block just because they weren't getting paid, then I knew they weren't the soldiers I needed to take me to the level I planned to go. My entire crew and me hustled those blocks together until we fed every last customer and shut the streets down.

Chapter 10

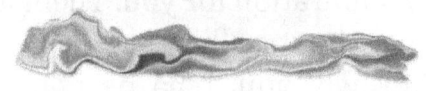

Spread My Wings

"Damn, what the fuck is you putting in that crack? Ya making a killing out there." Uncle Marvin shook his head as he counted the money I made for him that day. "Every week the profit keeps increasing."

"I told you I wouldn't let you down, Uncle Marvin."

"Hell, if I knew you would be flipping money like this, I would've gotten rid of Corey a long time ago."

"Maybe now you'll never sleep on me again." I shrugged.

"Boy, I'm scared of you."

"Stop playing, Uncle Marvin." I chuckled.

"I ain't playing. Boy, you dangerous. You done

taken a group of knuckleheads and turned them into moneymakers. Do you know what sort of leadership skills a man has to possess to pull something like that off?" my uncle said as if amazed.

"My crew ain't knuckleheads," I said, feeling some type of way about that jab.

"Don't take it as an insult to your crew, Nico. Take it as my admiration for you. Them folks didn't know nothing about selling no dope until they started fuckin' wit' you. I'ma be honest. I didn't think the shit was gon' work. But like I always teach you, be a man of your word and so I wanted to keep mine. You have proved me wrong all the way and honestly, I'm proud of you. Now I see why your father always wanted you to stay in school and go to college, 'cause you smart as a whip."

"You know how much I love and miss my father, but school was never my thing. It couldn't hold my attention, but hustling these streets do. I just hope my father ain't looking down on me disappointed," I said somberly.

"Let me tell you something, Nico. Your father loved you more than anything on this earth. You getting up everyday and grinding for yours. It may not be the way your father would've preferred, but you can't never be disappointed in a man that works for his. So get that bullshit out your head. You hear me?"

"Yes, I do, and thanks for saying it."

"Shiiit, thanks for all this money you making

me. Here's your cut and a little extra."

"That's what's up, Uncle Marvin," I said, taking the money with a huge smile on my face.

"Also, I know I never mentioned this, but I respect how you handled that Corey situation. You got a lot of balls. I be forgetting you only 16. You a bad boy. I wish you was my son."

"In a lot of ways I am," I said, giving Uncle Marvin a hug. "Now, let me get outta here. I got work to do." Uncle Marvin couldn't take the place of my father, but he was a great runner up. I had so much love for that man and it was mainly because he accepted me for who I was. He never tried to change me, but only kicked his knowledge and let me decide if and how I wanted to apply it. I respected that and respected him for it.

♛ ♛ ♛

"Awww shit, we gettin' bonuses now!" Tracy popped, snapping her fingers and dancing.

"Good looking out." Ritchie grinned.

"Yeah, man, I appreciate it. You didn't have to do this," Lance added.

"You the best boss ever," Alton added.

"Most def appreciate it," Reese then said.

"Each of you have been puttin' in that work and I wanted to show my gratitude. This is only the beginning. In a couple months after we keep bringing in the profits, I'ma ask my uncle if we can expand," I said.

"What you mean expand?" Alton asked.

"That we not only work the blocks we have, but we run some more which will mean more money for us."

"You think your uncle will let that happen?" Ritchie wondered.

"My uncle is a businessman. If we keep bringing in those dollars then for sure. Why let someone else work a certain area if you have another team that can double or triple your profits," I said.

"Sounds about right to me. Plus, we have enough manpower and woman," Lance quickly added eyeing Tracy.

"Okay enough talking, time for work," I said, clapping my hands."

On the weekends business had gotten so crazy that I had all five of them working at the same time. It had actually been extremely beneficial. They had become so competitive with each other, but in a very good way. They also had each other's back. In the last few months we had become like a family. We hustled together, ate together, and hung out with each other. Because they had proven to be great workers I didn't have to be on the blocks as much. But instead of bullshitting with the extra time, I was putting it to good use by scoping out new opportunities to set up shop.

After I stayed on the blocks for a few with my crew I headed towards the train station to check out this spot I had been eyeing in East Flatbush. From what I heard, the previous crew that had been selling over there had got jammed up a few months ago and nobody had taken over since. For the last few weeks I had been going over there for a couple hours a day just checking out how shit was moving. I came to the conclusion, there was way too much money over on them block to be made and I couldn't let it go to waste. Now all I was trying to do was figure out the best way to have my team invade without it being hostile.

"Nico! Nico!" I heard someone calling out as I was headed to the train. I was so caught up in my thoughts that at first I didn't even hear them. When I turned around, I wished that I hadn't. "Nico, you didn't hear me calling you?"

"Nah... what do you want?"

"Does a mother need a reason to want to talk to her son," my mom said, standing in front of me. I hadn't seen her face since I walked out the apartment that day and I had no interest in seeing her now.

"We don't have nothing to talk about," I said point blank.

"I miss you, Nico. I thought you would've come home by now, but as the days and months passed I realized it wasn't gon' happen."

"Yep."

"You still mad at me?" she asked as if she had put me on a bullshit punishment for no reason and hoped I was over it.

"Mad? Mad doesn't begin to describe how I feel about you."

"I told you how sorry I was."

"Did you... if so I didn't care then and I still don't care now. I told you as far as I was concerned I no longer had a mother and I meant that. Ain't nothing changed. So if there's nothing else, I got a train to catch," I said ready to walk away.

"Nico, wait," she said taking my arm. "I ain't doing too good."

"That ain't my problem," I shot back pulling my arm away.

"You might hate me, but I'm still yo' mama. I heard you out here makin' money well I ain't got none."

"You shoulda thought about that before you had my father killed." My mom put her head down as if ashamed.

"I know I let you down and I'll never forgive myself for it. But please help me. I'm doing real bad, son." I glanced down at my mom and she did look like shit. I even wondered for a second was she using. She was always a petite woman, but now she was just skinny and her face seemed sunken in. She used to always keep her hair done, but now it was in a messy bun on top of her head. But no matter how bad she looked I felt absolutely zero sympathy for her.

"Take this," I said, handing my mom a wad of money. "I ain't giving you this because I want you back in my life. I'm giving you this money to make sure you stay out of it. This is the one and only time you'll ever get a dime from me, so don't come back," I said and walked away.

♕ ♕ ♕

After scoping out the neighborhood in East Flatbush for one more week, I was ready to bring my idea to Uncle Marvin. I was confident that my crew and I could handle the territory, now we would just need the additional product. Before I stepped to my uncle I wanted to make sure I could answer all the questions I knew he would throw my way. I was waiting patiently for him to come home, and when I heard the front door opening, I immediately turned off the television and stood up.

"What's up, Uncle Marvin!" I could feel myself smiling too hard. I couldn't front discussing new business excited me. Plus, this was the first time I was branching out and basically starting a project from scratch so I was extra excited.

"You seem like you're in an awfully good mood," my uncle said putting his keys down on the table.

"I am! I was waiting for you to get home because there was something I wanted to talk to you about," I said pacing back and forth.

"It's funny you say that because there was something I needed to talk to you about, too."

"Let me go first because I'm sure you gonna have a lot of questions," I said. My uncle simply nodded his head so I started running off at the mouth. "There is this neighborhood I've been eyeing for weeks. It's a new spot I want us to take over in East Flatbush. I know we can make a killing over there. My crew already has the current blocks in Bedford Stuyvesant on lock so we're more than capable of expanding. I was thinking of initially starting with Tracy, Lance, and Reese and then rotating with Ritchie and Alton once things get rolling. What you think?"

"Sounds like a plan and a good one," Uncle Marvin said casually.

"I'm glad you think so! I'm sure you have some questions so shoot," I said rubbing my hands together, prepared for whatever my uncle threw my way.

"I don't have any questions. I know what you're capable of and if you believe your crew is ready to expand then I say move forward."

"Really?" I had over prepared myself for this discussion with my uncle that I was disappointed he wasn't giving me the opportunity to put it on display.

"Is that all you wanted to talk to me about?

If so I wanted to have an important conversation with you."

"I'm finished. You have the floor," I said, wondering what was so important.

"I recently found out I have Stage IV lung cancer. I'm going to begin chemo treatments, but I'll be honest, Nico it's not looking good for me."

"What are you saying... are you gonna die?" I asked stunned by what my uncle said.

"We gon' all die, son but my death is coming a lot sooner than expected. I always thought the streets would kill me, not these damn cigarettes," he joked. "I've known something was wrong with me for awhile now, but I was in denial. I should've taken my ass to the doctor a long time ago."

"What will I do? You're all the family I have left."

"You have a family. Your crew is your family. You have Chrissy and don't forget about your mother."

"You're the closest person I have to my father left. Being around you makes me feel like he's still here with me," I revealed.

"Your father is with you. Right in here," Uncle Marvin said pointing at his chest. "Just like I will be too, when I pass away."

"You sound like you're giving up."

"Nah, I'ma give this a good fight. Hell, I might even whoop this cancer's ass, but I might not. Regardless, I want you to be prepared to carry on without me."

"This is too much," I said, shaking my head.

"I've said it before and I'll say it again… you a bad boy. You dangerous… you ahead of your time. These streets ain't ready for you. Don't you dare start getting scared now. You bet not let me down."

"I would never let you down, but I hate to do this without you."

"I felt the same way when Royce got killed, but I knew he would want me to carry on and you will do the same and I'm going to make sure of that."

"What you mean?"

"I've already told my plug about you, but I'm going to introduce you to him. He'll give you the product at the same price he's been giving it to me. I have already begun to let my buyers know that you will be their new supplier."

"Wait, you want me to takeover for you?"

"Of course. You've been groomed for this. Nobody can do this better than you and we both know it. I'm going to start treatment immediately so things will be rough on me pretty quickly. So get ready, you're the new boss," Uncle Marvin said shaking my hand. I shook his hand back, but I was still in shock. I always wanted to be the boss, but not like this, not because my uncle was sick. I was trying to take it all in stride, but it was difficult.

"I'll step up and do what I have to do to keep business going, but you'll beat this, Uncle Marvin. I know it. You'll beat this cancer and be back bossing everyone around in no time," I said giving him a hug.

Three months later Uncle Marvin died. Besides my father being murdered it was the saddest day of my life. But unlike then, I didn't stay in my room and mourn for weeks. Instead, I used the pain to grind even harder.

Chapter 11

Drug Dealer's Dream

5 Years Later...

"Happy Birthday, Nico Carter," the DJ blasted over the microphone as the club when crazy. I was celebrating my 21st birthday and I made sure to show out. I shut the club down and it belonged to me and my people for the night. I had champagne flowing, open bar, and everybody was partying like it was New Year's Eve in Times Square.

"Nico, this the best party ever, man!" Lance yelled, holding up his bottle of bubbly.

"He ain't lyin'!" Tracy said giving me a hug.

"You finally decided to show yo' ass up." I

laughed, hugging her back.

"Sorry 'bout that, but my girl here took forever to get dressed," Tracy said, nodding her head at the young lady behind her. I gave a quick glance to her friend and I couldn't help, but notice how pretty she was. I laughed to myself when I saw both Alton and Reese swooping in on her like hawks.

"No problem, just glad you made it. A party ain't a party without my number one girl." I smiled.

"I wouldn't have missed this party for nothing. Where Ritchie at?" Tracy asked looking around.

"He saw some girl in here he was checking for and went to talk to her."

"Oh yeah, there he is," Tracy said pointing at the bar across from our booth. "Ritchie stay whispering in some chicks ear." She giggled.

Tracy was right, Ritchie kept women in rotation. It was crazy because I still remembered Ritchie being the goofy, naïve teenager, but in the last few years after he started making real money and being in the streets all that shit changed. It's like he grew some balls and never looked back. But I was happy for my best friend. Although I thought he could slow down a tad on all the different females, I was happy he found his confidence and broke out of his shell because he damn sure was a late bloomer.

I couldn't help, but stand back, observe my crew, and smile. We had been going strong for years and now we were here tonight, celebrating my birthday, together as a family. They were all having a good time, laughing, smiling and our bond was stronger than ever. I knew both my dad and Uncle Marvin would be proud of what we had accomplished and me. We had managed to do what many would say was impossible in this game—stay alive, out of jail, and on top. That was because we always watched each other's back and stayed loyal not just to the game, but to our crew and it paid off. I had become one of the biggest players in these streets, moving more product than just about anybody. Things were going so well, we had begun expanding to Philly, Virginia, and North Carolina. I had become the epitome of a true boss and my drug dealer dreams were only beginning.

"Man, I can't believe after all that partying we did last night, you already up and out," Lance said, sounding like he was still sleep when I called him.

"Can't no business get done sleeping, nigga," I said getting out the car to hit up my favorite deli.

"You got me feeling like shit. Like I need to get my ass out of bed." Lance chuckled. "But then again, that's why you the boss. 'Cause while we sleepin' you up thinkin'."

"Pretty much, but don't forget Reese wanted us

to meet with a potential new buyer later on today."

"Damn, that shit is today. What time?"

"Five, you think you can have yo' lazy ass out the bed by then?" I joked.

"Yeah, I'll be up. Shiiit you done already fucked up my sleep. I'm 'bout to get up now. I'll hit you back when I hit the street."

"Cool," I said ending the call on my cell phone right as I stepped into the deli to get my favorite turkey bacon and egg sandwich. There was no need for me to place an order because soon as I walked through the door, they already knew what I wanted. I was what you would call a regular. After paying for my sandwich and orange juice, I was caught off guard when I turned around to leave.

"Hi, Nico," a vaguely familiar face said to me before I even made it to the exit door.

"Hey," I replied, trying to figure out where I recognized her face because I knew I had seen her before, but I couldn't place where.

"I guess you don't remember me. But that's not surprising since Tracy didn't introduce us."

"That's right. You're the girl that made Tracy late to my birthday party." I smiled.

"I'm sorry about that." She blushed. "I hope you don't hold it against me."

"No. I was just messing with you. So what's your name so I can call you something other than Tracy's girl."

"Angela, but everybody calls me Angie."

"So do you come to this deli often?"

"Not really, but I actually work in this office building around the corner."

"I guess it was a nice coincidence that we ran into each other."

"To be honest, it wasn't really a coincidence. I remembered a while ago when Tracy came to see me at work; she mentioned every morning you stopped by this deli around the corner from me. This is the only deli." Angela laughed nervously. "When I saw you yesterday at the club, I figured I take a chance to see if you were still coming here. I guess you are."

"Why didn't you introduce yourself yesterday at the party?"

"Nervous I guess. Then people kept coming up to you and I didn't want to be just another person you would forget."

"As pretty as your face is, I think you would be hard to forget. I mean, at first I couldn't remember where I had seen you, but it didn't take me long once you said Tracy's name. I see you're blushing again."

"Is it that obvious? Now I'm feeling embarrassed."

"Don't be embarrassed."

"I hope me showing up here doesn't make you think I'm some sort of stalker because I'm not... I promise." Angela giggled then gave me a cute smirk.

"I don't think you're a stalker. I actually respect the fact that you saw something you wanted and made a play for it."

"You make it sound like some sort of a game."

"Don't mind me, it's just how I talk. But listen, I have someplace I need to be."

"No, of course, I understand. I didn't mean to hold you up."

"I'm glad you did. Can I call you?"

"Of course," Angela said, writing her number down on a napkin before I could even pull out my cell phone. I found her eagerness cute and refreshing. Most of the women I came in contact with would be on some fake uppity shit, but be ready to fuck and suck the first night we went out. It was like they thought acting stuck up made them appealing, but all it did was make me want to dismiss they asses.

"I'ma call you. Maybe we can go out to dinner when you get off of work one day this week."

"I would love that."

"Cool, I'll call you tonight," I said walking off. "You really are pretty." I looked back and smiled. I could hear Angela giggling again and for the first that I could remember I was actually looking forward to our date.

♛ ♛ ♛

By the time I finished running around and handling

most of my business it was almost five o'clock and time to meet up with Reese. At first I was tempted to postpone the meeting as I had a couple more things I needed to do, but I had already rescheduled two times before and I didn't want Reese to feel like I was giving him the runaround. Right when I was about to get on the bridge headed back to Brooklyn I saw Lance calling me.

"What's up, Lance?"

"I'm pulling up to the warehouse. Reese is already here and I'm guessing the other car is the guy we meeting with. You still coming right?"

"Man, you know I don't miss meetings. I am running late. I had a lot of shit to handle today. You go inside and talk to the dude. Give him our prices although I'm sure Reese already did and let them know I'll be there shortly."

"Will do. I see Tracy and Ritchie pulling in now too. I'll see you in a minute," Lance said before hanging up.

On my drive to the warehouse all I kept thinking was I hoped this dude Reese had us meeting wasn't a waste of my time. I spent each day wheeling and dealing for the next come up, I had zero time to waste. The only reason I was even entertaining dude was because Reese vouched for him and Reese was family, so I hoped he was the real deal.

Chapter 12

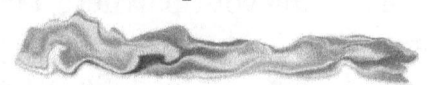

Nice To Meet You

"There's the man that makes everything happen," Alton said when I stepped in the warehouse.

"I was beginning to wonder if you was gon' make it," Reese added.

"My fault. Today was a lot more hectic than I anticipated. But I'm here now, let's get to it," I said walking over to where everyone was standing.

"Bink, this is Nico, Nico this is the new buyer I was telling you about." We shook hands and I was trying to size the dude up without seeming obvious.

"It's good to meet you, Bink. I know this was supposed to have happened awhile ago," I said upon releasing his hand.

"You a busy man and shit happens," Bink said

with ease. "Now that I finally have an opportunity to meet with you, I'm hoping we can do some business."

'That's the plan. Reese speaks highly of you and we all fam here so if the numbers make sense then I don't see why there would be a problem," I said getting a decent vibe from the dude.

"Like I was telling your partners, I have a huge crew in Upstate New York all they way on the other side of Maryland I have to feed. So we not talking small numbers. I have a large quantity of people I need to supply and if we can agree on a fair price I want you to be the sole distributor."

"I see." I glanced over at Lance and Ritchie who gave me the nod of approval. "Where's Tracy?" I asked wanting to get her input too. Although I could make or break any deals brought to the table, I preferred getting the okay from every member of my team so we were all in agreement. Before anyone could answer my question, Tracy came prancing out the back as if she heard me calling her name.

"There's my boo, what up, Nico." Tracy smiled. The sun hadn't even gone down and Tracy was already dressed to impress in her signature stiletto heels. She always had the appearance of a well-kept wife, little did people know she was lethal with a gun and would end your life without thinking twice. Besides me, Tracy was hands-down the best shooter in the crew.

"I was just asking about your whereabouts," I said.

"I had to freshen up in the bathroom. You know lady shit that ya don't know nothing about," she joked.

"Yeah, yeah, yeah… but um, Bink was telling me about the business he wanted to do with us."

"Yeah, I talked to him for a minute while we were waiting for the King's arrival," Tracy sniped, playfully frowning at me. "But he talking the right numbers and of course Reese already gave him the stamp of approval, so I say let's do this."

"So when you trying to get started?" Lance jumped in and asked.

"Based on the prices you all gave me, I'm ready to make my first order today," Bink let it be known.

"Well we don't keep no product at this warehouse, but we can make the trade tomorrow. Lance you go with Reese tomorrow to make the drop," I said feeling decent about the situation, but wanting to have someone keep a watchful eye until I felt good. Everybody in the crew had their strengths and one that Lance had was he analyzed everything. To the point that most of the time he over-analyzed. But he was sharp and it paid off for us on numerous occasions.

"That works for me. I'll see the two of you tomorrow," Bink said, nodding his head at Reese and Lance. "Nico, it was a pleasure. Let this be the beginning of a long and profitable business relationship."

"Yes, indeed," I said shaking his hand.

"I'll walk him out," Reese said following behind Bink.

"That money don't stop," Ritchie said once Reese and Bink had left the building.

"Pretty soon won't nobody be able to move drugs in New York without coming through us," Alton added.

"Boss, you awfully quiet. You got something on yo' mind," Lance questioned.

"I'm straight. Dude want a lot of product, but if he got the money to pay then he can play. We'll see," I said not yet convinced how legitimate Bink was.

"I think nigga legit," Ritchie said.

"Me too," Alton cosigned.

"Hell he better be! Don't nobody got time for a motherfucker to be playing," Tracy popped.

"Exactly, but enough of this shit. I got some other things to handle. Everything straight with business?" I asked before I headed out.

"I already checked in with all our workers and shit is running smoothly. I'll do another check in a few hours," Ritchie informed me.

"Cool. Running smoothly is always music to my ears," I said.

"Well, I'm right behind you, Nico. I'm picking my girl Angie up from work today so we can go have some drinks."

"Angela. I actually ran into her this morning."

"Where the hell did you run into Angie at?"

"At the deli around the corner from her job."

"Oh really?! Ain't that some shit. What the hell did you all talk about?"

"Calm down pitbull, you letting that green eye monster show." Alton laughed.

"Oh shut the hell up, Alton. Mind yo' business. This between me and Nico," Tracy snapped. "So tell me, Nico what did you all talk about?" Tracy continued, not letting up.

"I got her number and I plan on taking her out on a date."

"So you know, it won't no damn coincidence that Angie ran into you. I told her you be going to that deli."

"I know she told me."

"I should've known, Angie can't hold water. Nico, don't mess with that girl. I know she might appear like she about that life, but she ain't."

"Tracy, what you mean by that?"

"You know what the fuck I mean, Nico. Angie is my girl and I know you think because we're friends she must be hip, but she ain't."

"Tracy, it's a date. Calm down." I chuckled. "You getting all worked up over nothing."

"Okay, you say that now... that damn Angie, she just had to track you down," Tracy said shaking her head. "Let me get outta here."

"Don't go messing shit up for me neither and scare that girl off. I promise I'ma treat her right," I said putting my arms up. Tracy simply gave me the nigga face and left.

"Man, you know that girl like you. I don't know why you be playin' wit' her." Alton laughed, then slapped hands with Ritchie.

"We all know the rules including Tracy. No dating amongst the crew," I said without hesitation.

"That don't stop her from liking you though," Ritchie said.

"I like Tracy too but rules are rules. She's more like a sister to me anyway. A fine ass sister, but still a sister. Now Angie on the other hand, is fine too and she's not off limits. Tracy will be a'ight, trust me. Now enough fuckin' around wit' you knuckleheads, let me go." I swung my hand, dismissing them in a joking way.

On the way to my car I noticed Reese, Bink, and Tracy talking outside. They waved in my direction and I put my hand up saluting them. Bink seemed to be fitting right in nicely making me slightly optimistic that this might be the beginning of a profitable business relationship.

Chapter 13

Don't Be Afraid

"First you call, now we're here having dinner. All within two days, although it took three weeks to make it happen," Angela commented as she took another sip of her wine.

"I apologize for that. Business got crazy. I had to go out of town a few times and every time I was about to call you I got sidetracked. But I'm glad you still picked up once I finally did."

"Can't lie, I was reluctant, but how could I resist dinner at some super fancy restaurant in the city. First you bring flowers now this place. You really do know how to show a girl a good time."

"You deserve more, but I didn't want to over do it. You know, come on too strong."

"From what I heard, going strong is what Nico Carter does best."

"Is that right? Let me guess, you heard that from Tracy."

"Tracy only speaks highly of you. Between you and me, I think Tracy has a crush on you, but she would never admit it. But I guess it would be hard for any woman not to."

"I don't know about that, Angela. I know you said everybody calls you Angie, but you look like an Angela to me. Do you mind that?"

"Of course not, it's my name and I like the way you say it anyway." Angela blushed.

"There you go blushing again."

"For some reason every time I'm around you, I find myself blushing."

"Why is that?"

"Maybe because you have looks, money, charm, and if what the streets say are true, a lot of power. That can be very alluring and also very scary."

"Don't be afraid, Angela," I said, putting my hand across the table to touch hers. There were candles placed on each table and the way the light hit her face, she seemed to be glowing. Her pink lip-gloss made her plump full lips even more inviting. Her short, jet-black tapered haircut accentuated her high cheekbones and the fitted black dress she was wearing accentuated Angela's other assets too.

"This is going to sound crazy, but I know I should be afraid of you. I know you're probably going to break my heart, but I don't care. I've played it safe all my life, but I don't want to do that with you."

"Then don't. I'm young, I'm making moves and I'm not really in the position to be in a serious relationship. But I can promise that I'll always try to show you a good time. There's something about you that I like, Angela and I want the chance for us to get to know each other better."

"I want that, too. I won't put any pressure on you. I'll follow your lead and whatever happens... happens."

"If you keep that attitude we might go far." I winked before calling the waiter over so we could place our dinner order. I made that statement to Angela in a joking way, but I was being serious on the low. Angela's laid back calm demeanor fit how I was living right now perfectly. She seemed headache free and that was the number one criteria for any woman to be in my life. Most women didn't even make it to a first date with me. After a couple of phone conversations they were quickly deleted off the list because it was obvious to me that emotionally they were too high maintenance. Angela seemed different which was what I needed because street niggas need love too.

♛ ♛ ♛

"So we low on product already?" I huffed as Lance and I stood by our cars talking in front of Fulton Park.

"I know, but since Bink became a customer he be re-upping damn near every week which seems to now be interfering with our other clients. We need more product man. That ain't a bad thing."

"It is if you can't get it. I think I'm maxing out my connect. It might be time for me to get another." I sighed.

"You been dealing wit' yo' guy since Uncle Marvin and he was your uncle's connect. You really want to replace him?"

"I didn't say nothing about replacing him just having a back up. Business is growing. We have to keep up or risk leaving the door cracked for someone else to come in and take some of our business. I just want to be proactive," I explained.

"That makes sense. Do you have somebody in mind?"

"A couple people. But this dude Fernando that I've done some business with told me about this one connect that seems promising. I have to see who has the better product, best prices, and how quickly they can deliver though. Finding a new connect is now at the top of my priority list. Until then slow down how much product you give Bink. I have to make sure our other clients get served too."

"I'll handle it," Lance said tossing the soda he was drinking in the trashcan. "It won't be a problem."

"It's only temporary, at least that's what I'm hoping. Regardless, we'll make it work. But let me get outta here, I'm taking Angela to lunch."

"Angela... I've heard you mention her name quite a few times lately. What's up with that?"

"She's cool, I like her. I took her out to dinner for the first time a few weeks ago and we've been kickin' it ever since."

"This is a first for you. I ain't never known you to make time for no female and we been friends for years. All you think about is makin' money."

"And that ain't changed. I said I liked her. I ain't said we gettin' married. She a sweet girl and I can't lie, I enjoy her company. She don't give me no headaches either and it don't hurt that she easy on the eyes."

"You crazy." Lance laughed. "Hell, I'm just glad to know you still interested in women. I was gettin' worried," Lance cracked.

"Nigga, get off my dick. Don't worry 'bout my female situation. I'm straight over here. Don't be mad at me 'cause yo' ass been on lockdown wit' the same chick since high school," I joked.

"Fuck you! I thought you liked Morgan."

"Man, I do. I was jokin' wit' yo' sensitive ass. Morgan's a good girl. She gotta be to put up wit' yo' anal ass. Trust me, ain't that many good girls left so stick with what you got," I advised Lance. I meant that shit too. The line of business we were in, you rarely ran across a decent chick, especially one you could trust. Lance lucked out by still being with Morgan after all these years and I hoped he appreciated what he had. If not, I def wanted to remind him.

"I know I got a good woman. I didn't wanna say nothing 'cause she won't know for sure until she goes to the doctor tomorrow, but Morgan thinks she's pregnant," Lance revealed with the biggest smile on his face that I had ever seen.

"Word! Nigga, you gon' be a daddy!"

"I think so, at least I hope so. I've been wantin' a seed for a minute now, but Morgan insisted we wait until she finished college. Then she got a job and wanted to wait some more. I guess all that lovemaking I put on her finally paid off," Lance bragged.

"Shut yo' corny ass up," I clowned. "But on the real if Morgan is pregnant, congratulations. You gon' be a hell of a father. You a good dude," I said patting Lance's shoulder.

"Thank you. I appreciate that, especially coming from you. Does that mean you'll be the Godfather? I mean you do got all the money." Lance laughed. "So what you say." Lance continued laughing, rubbing his hands together. "But seriously, if Morgan and I are blessed with a baby, there is nobody else I would want to be the Godfather but you."

"I wouldn't have it no other way. We family, I got nothing but love for you. Now let me get the hell out of here," I said looking down at my watch.

"You 'bout to make me late for my lunch date with Angela."

"The way things are going with Angela, a lil' Nico might be next."

"Save your jokes. It'll be a long time before we see a lil' Nico," I said and drove off.

Chapter 14

Connect

"I'll be out of town for five days. While I'm gone, I need for ya to stay on top of shit. As we all know product is low so we have to move what we got with caution," I informed my crew as I sat at the round table with Lance, Ritchie, Alton, Reese, and Tracy.

"We gettin' a lot of complaints in the streets. They saying we dried up. How long you think this drought gon' last?" Ritchie questioned.

"That's the reason I'm going to the Dominican Republic, to fix this shit."

"Are you sure you'll be able to?" Reese then asked.

"I won't be sure of nothing until I get that

motherfuckin' product in my hand. But I am optimistic. If I wasn't I wouldn't be making this trip."

"Nico, I learned a long time ago not to ever doubt you 'cause you always come through. This ain't nothing but a slight bump in the road. I know you got this," Alton said pumping up his fist.

"I'll be in touch with Lance on a daily basis checking in, but of course get at me," I said, making eye contact with each of them, "if anything comes up. Other than that, we done here. I'll see you when I get back."

As we all got up from the table, Tracy strutted her ass in my direction. She was mad quiet during our meeting and I had a pretty good idea why.

"So you taking Angie with you to the Dominican Republic?" Tracy said in an accusatory type way.

"Tracy, you obviously already know the answer to that question so why are you even asking me?"

"Why are you doing this, Nico?"

"Doing what... living my life?"

"No, playing with Angie's."

"Tracy, you know I love you, we family, but don't nobody question me about my personal life. I don't owe you or anybody else an explanation. I'ma need you to slow down, 'cause you pushing it and it's rubbing me the wrong way."

"Sorry to be rubbing you the wrong way, Nico, but I have every right to be concerned about my girl."

"Concerned? She's a grown fuckin' woman. What's the real issue, Tracy?"

"I told you what my issue is. Oh I get it... you think I'm jealous of your relationship with Angie."

"I don't know what to think... are you jealous?" I straight up asked.

"No, that's some bullshit. Angie's mother used to babysit me. Angie was a few years younger than me, but we became really close. I was like a big sister to her. When she was 14, Angie's mother died, but while she was sick she made me promise to watch over her daughter and not let anything happen to her. Like you, Nico, I try to keep my promises. I'm a woman of my word."

"I get that and I respect it, but you know me. I have no intentions of hurting Angela so stop worrying. Your girl is good in my hands... I promise."

"I'ma hold you to that, Nico, but my gut is telling me, this shit ain't gon' end well. Have a good trip," Tracy said sarcastically before grabbing her purse and leaving.

I stood there shaking my head for a few seconds. I now had a better understanding of why Tracy was so protective of Angela, but I still felt she was out of pocket. I felt she was overreacting and coming at me like I was some type of bad guy. But I had to accept the fact that only time would ease Tracy's mind. Tracy was fair and once she realized that I wasn't going to bring Angela any harm, her attitude would change.

When we arrived at the resort in Punta Cana, the first thing Angela wanted to do was chill on the beach until we arrived at the private luxury home located in a gated community. This was the first time I had ever been to the Dominican Republic, but the potential connect I was meeting with suggested this is where I should stay and I'm glad I listened. I had never seen such beauty in person before. Growing up in the grimy streets of Brooklyn, I almost forgot places like this existed.

After handling my business, I planned on spending the duration of the trip with Angela racing on speedboats, deep-sea sport fishing, snorkeling, whale watching, catamaran sailing, and even swimming with dolphins. On our final night there, I was going to surprise her with a candlelight dinner on a small island called Catalina. I had everything figured out and I was looking forward to making this a trip Angela would never forget.

"Did I die and go to heaven because this can't be real." Angela gasped when she stepped out on the humongous balcony that overlooked a golf course, private pool, gazebo, and white sandy beaches with the bluest water I had ever seen.

"If this is what heaven looks like, I see why everybody tryna get there. You still want to hit the beach or do you wanna take a dip in that pool?" I said, hugging Angela from behind.

"I think I'll pass on the beach and dive into that pool instead," Angela replied, turning her head to kiss me.

"Then I guess you better go put on that bikini," I said kissing her back.

"Who needs a bathing suit." Angela giggled slipping out of her halter dress and panties right there before heading towards the pool. "Are you just going to stand there or are you coming?" Angela giggled some more, running towards the pool.

The way the hot sun was hitting her golden brown skin had a nigga feeling some type of way. Her body was glistening and I couldn't do nothing, but watch as Angela's curvy body dived in the water. After soaking in how damn sexy she was, I stepped out of my linen shorts and shirt and joined her.

"Did I tell you how amazing you are," were the first words out of Angela's mouth when she rose from the water to catch her breath.

"Nah, you haven't," I said pulling her body close to me.

"You are. You didn't have to bring me to this amazing place, but you did. This is the nicest thing anyone has ever done for me."

"This is only the beginning. I have big plans for you."

"That's funny because I have plans for you too," Angela teased biting down on my bottom lip.

That night Angela showed me exactly what her plans were. She gave me the best head of my life. I don't know if being in a fucking five bedroom beachfront palace heightened the sexiness, but Angela's lips wrapped around my rock hard dick felt even better than usual. She must've felt the same way because her moans of pleasure were on fever pitch when I slid inside. Her pussy was even wetter than the pool we had just finished swimming in. After that night, there was no doubt in my mind that Angela was a keeper.

The next day on my way to meet with my potential connect, Marco, I placed a call to Lance to see how shit was going. "What up my dude... how's it going?"

"Everything is cool under the circumstances. How did things go on your end?"

"I'm on my way to meet with Marco now. I'll hit you up as soon as I'm done," I said trying to pay attention to where I was going while talking to Lance.

"Cool. I'm keeping my fingers crossed this shit works out 'cause man we need it, we need it bad," Lance said sounding somewhat antsy.

"You sure everything a'ight over there. I ain't

been gone, but for a day and you sounding mad shaky."

"I'm straight just looking into a few things."

"Looking into what? Is there something going on that I need to know about?"

"Not right now. You know I'll let you know if that changes."

"You better."

"Nico, you already know how we do. I'm not gonna keep you in the dark about shit. It's probably nothing, but if I'm wrong you'll be the second to know."

"Okay. I'm here so I gotta go, but I'ma call you when I'm done."

"I'll be waiting on that call," Lance said and then hung up. He left me with a funny feeling when we got off the phone. I didn't know what was going on with Lance, but he didn't sound like himself. I couldn't worry about that right now though because I had to handle this meeting. But finding out what had Lance sounding shaky was next on my agenda.

"You finally made it," Marco said greeting me at the door, which surprised me. For some reason I thought bodyguards would surround him and he would have an entourage, but it wasn't the type of party. Marco was on some real chill shit. He lived in what I would consider a modest house on the beach, especially since he was supposed to be one of the largest coke and heroin distributors in the

Dominican Republic. He was also much older than I expected.

"I appreciate you seeing me, Marco," I said taking a seat in the living room area. The doors were wide open and the breeze from the beach was blowing the cream sheer silk curtains. The vibe was so tranquil that I almost forgot what the fuck I was there for. Now I understood why Marco lived here. There was something about the place that completely put your mind at ease.

"Of course. Fernando speaks very highly of you. He says you are in a bit of a bind, I believe I can help," Marco said speaking in broken English.

"That's what I needed to hear," I said, welcoming the good news. If Marco could be my new connect and I could get the product at the prices I wanted, I would be much closer to building my multi-million dollar drug empire.

Chapter 15

Guilt Trip

"Man, I'm happy you back," Lance said when we met up at a bar over in Queens. It was a low-key spot we would go to periodically to discuss business over drinks.

"It's good to be back."

"If it was me... the beaches, the sun... I would've stayed my ass over there."

"A little relaxation is nice once in awhile, but my high comes from these streets. Although it was a business trip mixed wit' pleasure, I won't need to take a vacation for at least another two or three years."

"Man you ain't right, but your way of thinking makes you the great Nico Carter. So let's get down to what you really came to discuss... business." Lance smiled.

"Before we get to that, how's Morgan doing?"

"She driving me crazy, but her pregnancy is going great."

"Ain't that what pregnant women supposed to do... drive you crazy." We laughed. "But good, you know I gotta check on my future Godchild. You let me know if you guys need anything. Now that we got that out the way, let's discuss business," I said, signaling my hand for another round of drinks.

"Shit is looking good now that you came through with this new connect. Do you have any idea when the first shipment will arrive?"

"No later than Friday, Marco said."

"Well, motherfuckers just gon' have to wait. I mean ain't nothing we can do."

"How bad is it? We don't have enough to maintain until Friday? I told you to spread that shit out. We can't be completely wiped out."

"There was a slight problem, nothing major."

"Is that why you were sounding all shaky when I spoke to you in the Dominican Republic? When I called you back you said everything had been handled and shit was straight. Was that a lie?" I grilled Lance.

"No, it wasn't a lie. At first I thought there was a problem, but then Reese told me everything was good, but then..." Lance hesitated.

"But then what?"

"But then Reese told me that he fulfilled Bink's order not realizing that was the last bit of product we had. It was a miscommunication."

"So wait, we runnin' 'round here dry while Bink got all the product? What type of shit does that make? We supposed to be the distributor not the other fuckin' way around."

"Nico, I know. It was an honest mistake. But luckily things came through with Marco and we'll have plenty of product to fulfill orders no later than Friday. Nobody got our quality of product and prices so our customers will wait."

"That ain't the point, Lance. Ya can't be making mistakes like that. We running a drug operation, but ain't got no drugs. I specifically said to slow down how much product we give Bink until I got this situation under control. Yet that nigga end up wit' the last bit of what we got. Don't neva let no dumb shit like that happen again."

"It won't."

"It bet not. I count on you to stay on top of shit, Lance. This some knucklehead shit I would expect from Alton, or maybe Ritchie 'cause he caught up in some pussy, but not you." I huffed.

"I know. I thought I had told Reese that was all we had left and we couldn't sell to Bink, but I fucked up. I guess my mind has been on the baby and Morgan's pregnancy. I apologize, Nico, but I'm back focused, man."

"I understand. Luckily more product is on the

way, but just know you've used your one free pass. Now let me finish this drink," I said, needing something to take the edge off.

♛ ♛ ♛

"I can't believe how good you treat me." Angela grinned as I paid for the clothes I just bought her. We left with so many bags you would've thought we shut down the store.

"I like treating you good," I said holding the door open for her.

"I like you treating me good, too. I can't wait to wear that red dress tonight when we go to Tracy's birthday party.

"I can't wait to take it off of you," I said about to open the passenger car door for Angela.

"Babe, wait," Angela said looking down. "What's wrong?"

"I left one of the bags in the store."

"You sure?"

"Positive. I don't see the bag that had two pairs of shoes in it."

"You get in the car, I'll go back inside and get the bag," I said heading back towards the store. Those were the last words I said before everything seemed to move in slow motion. Out of nowhere, a car pulled up next to mine with a guy wearing a black ski mask. His eyes locked with mine before he stuck his head out and began blasting. It all happened so fast that I didn't even have an opportunity to reach in the car to retrieve my gun.

"Angela, get down!" I yelled out, leaping towards her. All I heard was glass shattering. Then I saw bags and clothes flying everywhere. As quickly as the gunshots rang out they instantly came to a halt. When I reached Angela all the clothes concealed her. In rapid speed I began tossing the clothes off of her and underneath there was Angela's dead body covered in blood.

♛ ♛ ♛

By the time I finished getting interviewed by the cops, it was nighttime and I was in a daze. Just a few hours earlier, Angela was shopping, smiling, and giving me her signature giggle and now she was dead. I had killed before, had seen people get killed, but holding Angela's dead body in my arms fucked with me in a way that I had never experienced.

"Where's Tracy?" I asked Alton when I got to the lounge where Tracy was having her birthday party.

"Damn, it's good to see you too, Nico, what happened to hello?" Alton joked.

"Not right now, Alton. I'm not in the mood," I said, dreading the conversation I was about to have with Tracy.

"Is everything okay?" Alton asked with concern.

"No, now where is Tracy?"

"She's over in the back. Listen, I..." Before Alton could even finish his sentence I was headed to the back to find Tracy. She was sitting with two of her girlfriends drinking champagne when I walked up.

"Hey, Nico! Where's my girl Angie?" she beamed, standing up and coming in my direction. "And where is my present? I know you didn't show up to my birthday party empty handed," Tracy continued, sipping on her glass of champagne.

"We need to talk... in private." I sighed.

"Awww damn! You and Angie got into an argument and now she not coming to my party? Fuck that! I'm calling her right now," Tracy said, reaching into her purse to retrieve her cell phone.

"You can't call her, Tracy," I said, putting my hand over her purse.

"Why the fuck not? What is going on, Nico and why you actin' so fuckin' strange?"

"Can we just go talk in private," I said, leading Tracy by the arm towards a hallway I noticed. It led to some bathrooms and I pulled Tracy into one of them.

"Yo, what the fuck is going on?" Tracy snapped.

"There's no easy way to tell you this."

"Tell me what, Nico?"

"Angela is dead." The shock of hearing what I said caused Tracy to drop her glass and she stood in front of me with her mouth open, but no words were coming out. "It happened a few hours ago. We had just left the store and then there was a drive-by-shooting."

"A drive by! Damn, ya got caught up in somebody else's bullshit. Who was they shooting at?"

"Me."

"Wait, somebody was shooting at you and Angie got killed?" Tracy questioned as her bottom lip shivered.

"Yes. I'm sorry, Tracy. I know how much you cared about Angela and so did I," I said putting my hand on her shoulder.

"Don't touch me!" she yelled, jerking her body away from me. I told you this wasn't gon' end well. We live such a fucked up life, but we signed up for this shit, Angie didn't. I knew..." Tracy pointed her finger at my chest and paused for a second as she tried to hold back tears from flowing. "I knew no good would come from this relationship."

"Don't you think I feel fucked up about what happened too. I saw her die. I held her dead body in my arms. The guilt is eatin' my ass up inside. Yeah she died because of me, but I didn't pull the trigger."

"The moment you started dating Angie, you pulled the trigger. This is the shit I was talkin' 'bout, Nico. You the main one always stressing to us that this business ain't set up for love and relationships, but yet you had to get involved with someone who was like family to me, my own sister. I guess you understand why I practically begged you to let it go and not get involved with her. Now it's too late. My birthdays will never be the same again. Thanks for ruining it," Tracy stated, walking out the bathroom and leaving me standing in my own misery.

When I looked up I could see my reflection in the mirror. For the first time I didn't like what was staring back at me. No, I wasn't the ski-masked shooter, but Tracy was right, in a lot of ways I was the one that pulled the trigger.

Chapter 16

War Ready

"Any leads on who shot at me and killed Angela?" I asked Lance when he stopped by an office I had in downtown Brooklyn.

"Not yet," Lance admitted, taking a seat in the chair in front of my desk. He put his head down into his hands as completely stressed the fuck out.

"Has something else happened? 'Cause you seem out of your element."

"One of our trap houses got hit up late last night. I just found out about it on my way over here to see you."

"What the fuck!" I barked, pounding my fist down on the desk. "Which stash house?"

"Brownsville."

"How much product was there?"

"A lot. The shipment from Marco came in a couple of days ago and a big portion was at the Brownsville spot because we were expecting three big pickups today. It gets worse. They killed four of our workers that were there," Lance revealed.

"You can't be serious," I said standing in front of the window and staring outside. The sun was shining, but shit over my head was fuckin' gloomy.

"I don't think what happened is a coincidence or random. I think the same people that tried to kill you, hit up the stash house."

"No shit, Sherlock. Of course it ain't no fuckin' coincidence. It's the same motherfuckers. So you know what this means."

"What?" Lance said, looking up at me.

"It's means we 'bout to go to war."

"So you think it's a crew behind this?"

"Fuck yeah! Ain't one or two motherfuckers got enough balls to come at me like this. They tryna take me down and only a crew would think they have enough manpower to do so."

"So, what do you want to do?"

"First, we have to call a meeting and let everybody know what's going on because we all have to be on alert. They might've come at me first, but you, Tracy, Alton, Reese, and Ritchie could be next. We have to up security. Keep extra men posted outside each of the stash houses."

"I'll get on top of that immediately, but it's

gonna be hard to fight a war when we don't know who the enemy is," Lance said.

"You right. But let me handle that."

"Got you."

"In the meantime, let's get everybody war ready."

♔ ♔ ♔

"It was a pleasant surprise to hear from you." I heard a familiar voice say behind me.

"My man, Bennie. I see you still like sneaking up on motherfuckers." I chuckled, shaking Bennie's hand. "Have a seat," I said, moving over so Bennie could sit next to me on the park bench.

"I haven't seen you since your Uncle Marvin passed away. You was just a boy, now you a man. Look at you." Bennie grinned. "You clean and handsome just like yo' daddy was. Yo' father sure was a good man," Bennie continued.

"He sure was."

"But I know you didn't call me to talk about yo' old man, may he rest in peace. They never did find the piece of shit responsible for killing him. That's a damn shame," Bennie said, shaking his head.

"Trust me, Bennie. I'm sure karma has found them and justice was served."

"I hope you right 'cause your father was a hell

of a man. But enough talkin' 'bout that, what can I do for you, Nico?"

"I need to utilize some of your street informants, that is if you're still in the business of handling that?"

"I am. Although I considered retiring that part of my business, after I couldn't find out any information about who killed your father. That shit ate me up for years." Bennie groaned.

"Don't be so hard on yourself. Things have a way of working themselves out. But I do hope you'll have better luck with me."

"Tell me what's going on?"

"A few weeks ago someone tried to kill me. They end up killing a young lady I was dating instead."

"Sorry to hear that."

"Yeah, she was a good girl who most def didn't deserve to die."

"So you looking to know who killed her so you can get that situation handled?"

"Yes, but I think it's a little deeper then one shooter. The other day one of my stash houses was hit and four of my men were killed. I think a competitor crew is tryna take me out. But I can't figure out who would even have the audacity to come at me."

"This new young cats out here so crazy. I don't know what they be thinking. Hell, they don't be thinking, but I believe I can help. I got some new kids working for me that I know if they had been around when your daddy had gotten killed, they would've got the motherfucker. They sharp and got their ears in everythang."

"Good. That's what I need. The sooner you can find out the better. My business is under attack. This shit ain't just taken money, it's taken lives. I don't want nobody else to die except for the people responsible for this mayhem."

"I'm about to put my people on it right now. Do you have any enemies you can think of?"

"None that I think is capable of pulling something like this off. But I could be wrong so don't sleep on nobody. Have your people check into everybody. Somebody knows what the fuck is going on who's behind it. So find out for me, Bennie."

"I got you, Nico. Your father came through for me on numerous occasions, so I owe it to him to help out his son."

"I appreciate that but best believe you come through for me you will be very well compensated."

"Thank you and I'll be in touch," Bennie said, shaking my hand before leaving.

♛ ♛ ♛

After meeting with Bennie, I headed to the warehouse to meet up with my crew. When I pulled up, I saw that all their cars were parked out front so the only person they were waiting on was me.

"What's up fam," I said when I walked inside. They were immersed in a deep conversation so at first they didn't hear me. It took them a second to notice I had even come in.

"Nico, I'm glad you here," Alton said being the first person to spot me. "They over here arguing wit' each other," he explained.

"Listen, this ain't the time to be arguing amongst each other. What the fuck is you bickering about?" I barked, already annoyed before the meeting even started.

"Lance over here tryna dictate shit, when it's his fault four of our workers are dead," Ritchie spat.

"How the fuck is it my fault?" Lance shot back.

"You should've never had all that product in Brownsville. That ain't even our main spot. Normally only one at the most two men are posted there, but because you insisted on having all that product brought there we put more men on it. Now we lost money, our men, and drugs."

"Reese told me that we had three buyers coming through the next day to pick up their product," Lance explained.

"But I didn't say for you to have all their drugs there," Reese countered.

"It only made fuckin' sense to do it that way. The three buyers were closer to the Brownsville location," Lance said defending his decision.

"You mean it made sense to you," Ritchie grumbled.

"What the fuck would you have done, Ritchie? Oh I forgot, you be too busy running up in pussy to make a business decision," Lance quipped.

"Nigga, fuck you! My dick ain't got shit to do wit' the dumbass decision you made." Ritchie frowned.

"Everybody shut the fuck up!" I finally said. "You all are arguing over irrelevant shit. Whether or not Lance made the right decision having all that product at the Brownsville location don't change the fact that somebody tried to kill me and robbed one of the stash spots. We need to be spending our energy on tryna figure who the fuck is behind that shit instead of blaming each other. This shit is counterproductive. So have we amped up security?" I wanted to start discussing the important shit instead of the things we could no longer do anything about.

"Yes, I rallied a bunch of our men up and got them doubled up on the outside and inside for all locations. I even tripled them up on some of our busier spots," Reese said.

"That's good, Reese. I'm assuming you made sure everyone is properly armed?"

"No doubt. I even made sure they had plenty of backup on deck. Whoever these motherfuckers are that's coming for us, they'll be in for a rude awakening when they show up," Reese said confidently.

"I want each of you to have extra security on you too," I said.

"I don't need no extra security. I wish a motherfucker would step to me, they'll regret the day," Tracy popped, after being quiet for the entire time.

"That wasn't a suggestion, it's mandatory."

"What do you mean 'it's mandatory'?"

"We all know what the word mandatory means, including you, Tracy. So like I said, each of you have extra security at all time until this situation is resolved," I made clear. I caught Tracy rolling her eyes, but I didn't care because being cautious was more important. I didn't want any more lives lost.

Chapter 17

Climax

It had been two weeks since the hit in Brownsville and we were no closer to finding out who was responsible. The only bright side was there hadn't been any new attacks, but in my gut, I had a bad feeling that something was about to go down. I didn't know why and the shit was fucking with me. As I sat alone in a booth at the bar in Queens, I felt I was about to go out of my mind trying to figure this thing out. So much wasn't adding up to me, like I was missing something, but I couldn't put my finger on it. I kept the drinks flowing determined to come up with something.

"Let me get what he's having."

"Tracy, what are you doing here?" I looked up

and said when I heard her talking to the waitress. "And where is your security?'

"Where is yours?" she asked right back.

"Nobody knows about this spot."

"Exactly. I thought it was the perfect opportunity to shake them motherfuckers and have some alone time. So, can I join you?"

"Be my guest. How did you know I was here?"

"Lance told me."

"I guess he didn't mention that I don't want to be bothered," I said knocking back another shot.

"He did, but I was hoping you would make an exception for me."

"Tracy, if you came here to talk more shit to me about Angela you can go 'head and leave now, 'cause I ain't here for it."

"I know I've been hard on you these last few months and I wanted to apologize."

"Apologize? Hmm, why apologize when you meant every word you said?"

"It's true I didn't want you to get involved with Angie, but it's not your fault that she's dead and I'm sorry for even putting that out there. I was hurt and angry, but I shouldn't have lashed out at you."

"I appreciate you saying that, but if Angela hadn't gotten involved with me, she would still be alive, living her life."

"Nico, Angela was well aware of the lifestyle you were living and she chose to get involved with you. I mean she was the one that came after you...

remember. I remind myself of that every time I want to blame you for what happened to her."

"I guess…" I said as my voice trailed off.

"Don't do this to yourself, Nico. I know for a fact that Angela enjoyed every moment she spent with you. She said you made her feel more special than anyone has ever in her life."

"She said that?"

"Yes, she did. I have love for you anyway, but knowing that made me love you even more. You're one of the good guys, Nico. No matter how tough you try to act."

"One more, then I'm done," I said to the waitress when she stopped by the table to bring Tracy's drink. "How did shit get so bad so fast, Tracy? A couple months ago I felt we was unstoppable. Now…" I took a deep breath and shook my head.

"Now what?"

"Now I don't know what's gon' happen next."

"I know. We gonna find out who's behind all this bullshit and fuck them motherfuckers up. That's what's gon' happen next."

"Your feisty attitude is what I always loved most about you."

"And I thought it was the way I was able to handle a gun and look damn sexy doing it."

"That's a close second." I smiled. "But seriously, I hope you right, Tracy. "I'm ready for shit to get back to how it used to be."

"It will, Nico. Sooner than you think… watch.

We run these streets and whoever these dumb fucks are that decided to start a war with us, they will regret the day they made that decision."

"True dat," I said gulping down my last shot. "Now, let's go, 'cause if I have one more drink they'll have to drag me outta here."

"Don't let me find out you gettin' soft," Tracy joked, punching me in the arm.

"Never soft and you better take that back before I let this door hit you." I laughed, as I held the door open for Tracy.

"I ain't worried. All this ass I got will make that door bounce right back." She winked.

"Tracy, get down!" I yelled out.

"Huh!" she screamed, glancing back at me before looking in the direction I was staring at. Luckily, this time I was prepared and pulled out my gun shooting towards the man who was firing at us.

"Fuck you motherfucker!" Tracy bawled, pulling a gat from her purse and returning fire. At the exact same time both Tracy and me hit our mark. My bullet hit his chest and Tracy got the neck. After his body dropped, we didn't have a second to regroup when two more shooters popped out of nowhere with guns blazing.

"Tracy, you good?" I shouted to her as we both took cover behind a car.

"Of course I'm good. These niggas going down."

"You ready?" I said, motioning for us to come from behind the car and start blasting.

"Let's do this." Tracy nodded, as we began firing one shot after another. On the third try, Tracy put a bullet in the back of one of the shooters as he was turning away to take cover. I was able to shoot the other guy in his leg, which caused him to fall down in the middle of the street. I quickly ran towards him and put a bullet in his head to finish him off.

"Tracy, behind you! I yelled out when I noticed another gunman sneaking up on her. I fired off three more shots, but I wasn't fast enough. The gunman was able to release his shots, riddling Tracy's upper body with bullets before my shot blew his brains out.

"Nico," Tracy mumbled as blood flowed from her mouth.

"Shhh... shhh, don't say anything. Everything is gonna be fine. Tracy, I'ma get you some help," I reassured her.

"It's too late," she said softly. "We did good... if only that last motherfucker didn't show up," Tracy said, barely audible.

"Don't say another word. You have to keep your strength," I said, trying to stay strong.

"I love you, Nico, and make sure you get the motherfuckers who did this to me," Tracy said before closing her eyes.

"Tracy... Tracy... Tracy!" I kept yelling as I held her limp body. This was like reliving Angela's murder all over again only worse.

Nico Carter

♔ ♔ ♔

"This was a beautiful service, Nico," one of the guests at Tracy's funeral came over and said to me as I watched her coffin lowered in the ground.

"Thank you," I said not looking up. Even with the dark tinted sunglasses I was wearing, I felt it couldn't conceal the pain I was in. I must've been standing there forever because by the time I looked up, the only people left there was my security, Lance, Reese, Alton, and Ritchie.

"We need to get going, Nico," Lance said, putting his hand on my shoulder.

"Just give me a few more minutes." I needed a little bit more time to say goodbye to Tracy. Out of all the people to die, I didn't understand why it had to be her. First Angela and now Tracy, it was all too much. For the first time since I stepped into the drug game, I was asking myself was it really worth it? Was the high I got from hustling worth the lives of people I loved?

"What's next, boss?" Alton questioned as we all rode in the limo, headed towards a restaurant where a gathering was being held in Tracy's honor. I wasn't in the mood to attend, but I knew it was expected of me to show up. I'm sure Tracy would've wanted a party, but her family, specifically her mother, wanted a luncheon so I obliged. None of it mattered though because it wouldn't bring Tracy back.

"We've already beefed up security, all we can do is keep our ears to the streets and pray that we're prepared for whatever comes next," I said, staring out the window.

"Man, these pieces of shit are gonna burn for what they did to Tracy," Reese said bawling his fist.

"We have to find them first. These niggas startin' to feel like ghosts." Ritchie grumbled.

"I know right," Lance said, leaning down on his hand as if in deep thought. While they continued talking amongst each other, a text came through on my phone from Bennie asking me to call him. I didn't want to talk to him in front of my crew since no one was aware that I had hired Bennie.

"I'll be in there shortly," I told everyone when we arrived to the restaurant. Once they were all out of the limo and I was alone, I immediately called Bennie.

"I was beginning to worry when it took so long for you to call me," was the first thing Bennie said when he answered his phone.

"I was around some people and couldn't talk. I hope this call isn't a waste of my time."

"Not at all. I have some information that you definitely want to hear, but I prefer to tell you in person," Bennie said.

"I prefer that, too. I have to go inside to this restaurant for a second and then I'm coming straight to you."

"Meet at the regular spot?"

"Yep, I'll see you in about an hour," I said, ending the call. I planned on spending no more than 15 minutes inside the restaurant because the only thing on my mind, was finding out what Bennie had to say.

Chapter 18

Broken

"Bennie, I apologize for being late, but I got tied up," I said when I sat down next to him on the park bench.

"No problem, I know you a busy man, Nico."

"That had nothing to do with it. Today was a member of my crew's funeral. Her name was Tracy. She was family to me and now she's gone. That's why I hope you have something for me because this is hitting way too close to home now."

"I do. I know exactly who is trying to bring you and your crew down. His name is Bink."

"The nigga that buys product from me... that Bink?"

"That's the one. A few weeks ago you went

through a time when you ran out of product, correct?"

"Yeah, how did you know that?"

"Well, that Bink fella used that to his advantage and was supplying to some of your clientele during your drought. He used a middleman of course so you wouldn't know it was coming from him."

"So Bink was buying up all my product so he could then sell to my clients. That sonofabitch."

"From what my street informant found out, you were able to get a new connect."

"True."

"Once Bink knew you would have enough product to supply your customers, he decided it was time to take you out," Bennie explained.

"That motherfucker," I said, feeling my blood boil. "But something ain't adding up," I said, looking over at Bennie.

"There's more. This is the final piece to the puzzle," Bennie said, leaning forward.

"I'm listening."

♛ ♛ ♛

On my way to the warehouse, I kept replaying every word Bennie said to me. I remembered each detail as if it had been engraved in my brain. I had already made the necessary calls to track Bink down and now I was on my way to meet with my crew. When I arrived at the warehouse, I damn near jumped out the car before my driver even had an opportunity to turn it off.

"I'm glad all of you are here," I said when I got inside.

"You said it was an emergency, so we all got here as soon as possible," Lance said.

"Yeah, what's going on? Don't tell me somebody else has been killed?" Ritchie asked nervously.

"No, not yet. But I know who's responsible for all the fucked up shit that's been going on."

"Get out! Who? Let's go kill them motherfuckers," Alton shouted. "I knew you'd find out who it was, Nico," Alton continued getting amped.

"Bink."

"Bink, as in the nigga that buy product from us?" Ritchie asked, looking shocked.

"Yeah, that Bink."

"Are you sure, Nico?" Reese questioned.

"I'm positive."

"Then we need to make our move... now!" Alton barked.

"I'm working on it, but I don't know his location. It's like he disappeared. When is the last time he made a buy?"

"A few days ago. So unless he got wind that you were on to him and decided to leave town, he has to still be around," Lance reasoned.

"I only found out today so Bink shouldn't know

anything is up. As far as he's concerned, shit is still sweet for him and I want to keep it that way until we locate him."

"That slick motherfucker. I can't believe this nigga was doing business wit' us and plotting on us at the same time. That bitch ass nigga going down," Alton sulked.

"Yeah, that nigga do got a lot of balls. I'm just glad you figured this shit out, Nico, so we can shut him down for good," Reese said. "So how do you want to move on this?"

"Since you and Lance are the ones he primarily deals with, hit him up and see if he can meet with you tonight. If he can't meet with you then at least try and get his whereabouts."

"Sure, you want me to call him now?" Reese asked.

"Yeah, call him now."

"It's ringing," Reese mouthed as he held the phone to his ear. "He ain't answering," he said.

"Hang up," I said.

"Do you want me to try and call him?" Lance suggested.

"No, that might raise suspicions with Reese calling first and then you calling right behind him."

"You want me to send him a text message telling him to call me back?" Reese asked.

"That's a good idea. Send the text and if he responds you know what to do," I said.

"I'm on it."

"Is there anything you want us to do?" Lance wanted to know.

"Not right now."

"At least we finally know who the enemy is. Only if we had found out sooner, Tracy would still be alive," Ritchie said sadly.

"I know. We weren't able to save Tracy, but we will make sure everybody responsible for her death pays with their life," I stated. "I wanted to keep everybody in the loop on what was going on. Now that I have, you all can go and we'll meet back up tomorrow."

"Nico, is there anything you need me to do?" Lance came over and asked me as everyone was heading out.

"Just be careful. We'll talk tomorrow," I said walking out with him.

"I will. I'll be home chillin' with Morgan, rubbing on her pregnant belly." Lance smiled. "But call me if anything comes up," Lance said before getting in his car.

"Take me to my office," I directed my driver. I then placed a phone call to see if the men I had hunting down Bink made any progress. "Any news?"

"Not yet, but we're on it," he assured me.

"Trust me, they'll be movement very soon... I promise you. I'll be expecting a call soon."

"Okay," the worker said not sounding as confident as me, but I wasn't worried.

I wasn't at my office for more than an hour

when my cell went off. As I expected, it was one of my workers calling me back. "You got a location?"

"Yep, just like you said we would."

"Good, text me the address. Don't let them leave. I'm on the way," I said, putting on my bulletproof vest.

When I arrived at the address the worker gave me, I had my driver park next to the men I had keeping an eye on Bink. Luckily, it wasn't far so I was able to get there quickly. "How many inside?" I asked.

"We've counted four."

"Cool. I'm sure they're armed, but they won't be a match for us. How many men we got?"

"I already have seven surrounding the back of the apartment building and another seven parked up the street, waiting for the green light."

"Give them the green light then and let's go." With my two bodyguards we were over 15 men deep, about to ambush Bink and what made the shit so beautiful was he didn't even see it coming. "Kick that door down," I ordered, knowing the element of surprise would work in our favor.

"What the fuck!" Bink stood up and barked as his front door busted open. His immediate reaction was to reach for his firearm that was on the couch, but when he saw all the guns pointing at his head he knew better.

"Don't even think about it," I said to Bink who looked like he was about to shit on himself.

"I knew you would lead me to him, Reese. Thank you."

"Yo, Nico, I was just about to call you and let you know I found Bink. I'm glad you finally here," Reese said, standing up from the chair he was sitting in and coming towards me. I nodded my head to one of the gunmen and he immediately put the gun to Reese's head. "Why the fuck you got that gun pointed in my face?" Reese shrugged and then looked over at me as if he thought I would tell the gunmen to aim his weapon elsewhere.

"Killing you," I said pointing at Reese, "is what I'm most looking forward to."

"Nico, what the fuck is you talkin' about?" Reese was trying to give his best impression of a confused individual, but the shit wasn't working.

"The jig is up, so stop. I know it was you orchestrating all this bullshit wit' Bink. Nigga, you was part of a team and you killed one of the members. Tracy is dead because of yo' punk ass. I should shoot you right now, but that would be too easy. You will suffer… I promise. Your death will be long, painful, and slow."

"Nico, man this is all a misunderstanding. I can explain everything. If you hear me out it will all make sense… please," Reese begged.

"And Bink, for yo' fat ass to think you could take my spot. Oh wait, did dumb and dumber plan to share the position. You clowns disgust me. Tie all these niggas up, including these two motherfuckers sitting there not saying shit," I directed my men. I figured the two men were some workers of Bink, but I didn't give a fuck who they were because they were dying tonight too.

"Nico, it was all Reese's idea. He set this shit in motion from the jump. He brought me on. I wasn't even buying the drugs. He was stealing from you. It was him that wanted to takeover. When you found that new connect Reese decided it was time for you to go and make his move. It was all him... I swear."

"Bink, shut the fuck up! He's lyin', Nico!" Reese shouted sounding like the snake he was.

"None of this shit matters, both of you are gonna die."

"Man, I don't wanna die. It wasn't supposed to end like this," Bink said, sounding like he was about to break down in tears.

"Tie these niggas up," I said, ready to get this over with."

"Wait... wait... wait," Bink said nervously as one of the men was about to place tape over his mouth. "I know something. I'll tell you if you just let me live."

I saw Reese's face frown up and his jaw start flinching. "Nico, you don't need to listen or believe anything this nigga has to say. He making up bullshit to try and take the crew down. It's divide and conquer. I promise I'm not working wit' this nigga. He got a partner, but it ain't me," Reese said, pleading his case.

"All lies," I scuffed. "Tell me what you know, Bink, and I might consider letting you live."

"Once Reese realized my cover was blown, he said he needed to move quickly so he had me call some guys to take care of Ritchie and Lance," Bink revealed.

"Take care how?" I asked, but was afraid to hear the answer.

"Kill..."

Before Bink could even complete his thought, I was on the phone calling Lance. "Pick up the phone, Lance!" I called him again, and when he still didn't answer I called Ritchie.

"What up, man," Ritchie answered.

"Has anybody been to your crib?"

"I don't know, I'm not home. I'm at this chick's crib," Ritchie said.

"Have you heard from Lance?"

"No, not since we left the warehouse, why what's wrong?"

"Listen, get over to Lance's crib ASAP. Reese sent some men over there to kill him."

"What the fuck! Our nigga, Reese? Nah, man you must be mistaken," Ritchie said in denial.

"I'll explain the shit to you later. Right now you just get over to Lance's crib and bring some backup. I'll keep trying his cell, but call me as soon as you get to his place," I said, ready to break my phone out of anger, but instead used the butt of my gun to pistol whip Reese. Blood instantly gushed from the side of his head. I was tempted to finish him off right then, but that would be letting him off too easy.

"Get these motherfuckers and take them to the spot. When you get there, you can go 'head and kill Bink and these two other fucks, but don't kill Reese. Torture his ass, but leave him alive and lucid. I'll finish him off once I get there. I'ma stop by Lance's crib first. Call me if there's a problem, but don't fuck this shit up," I said rushing out.

On the way over to Lance's crib, I kept calling him, but wasn't getting an answer and now Ritchie wasn't answering his phone. After about 15 minute, we finally arrived to Lance's crib and when we turned onto the street there was an ambulance and several police cars out front.

"Stop the car!" I shouted, jumping out the back of the SVU and running over to the crowd of people.

"Nico, man I was just about to call you, but I was trying to find out what happened first," Ritchie said, stepping away from the large group of people standing around.

"What happened?"

"I'm not sure. All I know is there was a shooting and it came from Lance's brownstone. I haven't found out anything else yet," Ritchie explained.

Right after Ritchie spoke, I saw them bringing

out the first body on the stretcher. The body was covered up and I was praying that Lance managed to turn the table and kill the intruder. "Excuse me," I said walking away from Ritchie and over to a crime scene unit member who was carrying out the body on a gurney.

"Yes?"

"My brother lives there, can I please see if that's him?" He looked at me for a second then down at the body as if debating my request. "Please?" I guess he could hear the pleading in my voice because without saying a word he showed me the face. He quickly recovered it and proceeded out.

For a second I thought my knees were about to buckle as I felt my legs were locked and I couldn't move. Then I noticed them bringing out another body covered up and the large pregnant stomach was obvious. "Not Morgan and the baby too," I said as this sharp pain shot through my chest. "They got them... Lance and Morgan. Man, she was pregnant. How they kill that woman knowing she had a child growing inside of her," I said to Ritchie when he came over to me.

"And Reese is responsible for this bullshit! What the fuck! Damn," Ritchie said shaking his head in dismay. "What part of the game is this?"

I didn't even know how to respond to what Ritchie said because I didn't know what part of the game this was myself. We were a family, a crew. We came up together and built an empire and now the shit had completely crumbled. This part of the game had left me broken.

♛ ♛ ♛

When I got to the spot we used to dispose of bodies before calling in the cleanup crew, Reese was sitting in a chair, bloody and battered, but very much alive. His eyes were halfway closed. Partly because they were bloody and busted and also it appeared he was falling asleep.

"Wake his ass up," I said to one of my workers. They splashed a bucket of water over his face, which shook him out of his slump.

"Man, can you go 'head and kill me so we can get this shit over wit'," Reese mumbled.

"If I had the time, I would keep you alive for the next 10 years and damn near kill you and bring you back to life to only damn near kill you again. Unfortunately, I have too much shit to take care and honestly, you ain't even worth the stress. I mean, you have to be the foulest type of nigga to have a pregnant woman killed."

"Fuck you, Nico! These streets got you thinking you Mr. Untouchable. Now you wanna act like you a saint. We supposed to be a crew, but we all gotta kiss yo' ass and bow down to you. I could've stepped in your shoes and ran this shit."

"Is that right? You would've run this shit with who? Your cousin Alton, is that who? Was he in on this with you too?"

"Hell no! His punk ass is another Nico Carter ass kisser. That nigga would've ran and told you everything."

"So why not kill him? I get why you tried to kill me. But you took out Tracy, then Lance, and you would've got Ritchie if he had been home so why not Alton?"

"'Cause he family. He work my nerve, but we do have the same blood and my mom would've killed me if she ever found out I had my own cousin murdered. 'Cause like I said, we are family."

"And to think I thought we were family, too," I said and just put one bullet between his eyes. Reese wasn't even worth more than that.

A few minutes later my men brought Alton in who seemed completely baffled. "Nico, what's going on? These guys just showed up at my crib and brought me here. Is something…" before he finished his sentence, Alton spotted Reese's slumped over dead body on the chair. "What happened to Reese? What the fuck is going on?" Alton asked, sounding like he was about to hyperventilate.

"Your cousin was the one that orchestrated all this bullshit to bring me down. He's the one that killed Tracy, Reese, Lance, Angie, Morgan and of course tried to murder me."

"Are you serious! I swear, Nico, I didn't know

nothing about it. You know my loyalty is to you. I would've never been a part of that bullshit. You have to believe me, Nico," Alton said sincerely.

"I do believe you, Alton."

"Oh good, man. I was worried for a minute," Alton said, easing up.

"I'll always have love for you, Alton, and it pains me to do this, but Reese is your family. I can't take the chance that your conscious will start fuckin' wit' you and you try to retaliate against me or you slip up and tell one of your family members and they choose to see revenge."

"Never that, Nico! I promise you, I won't say shit to nobody about this and I give you my word that I would never try to retaliate against you. I love you like a brother. I put that on everything."

"I love you like a brother too, but the thing is you're not my brother. Rest in peace, Alton." I then pulled the trigger ending his life. I closed my eyes for a second and there was only one thing I wanted to say, "God forgive me."

Chapter 19

Precious Cummings

5 Years Later...

"I think I'm in love," I said out loud when I laid eyes on one of the sexiest women I had ever seen in my life. The way the sun hit her butterscotch complexion and the wind blew through her golden brown hair as she strutted down 125th Street in Harlem had a nigga open. She had to be one of the sexiest women I had ever seen with her glossy lips, sensual looks, and curvy figure. I watched her for a few minutes before I decided to make my move. All I wanted was her name. Five minutes later, I had it. Precious Cummings. She didn't know it yet, but

Precious was going to be mine.

♔ ♔ ♔

"Damn, nigga, you in an awfully good mood," Ritchie commented when I came through one of the blocks to check on some things. After all these years, I still felt like I had to be more hands on with shit after everything that had went down with Reese. He was this close to destroying everything I had worked so hard to build and I never wanted that shit to happen again. The only people left standing were Ritchie and I and together we running these streets and keeping the drug game on lock.

"I just got off the phone with this girl I've been seeing. She mad crazy, but in a good way."

"Well you know they say crazy women have the best pussy," Ritchie joked.

"I can attest to that being true, at least when it comes to Precious," I said thinking about how wet she felt the first time I slid inside. It was crazy because we had sex the night of our very first date and I wasn't expecting that. With her slick mouth and get money attitude, I figured she would've tried to make a nigga trick before giving up the panties, but I was wrong. But she played her cards right because I planned on doing more than trick on her. I was going to give her the world.

"So that's her name, Precious. She got any friends?" Ritchie questioned.

"Ain't you juggling enough women already."

"Can always make room for more, especially if she bad."

"I'll find out for you, but in the meantime how they handling business over here today? You know I had to come through and check on shit."

"It's all good. You know I be keeping these motherfuckers in check. I don't let shit slide," Ritchie said.

"Yeah, yeah, yeah don't go overboard now. But I was just passing through and since everything is good, I'ma go check on some of the other spots," I said getting back in my car.

"Cool. Don't forget to find out if yo' girl has a friend."

"I won't and call me if anything comes up." As I was driving to the next location my mind wandered to Precious. She was different then the other women I had been dating and the first woman that I knew I would eventually wife up. I dated and I even cared about a few chicks, but I didn't want to be tied down to any of them, but all that had changed.

♛ ♛ ♛

"Yo, I've been sitting here waiting for you for over

an hour. Your phone going straight to voicemail, you can't pick up the phone and call a bitch, like what's really good?" Precious said when I arrived at her apartment.

"You still sexy as fuck even when you pissed. Sorry baby," I said leaning in to kiss her, but she stepped back. "What? I can't get a kiss?"

"Nope. I don't like waiting around for no motherfuckin' body. Like my time is valuable."

"I understand. So, I'm an hour late. How much time is that worth?"

"Maybe like a g. Actually more, but a g will suffice." I pulled out 10 one hundred dollar bills and handed them to her.

"Now can I have a kiss?"

"Nope. That g only made up for the hour you had me waiting. I'm still mad. Why was your phone off and why didn't you call me?"

"Honestly, my cell died. I've been running around all day. The car I'm in, I just got it, and I still haven't gotten a car charger. What more can I say but that I'm sorry. The whole day I was dealing wit' bullshit and there was only one thing that kept me smiling."

"What's that?"

"Knowing I was gonna see you."

"Word?"

"Word."

"I guess you can get a kiss then," Precious said, placing her soft lips on mine. I positioned my hand behind her neck pulling her in even closer. The scent of the perfume she was wearing though unintentional was seducing me. I was ready to skip our date and instead lay her down and make love. But Precious was dressed for a night out and I knew she was ready to go, especially after waiting for over an hour.

"You sure you want to go out?" I whispered in her ear.

"Do you not see this fuckin' dress I got on? Oh you taking me out and someplace super nice too. Now let's go," she hissed, grabbing her purse.

"You gets no argument from me. I can't lie, you look exceptional tonight."

"I'm glad you noticed. I did it for you. From what I've been hearing in the streets, Nico Carter is that nigga. I just wanna represent. Let motherfuckers out here know, you have great taste across the board." Precious playfully winked her eye.

"So you representing for me now?"

"You tell me, am I?"

"I don't know if you ready for all that," I remarked.

"What you mean by that?" She frowned as I opened the passenger car door for her.

"Are you getting in?" I laughed after she stood outside the car, not moving.

"Not until you answer my question."

"Real talk, I've never had a girlfriend in my life and there's a reason for that. I'm a complicated dude and to be my woman requires a lot. I've never met a woman that I felt qualified for the position."

"You mean you never met a woman that qualified until me," Precious said without hesitation before getting in the car. I couldn't help but smile because that was one of the reasons I was so drawn to Precious—her cocky, confident attitude.

"Is this place nice enough?" I asked when we entered the upscale restaurant on the Upper East Side.

"This place is sexy, sophisticated, and has a little edge to it... definitely a good look."

"I thought it was a good fit. Reminded me of you." The soaring ceilings and garden windows created a grand setting that I knew would fit her taste. She liked for things to be a little over the top, but not overwhelming, which described this place perfectly. As the hostess showed us to the table, I watched Precious walking. I loved how she was such a feisty hood chick, but yet she fit in perfectly with the ambiance.

"Baby, are we poppin' bottles of champagne or what," she stated after the hostess left.

"Whatever you want."

"Is that only for tonight or always?" She smirked.

"That depends on how you play the game."

"Oh so we playing a game now? You shoulda

said that from jump so I could've been wearing my poker face."

"I thought you already was."

"I don't know whether to be flattered or offended by your comment."

"I was thinking... why don't you move in with me?"

"Excuse me! My fault, I didn't mean to say that so loud but umm, you caught me completely off guard. Less than an hour ago you was telling me you wasn't sure if I was ready to represent you now you're asking me to move in. Like what the fuck."

"I never said I wasn't ready, I said I wasn't sure if you were. I wanted you from the moment I saw you walking down 125th Street."

"Really?"

"You say that like you don't believe me."

"I guess I don't. I mean I def think you want me, but wanting somebody physically and asking them to move in is two different things."

"Maybe I'm moving fast." I shrugged.

"Maybe? We've only been on a handful of dates," Precious pointed out.

'True, but what about all those hours we spent on the phone talking, getting to know each other. Or the night we went on our first date and afterwards we chilled at the park and I opened up to you about my childhood and how I became the man I am today. Or later on that night you put it on me like you wanted to own it."

"Let's go for it. What we got to lose," Precious said leaning over the table to kiss me.

"I was hoping you would say that."

"I can't believe I'm moving in to Nico Carter's brownstone in Brooklyn Heights. I am truly moving on up in the world." She giggled. "Have the waitress bring out the champagne so we can celebrate."

"Before we start getting drunk on love, I want you to really understand what you're jumping into. We about to make a serious leap and once we do there's no turning back."

"I don't want to turn back. I'm all in. I'm sure you got some shit wit' you, but hell so do I. I'll be true to you and as long as you stay true to me then life will be sweet."

I took Precious's hand and stroked her slender fingers. It was the first time I looked at a woman's hand imagining putting a ring on it. I knew I was probably moving too fast because although we shared a lot of our deepest thoughts and the sex was amazing, there was a lot I didn't know about her. What I did know was I wanted Precious Cummings to be my woman and that trumped all my hesitation.

Chapter 20

Caught Out There

It seemed from the moment I laid eyes on Precious our relationship went from zero to sixty in record setting speed. I normally moved with caution and preferred to take things slowly, but with her, I threw caution to the wind and jumped right out the window. Honestly, it had me scratching my head sometimes, but once she got settled in my crib it felt right.

"So what you got planned for the day?" Precious asked, sitting up in bed.

"Regular shit. I'm considering investing in this club in Queens so I'm going by there to check shit out. Other than that same ole' thing."

"Are we still going out with Ritchie and Inga

this weekend?"

"Oh, I forgot about that. So things must be going a'ight wit' them, huh?"

"From what Inga said, it is. Why, Ritchie saying something different?"

"I haven't talked to Ritchie about Inga since we first hooked them up and he said he was feeling her."

"But that was months ago," Precious said, looking puzzled.

"I know that. I stay out of relationship shit, especially when it comes to Ritchie," I said buttoning up my shirt.

"Why, because he be fucking wit' mad bitches?"

"I don't know what that man do wit' his dick and as long as he ain't touching nothing of mine, I don't care and neither should you."

"Inga, my girl. You know I gotta look out for her."

"Then school her ass. If he ain't yo' nigga he don't owe you shit so do you and even if he is yo' nigga still do you, just in case you need to bounce."

"So wait. You sayin' I should be doing me instead always waitin' around on you?" Precious asked.

"Babe, I ain't the typical nigga. You ain't gon' neva wanna bounce and I'm not gon' let you anyway." I smiled.

"So if you do some fucked up shit and I'm ready

to cut you off, you gon' what, hold me hostage." She laughed.

"Exactly. I'll keep yo' ass tied up in this bedroom until you come to your senses."

"You are so crazy."

"Yep, crazy about you. Now let me get outta here. Call me if you need me."

"You do the same." She grinned. Wait!" Precious shouted when I was almost out the door.

"What's up?" I asked, coming back in the bedroom.

"You not gon' leave me nothing? You know I'm about to hit these streets."

"I just hit you off heavy the other day."

"Baby, that shit been spent. What can I say, I have expensive taste."

"That's another reason why I know you ain't going nowhere. I got you so spoiled, can't nobody else afford you… here," I said dropping a wad a cash on the bed.

"Thank you, baby," I heard her yell out.

"Just make sure you buy something sexy to wear for me tonight," I yelled back.

♔ ♔ ♔

"I was beginning to think you wasn't coming," Marshawn said when I finally arrived at the club.

"Man, I had so much going on today. I got here as soon as I could. This a nice spot you got here," I said, looking around before following Marshawn to the back of the club. It had a sexy high-end atmosphere. The interior was lush yet cozy with three bars, leather banquettes, elevated dance floor, metal DJ booth, secluded alcoves, and exposed brick with elegant chandeliers.

"Thank you. I've put everything into this club and business is really booming, but it cost money to run a business, promote, pay to get the hottest artist, and with my business partner gone, this overhead is taking me under," Marshawn admitted.

"It's messed up what happened to Malcolm. I didn't know him that well, but he seemed like a good dude."

"He was. The crazy part is I was supposed to be in the car with him, but at the last minute something came up and I had to stay here. That could've been me killed in that accident too."

"I feel you man that's why you gotta always count your blessings and live life to the fullest. You never know when your time is up."

"True dat. That's why I love living mine in this club. It comes with headaches, but I also have a lot of fun."

"I feel you."

"When we met last week, we went over the numbers and your share of the profits, but you wanted to come by and look at the place before making a final decision. So what do you think?"

"I think I would definitely like to be a partner. I like the location. As I said, this spot is nice, much nicer than what you described. I'm impressed."

"Does that mean we have a deal?"

"Yep, we have a deal," I said shaking Marshawn's hand.

"Let's have a drink. You know, a toast to our new partnership," he suggested.

"I have someplace I need to be, but I guess one drink wouldn't hurt."

"Porscha, pour me the usual, but make it two. "I want you to meet my new partner. This is Nico Carter."

"It's a pleasure. Your name rings bells out here in these streets," she said smiling.

"Porscha is our most popular bartender," Marshawn said taking his drink.

"I can believe that. Pretty girl, pretty smile," I said.

"Thank you," she said shyly. I could see she was blushing so she put her head down while pouring my drink. "Here you go," she said finally looking back up with a sweet smile across her face. There was something I definitely liked about Porscha.

♛ ♛ ♛

"Baby, these diamond earrings are beautiful. Thank you," Precious said leaning over the table and giving me a kiss. "Last week you bought that incredible diamond tennis bracelet, now these earrings. If I didn't know better I would think you had a guilty conscious about something." I sat there with a blank stare on my face. "It was a joke, Nico, lighten up." She laughed.

"I know you was jokin'. That was my poker face."

"Oh really." Precious smiled as she took off her earrings to put on her new diamond studs. "So I was thinking we could go to the movies tonight. Inga was telling me about some new movie she saw with Ritchie and it's supposed to be really good."

"I would babe, but I have to stop by the club tonight."

"Ever since you became a partner in that club, you're always there. I thought you said you were more like an investor and you wouldn't be dealing with the day to day operations?"

"I am, but I have to check on my investment. Make sure shit is running properly. I don't want them running through my money and not maintaining shit properly."

"I suppose."

"I'll make it up to you, baby. We can go to the movies tomorrow and do whatever else you want to do."

"I guess that means we'll be going on a shop-

ping spree. Fifth Avenue here we come."
"You know I love you."
"You better," she smacked.
"I don't get an I love you too?"
"I love you too, Nico."

I did love Precious and me fucking Porscha didn't taint that one bit, I thought to myself as I watched Porscha in action. "How does that feel baby," she purred between deep throating my dick.

"You doing it just right," I said stroking Porscha's hair as I watched her wet lips massage my tool. Her dick sucking skills were excellent. She had some good pussy too, but it was her head game that had me dealing with Porscha on a regular. After that day Marshawn introduced her at the bar, the next few times I came through, she would flirt with me and I would entertain it. It took me a couple months before I actually decided to deal with her on that level because I wanted to make sure she wasn't one of those stalker type chicks.

Everybody knew Precious was wifey and I didn't need nobody fuckin' up our happy home. So I had to be extremely careful about how I moved. Porscha was the first chick that I messed around on Precious with and I had no intention of making it a regular thing. I knew eventually it would come to an end and I hope Porscha did too.

"I gotta go," I said after finishing things up with Porscha.

"But we just finished having sex. Can't you lay with me for a little while?" she asked patting the spot next to her on the bed.

"Do I ever lay with you after we have sex," I stated as I was getting dressed.

"We've been messing around for a few months now, I thought things might change."

"Nothing has changed, but if you push things they might."

"I'm not trying to push things, Nico, but I know you must be developing some sort of feelings for me. I can feel it when we're making love."

"Listen, Porscha," I said, sitting down on the edge of the bed. "You see where we're at, we're in a hotel room. This ain't my crib and you're not my girl. Precious is the only woman I make love to. I enjoy your company. You're a sweet girl, but that feeling you said you get from me when we're making love, is just me enjoying the sex, nothing more."

"That's cold, Nico."

"We both grown and I'm not gon' sugar coat shit for you. If you can't handle the situation the way it is right now then let me know so we can end things because it ain't gon' change. This is what it is."

"I can handle things. I'm not gonna lie, I did think there was a chance of things getting more serious between us. I mean, I have genuine feelings for you. But you were always upfront about having a girl so it is what it is. If this is how it has to be, then I can deal with it," Porscha finally said, after sitting on the bed quiet for a few minutes.

"Okay," I kissed her on the forehead. "Go buy yourself something nice," I said, leaving some money on the nightstand like I always did. I didn't leave Porscha money because I thought of her as a prostitute because I did care about her. I left her money because I thought everyone should be paid for their services and Porscha was providing a service.

♛ ♛ ♛

When I got home later on that night Precious was lying peacefully in the bed. She looked so beautiful, almost angelic. I took a shower and got in the bed completely exhausted. I had been running around all day and coming home and going to sleep had been the one thing I was looking forward to.

"I was calling you all night, but your phone kept going to voicemail," Precious said before I even had a chance to close my eyes.

"Babe, my phone died in the club and I didn't have a charger."

"Nico, are you fuckin' around on me?" she asked point blank.

"Why would you ask me that?"

"Because for the last few weeks, things have seemed off and my gut is telling me that you fuckin' around. My gut is usually always right. But a bitch wanna be wrong 'cause if I'm not..." her voice trailed off.

"Baby, I've had a long day and night. I'm tired. Can't we talk about this in the morning."

"If you ain't fuckin' around then the conversation don't have to be that long, unless the answer is yes. If that's the case, then you need to wake the fuck up."

"The answer is no."

"No what?"

"No, I'm not fuckin' around on you, Precious. I love you... goodnight." I wasn't sure if Precious believed me or not, but what could I do? Tell her truth? No good would come from that. Plus, I was never going to let her go. It was 'til death do us part.

Chapter 21

She Loves Me, She Loves Me Not

Ritchie and I were out of town handling business when I got the phone call that seemed to be the beginning of my life spinning out of control. "Porscha, I'm in the middle of something. Let me call you back," I said about to hang up until I realized she was crying.

"Nico, I swear it wasn't my fault," she mumbled between sniffles. "She jumped on me and just went crazy."

"Who jumped on you?"

"Your girlfriend."

"Precious jumped on you? Hold up, tell me exactly what happened."

"This happened like an hour ago. I was at the club with my cousin and a friend. They knew the girl she was with and my cousin introduced me to her. Then she just came at me asking was I fucking her man. I was like, who is your man and she said Nico Carter. I told her I wasn't, but she didn't believe me. She swung a champagne bottle at me. Luckily, my cousin knocked it away before it hit me, but then Precious jumped on me and started punching me and wouldn't stop. The shit was a fuckin' nightmare," she cried.

"Where is Precious at now?"

"I don't know, security made her leave. They said I should call the police and press charges."

"Don't do that shit, Porscha. You understand? Do you understand?" I barked again when she didn't answer the first time.

"Yeah, I understand. I won't press charges, but I'm only doing it for you, Nico."

"A'ight. I'll call you when I get back in town." The second I hung up with Porscha I called Precious. "Answer your fuckin' phone," I yelled out loud in frustration when it kept ringing and then going to voicemail. I knew she saw it was me and was ignoring my call.

"Is everything okay?" Ritchie questioned, when I got back in the car.

"No. Some shit went down with Precious. I

gotta get back home."

"But we haven't finished handling our business here."

"You can stay and finish. I trust you can handle this shit. But I gotta go."

"Man, is she worth it?" Ritchie huffed.

"Excuse me?" I questioned with a raised eyebrow.

"I'm just saying. Ever since I've known you, you've always put business first. Now this chick got you breakin' out early before we've gotten our shit handled. That ain't the Nico I know."

"Precious ain't some chick, she's my woman. And business is being dealt with, that's what I got you for. And I'm the same Nico, so don't come at me like that again," I said before driving off.

♛ ♛ ♛

The entire time I was on my way back to New York I thought about how I was going to come at Precious. She still wasn't answering my calls so I knew she was pissed. I wasn't sure how this was going to unfold so I decided to play it by ear. When I arrived to the crib it was the middle of the afternoon, but Precious was still in bed asleep.

"Baby, are you okay?" She shrugged her arm as if wanting me to get out of her face, but I continued.

"I came home as soon as I heard what happened."

"I'm fine. You need to go check on yo' bitch."

"Precious, what are you talking about?"

"Don't play wit' me, Nico. I know all about you and Porscha. That's why yo' phone always be going to voicemail 'cause you laying up wit' that bitch. Nigga, fuck you." She pulled the blankets over her head as if she was going back to sleep.

I grabbed the covers and threw them on the floor. "I told you about that slick-ass mouth of yours," I said, pointing my finger at her. By the crazed look on her face it was obvious that pissed her the fuck off. She was now wide awake and seemed ready for a battle.

"I don't give a fuck whether you like what is coming out my mouth or not. You running round here fucking that cunt, and then the dumb bitch wanna step to me at the club. You lucky I didn't kill the bitch."

"Precious, I'm not fucking that girl. I barely know the chick. Whatever she told you was a lie."

"Nico, you must think you dealing wit' a straight fool. Who's the one that called you about the fight I was in?"

I paused for a minute because her question caught me off guard. "Inga called Ritchie and told him, and then he told me," I said, quickly coming up with an answer off the top of my head that sounded plausible.

Precious just nodded her head as she walked

over to her purse and retrieved her cell phone.

"Who you calling?" I asked.

"Inga. I'ma ask her if she called Ritchie and told him what happened."

I grabbed the phone out of her hand, so she went and picked up the cordless and I grabbed that too.

"What the fuck you need to call Inga for? There is no reason to get her in the middle of our shit."

"Bitch, you put her in the middle. You know damn well you didn't find out from Ritchie. That trifling Porscha called you crying the blues, and that's how yo' lyin' ass found out what happened. I'm done wit' yo' punk-ass. Go be wit' her, 'cause I won't have no problem replacing yo' bitch ass."

I grabbed Precious by her throat and slammed her against the wall. I could feel my eyes bulging and beads of sweat gathering on my forehead.

"If you trying to instill fear in me, the shit ain't working. I could really give a fuck. Nigga you's a clown as far as I was concerned," Precious spit at me full of rage.

"Precious, first of all get all that leaving and being with the next man out of your head. We family now. It's 'til death do us part. How many times do I have to tell you that? I'm sorry I had to grab on you like this, but you was flying off the handle, and I need your full attention. Baby, I'm sorry. I did fuck around with that girl, Porscha, but it was only a couple of times, nothing serious. She was out of line for even crossing your path, let alone saying a word to you, and she will be dealt with accordingly. But, Precious, you can't let these scandalous hoes come in and ruin our happy home. They just jealous and sitting around waiting and plotting to take your place. You smarter than that. You can't let that happen. I'm going to let go of your neck, but you have to promise me that you'll calm down and be mature about this shit."

She nodded her head yes to let me know she wouldn't black out on me when I let her go.

"So what you want me to do, Nico? Act like didn't nothing happen between you and that bitch?"

"Precious, I know that's easier said than done, but I'm begging you to be the bigger person and let it go. I promise I won't fuck with her ever again. I made a mistake. I'm a man. I can admit that. I'm asking for your forgiveness. I promise I'll make it up to you."

"You sound sincere, but the damage has been done," she said calmly.

"I can undo the damage. You know you love me and I love you, too. Let me make it up to you baby, please," I begged. I didn't want to lose her and in my heart I believed she felt the same way.

"Okay, I'll let you make it up to me, but you better not fuck up again, Nico," Precious warned, before getting in bed and going right back to sleep.

I spent the next few months doing everything I could to prove to Precious that I deserved her forgiveness. I bought her the new Benz she had been begging me to get her, took her to LA so she could go shopping on Rodeo Drive, and finally I took her on a vacation to Antigua and proposed. The five-carat rock sealed the deal. Precious accepted my marriage proposal and our relationship was finally back on track or at least it seemed to be.

"Where you going?" I asked Precious as she was grabbing her car keys to leave.

"To have drinks with my girl Tina."

"You've been going out a lot lately."

"No I haven't... maybe a little bit. I've been enjoying showing off my ridiculous rock." Precious smiled, flashing her finger.

"It does look good on you. Enjoy yourself, but don't be out too late."

"I won't. Bye babe," she said giving me a kiss. As I watched Precious leave I couldn't help but feel that something was slightly off. She was saying all the right things and on the surface we seemed to be more in love than ever. I wasn't able to put my finger on it so I brushed it off as me overanalyzing shit. Before I could think about it any further I saw that Ritchie was calling me.

"What's up?"

"I was calling to see if you were still interested in meeting with that new diesel connect I got?"

"Definitely, but like I said I want to start with a small order. See how shit moves on the street and then move forward from there."

"Cool, I'll set that up."

"A'ight, let me know when," I said before getting off the phone with Ritchie. Ritchie was another one that had seemed off for the last few weeks. He was coming up missing all the time and slacking on business, but lately he seemed to have snapped out of whatever funk he was in and was back handling shit like he was supposed to. With this potential new drug connect we had an excellent opportunity to make a shit load of money which made me respect Ritchie for getting his shit together and coming through.

Chapter 22

From Bad To Worse

When I woke up and started my day, if someone had said my night was going to end like this I would've said they were a motherfuckin' lie. It all started with a phone call.

"What's up, baby?" I said when I answered the phone.

"I was calling to tell you bye," Precious replied.

"What you mean, 'bye'? Where you going?"

"I can't do this no more, Nico."

"Do what? Stop talking in riddles, Precious."

"After we got back from Antigua I tried to put the whole Porscha situation behind me, but I couldn't. The only person that was able to console me was Ritchie."

"What the fuck did you say?"

"Nico, I've been seeing Ritchie for a few months now, and we're in love. I'm pregnant and the baby is his," she said with a slight sniffle in her voice as if holding back tears.

"Precious, don't fucking play with me. This shit ain't funny."

"It's not meant to be. I've packed my stuff. I'm leaving you."

"Where the fuck are you right now?"

"On my way to Ritchie's."

"I'm going to give you one more chance to take all this bullshit back before I lose it."

"I can't take it back, Nico, 'cause it's the truth. Why do you think Ritchie was showing you so much shade? He couldn't stand the fact that I refused to leave you. But once I found out I was pregnant, I decided it was time to let you go."

"That might be my seed. How you know I'm not the father?"

"I just know," she said, sounding confident.

"Then you a dead bitch," I said and hung up the phone. I bypassed my original destination and did a quick U-turn heading toward Ritchie's house. I knew shit had seemed shaky with Precious, but never did I expect this. I kept glancing down at my phone knowing that any second Precious was going to call me back saying this was all a bad joke, but that call never came.

When I pulled up to Ritchie's house I saw Precious' car parked across the street. I kicked the fuck out of that shit before running up the stairs and knocking on the front door.

"Nico… umm what are you doing here?" Ritchie questioned, looking shocked.

"Where the fuck is Precious!" I barked with my gun in hand.

"Yo, what's wrong wit' you and why would Precious be over here?"

"Nigga, kill that bullshit! Precious called me not too long ago saying you all been fucking and ya in love and having a baby together."

Ritchie seemed to be in complete shock. He was standing in his living room not saying shit, just standing there with a dumb ass look on his face.

"Man, I don't know what type of game Precious is playing, but ain't nothing going on between us. She's not here, I swear man."

"Don't play wit' me, Ritchie," I said, cocking the gun and putting it to his head. "If you tell me the truth, I'll let you live, but if you continue to lie, you a dead motherfucker."

"I wanted to tell you, but Precious begged me not to. It was an accident. She came on to me and I got caught up. I'm sorry, man. But this 'we're in love and having a baby,' I don't know where none of that is coming from. Precious must be tryna hurt you 'cause of that Porscha situation."

"We supposed to be brothers. We grew up together. We lost our entire crew because of betrayal.

Never did I believe you would betray me too. I hope fuckin' my woman was worth yo' life," I said before blasting Ritchie's brains out. By the time I did a quick search of his house making sure Precious wasn't there, police were surrounding Ritchie's crib. All I could do was shake my head and say, "This bitch set me up."

♔ ♔ ♔

As I sat in my jail cell, I kept replaying the last few months, trying to figure out how I didn't see this shit coming. I had dealt with the most ruthless criminals on the streets and couldn't none of them take me down, never did I think a scheming bitch would and that's exactly what happened to me. My attorney informed me that an anonymous female caller had tipped police off about the shooting at Ritchie's house. I knew that was nobody but Precious. I wondered at what point did she start plotting my demise. Did she ever forgive me for cheating with Porscha or was this her plan all along. She played the game like a pro because I was in jail facing first-degree murder charges for a double homicide. Come to find out a dude named Butch was killed right outside of Ritchie's house. My gut was telling me that Precious had something to do with that too.

"Tommy, man, did you go by the house and get that for me?" I asked one of my only workers that I trusted, when he came for a jail visit.

"It wasn't there."

"What you mean it wasn't there?" I asked, thinking maybe I was hearing Tommy incorrectly.

"The duffel bag was gone. The million wasn't there," he repeated.

"Precious took my fuckin' money."

"That's not all she took."

"What do you mean?"

"Her clothes, shoes, purses, jewelry, and your jewelry too."

"I should've learned from my mother that you can't trust no woman," I said shaking my head. "Remember that apartment Precious had in Harlem?"

"Sure do."

"She doesn't know that I know, but she kept it. I want you to put two men on it. She might be hiding out there with my money."

"If we find her do you want us…" I knew what Tommy was asking without him saying it.

"No. You leave that for me," I made clear. Precious would pay with her life for what she did to me, but I would be the one to end it.

"Nico, we requested a speedy trial so we need to start preparing for trial," my attorney said as I was halfway listening to him. I was still pissed that I was denied bail and I would have to sit in a jail cell while I awaited trial. The crazy part was that after all the dirt I had done in the streets since I was a teenager, I had never been to jail until now. "Nico are you listening to me? I know you're probably scared but..."

"I ain't neva scared," I said cutting my attorney off. "The worst thing that can happen is that I'm found guilty. But with the amount of money I'm paying you, you'll find a loophole to get me off on appeal. I'm charged with killing two drug dealers. When all the hype dies down, won't nobody give a fuck."

"I will do my best to get a not guilty verdict or at the very least a hung jury."

"Do what you have to do. There's a phone call I need to make so I'll see you tomorrow," I said to my attorney so I could go make my phone call.

"Nico, I was waiting for you to call me." I could hear Porscha smiling through the phone when she answered. I had cut her off, but when all this shit went down and I needed someone on the outside to keep me in the loop, she was there for me as if I had never walked out her life.

"Listen, I need you to do something for me."
"Sure, what is it, baby?"
"I need you to get in touch with Inga."

"You talking about Precious' friend?"

"Yes. I want you to let her know that Ritchie was fuckin' Precious behind both of our backs and that Precious is pregnant with his baby." I highly doubted the last part was true, but Inga didn't need to know that.

"Precious scandalous ass was fuckin' Ritchie. I knew she was a skeeze," Porscha said, sounding happy that she had some foul information about Precious.

"Then I want you to tell Inga I'll be in touch with her."

"I'm on it, baby."

"'Good, I'll be in touch."

As expected I was found guilty of all charges. The way the DA was gunning for me I wasn't surprised, but I wasn't worried either. I hated being caged up like an animal, but I knew in my heart that I would see the outside of these prison walls again and a lot sooner than anybody thought.

Even after the guilty verdict I was in touch with Inga as she had become somewhat of a street informant for me. After finding out about Ritchie and Precious, she was more than willing to try and bring Precious down. Inga had informed me that

Tommy had turned on me. He was trying to keep the million dollars for himself. Somehow him, Boogie—whom Precious used to work for—and his nephews all ended up dead. The money was never found. That meant Precious still had it and I figured those deaths were linked to her. Inga had even been in touch with Precious a few times, but she would never give Inga her location as if she knew her best friend had now become the enemy. I needed an update, but it seemed Inga had went ghost and I wanted to know why.

"Hello," a girl answered whose voice I didn't recognize.

"Can I speak to Porscha," I said, hoping Porscha could tell me if she had heard or seen Inga.

"Umm, Porsha ain't here."

"Do you know when she'll be back?"

"She ain't coming back."

"Who is this? What you mean she ain't coming back?" I questioned, confused by that response. "I spoke to her a month or so ago and she didn't say anything about leaving town."

"Nico, this is Porscha's cousin, Olivia. There is no easy way to say this. Porscha was killed a couple weeks ago."

"What... by who?"

"We don't know. She was found dead with another girl named Inga."

"Inga too... damn."

"You knew Inga?"

"Yeah, I did. I'm sorry about your cousin. Give Porscha's family my condolences," I said before hanging up. This shit was crazy. I knew for a fact Precious was behind the deaths of Porscha and Inga, but yet she was running around with my motherfuckin' money, free as a bird. I hope she was enjoying it because before I took my last breath, Precious Cummings would pay in blood for what she did to me.

Chapter 23

Against All Odds

Two Years Later...

The streets had counted me out and left me to rot in prison, but a nigga like me was built for this shit. Like I knew he would, my high priced attorney was able to get me off on a technicality. The DA's office didn't even want to spend the time or money to re-try the case, instead they gave me time served and my walking papers. I was a free man with a to do list and killing Precious was at the top of it.

Many things changed while I had been locked up. Precious was now married to a superstar rapper named Supreme. She was living every hood girls dream. She went from a project girl living in Brooklyn to being the queen of the streets as my woman and now the first lady of the biggest rapper out, but none of that would protect her from me. While I was locked up most had counted me out, but a few stayed loyal and was keeping tabs on Precious for me. Before she got married and was living on an estate she shared an apartment in Edgewater, New Jersey with a girl named Rhonda. I decided to pay her a visit.

"Hi, can I help you with something," a semi cute girl with a bubbly personality answered the door and said.

"I hope so. I'm old friend of Precious."

"Oh, Precious doesn't live here anymore."

"I know, Rhonda. That is your name... right?"

She gave me this baffled look. "How did you know my name and why..." Before she could say another word, I grabbed Rhonda by her throat and dragged her into the apartment with a gun to her head. I slammed the door shut and then put the gun to my mouth, motioning her to keep quiet.

"I'm going to release my hand from around your throat, but if you scream I will blow your brains out. Do you understand?"

She nodded her head yes as tears began to run down her face. "Why are you doing this?" she asked in a low voice, breathing hard.

"Because Precious did some fucked up shit

to me and it's time for her to deal with the consequences."

"I don't know anything about that," she cried.

"That might be true, but unfortunately for you Precious got you involved the day you became roommates."

"But she doesn't live here anymore."

"I know, but you're still friends. I want you to call Precious right now and tell her you need for her to come over."

"She's out of town, she won't be able to come over."

"I see we're going to have to do this the hard way, Rhonda."

"Wait! I'm telling you the truth."

"No, you're lying. Precious is not out of town. Do you want to try this again? This is your last chance."

"Please, don't do this," she pleaded. Precious is my friend. I can't call and lure her to her death. I wouldn't be able to live with myself."

"Have it your way," I said knocking her over the over the head with the butt of my gun. I then pulled her limp body into her bedroom, tying her arms and wrist to each bedpost. I put duct tape over her mouth. A few minutes after I was finished she began to come to. She was mumbling so I lifted the tape from her mouth.

"I don't want to die," she muttered.

"Then call Precious," I said, holding up her cell

phone. She shook her head no. "You're willing to die for your so-called friend. I hate to break it to you, but Precious has no loyalty to nobody but herself. Now make the call," I demanded.

"I can't do it knowing that you plan on hurting her. I think you're trying to scare me. I don't think you would really kill me. Please just go. I won't say anything about what happened."

"You must not know who I am. But that's cool. Honestly, I really don't need you. I know where Precious lives. I figured it would be easier to get her to this apartment then going to her crib. Guess I was wrong. I should've gone to her house first because now I have to kill you anyway."

"No! No!" Rhonda screamed out before I put the tape back over her mouth. I grabbed a pillow from behind her and placed it over her face to muzzle the sound of the bullet to her head when I pulled trigger. After Rhonda was dead I immediately got in my car and headed to the estate where Precious lived with her husband.

When I pulled up to the winding driving, there was no security at the front and the gate was open. It was as if the stars were aligned in my favor. I decided to park my car on the side of the road and walk up. When I got to the top of the hill, I noticed Precious getting out of her car.

"You've done very well for yourself. I'm proud of you, Precious." She closed her eyes as if she didn't believe I was real. "Baby, open your eyes. I'm not going anywhere. I'm the real deal."

"Nico, you can't be real."

"Precious, you're just as beautiful, if not more, than the first time I saw you walking the streets of Harlem. I knew you didn't belong there. Now look at you, married to a superstar, living in a mansion.

"You made Brooklyn proud. But as much as you cleaned yourself up, you still have those dark eyes just like me. Remember I told you besides me and my father you were the only other person I ever met with the same darkness in your eyes. That right there should've been enough incentive for me to let you walk away that day, but instead I wanted you more. Because of that, I had to pay the price for my decision. Now it's time for you to pay the price for yours."

"Nico, please. I was so immature back then and I made a mistake. But I'm a different person now. I've put the streets behind me and turned my life around."

"It's all good that you turned your life around, but you had to give my soul to the devil in order to get it. Not once did you think about the life you took away from me, and the money you stole. You destroyed everything we had over some pussy. A bitch I didn't even give a fuck about.

"But that didn't matter to you, because you're

like me. Your pride and your ego dictate your moves. But, Precious, with every decision you make in life, there are consequences. And your consequence is death."

"Nico, don't. What can I do to stop this? I don't want to die."

"You're already dead. I just came to take it in blood. But because I still have mad love for you Precious, I won't make you suffer the way I did your friend."

"What friend?"

"If I'm not mistaken her name was Rhonda," I said with a devious chuckle that I knew she would detest.

"You killed Rhonda, but why?"

"I really didn't want to take the chance and come here to kill you. I wasn't sure what type of security you were working with, but obviously not enough," he said, glancing around the estate. "So I paid her an unexpected visit.

"All I asked her to do was get you over to the apartment, and I would handle the rest, but she refused. She was a true friend to the end unlike Inga."

"Nico, hasn't there been enough death in our lives? I can give you back the million dollars and more, if you like. I have a husband, Nico, and I'm pregnant with his child. I'm living the life I never dreamed possible. Don't take that away from me."

"I came back to take what's mine, and that's your life." Not for one second did I believe Precious was pregnant. She was lying just like she lied about being pregnant by Ritchie knowing I would kill him. Once again, Precious was trying to scheme and manipulate her way out of trouble, but it wasn't going to work. Her luck had finally run out. I raised my gun, and we both turned when we heard a car pulling up.

As the car got closer, I could see what looked to be Supreme inside. He jumped out and his bodyguards followed with guns raised.

But it was too late. The loud explosion ripped through Precious' chest. The pressure jolted her back, and she hit her car before falling down to the ground. I started shooting in the direction of Supreme and his bodyguards as I ran vanishing in the darkness.

Chapter 24

On The Run

After shooting Precious and leaving her for dead I went on the run. I was determined not to go back to prison no matter what the cost. I soon learned that Precious survived the shooting, but after she was released and was leaving the hospital, her and Supreme were ambushed with gunshots. Once again Precious survived, but Supreme was pronounced dead at the scene.

During my time on the run I had reached out to a girl named Nina. She used to be a drug carrier for me and we also had a sexual relationship. Nina always wanted it to be more serious, but I wasn't checkin' for her like that. The good thing was she still was down for a nigga and when I needed her she was there.

"Nina, thank you for everything you've done for me," I said standing in the kitchen about to eat some Chinese food she had brought home for me. Nina let me stay at an apartment she had in Manhattan. It was nothing fancy, but comfortable and clean. Most importantly, it was no place anybody would think about coming to look for me.

"Nico, you know I would do anything for you. I'm just glad you trusted me enough to call and ask for my help."

"You were always loyal and with everything I was going through that's what I needed."

"I still can't believe all the bullshit Precious put you through. Because of her your life got fucked up. She need to pay for that shit," Nina snapped.

"Nina, I wanna put all that shit behind me."

"What you mean put it behind you?"

"There is no doubt Precious did the ultimate foul shit to me, but she's suffered enough. Her husband is dead and come to find out when I shot her, she really was pregnant so she lost her baby too. The fact that I'm responsible for Precious losing her baby is still eatin' me up. I want to put all this shit behind me and move on and after you make this final drop for me I'll have enough money to do that."

"You're leaving town?" Nina asked sounding panicked.

"I told you from day one that after I got enough money up I was outta here. New York is way too hot for me."

"Where will you go?"

"Either down south or the West Coast. I'm still deciding."

"I'll come with you," Nina proposed.

"Nina, I can't ask you to do that."

"You don't have to ask. I want to come."

"But your family and friends are all here. I don't want you putting you life on hold to go on the run with me," I said, thinking be giving up a lot.

"I want my life to be with you. I don't care about that other stuff. We never had a chance to make it work in the past. Maybe in a new state we can have a fresh start. Who wants to be on the run alone? You know I'll make a great partner." Nina smiled.

Nina did make a valid point. It would be nice to have someone by my side that I could trust while dodging the police. She had already proven to be an asset. When I got out of jail I had a connect set up to get back in the drug game, but after my confrontation with Precious didn't go as planned, I had to go underground. I couldn't afford to miss out on the opportunity to make some money and that was one of the main reasons I reached out to Nina. She had been in the drug game before working for me so she knew how to move. She handled my business since I wasn't able to show my face and it paid off. Last few months I had stacked enough money to get out of New York for good.

"You've convinced me. I guess we'll be leaving this motherfucker together," I said.

"Yes! You won't regret it," Nina beamed, wrapping her arms around me and giving me a hug. "I need to go and take care of some things. Do you need anything before I leave?"

"No, I'm straight. After that deal goes down tomorrow, I'm trying to be out a couple days after that. Will you be ready by then?"

"I'll be ready. I don't want you to have any excuses for leaving me behind. See you soon," Nina said before heading out.

♚ ♚ ♚

As I lay in bed before I was about to take a shower, I started reflecting on the rollercoaster ride my life had been on. Then I thought about how I had been hauled up in this apartment for the last few months but it was better then being locked up in a 6x8 jail cell. It was time for me to move on and I was ready.

When I got out the shower, I threw on some sweatpants and sat down on the couch to watch television. The TV was on, but my mind hadn't stopped wondering. I was so caught up in my thoughts that I didn't even notice that I had company.

"Long time no see," Precious said, sneaking up

on me with a nine-millimeter pointing directly at my head.

My eyes remained fixed on her, and I didn't flinch even with death staring me in the face. "My lovely Precious. I knew we'd meet again."

"I'm sure you did, just not under these circumstances."

"What do you mean by that?"

"Save the bullshit, Nico. Not in my worst nightmare did I believe you would come back and kill my husband. I can understand you seeking revenge on me and tryna end my life because I tried to end yours first by setting you up on that murder charge. I'll take that as settling the score, even though because of your actions I also lost my unborn child. That was foul. But to then come back and blaze Supreme while we're leaving the hospital. For that you gotta die."

I let out a deep sigh and shook my head. I put my hands over my mouth and rubbed my chin thinking about everything Precious had said.

She stepped back a little bit while keeping her finger firmly on the trigger.

"We've both done some fucked up shit to one another, but I swear on everything I've ever loved, which includes you, I ain't kill Supreme. And honestly, when you said you were pregnant I didn't believe you. I thought you were trying to manipulate the situation and have me pity you so I wouldn't finish you off. I'm sorry I took the life of your unborn child, but I swear I didn't kill Supreme. That's my word."

"You a fuckin' lie. Don't try to snake your way out this shit. You the only person that had reason, and is crazy enough to come at Supreme in broad daylight. I know it was you."

"In your heart, if you really believe I was the one, then go 'head and pull that trigger... go 'head," I pressed on.

Precious stepped forward and gripped the gun tighter wanting to blast off so badly, but something held her back.

"You know I'm speaking the truth. Whoever took out Supreme had their own agenda. It was just easy for the blame to fall on me because of what went down between us."

"Well if it wasn't you, then who?"

"Honestly, I don't know, but it wasn't me, that I can promise you."

As Precious digested what I said, neither of us heard the front door opening until she had a gun pointed in her face.

"Bitch, put that gun down before I waste you."

Precious turned to see who had her jammed up, "Yo, I know you ain't part of this bullshit!" she yelled, shaking her head.

"The two of you know each other?" I asked bewildered.

"Yeah, I know Precious very well. I was gonna surprise you, baby, and deliver this bitch to you, but

I see she found her way."

"Ain't this some bullshit! I knew you were a scandalous trick the first time I met you, but I let my guard down and now this." Precious switched her attention back to me. "I can't believe you got this hoe on your team. And Nina, aren't you supposed to be getting married today?"

"What the fuck is going on?" I seethed through clenched teeth.

"Precious, put that fuckin' gun down now and kick it towards me," Nina demanded, ignoring me. Precious did as she said.

"Nina, answer my fuckin' question. How do you and Precious know each other, and what's this about you getting married?"

"Oh, so you don't know about her fiancé? Yeah, I was supposed to be a bridesmaid and everything for this trick. So when did you decide you weren't showing up for the wedding, Nina? Before or after you planned on killing me?" I stared at Nina waiting for her to answer Precious' question. I was hearing all this shit for the first time and it had me completely perplexed.

"If you really want to know how this shit popped off, I'll break it down for you starting from the beginning," Nina began. "I was the one Nico called when he tried and failed to put you six feet under and had to go on the run. I'm sure he never got around to telling you this, but we used to fuck around until he got caught up in yo' silly ass. So when he needed me, I was there so I could prove to him I was a better bitch than you from day one, and he made the mistake choosing you over me. The night you came over to my fiancé's house for dinner, I immediately recognized your face from a picture that Nico still carries around of you. I wanted to kill your ass right there on the spot, but instead I decided that I would befriend you and finish the job that Nico couldn't."

"But Nina, I told you I had put that shit wit' Precious behind me and was moving on."

"Oh, please! And let this bitch get away with ruining your life? She's the reason that we broke up in the first place. She's why you went to jail and you're on the run. You might've decided to let her get away with it, but not me."

"Nah, Nina, you ain't takin' her out. Get that shit out yo' head."

"After everything Precious has done you're still choosing her over me? You're still in love with this poisonous bitch? I'm the one that's been holding it down for you while she's running around like she's queen bee. How can you defend her? I got a good man waiting at the altar for me because I want to be with you."

"Yo, don't put that shit on me. I didn't even know you was engaged. You the one that said you wanted to break out of New York wit' me. I told you to stay here and not put your life on hold to be on the run wit' me."

"You left your fiancé standing at the altar so you could run away with Nico?"

"Precious, shut the fuck up. This ain't none of your business. You're the cause of all this bullshit anyway. Nico and I would be married with children right now if he had never met you."

"Hold up, Nina. Now you're jumping into some other shit. I appreciate all you've done for me, but you can't blame Precious because she had my heart and you didn't. But even if I hadn't met Precious, I still didn't want to wife you. You were always cool people, and that's why when I was jammed up I reached out to you. Sorry shorty, but my feelings never ran deeper than that."

Nina looked crushed by what I said, but it was all true. I had no idea she had created this imaginary love affair between us, but then I didn't know Nina as well as I thought. All this time she had a fiancée that she never mentioned. Honestly, it would've made no difference to me, but the fact she had become cool with Precious and was plotting to kill her behind my back let me know she was unstable and not the woman I thought she was.

"Fuck that! Precious is a dead bitch!" Nina said coldly.

I walked forward. "If you shoot Precious, you have to kill me first," I stated, standing in front of Precious as a shield.

Nina had this bizarre look on her face. She seemed to have mentally checked out. I couldn't believe this was the same woman that I was having a conversation in the kitchen with the other day and planning to let go on the run with me. She was now standing in front of me and her anger for Precious ran so deep that there was a real possibility she would kill me just to get to her. But Nina wouldn't get that chance because a young girl I didn't recognize snuck up behind Nina and shot her from behind. Nina was lying in a puddle of her own blood.

"She's dead," I said after bending down and not feeling a pulse. "Who are you?" I asked the young girl responsible for Nina's death.

"That's Maya. She's a good friend of mine who just saved our lives," Precious said walking over to Maya and taking the gun out of her hand. The girl seemed to be in shock. "Yo, we got to get the fuck outta here. I know somebody heard those gunshots and called the police."

I knew Precious was right so I quickly disappeared into the bedroom, and got my suitcases that were already packed. I wasn't planning on leaving for a couple days to give Nina time to get her shit in order, but that was no longer necessary. I had my money so there was no need for me to wait.

"You couldn't have packed that fast," Precious said when I came out the bedroom.

"I was already packed. I just had to get my luggage from the bedroom closet."

"That's right. Nina did mention the reason she left her fiancée at the altar was so she could run off with you," Precious said sarcastically. "Well, come on, you can ride with us."

"I can't, Precious," I said solemnly.

"What do you mean, you can't?"

"There's too much heat on me right now. You need to go. I'll be in touch."

"You promise?"

"Yes, I promise."

"But where will you go? Do you need money?"

"Precious, I'll be fine. You know how I get down. You just take care of yourself and be careful. Supreme's killer is still out there."

"I'm sorry, Nico. I'm sorry for everything."

I put my finger over Precious lips and kissed her on the forehead before making my exit out the front door.

Chapter 25

Goodbye

I was headed out of town first thing in the morning, but I didn't want to leave without seeing Precious one last time. After all she put me through I was still very much in love with her. I don't think I ever stopped. The rage I was in for what she had done was only camouflaging it. I wasn't sure how Precious felt, but I didn't want to have any regrets so I reached out to her.

"Hello."

"Is anyone around you?"

"Nico, is that you?"

"Judging by the fact that you shouted out my name, I take it that you're alone."

Precious let out a slight chuckle. "Sorry 'bout

that, but I was so surprised to hear your voice. But yeah, I'm alone. How are you?"

"Just keepin' low."

"Are you still in the area?"

"Yeah, I'm tryna tie up some loose ends before I head out of here. If you don't mind, I would like to see you before I leave."

"I wanna see you too. When are you leaving?"

"Tomorrow morning. You think we can meet tonight?"

"Tonight is good."

"Cool. I'll call you around eight to let you know where to come. Make sure you're careful. I can't afford you being tracked by anybody."

"I got you. I'll be waiting for your call."

When I hung up with Precious I knew I had made the right decision. Obviously, we both needed closure and tonight we would get it.

Precious arrived looking beautiful. Her hair was slicked back in a ponytail with a metallic-colored jumpsuit that accentuated every curve. All I wanted to do was take her clothes off, but I tried to maintain my cool.

"Yo, this place didn't even come up in the navigation system," Precious commented of the nondescript spot I was staying at in Staten Island. "The only reason I was able to find it was because I used to hit up this mom and pop soul fool restaurant down the hill every once in awhile. "How did you find this place?"

"I still know a few people who got hideouts."

"This is definitely one of those. Ain't nobody gonna find you here."

"That's the point of a hideout spot. You hope nobody can find it." I smiled.

"True, but it looks nice inside. Hardwood and plush carpet, stainless steel kitchen appliances and a huge open space. You would never know all this was going on from the outside."

"Yeah, it's pretty official for what it is. But I'm ready to break out."

"Have you decided where you're going?"

"Yep, but don't ask me where. If you ever get yourself jammed up and they question you about my whereabouts, I really want you to be able to say you don't know. It's for your own protection."

"Am I gonna ever see you again?"

"I hope. I'll keep in touch from time to time. But if and when I get word that I'm able to show my face again, then you know I'm coming home. New York is truly all I know."

"Nico, you don't have to worry about the charges sticking for shooting me. If they do come at you, I'll tell them I made a mistake and you weren't the person who tried to kill me. I'll get on the stand and testify to that if I have to."

"I don't know what to say. Since I've been on

the run, all I've done was think. Think about my life, the past, and of course, you. It's still hard to believe that this is how everything turned out. When I first got out of jail I was so full of rage and had nothing but contempt towards you. But there is such a thin line between love and hate. And in my heart I never stopped loving you, and even now I wish we could be together and start our life all over again someplace else. But I know that's not possible. I have to clear my name, and maybe then if you still feel the same way, we can try again."

"I can't lie, my feelings for you do still run deep. Just like I hope you've forgiven me for fucking up your life, I've forgiven you for putting a bullet in my chest. I don't know if we can ever be together again, but I do believe the police will find Supreme's killer, whether the person is dead or alive. Then you'll be able to come back and fight the charges they have against you for attempted murder."

"What do you mean, find Supreme's killer either dead or alive? Do you know who took him out?"

"Just like you don't want to tell me where you're going, this is something that I need to keep to myself. But if it all works out, after you disappear, the next time you call me I'll have good news."

"I know how you are, Precious, so I'm not going to pressure you. All I will say is be careful. Whoever took out Supreme is ruthless, and they're playing for keeps. I don't want anything to happen to you,"

I said, now standing within kissing distance of Precious. I lifted her chin and softly brushed her lips against mine. I paused, waiting for Precious' reaction.

"Don't stop," she whispered. Those were the only words I needed Precious to say so I could proceed.

I lifted her up and carried Precious to the bedroom in the back. We both slowly undressed one another and I stood staring at her naked body remembering how good she felt when I was inside of her. I laid her down on the bed and trickled kisses from her soft lips to her neck, breasts, and stomach until reaching the sweetness of her wet pussy. I buried my face in her juices.

Precious let out moans of pleasure that made my dick get even harder. I then stopped and stared at her naked body again, but this time I took my finger and traced the faint scar down the middle of her chest. A pain struck my heart seeing what I had done to the only woman I had ever loved.

Precious pushed my hand away as if she could feel my guilt eating me up inside. She pulled me closer and said, "Baby, put it in. I need that dick inside of me now," she moaned. She sunk her nails deep into my skin as I entered inside of her. Feeling the warmth of her body with each thrust brought back so many memories of how lovely shit used to be between us. She was my woman, my everything back then. Now all I could do was make love to her like it would be our last time. After we both reached the height of pleasure, we climaxed simultaneously and fell asleep in each other's arms.

Early in the morning I could hear Precious get out of bed and get dressed. I pretended to still be asleep because I didn't want us to get caught up in goodbyes. Instead I wanted us to remember how perfect last night was. Before leaving, Precious kissed me on the forehead and softly said, "I love you."

I love you too, I said to myself as I watched Precious walk out hoping it wouldn't be the last time I'd see her again.

"You're back," Lisa said when I got back in the bed. "I wanted to feel you inside of me before I had to leave for work." She smiled, before wrapping her lips around my dick so I could feel the moistness of her mouth. Lisa had my dick rock hard. I brushed my hand against her thighs and her skin was so soft. Instead of waiting for her to finish giving me a blowjob. I flipped Lisa's body over and slid inside. Her pussy was even wetter than her mouth.

"Baby, you feel so good," I moaned, as each stroke got deeper and more forceful.

"Oh Nico, I love you so much," Lisa wailed in pleasure. She wrapped her legs around my back pulling me in closer to feel all my pressure deep inside of her. "Baby, I'm about to cum," she screamed, tugging her legs even tighter around me. Soon after Lisa came, I exploded inside of her. "I wish you could stay inside of me forever," Lisa said caressing the back of my head.

"As good as you feel right now got me feeling the same way."

"I hate to say this, but I have to get up. I don't want to be late for work."

"Why haven't you quit that job yet? I told you weeks ago that you don't need to work there anymore."

"Nico, you already do so much for me. I wouldn't feel right not working. I make really good tips there. No, it's not the kind of money you give me, but it's something."

"I understand. But just know you can always change your mind," I said kissing Lisa on the lips before sliding out of her so she could get out the bed. I watched as she went in the bathroom to take a shower. That was another reason Lisa was special to me, she let me spoil her, but she still wanted her own, no matter how little it was. I was so used to gimmie girls that wouldn't dare show up to a waitressing job if they lucked up and found a dude that was paying all their bills but not Lisa, she wasn't like that and I respected her for it.

♛ ♛ ♛

Since moving to Miami I was able to use the money I made with Nina while I was on the run in New York, to set up shop and get business poppin'. Fernando, whom I had dealings with back when I lived in Brooklyn, set me up with a local Dominican connect and we hit it off lovely. That was another reason why I hadn't moved back to New York. I had an operation going here that almost ran itself. There was so much drug money flowing in Miami that you only had to put in minimal work to reap the benefits.

On my way to meet with my connect I decided to check up on Precious and see how she was doing. "Hi, Precious, I'm happy for you and your family. I wanted to call sooner, but I knew you and Supreme would want some time alone after bringing your daughter home."

"Nico, thank you so much. I'm glad that you called. I was wondering if I would hear from you again. I..."

"Precious, are you there?" I could hear some ruckus like the phone had dropped, but I wasn't sure. I kept screaming out her name, but got nothing. I hung up and called back but after ringing a few times it went to voicemail. "Maybe Supreme walked in or something and she didn't want him to know she was talking to me," I thought out loud as I made a right turn on Biscayne Boulevard headed towards my destination. Although hesitant, I decided it was best for me to wait to hear from Precious instead of calling her back again. If this was about Supreme, I didn't want to cause Precious any problems because she had already been through enough.

♛ ♛ ♛

"Lisa, I have to go to LA," I said, packing up the last of my things.

"How long will you be gone?"

"I'm not sure. A very good friend of mine is in trouble and I have to go find out what happened to her," I explained, zipping up my bag.

"Let me guess, the she is Precious? Besides Tracy, she's the only female you've ever talked to me about. Since Tracy is dead that only leaves Precious."

"Yes, it is Precious. I called her a few days ago and the conversation ended abruptly. I thought maybe it had to do with her husband Supreme, but a detective has left me a few messages saying he wanted to speak to me about Precious. I've made a few phone calls and I think something bad has happened to her."

"You don't think you should let her husband and the police handle it?"

"They can do whatever they wanna do, but I got access to the streets and might be able to get information they ain't privy to. But I'm not taking no chances, not when it comes to Precious."

"I understand. I know you have a long history with her," Lisa said, putting her head down. I knew Lisa felt some type of way about me breaking out to go chase down my ex, but I always kept it one hundred with Lisa. I didn't sugar coat shit.

"If you want, you can stay here while I'm gone." Although I wasn't in a committed relationship with Lisa, she was the only woman I was dealing with in Miami so I had no issues with her staying here while I was away.

"Okay," she said nodding her head. "I'll stay."

"Cool. I'll leave some money for you, but if anything comes up you know you can call me. I'll also be checking in on you. Be good," I said kissing Lisa on the forehead before heading out to catch my flight.

On my way to the airport I thought about the last time I heard Precious' voice and what she said. I wondered if there was some sort of clue I was missing. All I did know was that Precious would never willingly leave her baby; she had just gotten her daughter back. She had been through hell and came out a survivor. If she was missing, it wasn't voluntarily, she was taken and I would do everything in my power to bring her back home.

Chapter 27

Aaliyah

Three Years Later...

"You're the most beautiful little girl in the entire world," I said holding my daughter Aaliyah. My life had completely changed in the past three years. After going to LA to find Precious, I ended up saving her life after she was beaten and left for dead in a burning house. Once I nursed her back to health, we found ourselves on the East Coast in search of Maya who had kidnapped our daughter. Of course at that time I thought Aaliyah was Supreme's daughter, but that didn't stop me from searching high and low like she was my own child. It's crazy how the universe can play tricks on you because come to find out Aaliyah was mine.

We didn't find out until Aaliyah was involved in a car accident and needed a blood transfusion. That's when Precious told me there was a possibility that I could be her father. She was just a baby and to think there was a chance I could lose her before even knowing if she was my child was the hardest thing I had ever dealt with. It was even harder than losing my father. But Aaliyah survived and through that tragedy I gained a daughter.

"Nico, you're gonna have her so spoiled. You tell her that all the time," Precious shook her head as we sat in the living room at her house.

"That's what a Daddy is supposed to do, ain't that right baby girl," I said, kissing Aaliyah on her cheek.

"Yes, Daddy, that's right." Aaliyah grinned kissing me back.

"It's always hard dropping her off. I wish I could spend every minute of the day with her." I exhaled, watching Aaliyah playing with her doll.

"Mrs. Mills, would you like me to get Aaliyah ready for bed?" the nanny came in and asked.

"Yes, that would be great. It's time for bed Aaliyah," Precious said standing up from the couch and walking over to pick Aaliyah up.

"Let me kiss Daddy goodbye," Aaliyah said, reaching over and giving me a hug and kiss as Precious held her. For a brief moment I wanted to reach over and kiss Precious too. It seemed right, in that moment we felt like a real family. I hated being a part-time Dad and sharing my daughter with another man.

"I guess I should be going," I said to Precious after the nanny took Aaliyah upstairs. "I'll see you next weekend."

"Nico," Precious called out when I was turning to leave. "I never tell you this, but thank you for not ever making this difficult. I know this isn't the ideal situation for you, but you always handle it like a gentleman. I respect you for that."

"You've given me the greatest gift. Instead of stressing about the negatives I try to focus on the blessing that is Aaliyah and you made that possible. Words can't describe how much I love you because of that. I'll talk to you later and give Aaliyah a goodnight kiss for me."

Walking out the door and leaving my daughter seemed to be getting more difficult. Maybe it was because she was getting older, talking more, and our bond was getting stronger. That little girl had become the most important person in my life.

"What are you doing here?" I heard a familiar voice ask as I was getting in my car.

"I was dropping off my daughter," I said to Supreme.

"You love saying that don't you... your daughter."

"That's what Aaliyah is, my daughter. I know it

"Yes, that's my child you have growing inside of you. I think it's nice Aaliyah will have a little brother or sister."

"You mean that?" Lisa asked sounding surprised by my response.

"I do. I wasn't expecting to be a father again so soon, but you're a good woman Lisa and I'm going to make sure I'm good to you and our baby."

"Nico, you're already good to me. I haven't wanted for anything since the day I met you."

It was easy to be good to a woman like Lisa. I had been dealing with her for over three years. Although I had never made myself exclusive to her she had always been exclusive to me. Because of my business sometimes I would go weeks without seeing her, but whenever I came back around she was right there waiting for me. I made sure she was rewarded for her loyalty. Lisa wanted for nothing and now that she was carrying my child I would give her even more.

"It's only going to get better," I promised Lisa.

"Are you coming by tonight," Lisa questioned.

"I'ma try to. Genesis is having a dinner party tonight that I have to attend. If it's not over too late then yes I'll definitely come by."

"Can I go to the dinner party with you? I've never met any of your friends."

"Lisa, we've talked about this before. The less people know about you, the safer you are especially now that you're carrying my seed. I want you and my baby to be protected."

"Okay. Hopefully you can come by tonight if not then tomorrow."

"For sure. I think it's time to get you out of your apartment."

"Why? I love that loft."

"It's nice for you, but when the baby comes you're going to need a house with a big backyard and a pool because my son or daughter will know how to swim." I smiled.

"You're going to get me a house?"

"Of course. My child will have everything and so will you. Now let's eat lunch."

♛ ♛ ♛

"Genesis, that was a nice dinner and very productive. I think we definitely closed the deal."

"I think you're right. We keep closing legitimate deals we can give up our drug empire."

"Neva that, man. I'ma die a hustler. It's all I know. I love that shit and it just isn't because it has made me a very rich man. The grind gives me the ultimate high," I admitted.

"I hear you, Nico and honestly I feel what you're saying. This life is addictive, but having a son now to raise I want to make sure that I'm around to see him grow up."

"Yeah, having a child does make a difference. Sometimes I can't believe that I'm a father. I mean finding out that Aaliyah was mine was the best thing that ever happened to me. She's so beautiful just like her mother."

"I guess it's safe to say that you still have it bad for your child's mother."

"Genesis, I've finally accepted that I'll probably love Precious 'til the day I die, but I gotta let that shit burn. She is happily married to Supreme."

"The heart wants what the heart wants, but I'm glad you let that go. It's for the best."

"I agree," I said thinking about Lisa and the baby we were going to have together.

♛ ♛ ♛

"I haven't seen you in over a week and you show up ready to take me house hunting," Lisa said, shaking her head.

"I'm sorry about that, but after that dinner Genesis had, I end up having to go out of town the next day. But I'm here to make it up to you," I said giving Lisa a kiss. "You're already starting to get that mommy glow."

"You're so full it." Lisa laughed.

"I'm being serious," I said pulling her closer. "So are you ready to go look at some houses?"

"Why not," she said grabbing her purse. "Let's go!"

"I need to take this call. Meet me in the car," I said handing Lisa my keys.

"Okay," she said cheerfully, giving me a quick kiss before leaving. I waited for a few moments to make sure Lisa had gone before answering the call.

"Precious, I'm surprised to hear from you. Is everything okay with Aaliyah?"

"She's great. I was calling because Supreme and I are going away for a couple days and I wanted to see if you wanted to keep Aaliyah. She could stay with Supreme's parents, but I wanted to give you the option first."

"Precious, I would love that. Thank you."

"You're her father and she adores you. I want you to be in her life as much as possible."

"I want that too. While I have you on the phone there is something I want to tell you."

"What is it?"

"You're actually the first person I'm sharing the news with."

"Do I need to sit down for this," Precious joked.

"I'm having a baby." Precious went dead silent. "Precious, are you there?" I finally asked after not hearing a word from her for a couple of minutes.

"I didn't even realize you had a girlfriend," she finally said.

"She's not my girlfriend."

"So who is she?"

"She's a girl I've been seeing off and on for the last few years."

"I see. Aaliyah is still so young, I hope you won't stop spending time with her once your new baby comes."

"That will never happen."

"Are you sure?" Precious asked. I could hear sadness in her voice, which surprised me because it let me know she still cared.

"You and Aaliyah are the loves of my life. Nothing or nobody will ever change that."

"I don't know what to say, Nico."

"You don't have to say anything. I know there is no chance for us, but that doesn't change the fact that I'll always love you, Precious."

"I love you too, Nico."

"That woman will always have my heart," I said out loud after ending our call. Precious Cummings was truly the love of my life.

Chapter 29

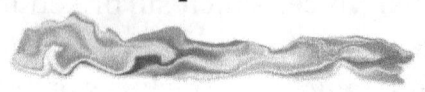

Look What You've Done

What I thought was supposed to be a happy time seemed to have changed in a matter of weeks. One day Lisa and I were looking at new homes for her, but lately the vibe was off and it was unexpected. Lisa and I never had problems before in our relationship because she didn't question me and played her position. Now all of a sudden she had concerns about Precious and I didn't understand why, especially since she was carrying my child.

"I don't know what you want me to say. I do care about you...."

"But you're still in love with Precious," Lisa said, cutting me off. "I can't deal with this anymore. You're still holding a torch for a woman that has moved on with her life."

"Of course I have love for Precious. We have history and we share a daughter together, but I want to try and make things work with you."

"Oh really, is it because you know Precious has no intentions of leaving her husband or is it because of the baby?"

"Why are you doing this?" I shrugged.

"Doing what... having a real conversation with you? I don't want to be your second choice, or for you to settle for me because of a baby. Nobody even knows about me. I'm a secret. You keep our relationship hidden like you're ashamed of me or something."

"I'm not ashamed of you. With the business I'm in and the lifestyle I'm in, I try to keep my personal life private. I don't want to make you a target."

"Whatever. I used to believe your excuses, but my eyes have been opened. I'm a lot wiser now. I've played my position for so long, believing that my loyalty would prove I was worthy of your love, but I'm done."

"Lisa, stop. Why are you crying?" I said, reaching for her hand, but she pulled away. "I was always upfront with you. I never sold you a dream."

"You're right. I sold myself a dream. More like a fairytale. But when I heard you on the phone with Precious that fairytale died and reality kicked in."

"What phone conversation?" I asked, hoping Lisa was bluffing.

"The one where you told Precious, she and Aaliyah were the loves of your life and nothing would change that, not even the baby you were having with me. It was obvious that was the first time you had ever even mentioned my name to her."

"Lisa, it wasn't like that," I said, stroking my hand over my face. "You didn't hear or understand the context of the entire conversation." I shook my head; hating that Lisa ever heard any of that. "That conversation was over a week ago, why are you just now saying something?"

"Because there was nothing to say. I needed to hear you say those words. I knew what I had to do and I did it."

"So what, you're deciding you don't want to deal with me anymore? It's too late for that. We're having a baby together. You gonna have to deal with me whether you want to or not."

"That's not true."

"Listen, Lisa. I'm sorry you heard what I said to Precious. I know that had to hurt, but again I think you read too much into that. I do care about you."

"Just save it, Nico. You care about me like a puppy," Lisa said sarcastically.

"I get it. Your feelings are hurt and you don't want to have an intimate relationship with me any longer, I have to respect that. But that doesn't change the fact you're carrying my child and I will be playing an active role in their life so I don't want us to be on bad terms. I want to be here for you and our baby."

"You don't have to worry about that anymore. You're free to pursue Precious and not feel obligated to me."

"It's not an obligation. We made the baby together and we'll take care of our child together."

"Don't you get it, there is no baby."

"Excuse me? Are you saying you lied about being pregnant?"

"No, I was pregnant, but…"

"But what, you had a miscarriage?"

"No, I had an abortion."

"You killed my child?"

"No, I aborted mine!"

"That was my child too."

"Fuck you! Fuck you, Nico! You want to stand there and act like you gave a damn about our baby and me. You're such a hypocrite and a liar."

"You had no right to make a decision like that without discussing it with me."

"I had every right. I heard you on the phone confessing your love to another woman and the child you all share together. Making it seem like our baby and me was some unwanted burden. Well now you no longer have that burden. Any child I bring into this world deserves better than that."

"You killed my child because of a phone conversation you overheard. You make me sick. I think I actually hate you."

"Now you know how I feel because I hate you, too," Lisa spit back with venom in her voice.

"You need to go before you meet the same demise as the baby you murdered."

"No worries, I have no intentions of staying. As a matter of fact, I came to say goodbye. I have no reason to stay in New York."

"You're leaving town?"

"Yes, for good. Like I said, there is nothing here for me. I don't want to be in the same city as you. It would be a constant reminder of all the time I wasted, waiting for you," Lisa said, as a single tear trickled down her cheek. "Goodbye, Nico."

I watched with contempt and pain as Lisa walked out the door. I couldn't lie to myself. I almost understood why she chose not to keep our baby. I wasn't in love with Lisa and couldn't see me spending the rest of my life with her. The fucked up part was it had nothing to do with her. Lisa was a good girl, but she was right, my heart still belonged to Precious. But I still hated her for aborting our baby. I guess that made me a selfish man. I wanted Lisa to bless me with another child that I could be a father to, but have her accept that she would never have my heart.

At this moment, it was all insignificant. That chapter was now closed. Lisa was out of my life. In the process she took our child with her and for that I would never forgive her.

Epilogue

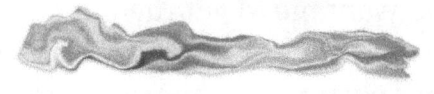

Angel

Seven Months Later...

"Look at her, mommy, she is so beautiful," Lisa said, holding her newborn baby in the hospital.

"She is beautiful," her mother said, nodding her head. "What are you going to name her?"

"Angel. She's my little Angel." Lisa smiled.

"That's a beautiful name and she is an angel," Lisa's mother said, admiring her granddaughter. "Lisa, are you okay?" she asked, noticing her daughter becoming pale and a pain-stricken expression on her face.

"I'm getting a headache, but I'll be fine," Lisa

said, trying to shake off the discomfort. "Can you hold Angel for a minute. I need to sit up and catch my breath," Lisa said, handing her baby to her mother.

"I would love to." Her mother smiled, gently rocking Angel.

"I feel a little nauseated," Lisa said, feeling hot.

"Do you want me to get the nurse?"

"No, just get me some water," Lisa said. Before Lisa's mother even had a chance to reach for a bottle of water, her daughter began to vomit. In a matter of seconds Lisa's arms and legs began jerking. Her entire body seemed to be having convulsions."

"Lisa… Lisa… what's the matter baby!" Lisa's mother said, her voice shaking, filled with fear. "Somebody get a doctor!" she screamed out, running to the door and holding her grandbaby close to her chest. "My daughter needs a doctor. She's sick! Somebody help her please!" she pleaded, yelling out as she held the door wide open.

"Ma'am, please step outside," a nurse said, rushing into Lisa's room with a couple of other nurses behind her and the doctor close behind.

Lisa's mother paced back and forth in front of her daughter's room for what seemed like an eternity. "It's gonna be okay, Angel. Your mother will be fine," she kept saying over and over again to her grandbaby. "You know they say babies are healing, and you healing your grandmother's soul right now," she said softly in Angel's ear.

"Ma'am."

"Yes... is my daughter okay?" she asked, rushing towards the doctor.

"Ma'am, your daughter was unconscious then her heart stopped."

"What are you saying?" she questioned as her bottom lip began trembling.

"We did everything we could do, but your daughter didn't make it. I'm sorry."

"No! No! She so young. She's just a baby herself. How did this happen?"

"I'm not sure, but we're going to do an autopsy. It will take a couple of weeks for the results to get back. It could be a placental abruption and amniotic fluid embolism, or a brain aneurysm, we don't know. Again, I'm sorry. Do you want us to contact the father of your granddaughter?" the doctor asked.

Lisa's mother gazed down at Angel, whose eyes were closed and she was sleeping peacefully in her arms. "I don't know who Angel's father is. That information died with my daughter."

"I understand. Again, I'm sorry about your daughter. Let us know if there is anything we can do for you," the doctor said before walking off.

"I just want to see my daughter and tell her goodbye," she said walking into Lisa's room. "My sweet baby girl. You look so peaceful." Lisa's mother rubbed her hand across the side of her face. "Don't you worry. I promise I will take care of Angel. I will give her all the love I know you would have. Rest in peace baby girl."

Follow Angel's Story In Female Hustler....

A KING PRODUCTION

All I See Is The Money...

Female Hustler

A Novel

Joy Deja King

Prologue

Nico Carter

"I don't know what you want me to say. I do care about you—"

"But you're still in love with Precious," Lisa said, cutting me off. "I can't deal with this anymore. You're still holding a torch for a woman that has moved on with her life."

"Of course I have love for Precious. We have history and we share a daughter together, but I want to try and make things work with you."

"Oh really, is it because you know Precious

has no intentions of leaving her husband or is it because of the baby?"

"Why are you doing this?" I shrugged.

"Doing what... having a real conversation with you? I don't want to be your second choice, or for you to settle for me because of a baby. Nobody even knows about me. I'm a secret. You keep our relationship hidden like you're ashamed of me or something."

"I'm not ashamed of you. With the business I'm in and the lifestyle I'm in, I try to keep my personal life private. I don't want to make you a target."

"Whatever. I used to believe your excuses, but my eyes have been opened. I'm a lot wiser now. I've played my position for so long, believing that my loyalty would prove I was worthy of your love, but I'm done."

"Lisa stop. Why are you crying," I said, reaching for her hand, but she pulled away. "I was always upfront with you. I never sold you a dream."

"You're right. I sold myself a dream. More like a fairytale. But when I heard you on the phone with Precious that fairytale died and reality kicked in."

"What phone conversation?" I asked, hoping Lisa was bluffing.

"The one where you told Precious she and Aaliyah were the loves of your life and nothing would change that, not even the baby you were having with me. It was obvious that was the first time you had ever even mentioned my name to her."

"Lisa, it wasn't like that," I said, stroking my hand over my face. "You didn't hear or understand the context of the entire conversation." I shook my head; hating Lisa ever heard any of that. "That conversation was over a week ago, why are you just now saying something?"

"Because there was nothing to say. I needed to hear you say those words. I knew what I had to do and I did it."

"So what, you're deciding you don't want to deal with me anymore? It's too late for that. We're having a baby together. You gonna have to deal with me whether you want to or not."

"That's not true."

"Listen, Lisa. I'm sorry you heard what I said to Precious. I know that had to hurt, but again I think you read too much into that. I do care about you."

"Just save it, Nico. You care about me like a puppy," Lisa said sarcastically.

"I get it. Your feelings are hurt and you don't want to have an intimate relationship with me any longer, I have to respect that. But that doesn't change the fact you're carrying my child and I will be playing an active role in their life so I don't want us to be on bad terms. I want to be here for you and our baby."

"You don't have to worry about that anymore. You're free to pursue Precious and not feel obligated to me."

"It's not an obligation. We made the baby together and we'll take care of our child together."

"Don't you get it, there is no baby."

"Excuse me? Are you saying you lied about being pregnant?"

"No, I was pregnant, but…"

"But what, you had a miscarriage?"

"No I had an abortion."

"You killed my child?"

"No, I aborted mine!"

"That was my child, too."

"Fuck you! Fuck you, Nico! You want to stand there and act like you gave a damn about our baby and me. You're such a hypocrite and a liar."

"You had no right to make a decision like that without discussing it with me."

"I had every right. I heard you on the phone confessing your love to another woman and the child you all share together. Making it seem like our baby and me was some unwanted burden.

Well now you no longer have that burden. Any child I bring into this world deserves better than that."

"You killed my child because of a phone conversation you overheard. You make me sick. I think I actually hate you."

"Now you know how I feel because I hate you too," Lisa spit back with venom in her voice.

"You need to go before you meet the same demise as the baby you murdered."

"No worries, I have no intentions of staying. As a matter of fact, I came to say goodbye. I have no reason to stay in New York."

"You're leaving town?"

"Yes, for good. Like I said, there is nothing here for me. I don't want to be in the same city as you. It would be a constant reminder of all the time I wasted waiting for you," Lisa said, as a single tear trickled down her cheek. "Goodbye, Nico."

I watched with contempt and pain as Lisa walked out the door. I couldn't lie to myself. I almost understood why she chose not to keep our baby. I wasn't in love with Lisa and couldn't see me spending the rest of my life with her. The fucked up part was it had nothing to do with her. Lisa was a good girl, but she was right, my heart still belonged to Precious. But I still hated her for aborting our baby. I guess that made me a selfish man. I wanted Lisa to bless me with another child that I could be a father to, but have her accept that she would never have my heart.

At this moment, it was all insignificant. That chapter was now closed. Lisa was out of my life. In the process, she took our child with her and for that I would never forgive her.

Seven Months Later...

"Look at her, mommy, she is so beautiful," Lisa said, holding her newborn daughter in the hospital.

"She is beautiful," her mother said, nodding her head. "What are you going to name her?"

"Angel. She's my little Angel." Lisa smiled.

"That's a beautiful name and she is an angel," Lisa's mother said, admiring her granddaughter. "Lisa, are you okay?" she asked, noticing her daughter becoming pale with a pain stricken expression on her face.

"I'm getting a headache, but I'll be fine," Lisa said, trying to shake off the discomfort. "Can you hold Angel for a minute. I need to sit up and catch my breath," Lisa said, handing her baby to her mother.

"I would love to." Her mother smiled, gently rocking Angel.

"I feel a little nauseated," Lisa said, feeling hot.

"Do you want me to get the nurse?"

"No, just get me some water," Lisa said. Before Lisa's mother even had a chance to reach for a bottle of water, her daughter began to vomit. In a matter of seconds Lisa's arms and legs began jerking. Her entire body seemed to be having convulsions."

"Lisa... Lisa... what's the matter baby!" Lisa's mother said, her voice shaking, filled with fear. "Somebody get a doctor!" she screamed out, running to the door and holding her grandbaby close to her chest. "My daughter needs a doctor. She's sick! Somebody help her please!" she pleaded, yelling out as she held the door wide open.

"Ma'am, please step outside," a nurse said, rushing into Lisa's room with a couple of other nurses behind her and the doctor close behind.

Lisa's mother paced back and forth in front of her daughter's room for what seemed like an eternity. "It's gonna be okay, Angel. Your mother will be fine," she kept saying over and over again to her grandbaby. "You know they say babies are healing, and you healing your grandmother's soul right now," she said softly in Angel's ear.

"Ma'am."

"Yes... is my daughter okay?" she asked rushing towards the doctor.

"Ma'am, your daughter was unconscious then her heart stopped."

"What are you saying?" she questioned as her bottom lip began trembling.

"We did everything we could do, but your daughter didn't make it. I'm sorry."

"No! No! She's so young. She's just a baby herself. How did this happen?"

"I'm not sure, but we're going to do an autopsy. It will take a couple of weeks for the results to get back. It could be a placental abruption and amniotic fluid embolism, or a brain aneurysm, we don't know. Again, I'm sorry. Do you want us to contact the father of your granddaughter?" the doctor asked.

Lisa's mother gazed down at Angel, whose eyes were closed as she slept peacefully in her arms. "I don't know who Angel's father is. That information died with my daughter."

"I understand. Again, I'm sorry about your daughter. Let us know if there is anything we can do for you," the doctor said before walking off.

"I just want to see my daughter and tell her goodbye," she said walking into Lisa's room. "My sweet baby girl. You look so peaceful." Lisa's mother rubbed her hand across the side of her face. "Don't you worry. I promise I will take care of Angel. I will give her all the love I know you would have. Rest in peace baby girl."

A KING PRODUCTION

Deadly Divorce...

A Titillating Tale

Toxic Series

A Novelette

Joy Deja King

Chapter One

Banking On Me

"What do you mean I didn't get the part?" Londyn swallowed hard. "You said the casting director loved me."

"Chris does," her agent Misty confirmed.

"Then what happened?!" Londyn's tone was loud and hostile, causing people in the restaurant to turnaround and briefly stare. She took a deep breath and lowered her voice. "When I got the callback and auditioned for the casting director and director, they both seemed extremely pleased with my audition. You even said I was a shoo-in for the role, so what happened?"

"You know I'm always transparent with you," Misty sighed. "Well, as you're aware the production is a big budget film and is supposed to be on track for box office gold."

"Exactly! This role was finally going to get me off the B-list and make me an A-list superstar."

"And you know I want that for you. You deserve it, and I still believe it will happen," she added.

"Stop bullshitting me and tell me why I didn't get the part," Londyn fumed.

"Supposedly, they're saying the producer requested a specific actress to be attached to the production who has the ability to fill up the movie theater. But off the record, Chris confided in me that the producer went over his head and the director, pulled some strings, and got the actress he wanted," Misty explained.

"Who is she?"

Misty hesitated for a moment. "Veronica Woods...I know I know," she put her hands up and said, knowing what Londyn was going to say next.

"Veronica! She can't fill up an elementary school play let alone a movie theater," Londyn seethed. "She's barely C-list!"

"Listen, everything you're saying, I said it and more with expletives. I'm being calm now, but I was livid. Chris finally admitted to me that whoever Veronica is dating, the producer owes him a huge favor and he called it in."

"So, Veronica got the part that I busted my ass off for, because of who she's fuckin'." Londyn rolled her eyes looking completely defeated.

"We both know this industry can be cruel and there's nothing fair about it. I hate seeing this disappointment on your face, but we'll push through like we always do," Misty said placing her hand on Londyn's arm.

"I just knew it was finally my time," Londyn's voice trailed off, she said shaking her head.

"Chris really is a fan of yours. He thought you were perfect for the lead but because of the Veronica situation, he offered you another part. Of course, it's a much smaller role but it will give you an opportunity to be seen by millions of people."

"I don't think I'm interested in his consolation prize."

"Londyn, don't look at it that way. View it as an opportunity to shine. This could lead to a bigger role in another movie."

"How many times have I heard that." Londyn's attitude had become cynical. "I'm not eighteen, just getting off the bus. I've been doing this for over ten years, and I feel like I've been stuck. My career seems to have reached a plateau. I'll never be a bankable actress."

"That's not necessarily true. Lots of talented and beautiful actresses don't reach superstar status until much later in their career," Misty said with optimism in her voice. From the dismal expression on Londyn's face, she could see her words of encouragement weren't working. "Just consider taking the other role Chris is offering you. And don't forget, ABC really wants you for their new crime drama."

"I'm not interested in doing a television show, plus the networks are saturated with crime dramas. The show will probably be cancelled after the first season," Londyn complained.

"Will you at least consider the smaller role Chris is offering...please," Misty pleaded.

"Sure, I'll think about it," Londyn exhaled, standing up. "But I have to go. I don't want to be late for Ryan's first major exhibit at that art gallery tonight, so I need to get to my hair appointment," she said grabbing her purse.

"That's right, Ryan's exhibit is tonight. Let him know I never received my invite."

"I told you he said that was an oversight and you are most definitely invited. He'll be disappointed if you don't show up."

"I highly doubt that, but if you insist, I guess I can come," Misty smirked. "Besides, I heard it's the place to be tonight. Ryan must be elated."

"More like thankful he is finally getting the recognition he deserves. Ryan has always had a vision and stayed focused. It's going to be amazing to see his vision come to life." Londyn smiled proudly at how far her friend had come, and the direction his career was heading in.

"A minute ago I was worried the frown on your face was permanent but now that winning smile is back. I'll have to thank Ryan when I see him tonight."

"Yeah, I'll have to thank him too. He inspires me. We both got to LA around the same time. After all the time and work he's put in at the studio, Ryan has finally gotten his big breakthrough. Maybe that means my big break is coming too," Londyn winked.

Misty desperately wanted the same thing for Londyn. She still remembered the day Londyn walked into her office begging for representation. She read a feature Variety Magazine had recently done on Misty and was adamant she was the only agent for her. She was so full of passion yet extremely stubborn, refusing to take no for an answer. That was the main reason Misty couldn't deny her request, although she was a complete unknown. Londyn soon became her favorite client. She had this sparkle and tenacity in her eyes that made you root for her. She still had that same spark, but Misty was afraid that if Londyn didn't reach the success she desired, that fire would soon burn out.

A KING PRODUCTION

Toxic...
A Titillating Tale

A Novelette

JOY DEJA KING

Chapter One

Got Time Today

"Look at that trifling nigga right there," Harper seethed. "He about to make me fuck my nails up." She glanced down at her freshly done, blush pink mountain peak nails with rhinestone swirls, as her fury continuied to simmer.

"Girl, let's just go. You don't need this drama. You got plenty of other options. You won't have no problem replacing him. Fuck Jamari!" Taliyah was doing her best to get her friend to leave the scene, but it wasn't working. When Harper got amped up, there was nothing nobody could do to lower her temperature.

"Nah, fuck that." Harper's tone had turned calm but icy, which only meant she was about to raise hell. "He ain't about to play me out here in these streets." She grabbed her purse and quickly jumped out her car with Taliyah trailing behind her.

Amina make me so sick! Why the hell did she have to call Harper and let her know Jamari was up in Phipps Plaza shopping wit' the next chick, Taliyah thought to herself as she watched Harper approach her boyfriend.

"What's good?!" Harper popped, sounding more like a dude than the prissy princess her outer appearance exuded. It was the main reason she always had problems with men. They thought they would be dating some submissive eye candy. By the time they realized she had the mindset of a nigga, who just so happened to look good in a dress, it was too late.

"Baby, what you doing here?" Jamari asked nervously, as he was putting shopping bags in the trunk of his car.

"I see you did some shopping. What you buy me?" Harper questioned, grabbing one of the Louis Vuitton bags.

"Umm, that's mine!" The chick with Jamari shouted trying to snatch the bag out Harper's hand.

"I advise you to let go of this bag, and stay the fuck outta this. This between me and Jamari. You don't want this smoke....I promise you," Harper warned.

The girl didn't know anything about Harper, but her instincts told her the bitch was crazy. So she stepped back, and directed her attention back to the man who had just taken her on a shopping spree. Her first one at that. She didn't want to mess things up with him, but she wasn't trying to scrap in the mall parking lot either.

"Jamari, what's going on... and who is she?" the girl smacked, folding her arms with an attitude.

"Yeah Jamari, who am I?" Harper smirked, enjoying how rattled he was. Although he was trying to act like he had everything under control, his eyes were telling a different story.

"Baby, let me speak to you for a minute." Jamari spoke smoothly, reaching out his hand, and gently taking Harper's arm.

"Get tha fuck off me!" She barked, yanking her arms out his grasp, before pulling out her baby Glock, that she never left home without.

"Yo, yo, yo!" Jamari put his hands up, slowly stepping back.

"I knew that bitch was crazy," the girl who was with Jamari mumbled, shaking her head. Her first thought was to get her phone and call the police, but quickly realized she had already put her purse in the car. She didn't want to draw unwanted attention to herself by opening the passenger door, so she remained in the background quiet.

"Harper, put the gun away and let's go," Taliyah sighed. She was used to her friend's antics but the shit was draining.

"You can go wait in the car for me, 'cause I got time today. We ain't done here, but this won't take much longer," Harper told her friend, keeping her gun aimed at Jamari.

"Baby, please calm down," Jamari pleaded, keeping his hands up. "It's not what you think. You know I love you."

"You so full of shit," Harper laughed wickedly. "It's always you pretty boys that think you can sweet talk yo' way out some lies."

Harper continued to laugh as she began grabbing the pricey items out of the shopping bags. One-by-one, she tossed them in the mud puddles that hadn't dried up from the storm the night before.

"No you fuckin' didn't!" The girl with Jamari screamed. Horrified seeing the luxury goods she envisioned showing off on the Gram being ruined, right in front of her eyes.

"Yo Harper, I can't believe you doing this dumb shit!" He roared, finally losing his cool. Jamari started to storm toward her, until she raised that Glock, aiming it firmly at his chest.

"Back tha fuck up, or else," Harper threatened, nodding her head, tossing out the last bag from the trunk. But she wasn't done yet. She reached back in her purse and brandished the knife she always kept on her too. She proceeded to walk around Jamari's brand new black on black Camaro Coupe ZL1 and slashed each tire.

"You bitch! I'ma fuck you up!" Jamari uttered viciously, ready to break Harper's neck. But she wasn't worried. She was the one holding the gun.

"Ya lovebirds can walk the fuck home, hand in hand. So who's the bitch now," Harper mocked, going back to her car.

"Harper, you are fuckin' certifiable, like seriously," Taliyah kept repeating as she stared back looking at Jamari. He was having a complete meltdown, while the girl he was with, was picking up purses, shoes and clothes, trying to salvage whatever items she could.

"Jamari betta be happy I didn't bust out them windows and key his car too," she snarled. "I bet that nigga learned today not to disrespect me," Harper scoffed, driving off.

A KING PRODUCTION

Bitch

The Beginning...

JOY DEJA KING

Can't Knock the Hustle

Coming from nothing and having nothing are two different things. Yeah, I came from nothing, but I was determined to have it all. And how couldn't I?

I exploded into this world when "Hood Rich" wasn't an afterthought, but the only thought. You turn on the television and every nigga is iced out with an exotic whip sitting on 24inch rims, surrounded by a bitch in a g-string, a weave down to her ass, poppin' that booty. So the chicks on the videos were dropping it like it's hot for the rappers and singers while the bitches around my way were dropping it for our own superstars. Dealing with a street nigga on say the Alpo status a legendary drug kingpin was like being Beyoncé herself on Jigga Man's arm.

A bitch like me was thirsty for that. I'd been on some type of hustle since I was in Pampers.

I grew up in the grimiest Brooklyn projects during the '90s. It was worse than being in prison because you knew there was something better out there; you just didn't know how to get it. You never saw green grass or flowers blooming. Instead of looking up to teachers, lawyers or doctors, you worshipped the local drug dealers who hustled to survive and escape their existence. Even as a little girl, I knew I wanted more out of life. Somehow hustling was in my blood.

First, I hustled for my moms' attention because she was too busy turning tricks to pay me any mind. I never knew who my daddy was, so while my moms was fucking in her bedroom, I would wait outside the door with my legs crossed, holding my favorite teddy bear in one arm as I sucked my thumb. When the tricks would come out, I would look at them with puppy-dog eyes and ask, "Are you my daddy?" The question would freak them out so badly they'd toss me a few dollars so I would shut the fuck up.

One day when I was five, my mother was looking for something in my drawers, she came across a bunch of fives and tens and some twenties. The total was five hundred and some change. Of course, she wanted to know where all the money came from. When I told her that the money came from her business clients (that's what my moms called them), she lit up. She tossed me up in the air and said, "Baby, you my good luck charm. I knew one day you'd make me some money."

On that rare occasion she showed me mad love. As young as I was, I equated my mother's newfound interest in me with love. From that moment on, I learned how to hustle for my moms' attention – that is, by providing her with money.

Where I grew up, everyone hated "The Man," so they wouldn't report shit, even child abuse or neglect. When I was really young, my neighbors helped look out for me, when necessary. One neighbor, Mr. Duncan, used to baby-sit me while my mother "Worked."

In the projects, we all minded our own business and had the same code of silence that the police have among themselves – we didn't snitch on each other.

Somehow, my moms' customers never messed with or even fondled me. I think it's because people say I got these funny looking eyes. Even when I was little I had an attitude that said, "Don't fuck wit' me."

By the time I was fifteen with all the tricks my moms pulled, we were still dead ass broke, living in the Brooklyn projects. She couldn't save a dime because with hooking comes drugging and my moms stayed high. I guess that's all you can do to escape the nightmare of having all types of nasty, greasy fat motherfuckers pounding your back out every damn day. The characters that I saw coming in and out of our apartment were enough to make me want to sew up my pussy so nobody could get between my legs.

One day when I came home from school, I found my moms sprawled out on the couch with a half empty bottle of whiskey in one hand, as she tried to toke her last pull off a roach in the other hand. Her once long, wavy sandy hair was now thin and straggly. The curves that once made every hood chick roll their eyes in envy were just a bag of bones. You wouldn't even recognize the one time ghetto queen unless you looked into the green eyes she inherited from her mulatto father.

Without a word, I gave the living room a lick and a promise. I emptied several full ashtrays, picked up the dirty glasses scattered about the floor and wiped off the cocktail table. Out of the corner of my eye, I watched my moms sit up and stare at me for a long five minutes. She had the strangest look on her face.

Finally she spoke up. "Precious, you sure are growing up to be a pretty girl." Although we were in each other's face on an everyday basis, it was as if this were the first time my mother had seen me in many years. I didn't know how to respond so I kept cleaning up. "Didn't you hear what yo' mama said?"

"Yes, I heard you."

"Well you betta say thank you."

"Thank you, Mama."

"You welcome, baby."

As I continued to clean I couldn't help but feel uncomfortable with the glare my moms was giving me. It was the same look she'd get when she was about to get her hands on some prime dope.

"Baby, you know that your mother is getting up there in age. I can't put it down like I used to."

I looked my moms directly in the eye, but I said nothing. I was thinking to myself, *What the fuck that got to do wit' me"*

"So, baby, I was thinking maybe you need to start helping me out a little more."

"Help out more how, I basically give you my whole paycheck?" I didn't understand what the fuck she was talking about. I barely went to school because I had what was supposed to be a part time job at a car detailing shop.

Damn near every cent I made, I used to pay bills and maintain my appearance. I couldn't afford to rock all the brand name hot shit, but because I had style, I was able to throw a few cheap pieces together to make it look real official. Luckily I inherited my moms' beauty and body so I could just about make a potato sack look sexy.

"Baby, that little job you got ain't bringing home no money. It's just enough to maintain. I'm talking about getting a real job."

"Mama, I'm only fifteen. It's only so many jobs I can get and so much money I can make. Boogie not even suppose to give me all the hours he have me doing at the shop. That's why he pays me under the table."

"Precious, as pretty as you are you can be making thousands of dollars."

"Doing what? What job you know is going to pay a fifteen-year-old high school student thousands of dollars?"

"The oldest profession in the book-sex," my moms said as if she was asking me to do something as innocent as baking cookies for a living.

"You 'un lost your damn mind. What you tryn' to be now - my pimp?"

"You betta watch yo' mouth, little girl. I'm yo' mama. Don't forget that."

"Don't you forget it. You must have if you asking me to sell my ass so I can take care of you."

"Not me - us. Shit, I took care of yo' ass for the last fifteen years. Breaking my back and wearing out my pussy to provide us with a good life."

"This is what you call a good life?" I said as I looked

around the small, broke down, two bedroom apartment. The hardwood floors were cracking, the walls had holes and the windows didn't even lock. It was nothing to catch a few roaches holding court in the kitchen and living room, or a couple of rats making a dash across the floor.

My moms stood up and started fixing her unruly hair, patting down her multicolored flannel pajamas and twisting her mouth in that 'how dare you' position as if she were an upstanding citizen who was being disrespected in her own home.

"You listen here," she began as she pointed her bony finger with its gnawed down nail. "A lot of these children around here don't even have a place to stay. It might not be much but it's mine."

That, too, was a lie. My moms didn't even own this raggedy-ass apartment; she rented it. But I didn't feel like reminding her of that because I wanted this going-nowhere conversation to be over.

"I hear you, Ma, but I don't know what to tell you. I'm not following in your footsteps by selling my pussy to some low down niggas for money."

"Well then you betta start looking for some place to live, 'cause I can't take care of the both of us."

"You tryna tell me you would put me out on the streets?"

"You ain't leaving me a choice, Precious. If you can't bring home some extra money, then I'll have to rent out your bedroom to pay the bills."

"Who is gon' pay you for that piece of shit of a room?"

"Listen, I ain't 'bout to sit up here and argue wit' you. Either you start bringing home some more money or find another place to live. It's up to you. But if you don't give me a thousand dollars by the first of the month, I need you out by the second."

With that my moms' skeletal body disappeared into her dungeon of a bedroom. She was practically sentencing me to the homeless shelter. There was no way I could give her a thousand dollars a month unless I worked twenty-four hours a day, seven days a week at the detail shop. But what made this so fucked up was that my moms basically wanted me to pay for her out-of-control drug habit. This wasn't even about the bills because our Section 8 rent and other bills totaled no more than four hundred dollars a month. Because the street life had beaten down my moms, she was beating me over the head with bullshit.

With my moms giving me no way out, I began my own hustle. I decided to get the money by selling my ass, but I was going to pick and choose who was able to play between my legs. My job at the car detailing shop came in handy. Nothing but top-of-the-line hustlers parlayed through, but before, I never gave them the time of day. They were always trying to holla at a sistah, but the shade I gave them was thick.

Boogie, my boss, appreciated that. He was an older dude who took his illegal drug money and opened up his shop. He was in his forties, donned a baldhead and wore two basketball sized diamond studs in each ear. He wore sweat suits and a new fresh pair of sneakers everyday. He could afford any type of car he wanted, but he remained loyal to Cadillac Devilles.

He had three: one in red, white and black.

"Boogie, who that nigga in the drop-top Beamer?" I asked when some dude I'd never seen before pulled up.

"Oh that's Azar. He moved here from Philly, why you ask?"

"I ain't neva seen him 'round here before, and I wanted to know who he was."

"Is that all, Precious?" Boogie asked, knowing it was more than that.

"Actually, to keep it real wit' you Boogie I'm looking for a man."

"What?" Boogie stopped dead in his tracks. "Looking for a man? One of the reasons I digged you so much, Precious, was because you wasn't fucking with none of these hustlers that came through here. Why the sudden change?"

"I'm not gonna get into all that Boogie, but I will tell you I really don't have a choice. I need money and fucking wit' a fo-sho nigga seems to be the only way to get it."

"Precious, you are much too young to have those types of worries. I could always give you a raise."

"Boogie, unless that raise is a few thousand dollars then it ain't gonna do me no good." Shit, I figured if I had to give my moms a thousand dollars a month, I might as well make a few for me. If I had to sell my ass, then I might as well get top dollar.

"I don't know what you need all that money for, Precious, but if you looking to fuck with a baller, then let me school you on a few things. For one, get your fuck game right."

"What you mean by that?"

"I mean if you want one of these niggas out here to spend

some serious paper on you, you gotta learn to sex them real good. You know you're a beautiful girl, so attracting a big timer's attention is the easy part. But to have a nigga willing to spend the way you want, your head and pussy game have to be on point. Just giving you something to think about."

I watched as Boogie went outside to talk to a few guys that just pulled up in G5's. I was still thinking about the advice he gave me. Boogie was right, if I wanted to really land a hustler and keep him, I had to get my fuck game in order. The funny thing was from watching my moms selling her ass all my life, it turned me off from sex. I was probably the last virgin in my hood. I definitely needed a lot of work, and I needed to find someone that I could practice on before I actually went out there and tried to find my baller.

After work I came home and my moms was lying in her regular spot on the dingy couch. She was so bad off that she would've had to pay a nigga to fuck her. I hated to see my moms so broken down. One thing I promised myself was that no matter what, I would never let myself go out like that. I would play niggas; they would never play me.

Bitch
Joy Deja King
Bitch Reloaded
Joy Deja King
Bitch Is Back
Queen
Last Bitch Standing
Joy Deja King
Dirty Little Secrets
Hooker to Housewife
Superstar
Joy Deja King
Paper
Joy Deja King
Trife Life to Lavish
Joy Deja King
Paper II
Joy Deja King
Paper
Paper
Paper
Joy Deja King
Trife Life to Lavish Part 2
Joy Deja King
Rich Famous
Joy Deja King
Joy Deja King
Bitch
Joy Deja King
Joy Deja King
Bitch
Mafia Princess
Joy Deja King
Chris Booker
Mafia Princess
Joy Deja King
Chris Booker
Baller Bitches Volume 1
Joy Deja King
Baller Bitches Volume 2
Joy Deja King
Baller Bitches Volume 3
Joy Deja King
Baller Bitches The Reunion
Joy Deja King
Power
Joy Deja King
Power 2
Joy Deja King
Drake
Chris Booker
Drake II
Joy Deja King
Chris Booker
Ride Wit' Me
Joy Deja King
Ride Wit' Me 2
Joy Deja King
Hustler
Hustler
Joy Deja King
Hustler 3
Joy Deja King
Hustler 5
Joy Deja King
Lovin Enemy
Joy Deja King
The Legacy
Joy Deja King
Assassins
Joy Deja King
Assassins
Joy Deja King
Assassins
Joy Deja King
Joy Deja King
Peter Mack
Joy Deja King
Peter Mack
Joy Deja King
Contagious
Hustler 7
Joy Deja King
Stackin' Paper VII
Joy Deja King
Toxic
Joy Deja King
Deadly Divorce
Joy Deja King

Read The Entire Bitch Series in This Order

P.O. Box 912
Collierville, TN 38027

A KING PRODUCTION

www.joydejaking.com
www.twitter.com/joydejaking

ORDER FORM

Name:
Address:
City/State:
Zip:

QUANTITY	TITLES	PRICE	TOTAL
	Bitch	$15.00	
	Bitch Reloaded	$15.00	
	The Bitch Is Back	$15.00	
	Queen Bitch	$15.00	
	Last Bitch Standing	$15.00	
	Superstar	$15.00	
	Ride Wit' Me	$12.00	
	Ride Wit' Me Part 2	$15.00	
	Stackin' Paper	$15.00	
	Trife Life To Lavish	$15.00	
	Trife Life To Lavish II	$15.00	
	Stackin' Paper II	$15.00	
	Rich or Famous	$15.00	
	Rich or Famous Part 2	$15.00	
	Rich or Famous Part 3	$15.00	
	Bitch A New Beginning	$15.00	
	Mafia Princess Part 1	$15.00	
	Mafia Princess Part 2	$15.00	
	Mafia Princess Part 3	$15.00	
	Mafia Princess Part 4	$15.00	
	Mafia Princess Part 5	$15.00	
	Boss Bitch	$15.00	
	Baller Bitches Vol. 1	$15.00	
	Baller Bitches Vol. 2	$15.00	
	Baller Bitches Vol. 3	$15.00	
	Bad Bitch	$15.00	
	Still The Baddest Bitch	$15.00	
	Power	$15.00	
	Power Part 2	$15.00	
	Drake	$15.00	
	Drake Part 2	$15.00	
	Female Hustler	$15.00	
	Female Hustler Part 2	$15.00	
	Female Hustler Part 3	$15.00	
	Female Hustler Part 4	$15.00	
	Female Hustler Part 5	$15.00	
	Female Hustler Part 6	$15.00	
	Princess Fever "Birthday Bash"	$6.00	
	Nico Carter The Men Of The Bitch Series	$15.00	
	Bitch The Beginning Of The End	$15.00	
	Supreme...Men Of The Bitch Series	$15.00	
	Bitch The Final Chapter	$15.00	
	Stackin' Paper III	$15.00	
	Men Of The Bitch Series And The Women Who Love Them	$15.00	
	Coke Like The 80s	$15.00	
	Baller Bitches The Reunion Vol. 4	$15.00	
	Stackin' Paper IV	$15.00	
	The Legacy	$15.00	
	Lovin' Thy Enemy	$15.00	
	Stackin' Paper V	$15.00	
	The Legacy Part 2	$15.00	
	Assassins - Episode 1	$11.00	
	Assassins - Episode 2	$11.00	
	Assassins - Episode 2	$11.00	
	Bitch Chronicles	$40.00	
	So Hood So Rich	$15.00	
	Stackin' Paper VI	$15.00	
	Female Hustler Part 7	$15.00	
	Toxic...	$11.99	
	Stackin' Paper VII	$15.00	
	Sugar Babies...	$9.99	
	Deadly Divorce...	$11.99	

Shipping/Handling (Via Priority Mail) $8.95 1-3 Books, $16.25 4-7 Books. For 7 or more $21.50. Total: $_____ FORMS OF
ACCEPTED PAYMENTS: Certified or government issued checks and money Orders, all mail in orders take 5-7 Business days to be delivered